OAKLAND COMMUNITY COLLEGE
3 2355 00357244 3

D0848125

FIREARMS AND

AMERICAN LAW ENFORCEMENT

DEADLY FORCE

FIREARMS AND
AMERICAN LAW ENFORCEMENT

DEADLY FORCE

FROM THE WILD WEST
TO THE STREETS OF TODAY

CHRIS MCNAB

First published in Great Britain in 2009 by Osprey Publishing, Midland House,
West Way, Botley, Oxford OX2 0PH, United Kingdom.
443 Park Avenue South, New York, NY 10016, USA.

Email: info@ospreypublishing.com

A CIP catalog record for this book is available from the British Library.

ISBN: 978 1 84603 376 6

Page layout by Myriam Bell Design, France
Index by Alison Worthington
Typeset in Perpetua and Walbaum LT
Originated by PPS Grasmere Ltd, Leeds, UK
Printed in China through Worldprint

09 10 11 12 13 10 9 8 7 6 5 4 3 2 1

For a catalog of all books published by Osprey please contact:

NORTH AMERICA
Osprey Direct, c/o Random House Distribution Center
400 Hahn Road, Westminster, MD 21157, USA
E-mail: uscustomerservice@ospreypublishing.com

ALL OTHER REGIONS
Osprey Direct, The Book Service Ltd., Distribution Centre, Colchester Road, Frating Green, Colchester, Essex, CO7 7DW
E-mail: customerservice@ospreypublishing.com

Osprey Publishing is supporting the Woodland Trust, the UK's leading woodland conservation charity, by funding the dedication of trees.

www.ospreypublishing.com

ACKNOWLEDGEMENTS

Writing this book has taken me into many complicated and dynamic areas of research, and I have numerous people to thank for providing me with both illumination and guidance. Warmest thanks go to 2nd Lieutenant Dan Courtney, who provided me with a program of invaluable research opportunities within facilities of the Fairfax County Police Department. Thanks go to all officers of the police department who assisted during my visit, including those of the Fairfax County Criminal Justice Academy Firearms Training Unit and the Police Helicopter Division, with specific thanks to the following officers: Lieutenant Jimmy Kellam, MPO Chuck Ponsart, 1st Lieutenant R. Wayne Inabinet, MPO Paul G. DeHaven, PFC John Debonis, Sergeant Mark J. Smith, and 2nd Lieutenant Ken May. I am grateful for the ride-along opportunities with Mason Station officer PFC Jose Morillo, who kept me both entertained and informed, and thanks also to patrol supervisor Lieutenant Gervais Reed.

Many other people assisted me with guidance through a complexity of issues ranging from suicide by cop to wound ballistics, and have given precious time in busy schedules for interviews. Thanks go to Thomas Aveni (Police Policy Studies Council), Gregory B. Morrison (Associate Professor of Criminal Justice & Criminology, Ball State University), Doug Whitland from the National Rifle Association (NRA) Museum, Massad Ayoob, Martin Fackler MD, and Shaun Dodson of the Firearms Tactical Institute.

I am also extremely grateful to those who have provided me with first-hand accounts of deadly force incidents, some of which are doubtless painful in the retelling. Special thanks go to Major Mike LoMonaco, Carl Stincelli, and also to Gary Bush, the latter for an insightful interview and permission to reuse his article explaining his powerful experience of suicide by cop. For additional insight into this topic, I would also like to thank Rebecca Stincelli of the Suicide by Cop organization (www.suicidebycop.com) for helping me understand something of the complexities behind this particular phenomenon.

A book like this relies heavily on written first-hand accounts, and on the work of others in the various fields of deadly force research. This book draws on an especially wide range of newspapers, magazines, articles, and books. Of the latter, the following are those which deserve special acknowledgement for their usefulness in this title, and are recommended reading for those wishing to explore more aspects of this complicated subject: David Killinger, *Into the Kill Zone: A Cop's Eye View of Deadly Force*; Mark Baker, *Cops*; Marilynn Johnson, *Street Justice – A History of Police Violence in New York City*; Daryl Gates, *Chief – My Life in the LAPD*; Bryan Vila and Cynthia Morris, *The Role of Police in American Society – A Documentary History*; Urey Patrick and John Hall, *In Defense of Self and Others ... Issues, Facts, & Fallacies – the Realities of Law Enforcement's Use of Deadly Force*; Geoffrey Albert and Lorie Fridell, *Police Vehicles and Firearms – Instruments of Deadly Force*; and Peter Scharf and Arnold Binder, *The Badge and the Bullet – Police Use of Deadly Force*. Rebecca Stincelli's book *Suicide by Cop: Victims on Both Sides of the Badge* also deserves a special mention. On top of such sources go a mass of invaluable articles. Those by Gregory Morrison, Thomas Aveni, Jeffrey Adler, Martin Fackler, Bill Lewinski, and John Hall have been especially useful, as have those published by the following organizations: The Police Policy Studies Council; National Institute of Justice/Department of Justice; FBI; Force Science Institute; FirearmsTactical.com; and PoliceOne.com.

I would also like to thank the many other people who have supported this project in various, invaluable ways. My sincere thanks go to all the staff at Osprey, particularly Anita Baker, Ruth Sheppard, Jaqueline Mitchell, and all the editorial team. I am also grateful to Hunter Keeter for both his friendship and his professional advice.

Writing for a living demands incessant long hours hidden away with a computer, and also absences from home. My wife, Mia, and my two wonderful young daughters have given me unfailing love, support, humor, and respite whatever the level of my working commitments. They remind me that despite the often cruel realities of my chosen subject areas, there is still much beauty in the world.

CONTENTS

INTRODUCTION

Sheriff James R. Barton needed his guns. By the time he took over as sheriff of Los Angeles County in 1851, his blood-and-dust territory was one of the most violent in an already light-triggered land. Its growth fueled by the California gold rush of the 1840s, Los Angeles was a town where furtively hidden wealth and openly displayed desperation lived uncomfortably side by side, and where young men half-crippled from work went to exorcise their demons in drink, whoring, and gambling. Racial tensions between Hispanics and European-stock Americans ran openly, events such as the Mexican-American War of 1846–48 being very recent memories for many in the region. Almost every day the newspapers and posters took murder as their headlines – *The Southern Californian*, for example, reported on March 5, 1855: "Last night was a brisk night for killing. Four men were shot and several more wounded in shooting frays."[1] One can almost sense the editorial glee that the town had provided a volume of death sufficient to distinguish it from the daily grind of individual killings.

Barton stepped into this blood-soaked arena with scant precedent and little guidance. Los Angeles had only had one previous sheriff, George T. Burrill (he served from April 1850 to September 1851), who had survived his term in the office through a mixture of grit, quick thinking and personal popularity. Yet Barton stepped into Burrill's big shoes with aplomb, and in total he took the position of sheriff six times between 1851 and 1857.

The frequency of his re-election to the post in such a dangerous town hints at a personal recklessness sometimes displayed in more open ways. Barton was, on more than a few occasions, a little too quick with his gun. Yet Los Angeles undoubtedly needed lawmen capable of violence, and the period between 1855 and 1856 when Barton was not sheriff (he stood down after a vigilante lynching of one of his prisoners) saw the rate of violence increase during the short terms of two other sheriffs. Thus many (although not all) amongst the town's population were relieved when he took the badge once again in November 1856. Then again, few could see how it would end...

On January 21, 1857, the notorious *Manillas* ('handcuffs') gang – led by outlaws Juan Flores and Pancho Daniel, and including others who had brushed with Barton before – launched one of their customary violent raids, this time on San Juan Capistrano near Los Angeles. They put bullets into a storekeeper, so this time Barton had a murder on his hands. In response, Barton gathered a posse (a group of men conscripted by a sheriff or other law enforcement officer in order to pursue a fugitive) of five other men, mounted their horses and headed out to apprehend the gunmen. Note the character of the man, and those who accompanied him. Barton was outnumbered by at least three to one, and by opponents short on mercy and big on firepower, facts that would have dissuaded most men from the pursuit.

The posse was 15 miles out from the town, and events were about to change pace. While cresting a hill, they accidentally ran headlong into the Flores/Daniel gang. Sensible men might have pulled on the reins and swung around, but that wasn't Barton's style. Undeterred, the posse leaned its horses into a full gallop and charged into what was immediately a smoking horseback gunfight, the cracks of gunpowder and bullet singeing the California air. Three outlaws were shot dead in the first few minutes of the gunfight before, in the swirl of the engagement, Daniel and Barton squared up to each other. It was the moment of truth for both men. They raised their pistols and dropped the hammers almost simultaneously – Barton missed his shot, but Daniel's heavy-caliber pistol round zipped into Barton's head with a horrible crack, dropping him from his horse into the dust below. While lying on the floor, dying, he still had enough grit to hurl his pistol uselessly at one of his attackers.

Only two of the lawmen escaped what became a massacre. By the time they raised the alarm and returned to the site of the battle with a substantial force of militia, the four men who had remained behind – Sheriff James R. Barton, Constable William H. Little, Constable Charles K. Barker and Charles Daly (a local blacksmith) – were nothing more than bullet-hacked bodies.

Sheriff James R. Barton was the first Los Angeles County sheriff to die in the line of duty. To modern civilians that fact may appear to be little more than a historical curiosity, with the passing impact of a 19th-century sepia print. Yet for serving Los Angeles police officers today, Barton's death still has resonance. The California Police Officers' Memorial society places Barton squarely in its Honor Roll, just one of the hundreds of names listed from the mid-1800s to the present day. At the time of writing, the Honor Roll has recently received a new name, 37-year-old Detective Vu Nguyen of the Sacramento County Sheriff's department. During a routine visit to a gang house in South Sacramento on December 19, 2007, Nguyen gave chase on foot to a criminal suspect. Shots were heard, and Nguyen was found shortly afterwards dying from a gunshot wound to the neck. His life ended in hospital, and a 16-year-old boy was subsequently arrested for wasting a good, young life.[2]

Vu Nguyen and James R. Barton share the same memorial because serving officers understand that although history plays itself out, the dangers stay the same. Every police officer in the world, but particularly one in such a heavily armed country as the United States, carries with him or her a background apprehension, however subdued, of violent assault and possible death every time he or she attends all but the most routine of calls. The National Law Enforcement Officers Memorial Fund states the dangers to police officers in the starkest of terms. A update recently posted on its internet database (April 3, 2006) displays as some of its core facts:

3. Crime fighting has taken its toll. Since the first recorded police death in 1792, there have been more than 17,000 law enforcement officers killed in the line of duty. Currently, there are 17,535 names engraved on the walls of the National Law Enforcement Officers Memorial.
4. A total of 1,635 law enforcement officers died in the line of duty during the past 10 years, an average of one death every 53.5 hours or 163 per year. There were 155 law enforcement officers killed in 2005.
5. On average, more than 56,000 law enforcement officers are assaulted each year, resulting in over 16,000 injuries.[3]

Since these figures were published, the death toll has continued to rise. In 2007, 188 officers died in the line of duty, 65 of them by gunfire and 48 by automobile accident (the latter showing the potential lethality of car chases). The following year, more than 120 officers fell, again the bulk of the fatalities spread between hostile gunfire and automobile accidents.[4] Such figures are the reason why officers will, as an ultimate resort, draw their own guns to stop either themselves, or innocent civilians, joining the ranks of Barton and Nguyen. In short, they will use force.

This book is about the history of the law enforcement armed response, and the use of deadly force – the application of potentially lethal firepower against the criminal or suspect. A word of warning and context is required at the outset. Police violence against citizens is highly scrutinized by the media, legal systems, and civil rights authorities, yet we who live much safer lives, often directly by virtue of the officers who maintain law and order, should be cautious looking at incidents that unfold *in extremis* and judging them from the comfort of a chair while watching the television or reading a book. It is something on which writer David Klinger, a former police officer who himself had to use deadly force, and today Associate Professor in the Department of Criminology & Criminal Justice at the University of Missouri–St Louis, has reflected:

> ... critics of the police typically gloss over or simply ignore an important fact about police work: it is an inherently dangerous job. According to FBI statistics, 644 police officers were murdered during the decade that ended in 2000. Most of these officers were slain with firearms: 452 of them with handguns, 114 with rifles, and 35 with shotguns. The other three-dozen-plus officers who were murdered during the decade were either stabbed or slashed to death with knives, swords or other cutting instruments; beaten to death with blunt instruments; purposely run down by motor vehicles; punched or kicked to death; or fell victim to some other form of gruesome fate. Tens of thousands of other officers survived assaults – many of them just barely – during the 1991 to 2000 span, including several thousand who were shot.[5]

Unless the violence or threat experienced by officers during the line of duty is appreciated, any analysis of deadly force incidence will be skewed and biased. This is not to condone those incidents where law enforcement officers have clearly, and criminally, overstepped the "acceptable" use of force, but it does at least give context to such actions – people operating in brutal worlds need exceptional mental strength if they too are not to slip into cruelty and indifference themselves.

* * *

The subject matter of this book is timely. Although there have been many excellent studies of deadly force in recent years, most have focused on contemporary issues or limited historical periods, rather than binding the whole together in an historical narrative. The reasons behind the general reluctance to tackle a comprehensive history are not too difficult to find. Statistical and procedural data for killings by law enforcement officers has often been only sketchily compiled over the decades – police departments generally being resistant to record, disclose, or discuss such incidents – liability and adverse public responses have dogged law enforcement since the earliest days. Furthermore, there is little obligation for most law enforcement agencies to log deadly force incidents, and consequently there is patchy access to hard long-term statistics. Such limitations are unavoidable, but using the records that are available, from press articles through academic data to government reports, we can still piece together a compelling narrative of how deadly force has fitted into US law enforcement since the end of the Civil War.

The start date for the main analysis, 1865, is somewhat arbitrary, as the foundations of much of the late 19th-century law enforcement system were established well before the Civil War began in 1861. (This introduction will fill in some of the blanks.) Yet the Civil War was a historical watershed for America, not least in that it went a long way toward completing the weaponization of society begun by firearms entrepreneurs such as Colt in the 1830s and 40s. The years 1865–1900 were some of the bloodiest in American history in terms of criminal use of firearms and police homicides, and so form a grim baseline for our subsequent analysis. The period also sees the attempted sharpening of federal control over state and county police actions, not always with a great deal of success, and this will be a theme to which we return again and again during this book.

The history of law enforcement use of force is, as we shall see, a case of continuity and change. The continuity part of the equation is primarily to do with the psychological realities of lethal engagements, which have scarcely changed since humans first stabbed each other with pointed sticks or bits of flint, or battered each other with rough clubs. Yet despite the ageless realities of violence, the nature of deadly force encounters is generally misrepresented not only on film and television, but also in the courtroom, where officers frequently have to unpack events with forensic precision, often for an unsympathetic audience, even though the events actually occurred in a terrifying blur that lasted one or two seconds. While the last two chapters of this book will attack many of these misrepresentations directly, they will emerge frequently throughout this book, from the Western 'dime novels' of the late 19th century to the cop films of the 2000s. Running on top of such continuity is, however, profound historical change. If we were to pick two themes that dominate policing in America over the last 150 years, they might be "professionalization" and "oversight." Increasing media visibility has steadily brightened the spotlight under which the police operate, and this in turn has required transparent professional standards and a greater awareness of civil liability. Such standards have been applied to deadly force procedures, with enhanced training providing much better tactical and psychological preparation for violent encounters. At the same time, however, each era of history presents new challenges to deadly force procedures, whether it be the labor riots of the late 19th/early 20th century (or the peace/race protests of the 1960s for that matter), the use of new forms of automatic weapon in the hands of 1920s gangsters or 1980s drug gangs, or modern phenomena such as "suicide by cop" and counterterrorist policing.

Yet before we begin our study in earnest, appreciate one fact – the vast majority of law enforcement officers will never draw their guns in anger. Nor do they wish to. Contrary to the rapid-fire fictional cops of TV and Hollywood, almost all law enforcement personnel have absolutely no desire to shoot anyone. Author Mark Baker describes this fact better than most in his work *Cops*:

> Rather than trigger happy, many cops are hesitant to use their weapons. Firing that pistol puts an officer in a no-win situation. If he handles a shooting incorrectly, makes the wrong decisions, his whole career will be in jeopardy. He could easily end up on the unemployment line, or worse, in prison. If, by care and good fortune, he shoots the right person at the right time for the right reasons, he still may suffer. He will be subjected to an investigation conducted as though he committed a criminal act. In all probability, he will be suspended from active duty and stuck at a desk job shuffling papers until the investigation is concluded. He is more likely to be excoriated by the media than praised. If he is involved in more than one such incident, he may be considered a troublemaker and be passed over for promotion. If the criminal survives, he may sue the officer for civil rights violations.[6]

Baker's accurate analysis of post-shooting problems perfectly summarizes why the right to use deadly force is actually a dead-weight vocational burden, not a liberty to be free with a gun. Moreover, and as Baker goes on to point out, professional consequences can be matched by psychological issues – the nightmares, anxiety attacks, anger, and inattention that characterize what we today label "post-traumatic stress disorder" (PTSD).

This book will explore how law enforcement officers have handled this burden through the changing political, social, cultural, and legal landscape of modern America. As such, it is as much about the sheer difficulties of policing a frequently violent and well-armed nation as it is about the dynamics of applying deadly force.

* * *

Early colonial life in 17th-century America was policed mainly by the aspirations and religious fidelity of the colonists. Living in relatively isolated communities, principally on America's eastern seaboard, and governed by respected groups of elders, the colonists had often fled the violence and turmoil of an internally combative Europe, and had little desire to replicate such strife within their own fledgling towns and villages – it was tough enough to cut life from an unforgiving sod, without turning on one another. Furthermore, the intimacy of small communities meant that it was difficult both practically and in terms of conscience to get away with substantial crime. Therefore violence and serious robbery, and the response to it, were not major issues in the mindset of the first immigrants (although the threat from Native Americans was a concern).

This situation would change via one of the most timeless social realities – add more people, get more problems. America's appetite for absorbing immigrants was ravenous. In 1700 the colonial population was around 275,000, but by 1720 that figure had flowered to 475,000 and by 1760 it was 1.5 million. Urban concentrations swelled, creating not homogenous communities but diverse stratified societies split into numerous ethnic groups and, in the competition to survive or prosper, spawning the inequalities in wealth that frequently act as spurs to crime.

During the 18th century, law enforcement consequently became a necessity, and for inspiration American society frequently looked back to the models of its homelands. The main influence was the English systems of shire reeves (later "sheriffs"), constables, and night watches that had emerged between the medieval period and the restored kingship of Charles II (r.1660–85). Colonial communities took up these models and began to appoint their own local law enforcement officers, constables, and sheriffs. We must not imbue these titles with our modern sense of professionalism. Early constables, for example, were simply appointed or elected from the town's local middle classes and turned out onto the streets to enforce the law on the basis of their own interpretation or through the frequently skewed dictates of the local judiciary. The service was generally unpaid (although there were some financial incentives for arrests, serving warrants etc), intrusive, time-consuming, and unappreciated, hence it is little surprise that many individuals served with less than total commitment. Furthermore, the low status of the job meant that it tended to be avoided by the more respectable members of society, and its ranks frequently contained rough-edged men who were as liable to bend the law as enforce it.

Constables were often in charge of recruitment to the "night watch," in effect the earliest form of organized law enforcement in North America. Night watches were a phenomenon of the towns and cities, and theoretically consisted of individuals committed to providing vigilance over the well-being of communities. Not only did they watch out for criminal activity, but their duties could also involve fire watch and weather reporting, an obvious dilution of their policing priorities.[7] One of the earliest night watches, that formed in Boston in February 1631, featured a seven-man team (one of whom was the leader) organized as a military guard, although later (1636) this was changed into a purely civilian body. Boston (and many other cities) worked on the basis that every adult male in the community would take his turn on the night watch on a rota basis. If a man couldn't attend for a particular night, then it was his responsibility to find a substitute (providing a tidy route for many people to avoid the duties altogether).

While nice and neat on paper, the system of the night watch had a different reality. Few people today would burn with enthusiasm at the idea of spending the twilight hours patrolling rough parts of town for no financial recompense, and the citizens of colonial America were no different. Consequently, constables in charge of hiring nightwatchmen often found temporary staff from the dregs of the local underworld, individuals who would either neglect their duties for the bottle or exploit the position to extort some money on the side. Urban lawmen were consequently widely disrespected, and most citizens were usually left with the law of the jungle as their only serious recourse against criminal activity.

A handful of civic leaders across the young nation, however, recognized the poor quality of law enforcement, and took the first toddling steps toward creating professional urban police units. During the 1730s, for example, Benjamin Franklin (1706–90) noted of the Philadelphia night watch system:

> The City Watch was one of the first things that I conceiv'd to want Regulation. It was managed by the Constables of the respective Wards in Turn. The Constable warn'd a Number of Housekeepers to attend him for the Night. Those who chose never to attend paid him Six Shillings a Year to be excus'd, which was supposed to be for hiring Substitutes; but was in reality much more than was necessary for that purpose, and made the Constableship a Place of Profit.[8]

Realizing that poor financial controls were at the heart of deficient policing, Franklin pushed through changes that by the mid-1740s drew police funding from direct taxation, thereby creating a police force that was more directly tied to municipal authority.

Beyond the major urban areas, in the dusty plains, cowtowns (towns dependent on the cattle industry), and on the frontiers, county sheriffs enjoyed what amounted to proper employment as law enforcement officers. Their legal jurisdiction was broader than constables, and extended to matters such as tax collection. Furthermore, sheriffs were generally elected by their local communities, at least providing the veneer of authority that comes with popular support (although elections could be manipulated). Nevertheless, few law enforcement positions of the 18th and 19th centuries could be described as "popular." Policing was necessary, and some individuals commanded more respect than others, but law enforcement officers found themselves straddling several social and political fault lines, many of which exist today – the divisions between races and gangs; the deeply entrenched belief in personal liberty versus the need for local, state and, later, federal control; the requirement that law enforcement didn't curtail the commercial vitality of a community with over-enthusiastic policing or law making.

Policing could also be plugged directly into military agenda or partisan interests – one man's law enforcement officer could be another man's persecutor. A good example of self-interested law enforcement was the slave patrols of America's South. Here were bodies employed not to police the masses, but to constrain a particular group – slaves. During the 17th century, slave revolts and the "problem" of fugitive slaves led to the formation, in the late 1600s and early 1700s, of slave patrol units designed to track down fugitives and return them to servitude, and to police potentially rebellious slave groups. First formed in states such as Virginia and South Carolina, the slave patrols hammered out their own unique brand of law enforcement (enforcing, that is, state laws on slave ownership) for well over 100 years and hence took on the function of a legitimate police force. The fear of slave patrols is apparent in many slave narratives, not just those of fugitive slaves but also those of slaves who, resembling citizens of occupied Europe during World War II, simply had to ensure correct paperwork to move freely. Clarissa Scales, a slave in Texas during the second half of the 19th century, remembered that:

> Mawster Vaughan was a great white man. He never had no overseer on his place. De slaves on his place didn't have to have no passes to go places. But dem patrols sure would whoop folks dat was caught without a pass. Many was de time dat de patrols sure would whoop 'em too.[9]

Slave patrols implemented state and county law, which didn't necessarily run in line with the desires of individual slave owners – there were frequent complaints by slave owners that the patrols abused slaves who had been given permission to travel. Furthermore, most of the slave patrols were staffed by people who were not slave owners, and therefore patrol service was one way for some of a state's more disadvantaged whites to get back at the "property" of more affluent neighbors. The other important factor in considering the status of the slave patrols was that they had military roots snaking deep into the local militia. Groups of individuals were often pulled from the militia for slave patrol duties, and the patrol itself was organized directly along military lines, with an officer in charge of a group of four or five men, similar to a military squad.[10] Later on, the slave patrols moved to a civilian volunteer basis, and in so doing the personnel were exempt from militia service, yet in many ways the slave patrols retained the sense of being a semi-military force, serving to enforce a wholesale social order rather than just police individual "crimes." Such is seen in an article from Virginia's *Norfolk Argus* in October 1860. In the heightened political environment of the antebellum South, the article recounts a clampdown on a potential slave insurrection:

> Every kind of instrument that could be procured was to be used on the occasion, such as pickaxes, pitchforks etc. One of the magistrates issued a warrant yesterday for a white man

> named Thomas Carroll, suspected of inciting the negroes to insurrection. There are about 21 negroes in jail, their ages running from 20 to 70. The surrounding country is under patrol day and night, and a strict guard is kept on the jail. The free negroes it is thought will be required to leave the country at short notice.[11]

This description has an operational feel similar to what the military terms "Operations Other Than War" (OOTW). The slave patrols are here enforcing armed 24-hour territorial control against a focused social group, with the operational remit of preventing what they would perceive as equivalent to a terrorist threat. For the black population, of course, this led to alienation from the law enforcement community in general, particularly as federal legislation progressively backed the slave patrol culture. A poster put up in Boston in 1851 illustrates something of how African-Americans feared police officers following the Fugitive Slave Act of 1850:

> CAUTION!! Colored people of Boston, one and all, you are respectfully cautioned and advised, to avoid conversing with the Watchmen and Police Officers of Boston. For since the recent order of the Mayor and Aldermen, they are empowered to act as Kidnappers and Slave Catchers, and they have already been involved in Kidnapping, Capturing and Keeping Slaves. Therefore, if you value your Liberty, and the Welfare of the Fugitives among you, Shun them in every possible manner, as so many Hounds on the track of the most unfortunate of your race. Keep a sharp lookout for Kidnappers and have Top Eye open.

The situation of the black community under the law in the 1850s raises the issue, to which we shall return with great regularity, of the relationship between state and federal law in matters of use of force and armed response. In general, the movement in the United States has been towards the increasing primacy of federal law, at least in the theoretical and constitutional framework – if anything warrants national oversight, it is the issue of putting bullets into people. In the aftermath of the American War of Independence (1775–83), the Constitution was framed and then ratified in 1788, after which the federal government introduced a series of ten amendments to reassure the American people of the limits of government power. These amendments collectively became the Bill of Rights in 1791, and a general thrust was made toward guaranteeing public freedom against unwarranted intrusions from law enforcement officials without due process of law. The constitutional amendments gave some frameworks for controlling excesses in the police use of deadly force, particularly in the Fifth Amendment statute that "No person shall be … deprived of life, liberty, or property without due process of law." Of course, one of the critical amendments from the perspective of this book is the Second Amendment, never far from the political headlines each year:

> A well regulated militia being necessary to the security of a free State, the right of the People to keep and bear arms shall not be infringed.

This book will not stir the can of worms that is Second Amendment analysis, but we shall touch on its implications. The most obvious implication for the future history of the United States was that the ability to own weapons would be barely restricted, thereby clearing the way for prodigious levels of gun ownership and the easy access to firearms for all of America's citizens, good and bad. As we shall see, when the Second Amendment was penned actual levels of gun ownership in the United States were surprisingly low, and it is only in the 19th century that the American population seriously began to arm itself. Nevertheless, what the Second Amendment implied was that the state and federal law enforcement agencies would be committed to police a *justifiably* armed society, meaning, in practical terms, that there was essentially a federally sanctioned equivalence of firepower between the civilian and the officer. Moreover, this equivalence was, and is, for many a matter of *moral* equivalence between the civilian and the police, as the twice governor of Virginia and passionate defender of civil rights, Patrick Henry (1736–99), argued vociferously:

> Are we at last brought to such humiliating and debasing degradation that we cannot be trusted with arms for our defense? Where is the difference between having our arms in possession and under our direction, and having them under the management of Congress? If our defense be the real object of having those arms, in whose hands can they be trusted with more propriety, or equal safety to us, as in our own hands?[12]

There is no discussion here of the types of weapons suited to the respective agencies, principally because at the time there was no practical distinction. Yet the distribution of *types* of weapons implied in the Second Amendment remains critically important to officers on the streets. While it is certainly now difficult for civilians to own military-grade automatic weapons, and while some 20th/21st century law enforcement agencies (such as the Coast Guard and some hostage rescue/SWAT units) can draw on military arsenals, generally a typical law enforcement officer can expect to face suspects that are potentially armed with just as much, or frequently more, firepower than he or she can bring to the fight. A brief example, to which we shall turn in greater depth in Chapter 4, is the infamous

Bank of America shootout in North Hollywood in 1997. During that incident, two bank robbers took on the police armed with numerous automatic weapons and thousands of rounds of ammunition. By contrast, the first police to arrive on the scene had nothing but 9mm Beretta pistols with 15 rounds apiece. Only later in the firefight were the police able to restore the firepower balance through SWAT teams and by requisitioning heavier firepower from a *civilian* gunstore. The point should not be lost that the gunstore was probably the best place for the officers to go because it could sell any legally distributed weapon on the marketplace, whereas the officers were restricted to weapon systems that had to balance firepower with all the other exacting social criteria for police weapons.

The Bill of Rights set the legal scene for the world of 19th-century policing. And a lively world it would prove to be. As much as the US Constitution and Bill of Rights painted a veneer of order across the American people, the reality was that law enforcement was a messy, violent business. Policing at the frontier and in the cities was often a lonely, self-responsible position, and with limited resources at his disposal an officer and his deputies would often implement law based on expediency rather than technicalities.

A new type of federal law enforcement officer made an emergence following the 1788 ratification of the Constitution – the US marshal. The term "marshal" could be applied to both federal and state officials. US marshals were specifically appointed to support the fledgling federal justice system under the terms of the Judiciary Act of 1789. Each US judicial district was to have a marshal appointed whose principal role was to execute federal judicial writs and facilitate the judicial process, including the pursuit and arrest of federal fugitives and even assisting in their execution. Section 27 of the Judiciary Act clarifies the marshal's status:

> *And be it further enacted*, That a marshal shall be appointed in and for each district for a term of four years, but shall be removable from office at pleasure, whose duty it shall be to attend the district and circuit courts when sitting therein, and also the Supreme Court in the district in which that court shall sit. (b) And to execute throughout the district, all lawful precepts directed to him, and issued under the authority of the United States, and he shall have the power to command all necessary assistance in the execution of his duty, and to appoint as shall be occasion, one or more deputies ...[13]

The US marshals proved a useful tool, and their ability to deputize duties indicated in this passage gave them some law enforcement muscle. In time, their roles would expand to include pursuing slaves (under the remit of the Fugitive Slaves Act), tracking Confederate spies during the Civil War, operating with the Internal Revenue Service (IRS) in pursuit of bootleggers, and, from the 1890s, protecting federal judges.[14] Some of their time was also spent on thundering hooves following gangs and desperadoes, and dangerous work could punctuate long periods of administrative duties. On January 11, 1794, US Marshal Robert Forsyth, marshal to the District of Georgia, and two deputies went to serve court papers on two brothers, Beverly and William Allen, who had been seen at an address in Georgia. The information proved correct – the marshals entered the house of one Mrs Dixon and discovered the Allens chatting with friends. The court papers related to the civil suit only, so Forsyth initially tried to keep the procedure low key by inviting the Allens elsewhere for a talk. Instead, the two brothers panicked and sprinted up the house stairs, locking themselves in a bedroom and loading a gun. Forsyth and his deputies set off in pursuit. Forsyth was first to the door, yet unfortunately for him Beverly Allen was aiming his pistol directly at the door. He fired, and the ball went through the wood and struck Forsyth in the head, killing him instantly, the first of over 200 US marshals killed in the line of duty to date.

The spread of the US marshals, the oldest federal law enforcement agency in the United States, was undoubtedly significant on a judicial level, but there remained the fact that they were just drops in the ocean of North American territory (during Washington's first period in office, for example, he established just 16 judicial districts, with a corresponding number of marshals). Even factoring in all other state and county agencies, law enforcement was still a sketchily distributed and unpredictably enforced business during the first half of the 19th century, particularly in the frontier regions and the gold towns and cowtowns, where officers could be quickly overwhelmed by the scale of territory or the levels of criminality. It is no surprise, therefore, that many towns and communities turned to private means of law enforcement – vigilantes, in short. Vigilantes have been popularly presented as gangs of partisan rogue gunmen who inhabit a shady world between moral uprightness and violent excess. As we shall see, some of this is true, but it is not the full picture. Often the "vigilance committees," to give them their proper title, were established not because they felt that the law was inadequate, but because they perceived the local lawmen as too corrupt to keep the peace. Nor were they an unruly rabble, as writer Roger McGrath has explained:

> Typically, vigilantes formed an executive committee and adopted a constitution. They had a chain of command and were often organized into companies and squads. Although impassioned and violent, vigilantes were usually highly disciplined, orderly, and deliberate. This was not accidental. Many of them had military experience, and some were combat veterans, having served in the Mexican War, the Civil War, or one or more of the Indian

> wars. Officially constituted authorities, realizing that they would have to oppose hundreds of well-organized and well-armed vigilantes, rarely attempted to interfere with such extralegal activities. Moreover, vigilantes generally represented the will of the majority of citizens in any particular community.[15]

Taking the image of the organized vigilante, McGrath further argues that "the actions of vigilantes should not be confused with those of a lynch mob," pointing to the fact that of the "ninety men taken into custody by the San Francisco vigilance committee of 1851, forty-one were exonerated and released, fifteen were remanded to the custody of the regular authorities, one was whipped, and twenty-eight were banished. Only four were executed."

This corrective appreciation of vigilantes is important, for they are usually associated with the worst type of deadly force procedures – the ability to kill outside of the official law. As we shall see, however, vigilantes always face the temptation to widen the remit of what is a capital crime, but during the 19th century in particular they often acted to protect the development of agriculture and mining, guarding these industries (and their own profits) from the depredations of gangs and opportunistic criminals. The research of Richard Maxwell Brown, an historian of American violence, has led him to conclude that:

> In the West of the middle and late nineteenth century, classic American vigilantism reached a peak as the economic elite and its middle-class compatriots converged in hundreds of local vigilante movements to purge the new country of outlaws so that fields, ranges, and mines could be worked in peace to produce raw materials for the factories of the East and profits for the middle and upper classes of the West.[16]

The role of vigilantes became quasi-legal often through the fact that local lawmen, town councils and civic leaders were involved with them, aiding their activities either through official support or by physically participating in them.

Yet we must not overstate the case for respectability and benefits of vigilance committees. There were certainly some responsible individuals in the world of vigilance, but equally there are plenty of examples to the contrary. The committees did indeed dish out their fair share of death via the bullet or hangman's noose. For example, the very first vigilance committee established – that around Piedmont in South Carolina – killed 16 people between 1767 and 1769. According to historian Michael Newton in *The Encyclopedia of American Law Enforcement* (New York, Checkmark Books, 2007, p.352), reported executions of vigilante groups between 1767 and 1902 number 728; these figures indicate those who were mostly hanged through quasi-judicial hearings, and does not include statistics for many hasty field killings. Individual accounts of clashes between criminals and vigilantes could exhibit almost medieval styles of persecution. One article published in the *New York Times* on December 19, 1857, based on information provided by the *Davenport* (Iowa) *Gazette*, talks of "Regulators" arresting a young man on suspicion of horse theft. One can sense a certain humor behind the article as the writer appreciates the horrible absurdities of the subsequent interrogation:

> He was threatened with immediate execution if he did not make a confession. He refused to confess anything about his companions, & c., and was swung up. He was let down gasping, but, refusing to make any confession, was again drawn up. On his feet again, the same demand of him was made the third time, and, as he had every reason to believe, the last time. Again he was pulled up into the air, and hung dangling to a slender cord, and again he was let down. Finally, recovering his breath, he told them coolly they "must be d....d fools" to try to get him to tell anything by *that* kind of process. He was tied up and thoroughly switched.[17]

The switching appears to have done the job, and the thief confessed his associate in crime, saving his own life (although one wonders whether he would have simply been tortured to death for not confessing). The Regulators then proceeded to apprehend the named third party, one Hiram Roberts, who was taken into a barn, where he too refused to make a confession. The outcome for him was chilling. Two men entered the barn, their faces ominously blackened. A few minutes later the doors of the barn opened, to picture Roberts swinging by the neck from a rope thrown over the rafters. Just for good measure, the executioners let the body hang for two days.

What is striking about this account is the way in which the vigilantes both embrace killing and yet seem to sense their shaky relationship to the law. Most of the committee withdraw for the final execution, leaving it up to two men with disguised faces, their hidden identities both terrifying to the victim yet also serving to conceal the executioners' identities, or perhaps psychologically distancing the killers from the killed. The hanging of the body for two days also suggests that with the killing done, the committee washes its hands of the incident, while also leaving a grim caution for those who might further consider horse theft as a career.

Another instability within the vigilantes was that different committees might literally divide communities, leading to feuds and what amounted to organized gang violence. For it was an inescapable reality that the power of running a large vigilante gang could go to some people's heads. The West's most famous vigilante gang gone bad is the Regulators of Shelby County, East Texas. (Note that, as in the news extract above, "Regulators" could be applied generally to vigilante groups.) The Regulators were founded by one Charles Jackson, actually a former fugitive from Louisiana, and Charles Moorman in *c.*1839, the official purpose of the sizeable gang being to prevent cattle and horse theft. By 1841, the Regulators had swelled to bullying levels of power. On July 12 of that year, for example, Jackson actually went on trial in Shelbyville for shooting a man, but his Regulators so intimidated the jury – even burning down some local houses – that the trial was abandoned. Even Jackson's assassination later in the year did not stop the violence; if anything, the number of killings rose as Moorman took command and the Regulators made more enemies.

The troubled situation grew to such an extent that a counter-Regulator force developed in Shelby County, named the Moderators and composed of various officials and citizens, including some local lawmen. What now developed was akin to outright war, a feud between two bodies over land and power. The clashes between the two sides approached levels similar to those of company-sized military engagements – in one famous clash on August 2, 1844, over 200 Regulators fought a gun battle with 62 Moderators. The conflict was only brought to a close by the intervention of the state militia, who arrested the ringleaders and effectively brought a five-year conflict to a close.

The Moderator-Regulator War, as it has become known, illustrates not only the dangers of vigilantism in general, but also the limits of law enforcement during the mid-19th century on the US frontiers. Away from the frontiers, however, deep in the growing cities, policing was achieving a measure of formalism. Utilizing models of policing developed over in England, urban America looked for some more satisfactory method of law enforcement than a largely unregulated nightwatch or constabulary. New York was the pioneer, with advocates for a professional, established police force making their voices heard as far back as 1812. However, it wasn't until *c.*1840 that mob violence and the "rising fear among the country's middle class,"[18] meant that policing became a political issue, as much as a legal one, for local mayors and aldermen. The result was that in 1845 New York became the first city in the United States to adopt a standing police force consisting of 800 officers, all full time. In 1853, moreover, the New York police adopted a formal uniform as a condition of service, setting the world of law enforcement visually apart from the rest of the population.

Other American cities soon followed suit – Chicago in 1851, Philadelphia and Boston in 1854, and Baltimore in 1857. Yet the one key distinction between Britain and the new US police forces was that the officers in the United States were *politically* beholden to local government, rather than operating under the umbrella of an independent central authority (such as the Home Secretary in the UK). The political allegiance of officers to local authorities is a theme to which we shall constantly return in this book for, as we shall see, politics and the expression of deadly force have often gone hand in hand. For the moment, it is worth noting the level of control local authorities had over policemen's careers, such as is highlighted by historian James Richardson concerning the formation of the New York police:

> To provide some over-all supervision, the act created the office of chief of police... But his supervisory powers over the police force were very limited. He could not appoint, assign, or remove policemen since these prerogatives were reserved to the mayor and the Common Council. Like the policemen, the chief was appointed for a term of only one year and could be removed before the expiration of his term. The appointment was to be made by the mayor with the approval of the council.

Policemen were to be chosen by the mayor upon the nomination of the alderman, assistant alderman, and the two tax assessors of each ward. The mayor could reject or accept such nominations, and in case of rejection new names would be submitted in the same manner as the original ones. In such a system the real power of appointment lay with the alderman and assistant alderman of each ward.[19]

In today's atmosphere of legal transparency, such open political power over the forces of law and order is unsettling. Combine that power with the deep Democrat/Republican divisions that often cracked open American society, and which fueled much of its violence in the Reconstruction era, and you have a deeply preferential police service in many places.

Yet this does not mean that the authorities welcomed their commitment to policing. Police were, and remain, a considerable drain on civic budgets, money that could be spent elsewhere. In the following extract from the *Brooklyn Daily Eagle*, dating from 1865, the mayor of the town delivers a statement on the annual budget, with some hesitant opinions about increases in police funding:

> Statement No. 6 is an estimate of the amount required for police purposes. It will be seen that as compared with the sum estimated for 1864, the amount is nearly double... The increase has been caused by the rate of compensation paid to the force and directing the addition of one hundred men to its strength. I have long felt convinced, and I believe that such is the conviction of the majority of our citizens, that some increase of the police force was indispensable to make it as efficient as is needed, and have urged action, having in view

> the accomplishment of that end. I confess, however, that in view of the unavoidable additions to our heavy burthen of taxation from various causes, I have lately felt some misgiving as to the propriety of incurring the great expense which an immediate increase of the force would entail upon the city. I had hoped, at least, that the addition of a less number than one hundred would suffice, but the Board of Aldermen have voted that number. The Police Commissioners also desire it, and as the law authorizes them to add them, whether the Common Council agrees to it or not, there was no room for an appeal from the decision.[20]

What is implicit here is how the police have gained a deeper relevance to the order of the city, and as such command greater authority to acquire investment and expansion. Debates leading up to the new budget highlighted that Brooklyn's 200 police officers were inadequate to perform crime-fighting duties, especially when large numbers of them were redirected to deal with fires or riots. The council debates also reflected on the fact that building projects had increased the value of housing in many areas, and the safety of the wealthy citizenry – with all its commercial and political muscle – had become paramount. It is further noteworthy to see that the police commissioners themselves had acquired powers of self-expansion by this time – the mayor's hand-wringing impotence on the matter is palpable.

By the time the Civil War broke out in 1861, the United States had, with many holes, anomalies, and imperfections, a system of policing both in the frontier regions and in the cities. The population of the country kept on growing, and the police would grow with it, as would the need for effective methods of social order. Taking this rough journey through early US policing forward into the next chapter, we will now wander into the world of deadly force. As we shall see, while the law of the gun was often genuinely necessary in a violent land, gunsmoke frequently blurred the line between legal killing and spur-of-the-moment execution.

1

WAR AND ORDER, 1865–1900

It's hard now to imagine the four years of horror unleashed by the American Civil War (1861–65). Civil wars are always bitter, internecine conflicts, and the American War, which took 900,000 lives, turned the original dream of a harmonious new world nation into a scarred and blood-soaked nightmare.

In terms of our story of the use of force, the Civil War was also a critical starting point for one simple reason – guns. For whichever way we look at it, the story of deadly force and armed response is ultimately about firearms. What we see following the Civil War is the perfection of a trend begun in the 1840s and 1850s – the arming of a nation. The combination of massive firearms acquisition amongst the people, plus a growing population and a concomitant rise in crime rates (particularly armed violence), made the police adoption of firearms a nationwide necessity rather than a preference. Once this shift had occurred, deadly force became an intrinsic part of police physical response.

A LAND OF GUNS

The popular view of US culture imagines a nation born from the barrel of the gun. This picture sees blue gunsmoke drifting pervasively over the early American landscape, with the colonial man claiming his own personal space against animals and aggressors through a faithful rifle. Careful research, however, has shown that this view is largely a myth. Gun ownership was not a birth gift to the American people, and America would not truly arm itself in earnest until the second half of the 19th century.

The historian Michael Bellesiles has done particularly interesting work in this area. Working through two forms of archives – county probate records and militia inventories – Bellesiles' research threw up some unexpected conclusions. The county probate records (property records compiled when a person died) for 38 counties between 1765 and 1850 indicate that the national average of gun ownership ran at only 14.7 percent for 1765–90, 16.1 percent for 1808–11, 17 percent for 1819–21 and 20.7 percent for 1830–32.[21] The figures show that firearm users were actually a minority amongst the American people for much of their early history, and the militia inventories deepen this picture. Backed by other documentary evidence, the inventories reveal militia forces throughout the United States plagued by both a lack of gun ownership and, significantly, a lack of familiarity with guns. (In this context, remember that in many states all white, property-owning males were obliged, with various exemptions, to serve in defense militias, bringing with them whatever firearms they owned.)

> In the first official inventory of American arms in 1793, Secretary of War Knox found that 37 per cent of the 44,442 muskets owned by the government were unusable, and an additional 25 per cent were either archaic or in serious need of repair and cleaning. The following year Knox estimated that there were 450,000 militia members in the United States, of whom no more than 100,000 either owned or had been supplied with guns. A decade later Secretary of War William Eustis, in what was probably the most thorough and exact of all the studies, found that almost nothing had changed: 45.4 per cent of the militia bore arms; the total number of guns recorded was sufficient for 4.3 per cent of the American population, or 20.9 per cent of white adult males.[22]

Bellesiles found this pattern of marginal gun ownership stretching on into the 1830s, and there are plenty of reports and letters from militia commanders bewailing their lack of an arsenal, and also the general lack of care shown by the militia towards what weapons they had.

Allowing for the inevitable error margins of such antique data, we can still be confident that prior to the 1830s, the US population was not a deeply armed people.

The reason for this is not difficult to see. Firearms technology before the 1830s was still dominated by flintlock weapons, either crudely made military types that had few applications outside mass battlefield volley fire, or bespoke hunting weapons that were simply too expensive for much of the American population. Yet this situation underwent a steady revolution as the country marched towards the middle of the decade. In 1836, the legendary Samuel Colt began production of his first revolver handguns, known as Colt-Patersons after the place of production – Paterson, New Jersey. The early Colts were bulky, heavy creations, but they were the beginning of a journey that would arm America. If any weapon could be purpose-designed to fuel crime and disorder, you could scarcely do better than the revolver. Good only for short-range shooting, the revolver offered several critical advantages over previous single-shot flintlock models or the cumbersome "pepperbox" revolvers. First, it provided a genuine multi-shot capability – the revolver's cylinder held five or six shots, fired in turn by simply drawing back the hammer and pulling the trigger. Second, Colt produced generally reliable weapons, meaning that killing became less of an unpredictable adventure. Third, and most important, they were affordable. While Henry Ford is often given the credit in American history for inventing the modern production-line process, that accolade might better be given to Samuel Colt. Colt invested in a system of production where individual workers focused entirely on producing specific parts in a fast, repetitious process, these parts being put together at a final assembly point.

Colt allied this production method to a slick marketing machine that equated gun ownership with manly virtues and the obligation to protect home and family. As with production, Colt was years ahead of his time in terms of marketing. He was a pioneer in using stirring artworks to sell his firearms – a classic example, relevant to our study here, pictures nothing but a rugged sheriff on horseback gazing across the prairies, the picture accompanied by the strapline "Colt – The arm of law and order." He also used a network of national and international agents and wholesalers, and applied strategic tools such as product sampling and public relations to push his brand.

After some financial fits and starts during the 1840s, sales rose (initially through military sales, then through private purchases) and the economies of scale subsequently pushed guns to within most people's budget. Regardless of your knowledge of firearms, you could buy a Colt revolver and, after reading the enclosed instructions printed on the cleaning rag (instructions were another of Colt's innovations), you were ready for battle, or crime. If the gun broke, then the fact that Colt revolvers were made of standardized parts meant that they were easy to repair and maintain.

Colt was soon joined by many other legendary names in the world of handgun production, such as Remington and Starr. From 1857 Smith & Wesson, by far Colt's greatest early competitor, introduced revolvers taking unitary metallic cartridges, improving the firepower of the common revolver exponentially. Previously the chambers of the gun were loaded individually with percussion cap, powder, and ball, but the cartridge combined all three elements into one, which could be dropped straight into the chambers. New ejector systems made reloading much faster. While rifles enabled people to hunt or take long-range battlefield shots, revolvers centered on the notion of self-defense. Whether that self was criminal, law enforcement, or just average citizen was another matter.

Some social commentators would later take a good, hard look at the revolver's legacy, and find in the process that America had arguably stepped off an ethical precipice. A journal article in the *Quincy Daily Whig*, dated August 18, 1906, reflects on the recent death of

Daniel B. Wesson, one half of a partnership that did every bit as much as Colt to arm America. Noting that Wesson "died with a fortune estimated at $30 million," the author then sees the blood in the money:

> Thirty million dollars is a big sum to be charged to a single dangerous and homicidal luxury. The revolver is that. It is of dubious service in war. Its only function there is as a cavalry weapon. It is effective only up to fifty yards. It has no value for hunting. The average man can do no more execution on birds and beasts with a slingshot. The only purpose which the revolver serves is to kill another man, and even for that its usefulness is over-estimated. A household armed with a pickhandle or baseball bat is in better shape to meet a burglar in his bedroom than if armed with a revolver; he can do pretty nearly as well with a heavy shoe, used as a bludgeon. The revolver is the anarch among weapons. It is dedicated to the idea of private justice. Private justice is mischievous in an age of law, and the revolver has done far more harm than good. The first impulse of anger finds in it a weapon ready to hand. It defeats the restraining second thought.[23]

The writer here raises a question to which we shall return in later chapters in more depth – "What is a handgun for?" Here the answer is that the revolver enables people to express aggression through its very convenience, its "ready to hand" quality. Furthermore, he points to the idea of "private justice" as a mental justification for handgun ownership, whereas the justice a handgun can deliver is far from sure.

The other seminal factor in the rise of armed America was the single greatest event in US history – the American Civil War. The social ramifications of the Civil War are profound and far-reaching. One effect of direct importance to police officers was that huge numbers of disbanded soldiers took their guns home with them, flooding society with arms and equal numbers of battle-hardened veterans. Production totals of firearms remained high even after the war. For example, Colt's most enduring 19th-century model, the Single Action Army or "Peacemaker," began production in 1873; by 1892 it was at serial number 144,000, and by 1900 at 192,000. New varieties of pocket pistols – small, easily concealed handguns – gave even the most urbane citizen lethal recourse. The brutalizing effects of war, and the sharp legacies of fear and mistrust between communities and factions, particularly between Democrat and Republican, meant that many people now viewed gun ownership as a sage necessity. Bellesiles sums the shift up perfectly:

> Prior to the war, the emerging middle class viewed with disdain the ugliness of personal confrontation and violence, though workers tended to find some defining manliness in the

> ability to fight well. Yet resorting to violence in antebellum America rarely involved the use of firearms. That attitude changed considerably after the war, most especially in the cities, with revolvers now small enough to fit in a coat pocket. Inexpensive and readily available guns changed many social equations...[24]

Methods of murder reflected this ascendant "way of the gun," and changed accordingly as the 19th century wound on. Bellesiles' collation of murder statistics for the 19th century, for instance, shows that between 1800 and 1845, beating, drowning, strangling, and stabbing were the principal methods of killing in the United States, with the gun accounting for just 17.2 percent of murders. Yet between 1846 and 1860, the figure for gun killings "nearly doubled, to 32.6 percent; for the remaining forty years of the century, it climbed to 47.5 percent."

For those law enforcement officers who had to police this new landscape, the escalation of gun ownership, combined with a multitude of other factors, expressed itself in a sharp rise in the number of line-of-duty fatalities. For the documented years between 1808 and 1864, a period of 56 years, the National Law Enforcement Memorial Fund lists the deaths of 61 officers killed in service. From 1864 to 1898, a period of 34 years, the Memorial charts 570 officers killed. Even allowing for years without accounting for the sheer growth in police departments and urban populations, the leap is striking. The data does not list the causes of death, but samplings of biographies from historical rolls of honor from various police departments give repetitive evidence of gun violence as the biggest culprit. For example, the Seattle Police Department gives one David Sires as the first officer killed in the department's history. He was shot dead on October 16, 1881, by (according to the official report) a "worthless loafer and desperado." The second to die was Police Detective James Wells on November 28, 1897. While Wells was transporting a suspect to custody the suspect suddenly produced a handgun, fired several volleys, and fatally wounded Wells. The very next year, Police Officer Thomas L. Roberts and his partner stopped two men for questioning in the Renton Hills Addition area of the city. One man pulled a gun and began blazing away, killing Roberts and seriously injuring his partner.

Jump outside of Seattle and the gun violence is much the same. In Austin, Texas, the first officer to die was Cornelius L. Fahey, shot on March 8, 1875, by a violent drunk. Of six officers of the Washington DC Metropolitan Police Department killed between 1871 and 1891, four were killed in shooting incidents. Of the remaining two, one was stabbed to death – reminding us that guns were far from the only lethal threat faced by police – and another drowned after tumbling from a police boat into a river.

The statistics mask some social complexities that will be revealed in due course, but the conditions of postbellum America meant one thing – law enforcement officers had to reach for their guns.

POLICING THE OLD WEST

Depending on your perspective, Dave Mather was either an ideal choice or a criminal misjudgment when he was appointed as the assistant marshal of Dodge City on June 1, 1883, also taking the title of deputy sheriff of Ford County. "Mysterious Dave," as he subsequently became nicknamed on account of his habitual silence and threatening demeanor, is one of those dark and impossibly colorful characters that seem to litter the pages of Wild West history. Born in Connecticut in 1851, Mather steered off the rails from his early 20s. He drifted through Arkansas, where he joined two other undesirables to form his own cattle-rustling gang, moving through to Texas after a warrant was issued on them for the murder of a rancher. Mather kept shifting across the landscape, and ended up in a city where he could indulge his love of saloons – Dodge City, Kansas.

By the early 1870s, Dodge City was on the up, commercially though not ethically. This regular cowtown had been transformed with the arrival of the Atchinson, Topeka, & Sante Fe Railroad by 1873, after which it became a major destination along the Chisholm cattle trail. An explosion of saloons, hotels, brothels, shops, and casinos made Dodge City a magnet for hardened men coming in from the plains, and for dissolute characters looking to make money in a place with a frequently tenuous grip on the law. The town was violent, as the historian Roger McGrath puts into context with details of homicide rates:

> Ellsworth, one of the Kansas cattle towns, had eight homicides following its establishment in 1867, and Dodge City, the queen of the cattle towns, had nine in its first year, 1872–1873. Since the populations of all these towns were small – never more than two or three thousand during the first year – their homicide rates would seem to have been very high. By contrast, Oakland, California, a western but by 1870 no longer a frontier town, had only two homicides during the entire first half of the 1870s, and its population was more than 11,000 in 1870 and nearly 25,000 in 1875.[25]

Mather's first period in Dodge was a lesson in brutality. He was seriously injured in a saloon knife fight, and then took up employment as a hired gun for the railroad. As part of a 70-strong gang headed by Bat Masterson, Mather took part in the violent "Railroad Wars" between the Atchinson Railroad and the Denver & Rio Grande Railroad, both of whom were competing to be the first to run their lines through the Raton Pass. The fighting was on a substantial scale, and was ultimately won by the Denver & Rio Grande, after which Mather cut his losses and journeyed on to Las Vegas. While there, he befriended the legendary Doc Holliday, who had also lived in Dodge. Holliday gave Mather some social representation, and despite the fact that Mather was already being studied by the law in connection with several robberies, he achieved the position of Deputy US Marshal.

While in Las Vegas, Mather gave further proof of his skill with a gun, an illustration of how easy it was in those days to slip from routine law enforcement into a major deadly force incident. On January 22, 1880, Mather and Marshal Joe Carson were called to deal with the presence of four known troublemakers – T. J. House, John Dorsey, William Randall, and James West – who had crashed into town and were cooking up trouble in the Close & Patterson Variety Hall. The two officers entered the hall and demanded that the four men check their guns. It seems that the suspects were far from compliant, for soon the saloon's smoky air was split open by gunfire. Carson was quickly shot dead by the four men, but Mather took cover and stoically returned fire. Against the heavily stacked odds, Mather shot and killed Randall, wounded West, and sufficiently scared Dorsey and House into flight. The two remaining fugitives were subsequently caught by a posse and imprisoned, but were later shot dead by Mrs Joe Carson, who was part of a lynch mob that dragged the men from their cells. Mather's reputation seemed assured, and he took Carson's rank, but his over-readiness to use a gun eventually bred unpopularity, and he traveled on to become an assistant marshal in El Paso, Texas. A violent incident in a brothel ejected him from that post, and so back he went to Dodge.

The lawmen who attempted to control Dodge City's violence were some of the most famous names of the West, including Bat Masterson and Wyatt Earp. Dodge City needed hard men to rule, and Mather was certainly that when he managed to engineer his law enforcement appointments. At first, life seemed good for Mather in Dodge. He was on a very respectable salary of $125 a month, which along with the $150 paid to the marshal (Jack Bridges) inspired some wry comments from local newspapers. The *Ford County Globe* commented: "Dodge City pays her marshal $150 per month and the assistant marshal $125 per month. Besides this, each of them is entitled to kill a cowboy or two each season."[26] Problems began, however, in April 1884 when the newly elected mayor, George M. Hoover, dismissed Mather and Bridges and replaced them, respectively, with Thomas C. Nixon and William M. "Bill" Tighman. (Note, however, that Mather retained his deputy sheriff position.) Further slaps in the face ensued. Mather and a friend attempted to open a dance hall in Dodge, but a new city ordinance prohibited "what is commonly known as a dance hall, or any other place where lewd women and men congregate for the purpose of dancing or otherwise." Yet the ordinance did not seem to extend to Thomas Nixon, who had no problem establishing and running the local Lady Gay saloon/dance hall.

Animosity between the Nixon and Mather men bubbled like a cesspool, and it was inevitable that guns would be drawn. The first to shoot was Nixon, when on July 18, 1884, he took a pot shot at Mather, who was standing in the doorway of the Opera House saloon. The bullet missed, and Nixon was shipped off to jail, subsequently being bailed for $800 but bound to appear in court on a charge of attempted murder.

Nixon never made it to the court house. Accounts of what happened vary somewhat, but what seems sure is that on July 21, 1884, Mather walked up behind Nixon, who was watching a game of cards, and shot him four times in the back with his Colt .45 revolver, killing him instantly.

Mather was arrested, and held without bail on the capital crime of first-degree murder. A reporter for the *Topeka Daily Commonwealth* observed that Mather sat in court "calm and collected, and being unrestrained, the best observer of human nature could not have selected him as the man whose life was in jeopardy."[27] The evidence initially seemed stacked against Mather. The testimony from the legendary Bat Masterson, who had quickly arrived on the scene, recounted what he found as he came across Nixon's body:

> I was probably the first that took hold of him. He was lying on his right side and back, with his head south west, and his feet north east. His right hand was up and his left was on his left hip. This was about a minute after the last shot was fired. He had his revolver on. He was lying on it. It was in his scabbard. It looked as if it might have fallen partly out or been drawn partly out. I did not see any other weapons on him or in his hands.

Even in the face of such incriminating evidence, which sketched Mather more as casual executioner than as someone who simply acted in self-defense, it took the jury only 27 minutes to find him not guilty, on December 31. Strict evidence of whether Mather acted to a threat probably didn't count for too much. Much jury-making in the late 1800s consisted of deciding whether someone "had it coming," and the rights of criminals and reprobates were a fairly distant concept. (The jury did accede that a bullet from Mather's gun had killed an old greyhound dog sleeping in the saloon, but wryly concluded that "the shooting was justified as any dog should have known better than go to sleep in a Dodge City Saloon."[28])

Despite the acquittal, it became apparent to the city authorities that "Mysterious Dave" Mather was not the ideal person to represent the stolid force of law and order, and he was essentially asked to leave the town. (Some more forceful accounts say he was given the choice of death or exile.) His subsequent life is largely conjecture, although a body

– complete with a bullet hole in the side of the head – found on the tracks of the Central Texas Railroad in 1886 was reputed to be that of Mather.

Whatever the case, Mather's trigger-happy career raises some notable themes for the study of 19th-century use of force. There seems to be, for example, a distinct lack of before-the-event policy restrictions on when deadly force might be applied. The expectation seems to be that in a violent frontier world, it was the character of the officer, guided by his own moral compass, that was the root of decision about whether to draw a gun and pull the trigger or not. By way of contrast, modern police forces have the limits and conditions of deadly force dictated to them in lengthy use-of-force policy documents, thus implying that the *law* is the groundwork for a shooting, not necessarily what an individual feels to be the right circumstances. Some of these documents will be examined in detail in later chapters, but for our study of the late 19th century one of the faultlines of the "moral shooter" idea lies in the nature of recruitment. For example, the life of Mather proves that having been a former criminal was no bar to work in law enforcement. In historian Bill O'Neal's recommended book *The Pimlico Encyclopedia of Western Gunfighters*, of the 255 gunfighters listed – who include many of the West's truly unpleasant characters – some 110 were employed as law officers at some point in their lives.[29] A random selection of the vocational listings for some of these individuals suggests that taking on the role of law officer was seldom a calling of conscience:

Brooks, William L. – stage driver, buffalo hunter, law officer, mule thief

Brown, Henry Newton – farmer, cowboy, buffalo hunter, cattle rustler, law officer, bank robber

Fisher, John King – bronco buster, cowboy, rancher, rustler, saloon partner, law officer, gunman

Leslie, Nashville Franklin – Indian scout, bartender, bouncer, jailer, law officer, ranch foreman, convict

Long, Steve – law officer, thief

Miller, James B. – cowboy, rustler, law officer, saloon keeper, gambler, hotel owner, professional killer[30]

The alarming picture from even such a short list is how the law enforcement career phase is sandwiched between both entry and relapse into criminality. Furthermore, it would be hard to argue that the quickness with a gun intrinsic to callings such as bank robber, gunman and professional killer would not rub off on the attitude to deadly force during the individual's period as a law officer.

The point that should not be lost here, however, is that such men had a clear and identifiable quality very useful for imposing order upon a town – fear. Take the second person on our list, Henry Newton Brown (1857–84). By the time he was appointed deputy marshal of Caldwell, Kansas, in July 1882, Brown had already killed numerous men (his first at the age of 19) and was a hired gun during the infamous Lincoln County War of the 1870s. During this conflict he was actually one of three men indicted for killing a sheriff and his deputy. He had also had some short-lived law officer experience: he was briefly appointed as deputy sheriff to Oldham County, but his tendency towards violence pushed him out of the profession.

It is hard to credit that a known killer, including a killer of law officers, plus someone who had already been ejected from police employment, would ever find work again as a law enforcement officer. Evidently the good authorities of Caldwell were desperate – and we should not underestimate how desperate life could become in the cowtowns, mining towns, and frontier settlements of the West. Gangs of gunmen could indeed rule a town without an equivalently violent force of law arraigned against them, and that's just what Brown gave Caldwell. O'Neal picks up the story:

> … within a few months he was appointed to city marshal. He imported a Texas hard case called Ben Wheeler (whose real name was Ben Robertson), to be his deputy, and the two gunmen immediately tamed Caldwell. On New Year's Day, 1883, Brown was presented a new Winchester with a silver plate saluting his "valuable services to the citizens of Caldwell, Kansas." Brown quieted the town still further by killing two troublemakers in ensuing months, and he otherwise enforced the law by helping track down area fugitives.[31]

This record of sterling service, however, masked a rather darker reality about the life of Henry Newton Brown. In June 1884, Brown was caught after robbing a bank in nearby Medicine, aided by Wheeler. Two bank staff were shot dead during the raid, resulting in a town posse chasing down the two men and apprehending them. Wheeler and Brown were subsequently lynched, bringing rough lives to a rough end.

Brown's example is far from rare when trawling through Western biographies. Although we mustn't overplay the influence of criminals within the US police forces during the second half of the 19th century – the vast majority were, and always had been, law-abiding citizens – the fact that criminals could so easily transition in and out of law enforcement must have made for a sketchy approach to the application of deadly force. Other factors heightened this effect. Remember that county sheriffs and city marshals were *elected* officials, and they regularly had to run for re-election. While the democratic process may seem relatively positive, in law enforcement it meant that the police officer had to court the popularity of the civic authorities and electorate, and what made an officer popular didn't always correspond with what made a law officer just. Furthermore, the performance of a sheriff, marshal, deputy, or constable would in turn reflect upon the authorities responsible for his appointment – it was in their interest to pin the badge on people who toed the political line. Hence an over-eagerness with the gun might be a vote-winner – what better way to please a population than providing a truly final solution to any anti-social elements.

A fine example of gun politics comes from an episode in the life of no less than James Butler Hickok, better known by his "Wild Bill" nickname. In April 1871, Hickok was appointed marshal of the utterly dire cowtown of Abilene, Kansas. If ever Clint Eastwood's mysterious gunman could have cherry-picked a violent, dusty town to ride into, he would have done no worse than Abilene. Abilene was born purely to serve the cattle industry, the town growing around a railhead built in the late 1860s by the Union Pacific Railway Company (Eastern Division), a railhead that sat at the end of a long Chisholm Trail across Texas. Texan cowboys would drive their cattle across hundreds of miles of plains, before finally unloading them in the pens at Abilene for rail shipment out to America's urban centers, while also unloading their inhibitions in Abilene's sprawl of saloons and brothels.[32] As cowtowns acquired ever-larger non-transient populations, the distaste and fear of the seasonal cowboy influx grew. One senses a lip-curling displeasure in the following extract from *The Kansas Daily Commonwealth*, which noted that each cowboy carried a pair of revolvers:

> … which he will use with as little hesitation on a man as on a wild animal. Such a character is dangerous and desperate, and each one generally has killed his man. There are good and even honorable men among them, but run-away boys and men who find it too hot for them even in Texas join the cattle drovers and constitute a large proportion of them. They drink, swear, and fight, and life with them is a round of boisterous gaiety and indulgence in sensual pleasure.[33]

It was into such a chaotic society that Hickok arrived. His appointment came at a specific political juncture. Joseph G. McCoy had just been elected to the position of mayor in the town's first municipal election, and McCoy had to make his mark on the rumbling issue of law and order. Hickok was stepping into a dead man's shoes. The previous marshal had been Thomas J. "Bear River" Smith, a granite-tough New York-Irish officer used to sorting out cowboys with either his fists or his guns. Smith came to a horrifying end while arresting one Andrew McConnell on the charge of murder. McConnell shot and injured Smith, whereupon one of McConnell's associates nearly decapitated Smith with an axe. Despite having Smith's ghost haunting him in the background, Hickok set about his policing with nerve and vigor. He was aided by the way the press lionized his reputation, expanding his actual tally of five men killed into dozens, thus giving his image added weight amongst the criminally minded. Wielding both his guns and his persona, Hickok imposed something approaching order upon Abilene during the cattle season, closing down disreputable brothels and dance halls, arresting the drunk and disorderly, and shutting down illegal gambling dens.

On a night in October 1871, however, Hickok demonstrated the cruel consequences of Wild West deadly force. On October 5, he was in the Alamo saloon with his part-time jailor Michael Williams, when he heard a shot outside. Stepping through the saloon doors into outdoor light, he found a gang of some 50 Texans, all pumped up with guns, alcohol, and adrenaline, headed by the owner of the Bull's Head Tavern, Phil Coe. The Texans had little affection for Hickok; he had spent most of the day attempting to disarm them as they became heavily drunk, enjoying themselves for one last day before returning to the trail. Hickok and Coe bristled and postured, standing only feet apart, with Hickok demanding that Coe drop his piece. Instead, Coe went for the shot, pulling the trigger twice but missing by inches each time. Hickok was more assured – his two shots went straight into Coe's stomach, dropping the man to the floor. Suddenly a figure rushed towards him from out of the darkness. Hickok moved fast, firing twice again – straight into Williams, who had sprinted outside to Hickok's aid. Once Hickok recognized the figure of his dying friend, he was nearly overcome with grief. He carried Williams back into the bar, but then returned outside and, fueled by despair, fearlessly manhandled the crowd into dispersing. By the time he returned to the bar Williams was dead. Coe would also die, but not until three days later.

The aftermath of the shooting was critical to Hickok's political status within Abilene. Unlike the lengthy legal processes such an incident would ignite today, what mattered in this case was how the public arena judged the event. Hickok did receive some threats following the shooting, but the balance of public judgment is best expressed by a local newspaper editorial, which noted that for criminals:

> ... there is no use in trying to override Wild Bill, the Marshal. His arrangements for policing the city are complete, and attempts to kill police officers or in any way create disturbance, must result in the loss of life on the part of violators of law. We hope that all, strangers as well as citizens, will aid by word and deed in maintaining peace and quietness.[34]

Hickok received the approbation of the local council as well as the local media. Frontier towns seemed fairly unanimous in their acceptance of deadly force as a means of engineering something approaching a functioning, lawful society, and acknowledged that the brutal delivery of this force by a hardened lawman was a necessity.

And yet, we mustn't think of the lawman operating in the judge, jury, and executioner role without oversight. Any killing would be subject to local scrutiny, both from the public and the media at large and from the coroner's court or local town authorities. (General police behavior was also analyzed; a town ordinance from Ellsworth dated April 1870 stipulated that any police officer found gambling, drinking, or whoring on duty would be fired.) In the case of questionable killings, the officer might well find that his personal safety became much more precarious – even editorials concerning the Hickok shooting noted that "Wild Bill" invested in a short-barrel shotgun as extra protection in the wake of the killing. Furthermore, the officers had to *prove* their value through effective policing – status was not automatically afforded with the job. Law enforcement salaries were often extremely low, particularly outside the cattle season and for deputy-level positions. Indeed, in many places officers were forced to supplement their salaries through fairly menial means, such as receiving fees for every stray dog they shot. Frequently, law enforcement salaries and expenses seemed given by town authorities with grinding reluctance, even when it came to ammunition allocations:

> Worse, the city fathers even begrudged the amount spent on ammunition for the police force. A typical example can be found at Wichita where, in 1871, according to city records, a measly six dollars was allocated for each policeman. Seventy-five cents was allowed either for a box of six paper or foil cartridges for a .36 or .44 caliber pistol, and a box of caps cost twenty cents. For powder, shot and cartridges, $1.35 was admissible. One can only assume that they were expected to make every shot count or be personally liable for unauthorized discharges.[35]

Financial hardship, danger, and public accountability must have imbued the position of law enforcement officer with more than its fair share of work-related stress. If we were to sum up how deadly force fitted into this career, it might be fair to say that an officer was free to use his judgment about whether to pull the trigger or not, but he could not afford to swim against the internal political and ethical currents of his town.

What we might term "political policing" – policing under the direct political supervision of a local elected authority – had, as we shall see, a whole host of dangers. In the years surrounding the Civil War, for example, being classified as Democrat or

Republican had explosive potential for polarizing communities into violent feuds. Representatives of federal law enforcement bodies also found themselves feeling distinctly unwelcome when venturing out into highly independent frontier communities, and attempting to impose law upon them.

A story from the *New York Times* dated April 22, 1860, although it sits just before our main period of consideration, illustrates this point well. The story centers on the shooting of a deputy US marshal, Leonard Arms, in Topeka, Kansas. The deputy marshal had been serving two writs upon a local "old citizen of Topeka," John Richey. The arrest turned into a violent argument, with both men going for their guns. Evidently, Richey may have been advancing in years but his competence with a gun was not diminished – he killed the officer by putting a bullet through his neck, severing his spinal cord. Newspaper accounts of killings during the 19th century were rarely impartial, and although the *Times* correspondent has a stab at rounded judgment ("Statements are contradictory as to what follows…"), there is little doubt as to where the balance of his interpretation lies. The writer is at pains to represent the stalwart character of Richey, describing him as someone with a "very warm, ardent temperament" who "has taken an active part in maintaining our defenses, and has never faltered at any post of duty." Arms, by contrast, is presented as a decent enough individual until he took the post of deputy marshal, at which he seems to have become positively villainous:

> One of his first efforts as a Government functionary was, when he came to Lawrence last February to attempt the kidnapping of a negro woman who was then living in a private family in this city. He at once encountered the indignation of nearly the whole of our population, and he was publicly posted in the streets the next day as a kidnapper, and the public were warned to "Beware". He was told plainly at that time that if he persisted in such business, he would soon find his level, and given to understand that such dirty business could not be followed in safety.[36]

The threat against a serving law enforcement officer in the last sentence is overt, and his ultimate death seems condoned in the tone and tenor of the article – moreover Richey was acquitted over the killing. Although this incident doubtless reflects some of the specific tensions building in antebellum America, there is also the understanding that the citizens retain the right to answer force with force. In this context deadly force ceases to be the ethical prerogative of the law enforcement officer, but is a potentially lethal version of the "checks and balances" of US government – the people's capacity for violence is the check on the officer's capacity for violence.

The atmosphere of mutual threat, plus the political management of police officers, are two reasons why on occasions police deadly force overstepped the boundaries of law enforcement into the realm of gang violence. The most egregious example of deadly force serving political ends comes from the grim chronology of what became known as the Lincoln County War. In the early 1870s two former army officers, Lawrence G. Murphy and Emil Fritz, founded a mercantile and banking operation in Lincoln, New Mexico (Lincoln County was the largest county in the United States at the time, covering around one fifth of New Mexico's territory). The two men had powerful political backing from the Santa Fe Ring, an organization of local politicians and entrepreneurs that effectively ran the county like a gangster's turf, being vehemently opposed to anything that threatened or diluted their financial interests.

Unfortunately for Lincoln County, the status quo was soon to be split apart. In 1877, lawyer Alexander McSween and English entrepreneur John Tunstall, both backed by the powerful cattle baron John Chisum (who settled his own ranch in Fort Sumner, New Mexico), established their own rival banking and goods company right in the heart of Lincoln. In 1874, following the death of Fritz, James Dolan of County Galway, Ireland, had taken over his share of the business to form the Murphy & Dolan company, better known locally as "the House." The bulk of their business was beef supply to the Mescalero Apache Reservation and the military base at Fort Stanton. Politically, the House was primarily Democrat, although that didn't prevent it from working with corrupt Republican politicians in local government, particularly Thomas B. Catron, attorney general of New Mexico Territory and president of the First National Bank of Santa Fe.

At first relations between the two rival companies appeared reasonably good-natured. McSween was employed for his legal skills as executor of Fritz's estate, but a powder keg smoldered at the heart of this situation. The House claimed some $2,000 of Fritz's $10,000 estate, but McSween retained the funds in order to satisfy future claimants. There were plenty of hotheads on both sides, and as verbal accusations flew guns were holstered and men mustered. The dispute snaked out into other areas, the rival commercial interests between the two sides underpinning the growing animosity. Each side began to build up its own private army for what would become a turf war.

When first blood came, it was a big name to fall, and law enforcement officers would aid in the killing. The House had already been flexing its muscles through the efforts of its puppet sheriff, William Brady, who had been systematically harassing McSween/Tunstall and their associates with multiple trumped-up charges and arrests. In February 1878, the House's legal team issued a $10,000 writ of attachment on McSween's property (and on Tunstall's, by implication of claims of partnership). The McSween/Tunstall store in Lincoln was appropriated, plus McSween's own house. The House then set its sights on Tunstall's horses, and a 44-man posse of hired guns was assembled for that purpose by Brady, under the leadership of Deputy Billy Matthews and accompanied by Dolan, who liked a good day out hunting.

Through a convoluted sequence of events the day led to a snow-laden New Mexico gorge, where Tunstall and a group of five hired guns – including the legendary William Bonney, "Billy the Kid" – were confronted by 18 men of the House's posse, with local cattle ranch foreman Billy "Buck" Morton in charge. A brief exchange of gunfire rattled around the gorge, and Tunstall's associates, seeing that they were heavily outnumbered, scattered into the scrub. The famous Pat Garrett, writing the life of Billy the Kid in 1884, recounts what happened next:

> On the approach of Morton and his party, Tunstall's men all deserted him – ran away. Morton afterwards claimed that Tunstall fired on him and his posse; at all events, Morton and party fired on Tunstall, killing both him and his horse. One Tom Hill, who was afterwards killed whilst robbing a sheep outfit, rode up as Tunstall was lying on his face, gasping, placed his rifle to the back of his head, fired, and scattered his brains over the ground.[37]

These early gunshots triggered the Lincoln County War, six months of killing and counter-killing. The war was little more than an exercise in sequential murder, but the killing required the veneer of legal propriety. Lincoln Justice of the Peace John B. Wilson authorized the arrest of Dolan, Morton, and several other House posse members for Tunstall's murder, but Brady had the town constable and his deputies (including the newly deputized Billy the Kid) themselves arrested and flung into the local jail. Brady made no attempt to explain why he hadn't gone after Tunstall's killers. Only with the use of troops from Fort Stanton were the men freed, at which point Brady himself was temporarily arrested.

The war between the respective law enforcement gangs escalated. Wilson appointed foreman Dick Brewer as a special constable with his own gang of deputies, and together with a large group of other hardmen these men formed themselves into the "Regulators." The House responded by calling in favors from Governor Samuel Axtell, who in a flying three-hour visit through Lincoln voided Wilson's authority, and hence the authority to make police appointments. Nevertheless, the Regulators were now effectively an independent force, out for war. And war they made. Morton and two other House gunmen were executed on March 9, and on April 1 Brady and his deputy were shot dead on Lincoln main street. By return, Brewer died on April 4, shot through the head from a long-range rifle shot fired by the House employee Andrew "Buckshot" Roberts, who in turn died the next day from injuries sustained in the action. Frank McNab took over, but he was ambushed and gunned down on April 29, after which one Doc Scurlock took over command.

It became apparent that the Lincoln County War was building up to a climactic battle. The House pulled its political strings to shift the balance of power firmly in its favor. Axtell was wheeled out again to sack Sheriff John Copeland, a man who had been sincerely attempting to bring some order out from the blood-spattered chaos, replacing him with House loyalist George Peppin.

The final act of the Lincoln County War began on July 15, 1878. Having been pursued by Peppin and his gang for several weeks, McSween and the Regulators finally chose to make a stand and took over Lincoln itself. They holed up in the McSween house and Regulator-allied stores, there to wait for a final shootout. Soon the Regulators found themselves under siege; Sheriff Peppin and his men put a cordon around Lincoln, with a twist. Thirty-five troops under one Lieutenant-Colonel N. A. M. Dudley, 9th Cavalry, were sent in from Fort Stanton to aid in the siege, these not only wielding their small arms but also a Gatling gun and a small howitzer. Leon Claire Metz has explained how "The military thus patrolled back and forth, making it difficult for McSween supporters to shoot over their heads, but easy for the deputies to fire into the buildings."[38]

Ella Davidson, a long-suffering resident of Lincoln in those days, gave an insightful interview in 1938 as to what happened next during the siege:

> On the Sunday evening before the terrible days that ended the Lincoln County War, Mother said: "Ella this is the week that will end all this bloodshed and fighting and, I thank God your father is away and won't be mixed up in the shooting, but I am afraid to stay here with you children unprotected." So that night after supper she took us to stay with the Ellis family, in their house which was built with all the rooms in one long row. About ten o'clock we heard someone with spurs on, come clattering down the whole length of the house. The door where we sat opened and there was Billy the Kid! He was followed by fourteen men who took possession of the house. We went back to our home but Mother was afraid to stay there after she thought our water supply would perhaps be cut off, so we went to Juan Patron's house and about midnight that house was taken over by some of the fighters. We then went to Montonna's store where we went to bed and when we got up the next morning about twenty men had taken possession there, but we stayed there from Sunday evening, until the next Friday morning. Mother got up and after we saw men fired on and one killed, she said, "I am going to take you children out of this danger!"
>
> So she took us two miles out of town to where there were some tall poplar trees – they are still there – and about noon we saw heavy smoke. It was the McSween store

> that had been set afire by the Murphy men to burn out the McSween men (one of them was the Kid) who were surrounded, so they couldn't escape. When the fire was under way Mr. McSween calmly walked to the door as if surrendering and was shot down. Then, two others that followed were riddled with bullets. George Coe, Henry Brown, and Charlie Bowdre were among the crowd that escaped. Billy the Kid was the last one left in the building. During the excitement of the roof crashing in, he rushed out with two pistols blazing. Bob Beckwith, whose shot had killed McSween, was killed by one flying bullet and two others were wounded. The Kid, with bullets whizzing all around him, made his escape.
>
> After this battle that took place in July, 1878 everything quieted down, and my mother took us home. Mrs. McSween, whose home was burned, stayed with us all night, and the next morning she asked me to go with her to see the ruins of her house. We found only the springs and other wires of her piano that was the pride of her life. She raked in the ashes where her bureau had stood and found her locket.[39]

Although the role of the Kid in this action is slightly embellished, it conveys not only the terrible drama, but also the home-front weariness and bitterness such internecine conflicts bred. The Lincoln County war was now effectively over. Dudley's men and the law enforcement officers stood by as McSween's stores were looted for hundreds of dollars of goods. Legacy violence rumbled on in Lincoln County, however, until the military was finally used to bring order rather than add to chaos. By this time Dudley had been removed from his post – his role in the war had painted neither him nor his troops in a favorable light. Governor Axtell was also dismissed and replaced by General Lew Wallace in September 1878 (the same Lew Wallace, incidentally, who later wrote *Ben Hur*).

If ever there was an episode that revealed the potential ethical void beneath frontier deadly force, the Lincoln County war was it. Here men were deputized essentially *because* they were killers or gunmen – the ability to deliver deadly force was the *raison d'etre* of their law enforcement service. Furthermore, these appointments were made to engineer political, feudal, and commercial results by powerful civic factions. The US Army itself became a party to the violence. Much will be said later in this chapter, and throughout the book, about the role of the military in law enforcement engagements, from controlling civic riots through to a more shadowy special forces presence at incidents such as the Waco siege in 1993. In this instance, the soldiers did not open fire, although doubtless the mouth of a 12-pounder brass mountain howitzer smiling at the McSween house did focus the thoughts of the occupants. The other element to this whole episode is how non-badged individuals could become involved in delivering lethal force on behalf of the police and their masters. Such easy license to kill became, admittedly, much less common as the century wore on and county, state, and federal law enforcement became more established and regularized throughout former frontier territories. As we shall now see, however, both the mob and the military did provide useful service both in lawless regions and in those territories that were supposedly more civilized.

CONTINUUM OF FORCE

A modern concept (developed primarily from the late 1970s) to which we shall return continually in this book is the "continuum of force" (CoF). Put simply, this is a categorization of the types of force response available to officers, ranging from the most benign – typically a verbal command – through to the most extreme: deadly force applied with firearms. Each force has subtle variations on the CoF, but a typical example from the San Diego sheriff's department provides a good general idea, starting from the softest and running to the hardest:

Deputy Presence
Verbal Direction
Soft Hand Control
Chemical Agents (e.g. pepper spray)
Hard Hand Control
Intermediate Weapons (such as tasers, batons)
Lethal Force[40]

Looking back in time, it is a fruitful exercise to try to reinvent a typical CoF for the law enforcement officers of the 19th century. This effort is admittedly complicated on account of the political and social conditions, already noted, of western parts of the United States. The modern CoF was designed to give some legal and educational framework to officers, and a clear sense of their accountability and of *appropriate* levels of force. In the 19th-century Wild West, what was appropriate force could be twisted to suit other purposes far more easily than in the 20th century, and the stages between "officer presence" and "lethal force" could be few and fast. Nevertheless, acknowledging that the larger percentage of 19th-century law enforcement officers were not psycho-eyed killers, what instruments and techniques of control were available?

Deputy Presence, Verbal Direction, and Soft Hand Control were doubtless the stock-in-trade of general officer compliance techniques – not much has changed there. There are numerous accounts of particularly brave or well-reputed officers quelling crowd unrest by presence alone, backed up by words laced with menace and the odd guiding hand. Hard Hand Control would equally have been an option for controlling belligerent, drunk cowboys or other unsociables. What would have been different was the absence of chemical agents such as pepper sprays, and also some of the intermediate options available today, particularly the taser. In short, if the suspect did not comply with verbal commands, the chances are that the officer would have to damage them to gain compliance.

Broadening our focus now to include the major urban zones of the United States, the baton, "straightstick," or nightstick was the primary tool in delivering pain compliance. (It appears far less in accounts of frontier policing, probably because of the amount of time spent on a horse and also because in semi-lawless regions of well-armed citizens, clashes would quickly go from Verbal Direction to Lethal Force, skipping the intervening stages.) Made of hardwood such as hickory, redwood, or locust wood, and measuring anywhere between 20 and 30in., the baton was not to be trifled with, especially as officers had little of the training in precision pain compliance areas that the police have today. An account of a clash between police and a mob in Chicago in 1877 at one point notes: "The Police used their clubs effectively, sparing no one. One fellow was hit with a telling blow that crushed the back of his skull. When he fell he was borne away by his comrades."[41] Such a blow was likely to have killed the victim.

Once the dispute escalated to a matter of deadly force – and it quickly could – then the officers reached for their guns. Their firearms generally fell into three categories. First, and the initial line of defense, was the handgun. Police handguns were many and varied in type, and usually ranged from .32 to .45 caliber, the larger calibers becoming more popular as the century wore on and firearms designs became more suited to firing large centerfire cartridges. It was also discovered from rather obvious practical experience that a large bullet made a correspondingly large hole in the target, giving greater chance for a quick takedown.

An abiding mythology has accrued around the way gunfighters of the West used their handguns. The image that we know and cinematically love is of two men squaring up to each other in the street, pistols holstered, ready to see who is quickest on the draw. The outcome – one man lies sprawled, dying, in the dust of a frontier street, while the victor stands with his reputation confirmed. Another impression given is that the Wild West shooter was fiendishly accurate, as writer Joe Zentner notes about Wild Bill Hickok:

> Today, Wild Bill's fame as a marksman seems secure, partly because of the publication, in the 1930s, of three biographies. In those, the celebrated "marksman" never missed his man. Moreover, we learn that Wild Bill could hit a running man with a bullet from his revolver every time at 100 yards and that he could crease a friend's hair at 50 paces, with no damage to the hair. Or its owner. According to his biographers, Wild Bill never made an outright poor shot. One time in Mesa, Arizona, a pair of murderers fled from him. A Hickok biographer states that, "One was running up the street, and the other down the street, in the opposite direction. Bill fired at the men simultaneously and killed them both." Another biographer says that, "Wild Bill shot an evenly spaced row of holes along the outside of a hat brim as it was falling off a man's head, before it touched the ground."[42]

While we cannot deny that the Wild West had plenty of good shots, talents on par with those described stretch credulity, especially if we unpack the realities behind 19th-century revolvers, and how they had an impact on the application of deadly force. Accurate range for a considered and relatively leisured aimed shot would be in the region of around 25 yards, at least in terms of striking a man-sized target, but the dynamics of a snap-shooting engagement would reduce such range considerably, probably to the 5–10 yards range. Accurate shooting was further complicated by the dynamics of operating the firearm. Revolvers were separated into single- or double-action versions. Single-action revolvers required the user to cock the hammer manually with his thumb before firing. The primary benefit of the single-action system was accuracy: drawing the hammer back left the user with a very short, light pull on the trigger to drop the hammer and fire the gun, and this in turn reduced the amount of time in which the shooter could wobble off target, and alleviated some of the tremble that often accompanied a heavy trigger pull. (Pulling back the hammer turned the gun's cylinder, placing the next live cartridge under the hammer ready for firing.) Cocking a hammer was also a useful psychological signal in its own right – a sharp click as the hammer went back might induce more compliance, as the gun-familiar audience would have understood that both lawman and firearm were ready for action.

All well and good, but in the adrenaline frenzy of a real shootout the single-action revolver brought its own set of problems. Cocking the hammer admittedly could be performed within a second, but such an interval could be critical in the split-second mortal struggle of a close-quarters gunfight. Furthermore, the light trigger pull involved with a single-action weapon could lead to accidental discharges, especially when the lawman was jumpy and nervous. A short article from the *New York Times* from 1880 recounts how Edward Daily, a watchman in the Eastern District, was exploring a Broadway jewelry store, having heard a suspicious noise. He cocked his revolver and in the low-light fumblings in a dark corridor knocked the light-set trigger, shooting himself in the leg.[43]

Single-action revolvers, once cocked, were prone to such unwelcome outbursts; then again, accidental discharges litter the pages of police reports and newspaper archives to this day, whatever the weapon carried. The Texas lawman/criminal William Sydney "Cap" Light, a man with at least three killings to his name during his career and an undoubtedly experienced gun handler, died on Christmas Eve 1893 when he accidentally pulled the trigger of his revolver in his pocket – his femoral artery was severed, and he bled out on the floor of a Missouri, Kansas & Texas traincar, never reaching his home for Christmas.

In contrast to the single-action revolver was the double-action version. Pioneered by British companies such as Adams in the 1850s and developed by the big American names during the rest of the century, double-action revolvers worked on trigger pull alone – pulling the trigger turned the cylinder and drew back and then released the hammer. The advantage of the double-action weapon, appreciated by many a lawman, was its speed in firing. Five or six quick trigger pulls discharged five or six quick shots, with no momentary pause between shots for manually cocking the hammer. Such a facility was found useful by military officers in close-quarters engagements during the Civil War, and law enforcement officers found it similarly practical in a gunfight. In balance, double-action revolvers were not as accurate as single-action weapons, although at the ranges at which most gunfights took place that was scarcely important. Double-action revolvers steadily took over from single-action ones in terms of popularity.

Alongside the handgun, frontier officers in particular might carry a rifle. In the post-Civil War period, these were typically one of the many varieties of repeating rifles on offer – lever-action, magazine-fed rifles of great durability and with an effective range of several hundred yards. (The most important manufacturers were Henry, Winchester, Sharps, Remington, Maynard, Whitney/Burgess-Whitney, and Spencer.) Rifles provided long-range shooting capability useful for policing the American wilderness, and the typically large, powerful bullets could successfully drop a buffalo, let alone a human. The magazine capacity was hugely appreciated – the Winchester 1873, for example, carried 15 rounds of .44-40 ammunition in its tubular, under-barrel magazine. Each round was cycled through the gun simply by swinging the under-lever back and forth, hence for a serious gunfight over any sort of distance the rifle was often the preferred weapon of choice. For close-range work, a shotgun was also a useful backup, and remains so to this day in most US police forces. Unlike those of today's police, the shotguns of the 19th century were mostly adapted civilian models, often with the barrels sawn short to aid both concealment and a vicious spread of shot at near ranges. Shotguns were disadvantaged by requiring reloading after every two shots – most of the shotguns were double-barreled, break-barrel types – although there were some lever-action shotguns on the market, and at the very end of the century pump-action shotguns made their entrance. A particularly popular model of lever-action shotgun was the Winchester Model 1887, gripped by many a lawman (including characters such as George Selman) and also by ever-vulnerable stagecoach drivers and guards, who valued the greater leniency regarding accuracy when firing a shotgun from horseback.

So how did gunfights play themselves out during this period? Roughly speaking, the pinnacle of modern CoF is a "shoot to stop" policy – keep pulling the trigger until the opponent is down. Such was largely true in the 19th century, but the dynamics of group policing cranked up the stakes and, often, the level of violence used. But first, we have to demolish many of the myths of the Wild West gunfight in particular. Rarely, if ever, did individual lawmen and bad men square up to each other in a street to fight out a quick-draw, prearranged duel to the death, "High Noon" style. Mutually exposing oneself to the other's shot was quite simply a bad idea, as it upped the chances of being hit – even the hardest of men were no fools. Furthermore, although it was advisable to practice pulling a gun quickly from a holster, there was little sense that being "fast on the draw" would automatically give you a survival advantage over the other person. Anyway, town and city ordinances frequently prohibited the carrying of guns openly displayed in holsters; it was just as common therefore for guns to be stored inside jackets or in trouser pockets.

In actuality, most one-on-one gunfights between lawmen and bad men were improvised, blurred events unfolding in chaotic, unplanned fashion within the confines of a street, saloon, or store. The overwhelming objective of the participants was not to prove who had the superior unholstering speed, but simply to fill the opponent with enough lead to put him down. Accuracy often went out the window, confounded by clouds of black powder smoke, as attested to by the high number of innocent bystanders often killed in shootouts. Nor did professional lawmen attempt to "fan" their revolvers – hold down the trigger and snap the hammer back and forth to achieve something approaching rapid fire. Such a technique would arguably qualify as the least accurate shooting technique in the world; far better was, if conditions allowed, the accurate aimed shot that went home. A telling comment on the realities of gunplay comes from no less a legend than Wyatt Earp, the American lawman (amongst other professions) most famous for his part in the shootout at the OK Corral (more about that below). About gunfights, Earp sagely commented:

> The most important lesson I learned was the winner of gunplay usually was the one who took his time. The second was that, if I hoped to live on the frontier, I would shun flashy

trick-shooting as I would poison. I did not know a really proficient gunfighter who had anything but contempt for the gun-fanner, or the man who literally shot from the hip.

Telling words indeed against the Hollywood cowboys and lawmen. This is not to say that rare incidents approaching the mythologized gunfight did not occur. In 1865, for example, Wild Bill Hickok fought a legendary gunfight with 26-year-old David Tutt, to whom Hickok lost at the gambling table in Springfield, Missouri. As so often happened, the gambling loss soon ran with bad blood (Hickok was slighted that Tutt took his pocket watch), and mutual threats were issued. Although a gunfight was not planned, the two men met on July 26, 1865, in the town square. To ratchet up the tension, Hickok's pocket watch was swinging from Tutt's waistcoat for all to see. At a distance of about 75 yards – a long range for a gunfight – both men fired. Tutt's bullet went wide, whereas Hickok, true to his future legendary status, shot the man clean through the heart. Although Hickok was not a law officer at this stage, he was unwittingly laying the groundwork for the reputation that would later make him a sought-after lawman.

As we have seen, however, subsequent gunfights in Hickok's career would be far less clean. Throughout the second half of the 1800s, newspaper reports give a grittier picture of the realities of lethal force engagements than those sketched out in the dime novels. For example, an article in the Iowan newspaper the *Adams County Union* from 1896 presents the following in its daily news round-up:

EGBERT KILLS FIVE PEOPLE

He Then Takes His Own Life – His Sister Dies Of Shock

Peter Egbert in Rockville, Ind., Carpenter, 22 years old and unmarried, Saturday morning, without apparent cause of provocation, shot and instantly killed Mrs. Herman Raschke and two children, next door neighbors. He then reloaded his gun, and going up town, saw Sheriff W. M. Mull and Deputy Sheriff William Sweem in the National Bank Stairway. Egbert shot the sheriff in the back of the head, killing him instantly. Deputy Sheriff Sweem was shot in the right side of the neck, being instantly killed. Egbert then made his escape to the fairgrounds, just outside of town. A posse was immediately organized and started in pursuit. Fifty or more men, armed with shotguns, rifles and pistols, surrounded the grounds. When he saw escape impossible, the murderer killed himself. Miss Florence Egbert, the sister of the murderer, when she heard the details of the horrible affair and that her own brother was the central figure of the various tragedies, became frantic and died immediately from the shock. She was in bed suffering from typhoid fever.[44]

The reality of this engagement is utterly removed from glamour of the Hollywood gunfight. The two officers killed appear to have almost no opening for defense, and are simply dropped on the spot with two shots. The posse assembled to track down and kill Egbert has no opportunity to acquit itself; the obviously psychopathic Egbert simply shoots himself rather than opt for "suicide by cop." His death signals a bloody and depressing end to a pointless bout of murder.

Even when the shootout was along more "traditional" lines, there was scarcely any romance involved. On April 14, 1881, for example, the great lawman Dallas Stoudenmire faced another call on his talents with a gun. Stoudenmire had been made the city marshal of El Paso on April 11, and was known as someone ready for action. Indicative of how gunfights could variously play themselves out, Stoudenmire carried two revolvers – one with a long barrel for more accurate shots over range, and another with a stubby barrel for use as a "belly gun" meaning, according to Leon Claire Metz, "that its short barrel made it suitable for close-in fighting – for ramming into an opponent's belly and pulling the trigger."[45] On April 14, an inquest was held in El Paso into the killing of two Mexicans by two men, George Campbell and Johnny Hale (Campbell was himself a former law enforcement officer). Stoudenmire was present. After the inquest, Campbell and Hale confronted the court translator, Gus Krempkau, in the street, accusing him of giving the evidence a slant in translation. After an argument, Hale quite simply shot Krempkau on the street, fatally wounding him. Alerted by the gunshots (he had been eating lunch in the Globe Restaurant), Stoudenmire here entered the picture. Running onto the scene, he took a long shot at Hale – the bullet flew past his target and killed an innocent Mexican who was in the process of sprinting away from the scene. Undeflected from his purpose, Stoudenmire took a second shot at Hale's head, which popped up from behind an adobe pillar where Hale had been taking cover. This bullet struck home, and Hale was killed outright. Campbell was by this time panicked, and protested that "Gentleman, this is not my fight" to Stoudenmire. The dying Krempkau now opened up from the ground with his own revolver, hitting Campbell in the hand and foot. Campbell dropped his gun, bent to pick it up, and as he straightened up Stoudenmire was on top of him, emptying his revolver into Campbell's stomach and ending the gunfight.

Such a narrative graphically illustrates how rapidly Wild West deadly force engagements could escalate, and there is a clear sense that once Stoudenmire heard the shots, his CoF understanding immediately went to lethal levels, which he prosecuted even though there were several possible moments when the shooting might have been stopped. As we have seen, when a police officer did have some measure of forewarning about impending violence, he had to rely on his own judgment and ethics to gauge his level of response. Remember that the CoF in today's police forces is a hard-copy document that every officer will study intently during his training phase, and by which he will be judged should he be required to pull his gun. In post-colonial America, there was typically no such codification, although some officers did attempt to put on paper what amounted to standard operating procedures (SOPs).

One of the most notable examples came from David J. Cook, who was a sheriff in Colorado during the 1860s and rose to become the Chief of Police in Denver in the subsequent decade. From a position of authority and experience, he put down his views on how officers should behave during an arrest in his 1882 book *Hands Up! or Twenty Years of Detective Life in the Mountains and on the Plains*:

> I. Never hit a prisoner over the head with your pistol, because you may afterwards want to use your weapon and find it disabled. Criminals often conceal weapons and sometimes draw one when they were supposed to have been disarmed.
>
> II. Never attempt to make an arrest without being sure of your authority. Either have a warrant or satisfy yourself thoroughly that the man whom you seek to arrest has committed the offense.
>
> III. When you attempt to make an arrest, be on your guard. Give your man no opportunity to draw a pistol. If the man is supposed to be a desperado, have your pistol in your hand or be ready to draw when you make yourself known. If he makes no resistance, there will be no harm done by your precaution. My motto has been, "It is better to kill two men than to allow one to kill you."
>
> IV. After your prisoner is arrested and disarmed, treat him as a prisoner should be treated – as kindly as his conduct will permit. You will find that if you do not protect your prisoners when they are in your possession, those whom you afterwards attempt to arrest will resist you more fiercely, and will be inclined to sell their lives as dearly as possible.
>
> V. Never trust much to the honor of prisoners. Give them no liberties which might endanger your own safety or afford them an opportunity to escape. Nine out of ten of them have no honor.[46]

Although this text was published in a biographical work rather than an official document, it is likely that his views were directly transferred to the officers under his command. Much about his guidelines has a very modern ring to it – the emphasis on treating the prisoner civilly once arrested, and being sure of the quality of the charge and information before making an arrest. The expectation and realities of deadly force are kept in focus, however. In the same way that a modern officer may well be prepared to draw his gun when, say, approaching a suspicious vehicle, the 19th-century officer is urged to make a pre-emptive preparation for a deadly force encounter. The only precept that truly dates this passage is the first one, which cautions the officer against pistol whipping suspects not on account of the hole it might leave in the victim's head, but because it might damage the gun. ("Buffaloed" was the informal term for pistol whipping.)

In a situation requiring, or likely to involve, deadly force, there was another resource available to law enforcement officers – sheer numbers. Particularly in the frontier regions, but also in some urban situations (see below), law enforcement departments simply had insufficient officers to meet the needs of major incidents, such as large-scale fugitive pursuits or tackling civil unrest. This is where the posse came in. The use of the posse – the conscription of individuals by a county sheriff or other law enforcement officer to pursue or apprehend a fugitive – could, like much of early US policing, contain very shady ethics.

On one level, the posse was simply a force expander, adding more men and guns to the mix in a time when police resources could be few. The challenge for the officer in charge was to control the various personalities that formed the posse, all armed and nervous. Part of the control came through judicious selection of personnel – the sheriff or marshal would choose men he trusted to behave in accordance with his wishes, although if the posse grew too large, as it often did, the limits of control were often stretched beyond breaking point. The following are two examples of posses used in deadly force incidents. In the first, we see the posse express its force in a fairly controlled manner, with generally good command and control. In the second, the posse unleashes criminal levels of violence that result in a massacre.

EUGENE BUNCH AND THE PINKERTONS

Born in Mississippi in 1841, Eugene Bunch turned out to be an unlikely villain. His first careers were as a teacher and a newspaper editor, and he was known as a cultured and affable man. Discovering that there was little money in his chosen professions, however, Bunch decided train robbery offered steeper profit opportunities. Along with a select gang, he began robbing trains in Mississippi, Louisiana, and Texas from 1888. He was something of a gentleman while conducting the robberies, tipping his hat even as he took ladies' purses, and issuing gently spoken but very real threats of violence to Express Car messengers to open their safes. The career change seemed to pay off: in one raid on November 3, Bunch and his gang took nearly $30,000 in cash.

Yet in true Western style, justice was hot on his heels. In 1892 he took $20,000 from a train heist in New Orleans, and the train companies poured money into the hands of agencies to track down and bring in Bunch, dead or alive. In this case the money was directed to the infamous Pinkerton National Detective Agency. Established by former presidential security officer Allan Pinkerton in 1860, the "Pinkerton Men" grew into one of the looming tools of cross-state US law enforcement before the advent of organizations such as the Federal Bureau of Investigation (FBI). Running under the motto "The Eye That Never Sleeps," the Pinkertons were generally employed by companies to protect their interests against criminals and labor disputes, in roles that included strike breaking, train robber pursuit, and stagecoach protection. Strictly speaking, their activities sat outside the central bodies of law enforcement, being a private, for-profit organization. Yet to omit the Pinkertons would be remiss. In the rather haphazard world of emerging US law enforcement, the lines between public and private were often hazy, and the Pinkertons were a significant recourse for those organizations that couldn't achieve their objectives by other means.

While the Pinkerton agency did have a large repository of highly resourceful detectives, it also had more than its fair share of hired thugs. Its results-oriented business practices (to use a cloying but apt phrase) often led to brutality, such as excessive force in suppressing strikers (in one incident in 1888, ten strikers were killed by Pinkerton men) and the quick resort to weaponry. Yet in other cases they acted with professionalism and resourcefulness.

In 1892, the Pinkertons were employed as agents for the Southern Express Company, charged with tracking down Bunch. A posse was gathered under detectives Thomas Jackson and C. O. Summers, and the group of men – all armed with Winchester rifles and revolvers – set out from Franklinton, Louisiana, just after midnight on August 21, 1892. The information regarding Bunch led the posse on a long trail to near the banks of the Pearl River, where they spread out along the bank and set up pickets to watch and wait for Bunch. Sitting in silence, and staring over the marshy ground, the Pinkerton men soon picked up voices punctuating the early morning air. The voices were those of Bunch and his chief accomplice, one "Colonel" Hopgood. As they drew closer, Bunch suddenly spotted a posse member squatting out in the vegetation. Straight away he pulled his gun and opened fire. He missed, and his criminal career then came to an end in a crackling volley of Winchester fire. Bunch had just enough strength to fire off two more ineffective shots from the ground, before he rolled over and died. Hopgood had the good sense not to retaliate, and thrust his hands skyward and prayed for mercy, which he received. The dead Bunch and living Hopgood were taken back to Franklinton and, according to the *New York Times*, "Jackson and his posse will be considerably richer by their day's work."[47]

The use of force here seems to follow lines that would be perfectly acceptable to any of today's US police forces. The fugitives were pursued and the posse only returned fatal fire when fired upon itself. Furthermore, the posse members honored the surviving outlaw's choice to surrender, and he was taken into custody and processed appropriately. Yet there is the possibility that the remuneration for a job well done might incline some private agencies to use deadly force more as a first resort – what better way to get your man, and insure against his future escape, than by killing him. In another Pinkerton action, this time in 1875, a group of detectives surrounded a cabin in Missouri that was believed to contain the outlaw Jesse James. The information was sketchy, but the detectives opted to throw a fire bomb through a window just to be safe. Jesse in fact wasn't there, but his mother and half-brother were. The former was severely injured and the latter killed, and the operation misfired in the media also – after this action, the public gave much more sympathy to Jesse.

THE LATTIMER MASSACRE

On September 10, 1897, an incident occurred that threw into relief the potential excesses of the posse system, and which changed the way law enforcement agencies could call on extra guns to multiply their deadly force potential. Postbellum United States was a place of deep industrial unrest. The awesome economic growth that the United States experienced in the last decades of the 19th century was matched by increasing resistance to poor, in some cases horrific, working conditions in key industries such as mining, steel production, and the railroads. Importation of foreign labor added to the friction, both by aggrieved indigenous workers, who felt that their wages were being flattened by the poorly paid foreigners, and amongst the foreigners themselves, who in many cases were treated little better than forced labor. Within the economic growth, there were also periods of banking collapse and unemployment, forcing discontented masses out onto the streets, where they scouted for trouble.

The consequence was continual civil unrest that ran well into the 20th century, with the big businesses using their political and financial influence to engineer some often brutal solutions to the disputes. The seeds of the Lattimer Massacre began with a strike by the mine workers at the Lattimer mine near Hazleton, Pennsylvania. The mine was principally worked by immigrant labor from Eastern Europe, mainly Poles, Slavs, and Lithuanians. All the workers were treated equally dreadfully. Referred to as "hunkies" by their owners and foremen, they toiled for terrible wages from which the company deducted housing, food, and other costs, plus a 3 percent "alien tax," to leave the workers and their families with practically nothing. (The workers were also forced to shop at company stores, which charged excessive prices for the goods.)

Enough was finally enough, and on September 1, 1897, several thousand miners came out on strike. Strike militancy spread to smaller neighboring mines throughout northeast Pennsylvania, and soon the total number of strikers reached towards 5,000, and they marched through the region, closing down many of the mines.

The man tasked with bringing the strike to a close was Sheriff James Martin of Lucerne County, who was whisked back from a holiday. Negotiation was not an option – the strikers were essentially viewed as a common rabble – so Martin looked at force options. He gathered a posse of some 87 men, deputized them, and armed them with brand new Winchester rifles loaded with metal-jacketed bullets (for better penetration, as well as leaving less lead deposit in the barrel) and shotguns for close-range work.[48] It was not only the choice of armament that would seem to predispose the posse towards using deadly force. Of the men chosen for the task of quelling the strike, none were of the ethnic groups of the strikers and all had vested commercial interests in seeing the mines restored to full operation. It was an incendiary combination…

On September 10, a group of about 400 striking miners headed out to the A. D. Pardee & Co. colliery at Lattimer, intent on closing it down. They were roughed up along the way by the police posse, but stoically continued their march. Sheriff Martin was in pursuit, heading over to the colliery with his full posse, and subsequent reports revealed that one deputy was overhead saying "I bet I drop six of them when I get over there."[49] Once they reached the colliery, other mine company security units swelled Martin's ranks to some 150 men.

Accounts are confused about what subsequently happened, but at around 3.45pm the 400 strikers marched up to the entrance of the colliery, completely unarmed. Martin ordered them to stop, but language confusions and the size of the crowd meant this was not heeded. Martin found himself in a scuffle with one of the men, and he pulled his pistol, which misfired as he attempted a shot. Then, from the ranks of the posse, a voice called out "Open Fire!" The ranks of the posse complied, shots ringing out for some 90 seconds, discharging up to 150 rounds. Many of those hit were sprinting away from the scene to take cover, and some deputies were observed to break out of the ranks of the posse to take better aim.[50] By the time the posse stopped its enthusiastic fire, 19 people were dead and 36 were wounded. In the immediate aftermath of the shooting, it seemed to dawn on some of the deputies just what they had done, and they started trying to help the injured. Others couldn't care less, delivering hefty kicks to some even as they lay on the ground, dying.

The Lattimer Massacre received huge national press coverage, with public opinion very much against Martin and his posse. The fact that the traumatized mining families did not retaliate, but showed dignity in their grief, added to the public sympathy. The government responded by effectively prohibiting the use of posses in civil disorder cases, the responsibility thereby being passed to the National Guard and the official police force. Whether this improved the management of deadly force incidents in the future is, as we shall see, questionable, but certainly there was an acceptance that ad hoc deputization was a potential recipe for bloodshed.

One of the other problems with the posse was that it could act as an extension of the vigilance committees, with the greater emotional momentum of a large group leading to more questionable justice. One sharp example of how the lines could blur comes from the town of Fort Griffin, Texas, along the Clear Fork River during the 1870s. The town was built upon buffalo hides, cattle, and the income from soldiers and cowboys making merry in the town's bars, saloons, and brothels. Proper civil authority only arrived in the town in 1874 with the formation of Shackleford County (previously law had been erratically administered by the local military), but by that time the town was plagued by cattle rustling and violence on a fairly epic scale.

In 1876 Fort Griffin duly elected John M. Larn to the position of sheriff. Larn's credentials seem to be a personality that fused charm and urbane intelligence with a murderous affection for violence. Prior to his arrival in Fort Griffin, Larn had either personally killed or taken part in the execution of more than 15 individuals, and had been a member of a vigilante gang around Griffin known as the Tin Hat Brigade.[51] His appointment as sheriff was very much business as usual, and the newly formed Shackleford County Vigilance Committee, almost certainly directed by Larn himself, started to deliver its own brand of retribution against cattle rustlers and horse thieves. An article in the *Frontier Echo* of May 12, 1876, spelled out how the law was to be enforced:

> Court Proceedings on the CLEAR FORK!
> Judge Lynch Presiding
> Special to the Echo
> FORT GRIFFIN TEXAS
> May 7th, 1876
>
> The notorious character known as "Reddy" of horse thief fame, was captured on the 2nd inst. at this place for horse stealing in Eastland county, and put in the military guardhouse for safe keeping. On Friday afternoon he was turned over to parties to be conveyed to

> Eastland county. Yesterday his body was found hanging to a tree three miles from here. On 23 June, a notice was posted near one of Fort Griffin's more popular saloons ordering prostitutes and their procurers to leave town immediately "or you are doomed – VIGILANCE."[52]

In recent years historian Charles M. Robinson III has reflected on how the dispensation of such ruthless justice would have been impossible without Larn's involvement. Furthermore, he also acknowledges how it would be all too easy for a town to benefit from this special brand of law enforcement:

> None of this could have happened without Larn's consent, and indeed, it was generally known that he was a leader of the Shackleford County Vigilance Committee. Nevertheless, as Edgar Rye, who served as a justice of the peace in the permanent county seat at Albany, 14 miles to the south, grudgingly admitted, "During the first six months of his term Laren [sic] did more to quell lawlessness than any man who served the people as sheriff, before and since his time."[53]

What we have in the case of Larn is effectively deadly force by proxy. (In an ironic sidenote, Larn himself was summarily executed by masked gunmen in 1878 while being held in jail for cattle rustling.) The vigilance committee could act as a buffer between the officer and accountability for a killing, while at the same time solving the problem of certain criminals in a very final way. In areas struggling with controlling criminality, this type of deadly force was useful, as it gave the authority of the lawman a far greater implicit threat and authority than if he stood alongside a few deputies as a solitary figure.

The ugliest side of deadly force by proxy was the outright lynch mob, which had plagued many states throughout US history. The rule of "Judge Lynch" has led to some of the worst human rights abuses in American history. The Deep South in particular saw lynchings of African-Americans on charges as mundane as "looking in the wrong way at a white woman," even into the first decades of the 20th century, and on many occasions local law officers either absented themselves, stood by and watched, or actively participated. Note, however, that the mob could prove just as dangerous to the straight-down-the-line officer as the criminal it had arrested, often more so, and some officers stood up to vigilante justice with almost insane bravery. On some occasions, the lynch mob would act directly against the law, threatening the law officer to stand aside while it enacted its own brand of justice or social engineering. An example is that of the Courthouse Riot of 1884, which took place in Cincinnati. On March 28, a full 8,000 people, incensed by a speech delivered in the Music Hall that claimed murderers got away with their crimes lightly, headed off to the city jail, brimming with blood lust. (It was a time when a series of particularly gruesome murders, including the killing of an entire family for the sale of their bodies to medical schools, had shocked the city. Several instances of juries acquitting accused murderers had further inflamed public opinion.) Their intention was to lynch two men, Joseph Palmer and William Berner, both accused of the murder of their employer. Many in the crowd were heavily armed with guns, and obviously meant business.

The police line over at the jail was led by Sheriff Morton Lytle Hawkins and his 13 deputies (he had boosted his deputy numbers in the expectation of trouble). The mob soon gathered around the jail. State police arrived in two wagons as backup, but only one of the wagons managed to make its way through, using brute force. The mob bristled with unused energy and began to open fire, and a 17-year-old boy was seriously injured. They then smashed their way into the jail, although they were unable to get at their prey owing to robust internal doors. Troops of the Ohio National Guard now arrived, commanded by Colonel C. B. Hunt – Hawkins had requested their help when he realized the scale of the onslaught. Four Guardsmen were shot, but eventually they drove the rioters out of the jail, aided in no small measure by shooting dead their ringleader. The mob then attempted to set the jail on fire for good measure; this failed, but another eight people were shot during the melee, including one police officer and four Guardsmen.

The day ended in stalemate, but Hawkins called in more reinforcements, knowing that further trouble was on the horizon. His numbers had risen to some 200 men, but the mob decided to attack an easier target – the nearby city courthouse was set on fire and burnt to the ground. As troops assisted the firefighters called to the scene, another two Guardsmen were shot, one of them fatally. Later that night, however, Hawkins finally began to receive reinforcements on a scale equal to the threat – 425 troops of the Ohio National Guard, who even brought with them a Gatling gun. The mob was far from cowed when the troops arrived, showering them with rocks and wounding ten troops with gunfire. The next day another 2,000 Guardsmen arrived; Governor George Hoadly had been initially reluctant to send in large numbers of troops for fear of hurting his political popularity, but the sight of the smoking shell of the courthouse was a firm persuader.

Although the violence abated for a short while, at 8.30pm on March 29 it reignited in a major riot. Under fire, the Guardsmen finally cranked the handle of the Gatling, sending hails of bullets into the crowd. The local *Daily Times Star* newspaper observed that "The deadly Gatling gun, the product of a Cincinnati inventor, yielded its thrumming voice to the yelp of the pack ... and that weapon, more than any other single agency, was responsible for the return to sanity of the thousands who had been swept off their feet by fiendish desire to kill." The troops then repelled a riotous charge with two massive volleys of rifle fire.

What became known as the Courthouse Riot was now nearing its end. On Monday, the troop numbers rose by another 500 men, and the crowd was running out of steam. Furthermore, the casualty levels had reached almost battlefield proportions – 56 people were dead, the vast majority of them townsfolk, and over 200 people had been seriously injured.[54]

The Courthouse Riot demonstrates that the instinct for people to take the law into their own hands could evolve into the policeman's nightmare. Another important fact is the implications of using a military force – the National Guard – as an instrument to restore order. The high final death toll was the result of military-grade weaponry, including rifle volleys and machine-gun fire, being employed without many of the political and legal restraints placed upon modern agencies. Here we arrive at a thorny issue in American politics – the use of the military in the control of civilian disturbances.

MILITARY MUSCLE

Up until the late 1870s, but arguably to this day, the US law enforcement community has shown a fondness for employing either the military directly or quasi-militaristic bodies (think SWAT teams). In our Introduction, we saw how state militias were put to work in policing duties during the 18th and 19th centuries, and how they influenced the formation of bodies such as the slave patrols. Some law enforcement organizations of the 1800s, in fact, were military units in all but name. The most famous example is that of the Texas Rangers, a group that has survived in a much modified form to this day. The Rangers were born in the early 1820s when US colonists in what is today Texas, but what was then Mexican territory, created a protection force to compensate for the lack of standing army and police force to oversee their well-being. The man behind the Rangers was Stephen F. Austin, and from an initial group of ten men the Rangers – so-called because they "ranged" far and wide across the territory – emerged and grew in authority. In October 1835, a more formalized and larger body of Rangers was established that directly reflected military structure: the Rangers were organized into companies, with each company commanded by a captain and first and second lieutenants, and by November 1835 were approaching 200 men in number. In terms of duties during the 1830s and the Civil War, the Texas Rangers were wielded primarily as combat troops, fighting in the relentless Indian Wars and also in the Mexican War as part of General Zachary Taylor's army.

The Civil War, or the War Between the States as native Texans prefer to call it, totally reframed the future of the Rangers. As many Rangers had naturally fought for the

Confederate forces, the Union government mistrusted their militaristic nature during the Reconstruction period (1865–73) and rebranded them as "State Police". In this capacity, the Rangers waned in terms of both morale and service. Their policing was poor and preferential, with racist groups such as the Ku Klux Klan allowed to continue most of their activities with relative impunity under the noses of the service. Yet as Reconstruction came to an end, the Ranger concept stirred and revived, and in May 1874 Governor Richard Coke pushed through legislation to form six companies of Texas Rangers, each company having 75 men. The Texas Department of Public Safety, under which the Rangers operated from 1935, admits in its own history that these new organizations straddled uncertain lines between military formation and regular police:

> They were stationed in districts at strategic points over the state in order to be on hand when ranches were raided. The service was known as the Frontier Battalion. Rangers were given the status of peace officers, whereas before this date the service was a semi-military organization.
>
> During this era, the Ranger Service held a place somewhere between that of an army and a police force. When a Ranger was going to meet an outside enemy, for example, the Indians or the Mexicans, he was very close to being a soldier; however, when he had to turn to the enemies within his own society – outlaws, train robbers, and highwaymen – he was a detective and policeman.
>
> The Rangers were organized into companies, but not regiments or brigades. The company was in the charge of a captain or a lieutenant and sometimes a sergeant. The headquarters was in Austin where the captains reported to the headquarters officer. Under the Republic of Texas this officer was the Secretary of War. Under the state, until 1935, he was the Adjutant General; since then, the Director of the Texas Department of Public Safety.[55]

The broader organization of the Rangers during this period – into the Frontier Battalion and Special Force Company – also reflected the sense that here was a dual-function formation. The Frontier Battalion was tasked with combating large-scale disorder, such as violent feuds, and quashing the diminishing bands of rebellious Indians, while the Special Force gave its attentions to bandits and outlaws. These two units were fused during the 1880s, simply titled the Texas Rangers.

In terms of their use of force, the Texas Rangers were not shy about drawing their guns. During the 1870s, they killed over 3,000 people in armed engagements and crushed Indian tribes such as the Comanche and Kiowa. Famous outlaws such as Sam Bass and John Wesley Hardin fell to the guns of the Rangers, and it was said amongst outlaws that "It is easy to see a graveyard in the muzzle of a Ranger's gun."

The curious balance between a military-style deadly force and the responsibility for enforcing the law can be seen in one Special Forces operation in May 1876. On the 25th, 40 Rangers, headed by Leander McNelly, set out from Laredo in hot pursuit of cattle rustler John King Fisher and his gang. One of the Rangers, Napoleon Augustus Jennings, left a fascinating first-hand account of the operation. After a substantial ride, the Rangers eventually surrounded Fisher's ranch house near the Nueces River. Inside were Fisher and eight other men, including Fisher and his right-hand man Frank Porter. After staking out the ranch house, the Rangers eventually upped and charged, and caught the outlaws as they scrambled to get their arms. Jennings takes up the story:

> "You'll have to surrender or be killed!" cried McNelly to Fisher, who stood halfway out of the door, with the lieutenant of his band, one Burd Obenchain, but known to his companions as Frank Porter.
>
> Fisher did not move, but Porter half raised his Winchester, and coolly looked along the line of Rangers.
>
> "Drop that gun!" yelled McNelly. "Drop it, I say, or I'll kill you."
>
> Porter looked McNelly squarely in the eyes, half raised his rifle again, and then slowly dropped it to his side, and with a sigh leaned it against the side of the house.
>
> "I reckon there's too many of yer to tackle," he said, calmly. "I only wisht I'd a-seen yer sooner."
>
> The other men gave up without a struggle. They were badly frightened at first, for they thought we were members of a vigilance committee, come to deal out swift justice to them and hang them by lynch law. They were agreeably disappointed when they discovered we were the Rangers, officers of the law of Texas.
>
> … Captain McNelly told us, in the hearing of the prisoners and of Fisher's wife – a pretty girl, with wonderfully fine, bold black eyes – that if any of our prisoners attempted to escape or if an attempt was made to rescue them, we were to kill them without warning or mercy. That is, or was, known on the frontier as *La ley de fuga*, the shooting of escaping or resisting prisoners. It was well understood among the outlaws, and was a great protection to the officers who were compelled to escort prisoners over long distances through the sparsely settled country. The knowledge of this condition of the border prevented members of a desperado gang from attempting to rescue prisoners, for such an attempt meant instant death to the captives.[56]

Much subsequent study of Jenning's reminiscences has revealed a large degree of elaboration, invention and outright misrepresentation in his work. Yet this account does reveal significant elements of Ranger "CoF." On this occasion, use of deadly force is restrained by the surrender of the fugitives, the responsibility of being "officers of the law of Texas" restraining the triggers. Yet in balance, the threat of quick execution for attempted escape or rescue delivers the threat of death in no uncertain terms. Almost implicit in *La ley de fuga* is the sense that any sort of resistance would bring swift summary execution to the group. Indeed it is true that the first 100 years of the Texas Rangers were dogged by instances of outright brutality, albeit brutality seen from the much safer perspective of the modern world.

McNelly himself could be a particularly cruel man when pushed, aided by the widespread view amongst the white population that killing a Mexican was perfectly acceptable under most circumstances, the entire race being branded as thieves and cut-throats.[57] When many fugitives were apprehended, McNelly turned them over to his own personal inquisitor, Jesús Sandoval, a Mexican in the ranks of the Rangers. Sandoval's specialty was interrogating prisoners with a distinctly persuasive technique – repeatedly hanging the suspect by the neck to just short of unconsciousness, and repeating the process until they were sufficiently motivated to tell what they knew. Once the interrogation/torture was over, some unfortunate individuals were then hanged again, but this time featuring a drop from the back of Sandoval's horse that usually snapped their necks.[58]

McNelly would also quite happily export his deadly force across the border into Mexico itself. In November 1875, McNelly and some 30 Rangers crossed into Mexico on an operation to crush a cattle rustling gang working from the Rancho Las Cuevas, near Camargo. After an arduous river crossing, the Rangers closed on the ranch buildings, and were met with a shot from a vigilant sentry. McNelly, in no mood to tolerate resistance, fired back and killed the sentry, then launched his men at the ranch, who quickly shot down at least five or six men (some reports put the death toll in double figures), whose hostile action appeared to be little more than chopping wood. Only once the gunfire stopped, and the pools of blood began to dry quickly under the Mexican sun, did a local woman inform them that they were in the wrong place – Las Cuevas was a mile away. McNelly cursed his loss of surprise, and simply redeployed his men to the correct location.[59]

A constant caution throughout this book is not to give the so-called atrocities committed by various law enforcement agencies a general status – put more simply, we shouldn't tar everyone with the same brush. The Texas Rangers performed a critical function in a land more brutal than we can imagine, and the standards of our time would be unlikely to carry much weight in an era where men reached quickly for their guns. Nonetheless, the CoF practiced by the Rangers wholly seems to reflect their semi-military status. The raid into foreign territory reads like a modern US Army Special Forces operation, and the use of deadly force seems to be the only option when operating in a foreign country that would be hostile to the attempted forced extradition of its citizens.

Looking beyond the Texas Rangers, for much of the 19th century the regular and reserve military forces of the United States were also on call to supplement the law enforcement community in the suppression of civil unrest. Sometimes this was done because the officers found that a local rebellion or feud meant few men were willing to join a posse, and therefore be identified with a particular side of a conflict. Furthermore, there were practical and financial limits to the size of posse a lawman could organize. The Judiciary Act of 1789 had given US marshals the right to *posse comitatus* ("right of the county"), and this right was further enshrined by Attorney General Caleb Cushing in 1854. Cushing's legislation, in an attempt to improve the efficacy of the Fugitive Slave Act of 1850, gave marshals or local sheriffs the right to summon a posse if necessary for the pursuit of fugitives. It also provided the right for militia and regular military forces to be included within that posse. If federal forces were utilized in what the officer could prove was a legitimate emergency, then the government would pick up the financial costs incurred.

The use of military forces in *posse comitatus* was all well and good in a country that was pushing back the frontier with limited legal resources. Real problems, however, arrived with the post-Civil War period, when the use of military units in law enforcement carried serious political implications. Historian Colonel (ret.) John R. Brinkerhoff elaborates:

> During Reconstruction, the Army exercised police and judicial functions, oversaw the local governments, and dealt with domestic violence. In effect, the Army governed the 11 defeated Confederate States and was the enforcer of national reconstruction policy during all or part of the period. Before the Civil War, the militia under state control was used to control local disorders throughout the United States, but during Reconstruction, there was no effective militia in the defeated states, so the Army protected the people (especially the newly emancipated slaves) and dealt with disturbances. This use of the Army was validated by the Civil Rights Act of 1866, which empowered U.S. marshals to summon and call to their aid the posse comitatus of the counties, or portions of the land or naval forces of the United States, or of the militia. As the former Confederate States were readmitted to the Union, the status of the Army changed, but its role remained much the same.[60]

The ability of local law enforcement officers to call up military forces – and they did so frequently during the many labor disputes and territorial range wars of the 1870s – gave them a power that naturally made many people deeply uneasy, and generated an abiding animosity amongst many peoples of the South. Furthermore, the US Army was frequently none too happy with its role; it classed itself as a war-fighting machine, and often resented being dragged into quelling squalid town riots and intervening in local feuds by the command decision of a local law enforcement officer. In 1878, therefore, came a ground-breaking piece of legislation from the US Congress. Known as the Posse Comitatus Act, it placed control of regular armed forces back into the hands of the federal government:

> 20 Stat. L., 145
>
> June 18, 1878
>
> CHAP. 263 – An act making appropriations for the support of the Army for the fiscal year ending June thirtieth, eighteen hundred and seventy-nine, and for other purposes.
>
> SEC. 15. From and after the passage of this act it shall not be lawful to employ any part of the Army of the United States, as a posse comitatus, or otherwise, for the purpose of executing the laws, except in such cases and under such circumstances as such employment of said force may be expressly authorized by the Constitution or by act of Congress; and no money appropriated by this act shall be used to pay any of the expenses incurred in the employment of any troops in violation of this section. And any person willfully violating the provisions of this section shall be deemed guilty of a misdemeanor and on conviction thereof shall be punished by fine not exceeding ten thousand dollars or imprisonment not exceeding two years or by both such fine and imprisonment.
>
> 10 U.S.C. (United States Code) 375
>
> Sec. 375. Restriction on direct participation by military personnel: The Secretary of Defense shall prescribe such regulations as may be necessary to ensure that any activity (including the provision of any equipment or facility or the assignment or detail of any personnel) under this chapter does not include or permit direct participation by a member of the Army, Navy, Air Force, or Marine Corps in a search, seizure, arrest, or other similar activity unless participation in such activity by such member is otherwise authorized by law.
>
> 18 U.S.C. 1385
>
> Sec. 1385. Use of Army and Air Force as posse comitatus: Whoever, except in cases and under circumstances expressly authorized by the Constitution or Act of Congress, willfully uses any part of the Army or the Air Force as a posse comitatus or otherwise to execute the laws shall be fined under this title or imprisoned not more than two years, or both.

The limitations and extent of the Posse Comitatus Act are issues to which we shall return in this book. We need to be clear, however, about what it is saying and what it isn't. Since the Act was passed, a popular understanding has developed that sees it as prohibiting the use of the military in the realm of domestic law enforcement. This view is erroneous. The Act stopped law enforcement officers themselves being able to call up regular military forces under their own jurisdiction, but it did not stop the federal government diverting military resources to support law and order should the government perceive the situation as serious enough. Note also – and it is a big exception – that the Posse Comitatus Act did not apply to the use of militia or, in the future, the US National Guard. Today a state governor can call up the local elements of the National Guard, a truly enormous military machine with every conceivable type of hardware, to aid in civil disturbances. The US Coast Guard also sits outside the act, awkwardly straddling the line between combat force and law enforcement agency. Technically, the Act also does not apply to the US Navy and Marine Corps, although there is an implicit understanding that for practical purposes both agencies should be treated as if restrained under the Act.[61]

Military forces, either in style or in official organization, make regular appearances throughout law enforcement history to this day, usually in the context of civil disorders but also in the modern contexts of the "War on Terrorism" post 9/11 or the "War on Drugs" in the 1980s and 90s. The critical point for our analysis here is that the CoF explored above alters depending on the level at which it is applied. At county level, the officers rely on their own personal CoF up to the use of firearms, but if the problem expands to state level then the more powerful weapon systems of the National Guard come into play. Should the disturbance escalate to federal relevance, then the CoF can go up to the full arsenal of US military resources, from artillery to tanks.

CITY POLICING

If we turn our focus away from the West, and more towards the urban Eastern cities, the patterns of police use of force change somewhat. In terms of deadly force, cities are not well suited to any sort of official gunplay. First, cities are crowded, claustrophobic places, and the consequences of bullet overflight (when the bullet has missed its target and continues to fly freely) are potentially far more serious in an urban sprawl packed with people than they are around some isolated rural ranch. Second, the high population density in a city typically means that there are more pairs of eyes to witness a beating or a shooting. Although this has obvious relevance to illegal or questionable shootings, it also affects perfectly legitimate use of weaponry, as the urban public is frequently quick to condemn or misjudge the way that lethal force engagements unfold (see Chapter 6). Third, there is the simple fact that the authorities and powers in a city understandably don't like to see guns discharged. Shots fired in a city unnerve the public, and a disquieted public is bad for politicians and other civic leaders, who may be seen as losing the war on crime. All these factors come into play when looking at how the police have applied the CoF on urban streets. (Note that in the subsequent analysis, I am imposing the idea of "Continuum of Force" on past policing; the actual use of the CoF concept did not materialize until the 1970s – see Chapter 3.)

The primary tool of physical law enforcement used in most encounters was not the firearm, but the nightstick, as already mentioned. By coming lower on the CoF in terms of its perceived lethality, the nightstick might be viewed as a less controversial instrument of force than the revolver or rifle, but such a perception is generally inaccurate. Wielded with force and precision, a locust wood nightstick was perfectly capable of killing someone through a fractured skull or ruptured internal organs, or at least of leaving the victim with a permanent physical injury. (Locust wood is an unusually dense and heavy material, and created fearsome nightsticks.) Furthermore, the ready recourse to nightsticks generated public controversy and adverse headlines that forced many city authorities and police forces to implement strict guidelines or restrictions as to their use. New York is a useful case study in this regard.

From the 1850s onwards, batons became an essential piece of kit for New York Police Department (NYPD) patrol officers, particularly in poor, violence-stricken districts such as the Five Points. Police appointments were made at a local level by aldermen, but in the process the police were often effectively controlled by their political masters, with corruption, graft, and the toleration of certain criminal practices driving down the police reputation. Patrolling tough neighborhoods, therefore, the police became targets for aggrieved citizens and criminal classes alike, and reached for their batons quickly when a threat was perceived. The liberal use of the baton also gave an instant form of respect that, it was felt, was immediately understood throughout the less salubrious parts of the city. Furthermore, inefficiencies in the criminal justice system, which often saw local criminals escaping prosecution, led to the application of "curbside justice," delivered via a severe beating.

Discussing the 1850s and 1860s in New York, Marilynn Johnson explains how the nature of New York politics and policing led to a spiraling brutality:

> This cycle of violence intensified under the administration of the Republican-controlled Metropolitan police. During these years, political, cultural, and class conflicts converged in an explosive way as the city's predominantly ethnic and Democratic working class chafed under the control of a police force administered by elite, native-born Republicans intent

> on enforcing excise, Sabbatarian, and vagrancy laws. The new emphasis on policing morality fueled bitter resentments among the city's large Irish and German populations, which viewed the police as an alien and coercive force.[62]

The result of the city's tensions, exacerbated during the 1860s and 1870s by periodic economic problems nationwide, was gang violence and rioting. Life became very dangerous for the police. Three policemen and 100 citizens died during the Draft Riots of 1863, and 60 people were killed during the Orange Riots of 1870–71. Although the bulk of the civilian death tolls came from internal violence, the police undoubtedly added their own tallies. A notorious example of the recourse to arms is the Tompkins Square Riot of 1874.

In the midst of an economic depression, some 7,000 unemployed protesters – mostly immigrants and socialist groups – gathered in Tompkins Park in the East Village, demanding the implementation of a public works policy from the city authorities to cure the economic woes. The police, assigned by a nervous local mayor to break up the gathering, dispersed the crowds through impact means rather than negotiations. The writer Samuel Gompers, present at the incident, described how "mounted police charged the crowd on Eighth Street, riding them down and attacking men, women, and children without discrimination. It was an orgy of brutality. I was caught in the crowd on the street and barely saved my head from being cracked by jumping down a cellarway."[63] Newspaper columns were full of denunciation for what was seen as a brutal culture amongst the New York police, and many labor organizations were radicalized by such actions, adopting constitutions and doctrines that advocated strong self-protection against police violence.

In 1870 the state legislature moved back to the Democrats, and complaints against police brutality intensified to levels that could no longer be ignored politically. Again, it was use of the baton that seemed to give most cause for concern. Johnson's search through the *New York Times* archives revealed 272 articles pertaining to police brutality between 1865 and 1894, of which a full 206 cases (72 percent) were related to clubbings; the next largest category was illegal shootings, which took only 7 percent of the cases (20 incidents).[64] The slightest provocation appears to have inspired brisk thumpings with the nightstick, and both men and women were recipients. The more affluent American public, by contrast, often condoned police strong-arm tactics as an unpalatable reality for controlling the febrile masses, and of protecting the ability of employers to guard and develop their capital. In an article from the *Brooklyn Daily Eagle* dated October 23, 1892, the correspondent observes in connection with a city parade: "No special instructions were issued to the police last week in regard to the use or rather non-use of clubs in the handling of the vast crowds which it was expected would view the parade."[65] It would be interesting to know what "special instructions" might be, and this at least implies that on occasions the NYPD would issue use of force policy to its officers. On this occasion, however, there is a disquieting sense of the batons restrained purely by individual judgment, a force easily imbalanced in crowd situations.

Matters truly came to a head in the Lexow Commission of 1894–95, a committee formed with the onerous task of rooting out corruption in the New York police and government. (The commission was named after its chairman, Senator Charles Lexow, and was powered by the Republicans taking control of the state legislature from the Democrats in 1893.) A critical phase in the proceedings came in October 1894, when the commission began to probe records of police violence. Committee representative John W. Goff advanced two critical claims at the start of his day's testimony:

> First – The attitude of the police toward the people, as disturbers and breakers of the peace, and as men dangerous to the liberty of the citizens. We will show the number of assaults committed by police on citizens, and the number of convictions for those assaults. In three years there have been but four dismissals from the police for assault. A most remarkable thing in view of the almost daily statements in the newspapers in reference to police assaults on citizens, is that only one of the four dismissals was for assault on a citizen. The three other dismissals were for police assaults on police officials themselves. This brings us to consideration of the next point.
>
> Second – The evidence that the police force of New York is, to all intents and purposes, and in practice, exempt from and above the law of the land. The police have committed felonies and misdemeanors, and they have gone for years unpunished for crimes which, if perpetrated by citizens, would have sent the latter to State prison... For a crime which would send a citizen to prison for four or five years, a police officer may get only a fine of ten days' pay – $30. This goes to show that a New York policeman may brain a citizen, and all the penalty he pays is $30.[66]

On the basis of these accusations, Goff then summoned a wide range of witnesses, including serving police officers, who delivered numerous harrowing tales of almost medieval violence. One officer, Thomas Coleman, revealed a personal, grotesque litany of assaults upon numerous citizens. His victims included: John Casey (Coleman was fined 28 days' pay), Henry Ott, beaten with a beer pitcher (Coleman was fined seven days' pay), 15-year-old Margaret Cox and her father, John Cox, both clubbed in the street seemingly without provocation (Coleman pleaded that his mental state had been affected by medication, and he was fined 30 days' pay).

Goff used the testimony of people like Coleman to illustrate how potentially lethal force was used on a casual basis, yet even if officers were found repeatedly guilty of misuse of force they could remain on staff. One officer alone had been summoned before the Police Board some 24 times on charges that included dragging a woman along by her hair while threatening her with his revolver. At the start of the Commission, records disclosed that there were 56 cases of police assault on the books that remained uninvestigated and largely forgotten by the police authorities.

The Lexow Commission, for all its undoubted political motivation, produced a report that made superbly grim reading to all US citizens. It highlighted the activities of unsavory characters such as Alexander "Clubber" Williams, a truly aggressive career cop who over 30 years of police service managed to batter dozens of New York's citizens, several of them simple bystanders at public events, while successfully rising up through the ranks. Other cases brought to light incidents of students, mothers, children, and other non-threatening elements all receiving the impact of the nightstick.

Yet for all its high profile and media coverage, the Lexow Commission had a limited impact upon the actual expression of police violence.[67] Theodore Roosevelt became New York police commissioner during the 1890s, and introduced several reforming measures across broad issues, including police use of nightsticks. In 1892, in a bold move, a ban on nightsticks was trialed. The ban was not entirely successful, due in part to officers showing a resilient spirit of innovation, as one officer described:

> I manned myself with a piece of rubber hose, about eighteen inches long, a piece that had been well used in the cellar or behind the bar of the saloon of that day. Yes and you can believe me it was better than a night stick, for when it was not in use I would carry it up the sleeve of my coat, ever ready for any emergency, and when the tough fellow would come up to me to give an argument … I would lead off with my left and soak him with the rubber hose with my right, and he would fly for his life, saying to himself, gee what the h– did he hit me with?[68]

Marilynn Johnson notes that while there is no evidence to suggest that the numbers of alleged police beating declined during the ban era (1892–95), the number of reported fatalities to clubbings did indeed drop, possibly because of the removal of the skull-cracking locust-wood nightsticks.[69] Later controls also prohibited officers from twirling their nightsticks in a "menacing fashion."

Roosevelt reversed the nightstick ban in 1895, and controversy over police brutality rose again. Johnson claims that "New Yorkers responded in kind, escalating the cycle of violence on the streets. Instead of defusing violence, Roosevelt's big stick approach probably helped perpetuate it, requiring greater police resources than before."[70] Such a claim is extremely hard to support, as much criminal violence is directed into the fight *between* criminals, not necessarily against the police. Yet it does seem to be the case that in New York the application of the nightstick was a little too free and easy, and it wasn't until the Progressive era (see next chapter) that the reformist spirit truly started to rein in excessive brutality.

Note that the case of New York shouldn't be applied blanket fashion to the United States as a whole. In a study of policing in Detroit around this period, for example, the writer John Schneider found that there was much restraint in the wielding of the club, especially as egregious beatings would be splashed all over the next day's headlines. He notes that:

> Out of a total of 849 policemen brought before the commissioners for misbehavior from 1865 to 1885, only fifty-two were accused of physically abusing a citizen, an arrestee, or a jailed prisoner. The police surgeon could still claim in 1868 that he had yet to dress the wounds of a person injured by a patrolman's club.[71]

URBAN GUNS

By the turn of the century, most of America's urban police were tooled up with firearms, but this process was gradual and often informal. In the aforementioned study of Detroit, for example, John Schneider makes the following notes about police being armed in the 1870s:

> Patrolmen were, in fact, not issued revolvers. Yet they were not forbidden to carry one of their own pistols. Officials warned, however, that they should use them "at their peril," since the department would assume no responsibility if an "accident" occurred. In his study of the New York police, Wilbur R. Miller found that the middle and upper classes in that city expected policemen to be tough in dealing with dangerous elements, even if it meant resorting to firearms. While this was also the case in Detroit, policemen were not really expected to brandish firearms on a routine basis in their control of the streets. In the 1870s, there were enough minor incidents of patrolmen using their revolvers without sufficient justification that the press of both parties complained specifically about it. The *Free Press* even suggested that the department forbid officers to carry guns, certainly concealed ones, which was a common practice among patrolmen. That a gun was not considered indispensable to efficient policing in Detroit may have been due in part to the fact that the

dangerous class there was not well armed. Only one of every one hundred arrested persons carried a gun, and only one of eight even had a knife.[72]

Most policing of even dangerous criminals was indeed accomplished by the use of non-lethal force – then, as now, it remains comparatively rare for an officer to draw his gun and fire, when seen in the total spectrum of arrests made.

Not every urban authority was as reticent about arming its officers. The Boston police force, for example, was given its first issue revolvers in 1863, five years after it had received its new uniforms. Yet Boston seems generally the exception. The NYPD, like that in Detroit, carried its own personal weapons for much of the second half of the 1800s, although this practice was only officially sanctioned in 1887 with Rule 503 of the Manual of Rules and Regulations: "In addition to the ordinary baton of the patrolman each member of the Police Force shall be armed while on duty with a revolving pistol of pattern and caliber approved by the board." The note about caliber is important. As we shall see at regular intervals throughout this book, the caliber of a police weapon carries with it controversy and political importance. As a rough guide until the more detailed analysis of Chapter 6, the smaller the caliber the less penetration and damage a handgun bullet causes (this is not always the case with high-velocity rifles), and therefore the smaller calibers have less lethality. In 1896, the NYPD received its first issue weapon, a compact 4in.-long Colt .32 revolver. (Financial constraints on the purchase of firearms, however, often meant that many police officers retained their own weapons even into the 20th century.) The previous year the NYPD had also opened a Pistol Practice school, aware that not every officer was familiar with handling firearms. An article from the *Brooklyn Daily Eagle* in 1893 recounts an incident in which a class of young officers, about to be lectured on the "careful use" of firearms, was disrupted when one of the officers accidentally shot himself.[73]

Standardizing the issue of firearms was a sensible measure, as it prevented officers taking to the streets with inappropriate weapons. An instance of inappropriate handgun use, fortunately amusing, comes from a *Brooklyn Daily Eagle* article of 1895:

SEYMOUR HAD THREE REVOLVERS

There was nearly a riot at Gwinette street and Lee avenue last evening, owing to the peculiar actions of David Howard Seymour, a special policeman attached to the Twelfth precinct. Seymour was standing at the switch at the point named, and when a crowd gathered and commenced to jeer the switchman Seymour became excited. He reached into his pockets, pulled out two big revolvers and flourished them about like a stage Hawkshaw.

> "Stand back," he yelled, "I will protect this man at the risk of my own life. You can only reach him by passing over my dead body."
>
> Instead of dispersing, the crowd grew larger, and in a few moments Seymour was surrounded. His pistols were taken away from him, he was pelted with snow balls, and finally, Officer Rickards arrived and placed him under arrest under a charge of carrying concealed weapons.
>
> Up to the time that Seymour landed in the Sixteenth precinct, no one had any idea what his business was. When Sergeant Pinkerton asked him his pedigree, however, Seymour unbuttoned his coat and vest, and after considerable trouble, extracted his special police badge from his suspender.
>
> Of course, Seymour was discharged, after being advised to keep his badge in sight thereafter. He was armed to the teeth, having three big revolvers in his possession and cartridges enough to settle a Central American war.[74]

The enthusiastic Seymour, ostentatiously waving around a bullish arsenal, obviously met a crowd that was relatively unfazed by firearms, or which clearly saw through his bravado. Although Seymour was a special policeman rather than regular beat officer, his weaponry illustrates the need for law enforcement firearms to be controlled. Had Seymour's blood run a little hotter, he could have unleashed his own private massacre.

Regarding urban deadly force, politics come to the fore, often even more so than in the skewed democracies of many cowtowns and mining settlements out West. With large population bases to satisfy politically, particularly the affluent and commercially prosperous sections of society, city governments frequently gave police unwritten permission to "clean up the neighborhood" with as much violence as they saw fit. Looking at New York, the controlling Democratic machine centered on Tammany Hall gave the police leeway to apply deadly force directly in the service of its political ends, particularly in the context of ending labor disputes and of ridding more well-off streets of "undesirables." The latter was aided significantly by the "fleeing felon" rule, which basically gave the officer permission to shoot any criminal who attempted to get away from him. David Caplan here elucidates the thinking behind the rule:

> The social policy encouraging deadly force to be used if factually necessary – or according to caselaw, even if not factually necessary – to prevent the escape of these felons fleeing from the scene was based upon the rational presumption that a dangerous felon at large threatens the peace and security of society – i.e., the next victims. Immediate stopping of the fleeing felon, whether actually or presumably dangerous, was deemed absolutely necessary for the security of the people in a free state, and for maintaining the "public security."[75]

The fleeing felon rule was to cause persistent controversy until its effective repeal in 1985 (see Chapter 4), but it was broadly appreciated by higher society as a good policy for tough policing. An editorial in the *New York Times* back in 1858 noted that "there is absolutely no safety but in summary and even lawless measures – that the police are our sole reliance, and that they must have the power to shoot down every ruffian who resists arrest or attempts to escape."[76] This is not to say, however, that city police were free to draw and fire on anyone, or that the criminals had a complete lack of rights. An article in the *Brooklyn Daily Eagle*, for example, recounts an episode in 1869 centered on one Patrolman John Burke, of the 42nd Precinct. While on night patrol, Burke was called to a bar altercation in Fulton Street, where laborer John Dougherty and friends were arguing with the manager over the payment of a bar bill. Burke arrested Dougherty, and led him off down the streets towards the station, Dougherty's friends forming a jeering pack following behind, no doubt whipping up the emotions of both officer and the apprehended. At some point during the journey, Dougherty broke away and ran:

> The officer immediately pursued the fugitive and called upon him to stop, but the escaping prisoner not heeding the call, the officer drew his revolver and fired two shots at the flying man, while in Pearl street, without effect. Unheeding the shots Dougherty turned into Front street, and appeared to be about to enter the building No. 120, when the officer fired a third shot, and the fugitive disappeared in the building and closed the door.[77]

When Burke reached and entered the building, he found Dougherty in the hallway, shot and dying. The post-shooting procedure is revealing. Burke himself appeared before the Police Justice and "surrendered himself," before being "committed to jail to await the result of the injuries of Dougherty." The incarceration was spurred by an official complaint by a member of the public (whether one of Dougherty's gang or a bystander is not clear).

The outcome of the legal incident is not revealed, but it is highly unlikely that Burke was prosecuted. Most available evidence shows that police were almost never convicted following deadly force incidents. In detailed records from Chicago, a comparable city, for example, historian Jeffrey Adler revealed that "for killings in which policemen used deadly force, local prosecutors secured convictions in only 1 percent of cases."[78] A glance through the headlines of papers such as the *Brooklyn Daily Eagle* and *New York Times* show numerous cases of police shootings, but very few accounts of police convictions as an outcome.

As is so often the case with research into police deadly force, specific figures for how many people were killed by New York police during the 19th century are not available. Fortunately, this is not true for the Chicago police, of whom we will say much more in our next chapter. The aforementioned Jeffrey Adler has worked on important collections of data concerning police homicides, classed as justifiable or otherwise, from 1870 through to the 1920s. Cross-checking these figures with other public data shows them to be accurate, and so they give us a fairly unique insight into urban deadly force policy in one of America's most violent cities. The results are blunt, and should be borne in mind during the analysis of the next chapter:

> Between 1875 and 1920, Chicago police officers killed 307 people, accounting for one homicide in every eighteen committed in the city. Chicago policemen claimed three times as many victims as local gangsters during this era. In a city renowned for its bloody strikes, local law enforcers killed almost two and half times as many Chicagoans as died in labor conflict.[79]

Adler unpacks the figures with a balanced perspective, and an eye to the emerging patterns. Between 1875 and 1890, it appears, police violence on the whole did not lead to the deaths of many suspects or fugitives – there were 20 police killings over the 15-year period, although the numbers of people wounded by club or bullet were doubtless much higher. Seemingly out of the blue, however, police homicides rocketed to 39 between 1890 and 1900. Adler plausibly argues for two major causes behind the surge. First, he indicates a city-wide leap in general homicide rates, climbing by "49 percent between the late 1880s and the early 1890s, and by an additional 90 percent between the early 1890s and 1920."[80] Within this leap in homicide was a major increase in the number of murders committed during robberies, a type of crime that directly impinged on both the reality and imaginations of the more affluent neighborhoods targeted by the burglars.

Against this backdrop, the press accused the police of being soft or ineffective in their work. In response, various Chicago police chiefs ordered the police to toughen up their act, deliberately encouraging the use of deadly force as the most visible way of demonstrating effective policing. A definite "shoot-to-kill" policy was expressed by several Chicago police leaders, including chiefs Joseph Kipley and George Shippy.[81] Killing was delivered on mere suspicion – Adler points out that in "41 percent of police homicides, Chicago law enforcers discharged their weapons specifically to apprehend fleeing suspects."[82] The least twitch of clothing could be interpreted as the drawing of a gun, with lethal consequences.

The undoubted tenor of Adler's argument, and one that we shall delve into further in the next chapter, is that the end of the 19th century saw Chicago's police enjoying an almost unrestricted capacity to pull guns and fire them. There is unquestionably something deeply unsettling about the application of deadly force in the dying years of the 19th century. And yet, while police deadly force is open to external manipulation and criminal excesses, it also usually reflects something of the wider trends in violence. Between 1875 and 1900, 40 Chicago Police Department officers were killed, primarily through violent acts and mostly by gunfire. Now bear in mind that the same department lost only five officers between 1853 and 1875, a period of roughly the same duration, and there must have been a clear sense amongst the officers that they were operating in a world where sudden death stalked the streets. Expectations of violence could therefore lead to deadly force as a preemptive measure, part of the reason that police homicides typically outstrip by decent margins the numbers of police officers killed by criminals.

The cycle of violence is graphically illustrated in what became known as the Haymarket Riot or Haymarket Massacre, the appellation selected usually on the bias of the historian. On May 1, 1886, labor strikes and demonstrations were launched throughout the United States as leverage to achieve an eight-hour day for workers. Two days later, members of a 400-strong police unit outside the McCormick Harvester Plant in Chicago fired on a surging crowd of protesters, killing several men. In an already febrile atmosphere, the deaths were an explosive catalyst for mob violence. The next day, police advanced towards a mass of demonstrators in the Haymarket Square. Suddenly a hand-thrown dynamite bomb was hurled into the law enforcement ranks, killing one officer instantly and fatally wounding two others. The square rippled with gunfire from both sides, and by the time the shooting stopped a total of eight police officers and four civilians were either dead or well on their way.

The US media placed its support squarely behind the police on this occasion, seeing the menace of socialism and anarchism in the actions of the striking mob. The police, for all the toughened characters in their ranks, were also deeply shaken by the bloodshed of that day, as testimony from the subsequent trial (termed Illinois vs. August Spies et al., the named party being an anarchist labor activist) made clear. The following is part of the testimony, under questioning, of Police Officer H. F. Krueger. Krueger was shot in the leg during the riot, and his testimony became confused as to whether he heard shots first, after which the bomb went off, or vice versa:

Q. The first noise that you heard was the explosion of the bomb?

A. Well, I don't recollect exactly.

Q. Didn't you know the first explosion – the first noise – first pistol shot – at least that the first noise that was heard was the explosion of the bomb?

A. Well, I am not certain of that.

Q. What is your best judgment?

A. There might have been a shot or two fired before that.

Q. I don't ask you what there might have been: what is your best recollection? Was the explosion of the bomb the first noise, according to your best judgment?

A. No; I could not judge of that.

Q. You could not say?

A. No.

Q. How long was it after Mr. Fielding got down out of the wagon before the bomb exploded? [Mr Fielding was one of the defendants, who had mounted a wagon to speak to the crowds.]

A. You might count three or four.

Q. That is, after he got on the ground, you might say "one- two- three- four"?

A. Yes.

Q. Or, "one, two, three"?

A. Yes, that is about it.

Q. After he got down?

A. Yes.

Q. If there was a pistol shot fired before the bomb was exploded it was just before, wasn't it – so near as to leave it in doubt in your mind?

A. Yes, it would have been, I should judge; but I am not a judge of that.

Q. You would not have had time to count one, two three after the pistol shot was fired before the bomb was exploded, would you?

A. Well, you might have had. I am not certain on that point.

Q. Now, your best judgment is, is it not, that the pistol shots and bomb exploded at about the time – almost simultaneously?

A. The bomb was fired or exploded when the gentleman was pretty near on the sidewalk; he got a couple of steps from the sidewalk.

Q. The question is whether or not the pistol firing and the bomb explosion did not commence about the same time – about the same instant?

A. I do not know anything about the pistol firing.

Q. You did not hear any pistol firing?

A. I don't recollect anything about that.

Q. You are not going to say there was any pistol fired until the bomb was exploded?

A. I did not hear it and I am not going to say it.

Q. Your judgment now is that you did not hear a pistol fired until you heard the bomb?

A. I don't say that.

Q. Do you remember now to have heard a pistol before the bomb? Did you hear a pistol before the bomb?

A. No sir; I cannot recollect that.

Q. You cannot recollect it?

A. No sir.

Q. Then your first recollection is that the explosion was the bomb?

A. That is my recollection.[83]

Knowing what we do now about shock and the way the human brain attempts to reconstruct or blot out traumatic events (see Chapter 6), the testimony here is painful to read. The sense of disorientation is clear, and the large numbers of officers involved in the riot that day meant that the collective memory for self-protection would have been carried forward through the rest of the century and beyond. Factor in the "regular" murder of an officer every one or two months, and it is hardly surprising that a sense of "us versus them" might have informed the dynamics of deadly force encounters.

The differences between the frontier law officer of the Old West, attempting to stamp his own brand of authority on a recalcitrant cowtown, and an urban officer using the power of mass and organization to achieve his force's aim, may seem distinct. Yet what unites them both is the instinctive sense that deadly force was entirely appropriate to achieving the aims of law and order, and that the criminal had little in the way of rights to defend himself against the use of such force. That perspective was about to change.

2

BLOOD AND WHISKY, 1900–45

On the early morning of May 23, 1934, a gray V8 Ford rumbled down the highway near Salines, Louisiana. It had two occupants – a 24-year-old man, who was driving, and a seductive 23-year-old woman in the passenger seat. Both were attractive individuals in their physical prime, the man dark with strong, clear facial lines, the women lithe and pretty, with blonde bobbed hair. They were heading for the home of Ivan Methin, the father of one of their associates. It was a place they had been to frequently before, a refuge to unwind and relax in the company of people they knew. A place to hide.

Further up the road, unknown to the young couple, were six men. In contrast to the young couple, these individuals had faces wired tight with tension and anxiety. Their leader was retired Texas Ranger Frank Hamer, and accompanying him were old friend B. M. Gault plus hand-picked crew Bob Alcorn, Ted Hinton, Henderson Jordan, and Paul Oakley. They had camouflaged themselves in the vegetation by the side of the road at 1.30am, and then simply waited for the dawn to streak the horizon. Seven interminable hours followed – a long time to hold in fear and nervous energy. Then, at around 9.10am, they heard what they had been waiting for.

The V8 Ford was coming. Amongst the men, muscles tightened and minds raced, trying to process what was about to happen. In the car, the normality of an everyday drive presided.

The car came into view, and two of the officers stepped forward to wave it down, hearts thumping. At first, the car slowed obediently, but then the world exploded in the blink of an eye. The driver accelerated, attempting to pull away, and both he and his passenger reached for guns inside the car. They had shot their way out of trouble before, after all. Not this time. The heavily armed officers, some clutching full-auto Browning Automatic Rifles (BARs), opened up on the car with a shattering barrage of fire. The windscreen and side windows were torn open, the bodywork shot through, and what eventually totaled a barrage of 167 steel-jacket bullets cut the occupants to ribbons, some 50 rounds finding their human marks. Even as the gunshot echoes died down, the officers were tense, not trusting that this was finally the end of a long criminal journey that had begun over a year before. Their caution was warranted: in the car the officers found three BARs, two shotguns, one Colt .45 revolver, eight Colt automatic pistols, and some 3,000 rounds of ammunition. They also found license plates from Illinois, Iowa, Missouri, Texas, Indiana, Kansas, Ohio, and Louisiana, and one saxophone.

The deaths of Clyde Champion Barrow and Bonnie Parker, the infamous Bonnie and Clyde, are notorious on many levels. Although the pair were wanted for murder, including the killing of police officers, they had become virtual media celebrities, the inspiration for poems and, later, Hollywood films. Such was the clamor around the small funeral parlor where their bodies were kept, that the undertaker had to resort to spraying embalming fluid over the crowd to keep them back. The bullet-ripped car became a freakish novelty, and traveled around the United States in fairs where the enterprising new owners charged 25 cents just for a look. Furthermore, there was something startling about the level of violence used by the law enforcement officers. This was no spur-of-the moment snap shooting on the street. Here was a military-style ambush using heavy automatic firepower and bullets designed to carve their way through the automobile – several rounds had passed through one side of the vehicle, gone through the occupants, and exited through the bodywork on the other side. In terms of the CoF, the use of deadly force could scarcely be more extreme, although the merciless trail of death that had followed Bonnie and Clyde made their ending oddly fitting.

The deaths of Bonnie and Clyde hit a chord that will reverberate throughout this chapter. The period from the beginning of the 20th century to the end of World War II is one of the most fascinating in US law enforcement history. Not only do we see the birth of new, powerful federal agencies; we also see these and regular state and city police exploring the limits of deadly force against some of the most violent criminal movements in US history. This period takes in an infamous and violent age of gangsters and prohibition, of police corruption and of good policing, and of new weaponry in the hands of both criminals and officers.

NEW AGE

Despite the new century, some things remained timeless. Bad guys still drew guns on good guys, and vice versa, with all the frenzied dynamics of lethal force encounters that apply today. Yet between 1900 and the end of World War II, there were also profound changes in the world of law enforcement. The era saw the founding or shaping of the great federal agencies that loom over the legal landscape of the United States today – the Federal Bureau of Investigation (FBI), the modern US Coast Guard (USCG), and various organizations that would eventually produce, in their merging, the Bureau of Alcohol, Tobacco and Firearms (BATF). A brief explanation of the early history of these organizations gives us a useful context for the analysis that follows.

The FBI was the child of the Department of Justice. Formed in 1870, the Department of Justice was created to handle federal prosecutions (although the office of Attorney General had existed since the late 18th century). Since its formation, the chief gripe of the Department of Justice had been that it lacked an effective enforcement arm. The primary reason for its lack of active field agents was the initial scarcity of federal cases to pursue, hence its caseload did not warrant a large, regular workforce of field officers. When it did need more boots on the ground, it solved this problem during the 1880s and 1890s by hiring muscle, such as men from the Pinkerton Agency or agents from the Treasury Department, although the brutal handling of strikers by such agencies did little for the Department of Justice's reputation. Yet with the steady expansion of Department of Justice responsibilities in response to legislation such as the Interstate Commerce Act of 1887 and the Sherman Anti-Trust Act of 1890, it soon became apparent that the Department of Justice needed its very own law enforcement arm.

In 1908 Attorney General Charles Joseph Bonaparte gained the backing of President Theodore Roosevelt to give the Department of Justice its own body of agents. This was no easy matter to pass through Congress – suspicion of extending federal powers still ran hot in government – but the legislation passed through, and the new force was born on July 26, 1908. It would take another year before the organization managed to acquire a title – on March 16, 1909, it became the Bureau of Investigation (BI).

The BI was meant to embody the spirit of "Progressivism" – the idealistic attempt by prominent politicians and civic leaders to improve the lot of American society from the laborer to the big business entrepreneur. Here, apparently, was a professional, well-trained body that was above the spirit of corruption infecting many US political and law enforcement institutions. In spite of its slick name, the BI was rather toothless in its early days, as it could investigate little more than crimes committed on federal property. Various government acts, however, steadily expanded the BI's jurisdiction to include cross-state prostitution and vice (the 1910 Mann Act), draft dodging (the 1917 Selective Service Act), and various wartime and post-World War I anti-espionage acts. It was during the 1920s and 1930s, however, that the BI rose in terms of public effect. This was the age of gangsterism and Prohibition, and from the end of 1924 the Bureau came under the directorship of that landmark figure, J. Edgar Hoover. Hoover did much to professionalize the BI (within his own rigid perspectives on race and gender, that is), investing more in the removal of corrupt officers, in training programs, and also in scientific forensic expertise – the Scientific Crime Detection Laboratory was opened in 1932. In 1932 the BI changed its name to the US Bureau of Investigation (USBI), which in 1933 also merged with the largely ineffective Prohibition Bureau (another Department of Justice agency).

The USBI, which evolved to become the FBI in July 1935, will feature prominently in this chapter, not least for its new approaches to firearms training but also because of its "war on crime," a systematic campaign against the gangster world launched in the aftermath of the Kansas City Massacre (see below).

The BATF, like the FBI, was an evolution of 19th-century institutions. It grew out of Treasury Department efforts to impose taxation on imported and domestically produced alcohol, in a country that enjoyed a lively bootlegging industry. With the passing of the Volstead Act in 1919, and the subsequent imposition of Prohibition on January 17, 1920, policing alcohol sale and distribution became a more high-stakes game. The Treasury Department's Prohibition Bureau tried to stem the flood, but deep-seated corruption rendered these efforts of limited success (some 10 percent of the Prohibition Bureau's agents were dismissed from duty between 1920 and 1930). Following the repeal of Prohibition in 1933, there was a spell of multi-agency confusion over the policing of alcohol. In 1940, the Alcohol Tax Unit (ATU) was born from the merging of a Department of Justice organization of the same name with the Treasury Department's Federal Alcohol Administration. Alongside the ATU was another federal agency, the mysteriously titled Miscellaneous Tax Unit (MTU). The MTU's primary responsibility was enforcing taxes over the transfer of tobacco and firearms, the latter of which took on greater political significance with the passage of the 1934 National Firearms Act, a policy designed to curtail the use of a more destructive breed of weaponry in the hands of gangsters and other criminals. The MTU would eventually dissolve in 1952, to be replaced by the Alcohol and Tobacco Unit (ATU), then the Alcohol and Tobacco Tax Division. Only in 1968 were the worlds of alcohol, tobacco, and firearms united under the jurisdiction of the newly created BATF.

The important point about these various agencies was that they, like the FBI, introduced a new tier of cross-state law enforcement. While these agencies were shiny new attempts to combat crime, the USCG had a far older ancestry, created as the Revenue Marine or Revenue Cutter Service back in 1790. From initial duties relating to the maritime collection of taxes and tariffs and activities against smuggling, the Revenue Cutter Service gradually acquired an extremely broad and frequently militaristic brief, which would later include open combat in wars alongside the US Navy; the Coast Guard has served with distinction in conflicts including World War II and the Vietnam War, and in the "War against Terrorism" in the Persian Gulf. The openly naval nature of its deployments meant that, in terms of its CoF, the Coast Guard had greater firepower available to it than any other law enforcement agency, and this largely remains true today. For a period during the 1970s, USCG vessels boasted not only naval gun systems, but also Harpoon antiship missiles, although the prospect of a large warhead parked on a ship at the end of jetty in a local fishing harbor, plus the sheer cost of training and upkeep, resulted in the missiles being ditched. Nonetheless, the USCG still has major firepower under its belt, and when it took its modern title in 1915, the result of fusing the Revenue Cutter Service with the Life-Saving Service, a powerful off-shore law enforcement body was born.

The new federal agencies outlined above had their work cut out for them in the first decades of the 20th century. It was a time not only of criminality on an industrial scale, spurred by the establishment of major mafia families, but also of deep civil unrest in the labor markets and amongst criminally inclined neighborhoods in some of the tougher urban districts of America. At the same time, a general, spluttering, and erratic movement began in the US law enforcement community in general – the shift towards professionalism. It was a movement that would have an effect on how officers utilized the means of force at their disposal.

DARK AGE

George Streeter (1837–1921) was one of those true characters in the history of Chicago. A former steam boat captain in Mississippi, he moved up to Chicago in the 1880s, where he ran his steamboat the *Reutan* along the shores of Lake Michigan. In July 1886, a storm forced the *Reutan* to ground itself on a sandbar, and there the vessel would sit for the coming years. As the decades passed, this apparently benign situation would curdle into an explosive and violent clash between Streeter and the law enforcement agencies of Chicago.

The sandbar on which the *Reutan* was embedded grew larger not only with steady accretions of silt, but also on account of rubble dumped around the sandbar from construction companies engaged in the rebuilding of Chicago after the Great Fire of 1871. Inexorably, Streeter's "island" grew ever larger, and he saw himself as its local ruler, even issuing deeds to those who wanted to live on his territory. Eventually the sandbar island grew so large that it connected with the shore, and by that point Chicago's authorities had realized that it had some valuable real estate – by the end of the century it would be valued at around $350,000 – that a maverick was holding outside its jurisdiction. In 1889 the industrialist N. K. Fairbank had claimed rights over the land, classifying Streeter as an illegal squatter, a claim assisted by the growth of vice (particularly prostitution) on the island. Streeter, backed by his own private army of "settlers," physically repelled Fairbanks' attempts to expel him, firing at officers with shotguns and hurling pots of boiling water at those who intruded.

The "war" – as several newspapers in the United States declared it – went on throughout the 1890s, with Streeter escaping prison sentences through pleading self-defense. Nonetheless, his holdings over his territory were steadily eroded by the authorities, about which Streeter was not happy. The scale of the dispute became clear on May 26, 1900, when Streeter felt that he had had enough. Early in the morning, he landed 20 armed men and two Gatling guns on a patch of contested ground at the foot of Superior Street. With some showmanship, Streeter raised the US flag and emplaced his Gatling guns in trench defenses. He was clearly ready for a showdown.

At around noon, a small party of city officials and policemen approached the captured land, backed by a healthy crowd of interested civilians. In true military style, Streeter had posted pickets as outer security, and as the Chicago police approached they received warnings to halt. The officers kept on coming, however, and were suddenly met with a barrage of rifle fire. One bullet struck a 14-year-old bystander, Reuben Manley, who received a severe injury to the knee. The officers scattered back to safety. A new approach was clearly needed.

The chosen solution was simply to scale up the force available to the officers, and thereby overwhelm the Streeter gang psychologically and, if necessary, in terms of firepower. The commanding officer, one Chief Kipley, upped his manpower to 300 officers, each one kitted out with a Winchester repeating rifle. Furthermore, he equipped a river boat with a Gatling gun, and floated this ominously behind the "enemy" positions, making it clear that for Streeter's men the river provided no avenue for escape.

For the rebels holding out, this demonstration of force did the trick. Surrenders began, but not without some nasty scuffles and minor injuries. Streeter himself did one of his characteristic vanishing acts, but the general outcome was mercifully benign considering the sheer amount of firepower available on both sides. The *New York Times* wrote an article on the clash entitled "Chicago has Real War."[84]

Throughout the history of US law enforcement, the police and other agencies have had to walk a difficult line in terms of firearms acquisition. Too little firepower, and you risk being outgunned by the criminals. Too much firepower, and you threaten overkill and collateral damage, with the resultant public condemnation. During the gangster age, this was a hard line to follow, as it was a period in which the criminals were armed with firepower approaching military levels. Responding to that threat with equal, and often greater, firepower tested the discipline of officers and commanders to the extreme.

The first three decades of the 20th century in the United States were a period of visionary ideology on the one hand and dire social circumstances on the other. A sweeping history of this period is not possible here, but we can highlight some keynotes. As the nation's wealth grew inexorably on the back of seemingly limitless natural resources, presidents such as Theodore Roosevelt (1901–09), William Taft (1909–13), and Woodrow Wilson (1913–21), in various ways and with contrasting degrees of commitment, improved the power of unions and workers, and placed pressure on big business to clean up its act in terms of exploitative working practices. At the same time, the Progressive movement promoted a more democratic momentum. In 1913 the Seventeenth Amendment to the US Constitution brought about the direct election of US Senators by the citizens (instead of state legislatures), the Nineteenth Amendment of 1920 gave women the right to vote, and various other pieces of legislation bolstered democracy with rights such as direct primaries for the election of party officials through to referenda on local issues. In terms of social justice, policies were implemented in the critical and long-neglected areas of employment conditions, including child labor laws, the development of a professional system of social service workers, occupational health and safety, working hours for laborers, and the protection of unionization.

Such developments were welcome indeed, and laid the foundations for subsequent US social progress, yet Progressivism was balanced by various counterweights. The US involvement in World War I, although it avoided the truly massive death tolls and territory destruction wrought across Europe, left a bitter taste in America's mouth, and the Republican "Return to Normalcy" slogan in the 1920 presidential election encapsulated a growing desire to reject rapid change and return to some of the perceived "traditional" American values. Consumerism became a dominant ideological trend, held in tension by the poverty that still ran deep in many quarters of American society, rural and urban.

Continuing and massive population growth, fueled particularly by huge waves of immigrants crossing the Atlantic from the violent world of Europe, was changing the social landscape. Between the 1880s and 1920s, something in the region of 12–15 million immigrants flooded into the United States, and while this influx doubtless led to greater commercial energies, it also bred racial polarization on the one hand, and the growth of an anti-communist suspicion from the government on the other. In terms of social wealth, in 1929 the Brookings Institute published a report that revealed that 60 percent of US families were surviving on less than the $2,000 per annum deemed necessary for basic living. The Great Depression of the late 1920s and the 1930s simply heightened the sense of financial fragility, and changed the status of millions of families from prosperity or subsistence to brute survival. It should also be remembered in the context of this chapter that policemen were not immune from such hardships. Policing in the early 20th century remained a blue-collar profession, and one that was poorly paid and under-respected. Officers who attempted to improve their lot through unionization did so at their peril. In September 1919, for example, 75 percent of Boston Police Department officers went on strike, challenging the authorities over their non-recognition of the new police union. In response, the Boston city authorities, led by the hardened governor Calvin Coolidge, simply shipped in the Massachusetts militia to continue the police work and sacked all those who had gone on strike.

Of course, the late 1910s and the early 1920s began one of the greatest waves of criminality to sweep US society. Nineteenth-century America had experienced more than its fair share of gangs, but the first decades of the next century brought organized criminality to US urban society on a scale never before seen. It rode partly on the back of the Volstead Act, which by 1920 had enforced the banning of alcohol across the whole of the United States, and partly on the waves of immigration mentioned earlier. Although the Italian-American gangsters such as Al Capone and John Torrio tend to capture much of the historical press, the gangs were just as likely to be of Eastern European or Jewish derivation. Prohibition, illegal gambling, and prostitution gave such gangs thriving enterprises, and by the mid-1920s bootlegging liquor alone was earning the criminal fraternity $2 billion a year. At the same time, inter-gang violence rose and with it violence directed towards the police. Death tolls amongst law enforcement officers for 1920–33 make sober reading (the figures in parenthesis indicate those killed by intentional gunfire, invariably the largest single cause of felonious death):

1920	185 (142)
1921	226 (163)
1922	225 (158)
1923	210 (140)
1924	246 (166)
1925	226 (146)
1926	228 (163)
1927	247 (146)
1928	247 (157)
1929	258 (144)
1930	288 (175)
1931	261 (163)

1932	268 (160)
1933	222 (147)[85]

Taking the 13 years prior to 1920 as a sample, during that period there were 1,599 officer deaths, with gunfire accounting for a roughly similar percentage of the casualties as the figures shown above. Between 1920 and 1933 (the date when Prohibition was repealed), however, the death toll runs to a prodigious 3,337 officers. Even allowing for an increase in police numbers, it is apparent that the gangster age was an extremely dangerous policing environment.

Any analysis of the first half of the 20th century must also admit that the period was one that presented troubling levels of excessive or seemingly unwarranted force amongst many police departments, and also significant patterns of corruption amongst both beat officers and police leadership. New York, for example, was plagued by a series of race riots from 1900, the product of racial hostility principally between "white" New Yorkers – i.e. those of European ancestry – and the Jewish and African-American communities with whom they jostled for employment and living space. Much of the reportage of the period indicates that during such riots, the police generally condoned or actively participated in the beatings of non-white people on the streets, regardless of their connection to the actual riot. The problem was exacerbated both by the large percentage of Irish-stock officers, who were naturally more likely to back the general hostility of New York's early Irish community toward the African-Americans, and also by the tendency of black men in particular to carry weapons as "equalizers" against other mobs and gangs, but which effectively increased their likelihood of being either beaten or shot.

Some specific incidents aggravated the problems in New York. In January 1905, a 26th Precinct officer, Frank McLaughlin, was found guilty of the murder of a black nightwatchman, John W. Patterson, the previous year. McLaughlin had been going to arrest Patterson at the time, but the nail in the coffin of McLaughlin's defense was witness evidence that he fired several shots into Patterson as he lay apparently lifeless on the ground.[86] Whatever the realities of the shooting, McLaughlin was convicted – such was a rare occurrence indeed amongst US police officers – and it appears that some other officers of the precinct were tempted to express their annoyance in physical terms.[87] A brick was thrown at a group of officers from a rooftop outside a saloon on West 62nd Street, following which the police unleashed a vigorous raid against both the saloon and a billiards hall opposite. Two men were shot, one of them fatally, and dozens placed under arrest. Those arrested were taken to the West 68th station house where, according to the later sworn statement of the billiard hall owner, they were made to run the gauntlet of police clubs. One at a time, each prisoner:

> ... was led to the back room, through which he had to pass to get to the cells. The lights were out in the room and it was filled with policemen with drawn clubs. Before it was my turn to go in, I heard the sound of clubs on the heads of other prisoners and heard them crying for mercy. I was frightened sick. When it came to my turn I was struck about a dozen blows. I am sore and black and blue all over yet. Several of the blows were on my head.[88]

Such accounts resulted in a series of civic protests against police brutality in New York, often resulting in high-profile public inquiries from which the police rarely emerged squeaky clean. By the 1920s, excessive force and corrupt policing came to be seen as the outward signs of the corruption at the heart of Tammany Hall politics, and the use of the "third degree" was publicly notorious. The origins of the term are uncertain, with possibilities being the series of tests applied in the Freemasons for someone to achieve the position of Master Mason, a terrible sweat punishment inflicted on criminals in the immediate post-Civil War period, or a simple description for the escalation of police force in interrogation.[89] Whatever the origins, it was defined by the police themselves as any method that would result in the successful coercion of a confession from an unwilling suspect. One officer, Captain Cornelius Willemse of the NYPD, acknowledged that the third degree could begin with merely scaring a confession out of the suspect through potentially violent posturing, but could graduate to harder measures if necessary: "The 'third degree,' too, means rough stuff when required ... against a hardened criminal. I never hesitated. I've forced confessions – with fist, blackjack and hose – from men who would have continued to rob and kill if I had not made them talk."[90]

Third degree methods came under the spotlight in the late 1920s via the Wickersham Commission, an investigative body established by the National Commission of Law Enforcement and Observance under lawyer George W. Wickersham. With statistical diligence, the Commission gathered hundreds of instances of third degree applications, with the NYPD coming out the worst offender. Figures from 1930 indicated that 23.5 percent of a 1,234-client sample had experienced police brutality, and the methods employed in interrogation also made unsettling reading, as Marilynn Johnson recounts:

> Some of the most chilling accounts combined physical and psychological torture. In one case reported by Emanuel Lavine, police assured a suspect they would not beat him, then hit him from behind with a club. When he came to, police sympathized with him and reassured him

> – only to have the same thing happen again and again until the subject confessed. In another method, known as "Taps," a suspect was tied to a chair and beaten with a rubber hose every thirty seconds, causing both pain and fear. Such beatings could be quite severe. A former district attorney told the commission of one case in which a police surgeon was called into a third-degree session to monitor the victim's pulse and advise police as to whether he could stand more blows.[91]

In balance, Johnson later points out that third degree tactics were generally used against suspects charged with felonies such as robbery, assault, burglary, and grand larceny; they were typically not used against those who had committed petty crimes nor, as a whole, against those charged with homicide, as in those cases the suspect would be given the extra power of paid counsel.[92] Furthermore, Johnson also acknowledges the fact that in those days there was no waiting to see what forensics would throw up – if the police failed to extract a confession, there was a strong likelihood that the suspect would walk free. Of course, this might seem largely fair to our modern sensibilities, but in an increasingly violent world, where many of the suspects were indeed hardened criminals, there must have been a sense in which getting a suspect off the streets meant a safer environment for the officers. This argument is buttressed by some alarming statistics that demonstrate just how violent the Prohibition world was for the NYPD. Between 1907 and 1919, a sample of 13 years, 56 NYPD officers died on duty from all causes, although the bulk of those causes was shooting. Between 1920 and 1933, however, the death toll rose by over 300 percent to 170 officers. Whereas in 1920 the NYPD suffered just four officer deaths, in 1930 it took 20 fatalities, with 18 deaths the following year. Interestingly, only in 1933, the year Prohibition was repealed, did the death toll drop back down to four officers.

Other police departments were having a similarly brutal time during the Prohibition. Like New York, the Chicago PD, for example, received the gaze of major investigations into corruption and brutality in 1898, 1904, 1912, 1917, and 1928, with final judgments including statements that the department was "rotten to the core."[93] Yet the violence against officers was escalating there too. A total of 160 officers were killed between 1920 and 1933. While this figure is marginally less than the NYPD numbers, the actual percentage of officers killed by intentional hostile gunfire was higher. Eighty-one percent of Chicago's fallen during this period were killed by criminals' bullets, whereas in the case of the NYPD the figure is forty-five percent. (NYPD officers, however, suffered a higher percentage of deaths due to accidents during vehicular pursuits and also vehicular assaults.)

Amongst the citizenry, violence was also in the ascendant. Organized crime, aided by the unpopularity of Prohibition, the easy availability of firearms, and the rise of the motor car (which made cross-state and interstate criminality easier), fueled the rise of massive criminal organizations with no compunction about killing. The result was over 500 gangland murders in the 1920s alone, and those are only the ones of which we are aware. At the same time, the number of individuals killed by the Chicago PD was probably also on the climb, although obtaining accurate figures for the Prohibition era specifically is difficult. Certainly, during the period immediately before Prohibition, officer-involved shootings were on the rise, largely for reasons outlined in the previous chapter. In his continuing analysis of shootings in Chicago between 1875 and 1920, Jeffrey Adler shows how police homicides roughly tripled between 1910 and 1920. This increase roughly parallels the expansion in robbery homicides – it is often the case that police shootings increase during times when the civilian world itself is becoming more violent. Operating in such a world, Adler presents a picture of police under active encouragement to take the shot:

> After a robber killed a police officer in 1915, Chief James Gleason advised his men "to carry their revolvers so they could draw them in a hurry." Gleason explained that Chicago policemen "must be ready to shoot first if necessary," a message underscored three years later, when police officials told local law enforcers "don't let them [criminals and suspicious characters] shoot first." Police chiefs promoted patrolmen who killed robbers, and one alderman proposed an immediate promotion for "all police who killed criminals," arguing that "some incentive is needed to quicken the trigger fingers of the police." The shoot-first policy, according to municipal leaders, would "protect the lives of the citizens of Chicago."[94]

Factor in the evidence that a full 41 percent of police homicides between 1890 and 1920 were the result of shooting at fleeing suspects, rather than self-defense, and the picture looks alarming.[95] Yet some of what is said here is actually common sense. Shootings tend to happen over the duration of a few seconds, so carrying a readied revolver was understandable. Shooting first is also a basic law of survival; if we change the phrasing and say the officer should shoot first rather than be shot first, the meaning changes significantly.

The drive to promote officers who killed is rather less easy to understand in terms of modern sensibilities, and rightly so. Certainly, many civil bodies seem to have questioned the legitimacy of police shootings during the first half of the 20th century, especially once Pandora's box was opened regarding officer corruption during the 1920s and 30s. Yet Adler also points out that many of the newspapers and much of the middle-class public were fairly behind the enforcement of a semi-official shoot-to-kill policy, even when there were repeated cases of mistaken shootings. Hence during the 1920s police homicides increased by 24 percent in tandem with a 33 percent climb in civil homicides.[96]

The fact that rates of police homicides often increase or decrease with rates of civil homicide should never be ignored in analysis of the use of deadly force (as opposed to more considered applications of force, such as the third degree). The police, although held to greater account than average citizens, still do not work in a vacuum, and the more brutal the world around them the more likely they are themselves to use violence. The 500+ gangland murders in Chicago in the 1920s brought people from all walks of life into a brute confrontation with the realities of violent death. A typical example is that recorded in the *Chicago Tribune* on August 11, 1932. The night before, Joe "Big Rabbit" Connell, a 35-year-old "entrepreneur," had stepped outside his saloon and cabaret, the Island Tavern on Hickory Avenue, Goode Island, to take a breath of fresh air. Connell had decided to go into the beer business, and this brought him into conflict with the businesses of the local crime syndicate. According to a local detective interviewed, "Connell used to buy his beer from two places. Then he started making the beer himself. This cost him only $7 a barrel. More recently he started out selling his beer at $30 a barrel to outsiders. The syndicate gets $55 a barrel."[97] Other sources implicated Connell in labor union rackets. In short, he was treading on powerful toes. It would prove to be a very bad choice in business diversification. As Connell stood there, drawing in the warm summer air of Chicago, a small sedan car pulled up, with three men inside. One of them called Connell over, and he obliged. As he approached the car, ripples of gunfire suddenly cracked out down the Chicago street, illuminating the interior of the car like flash bulbs popping randomly. Using what were later believed to be semi-automatic shotguns, the occupants of the car pumped some 30 slugs into Connell, who collapsed and bled out his life in a passageway running up the side of his saloon. Just another hit in Chicago's gangland.

Such incidents were repeated, with numerous grim variations, hundreds of times during the Prohibition period throughout Chicago and other major American cities. The sound of gunshots must have been a familiar resonance in entire neighborhoods, much in the same way as gunfire was in 1980s southcentral Los Angeles. The fact that police were quick to resort to their guns during such violent times, particularly as large numbers of their own were victims, is understandable, especially with the motivation to "clean up the streets," fueled by some degree of popular support. Yet we cannot extend the argument that police homicides simply reflect levels of civilian homicide too far. Ultimately, police are indeed held to higher ethical standards than the public they serve, and the reformers of the period had plenty to concern themselves about, of which use of force was but one element.

Reform came both from within the ranks of the law enforcement community itself, and from external civilian legislators and campaigners. The former included individuals such as Richard Sylvester, Arthur Woods, the vigorous J. Edgar Hoover, and August Vollmer. Between them they pushed new strategies for police professionalism, stretching across issues of training, education, conduct, investigative technique, and forensics. Chief Vollmer, of Berkeley, California, was a particularly high-impact reformer, and indeed laid the foundations for much of what we now witness or aspire to see in police behavior.

Vollmer was a tough, self-taught man who advocated high standards of moral and practical education for police officers, giving them the intellectual capacity to tackle crime not only with frontline investigation, but also in the more subtle capacities:

> … the pendulum is beginning to swing the other way, and the policeman is beginning to realize his power as a social worker, and the future is frought [sic] with wonderful possibilities, if all will realize their potential worth… If he would serve his community by reducing crime he must go up the stream a little further and dam it up at its source, and not wait until it is a rushing torrent, uncontrollable and resistless. Moreover, if he would succeed in his efforts he must utilize to the fullest extent every helpful agency in the community, such as schools, churches, recreation and juvenile departments, public welfare and employment bureaus, clinics, dispensaries, hospitals and fraternal and labor organizations. Cooperation is also necessary with character forming organizations, such as Boy Scouts, Campfire Girls, well organized boys' clubs, community social centers and auxiliary and junior police forces.[98]

Vollmer saw the police role in its most expansive terms, with the individual officer educated to understand the full social implications of his office. According to Vollmer, simply eradicating criminal behavior by (at one extreme) killing the suspect or at least brutalizing him into submission does not cut off the stream of criminal behavior at source, but merely rearranges its flow. Instead Vollmer advocated that police officers work with other social agencies to assist desperate individuals in their efforts to find housing and employment, and take youthful energies and channel them into a productive assistance of society and the police.

Although the educational aspirations of Vollmer's ideas led some to mock his officers as "college cops" (he founded a School of Criminology for his officers on Berkeley campus in 1916), Vollmer was no pie-in-the-sky thinker. Alongside his emphasis on social policing, Vollmer also pioneered grittier techniques of investigation and apprehension, including improved forensic handling of crime scene materials, the introduction of the polygraph lie detector, the use of fingerprint classification, and the installation of radios into police patrol cars.[99] Little wonder, therefore, that Vollmer was brought in to reform numerous other police departments around the United States, including Detroit, Minneapolis, Kansas City, Dallas, Portland, Chicago, Los Angeles, and San Diego, although in many places his vision met with a hostile reception, and Vollmer was dispirited on numerous occasions by inveterate corruption.

Richard Sylvester, superintendent of the Washington DC Police Department (1898–1915) and president of the International Association of Chiefs of Police (IACP; 1901–15), was another cornerstone reformer, with a special interest in the "third degree" tactics of interrogation. Sylvester argued that:

> There is no justification for personal violence, inhuman or unfair conduct, in order to extort confessions. The officer who understands his position will offer admissions obtained from prisoners in no other manner than that which is sanctioned by the law. If a confession, preceded by customary caution, obtains [sic] through remorse or a desire to make reparation for a crime, is advanced by a prisoner, it surely should not be regarded as unfair.[100]

Sylvester had been an officer long enough to know that not every cry of police brutality was warranted: "There are those who come in contact with the authorities who are always ready to condemn on slight provocation. Those who are waiting to even up for some fancied wrong, or for some contact with the police they may have had through their own wrong-doing, and who are ever ready to condemn the police."[101] Yet like Vollmer he was advocating that police reform is as much about the internal, moral life of the officer as it was about the structural and procedural life of any department. The IACP agreed, unanimously passing a resolution condemning the use of forced confessions. Federal legislation was also steadily tightening up the procedures by which police could obtain evidence for prosecutions. In Weeks v. United States in 1914, the US Supreme Court ruled that the acquisition of evidence without a search warrant rendered such material inadmissible in federal criminal prosecutions. This ruling sharpened respect for the Fourth Amendment, which protected citizens against "unlawful searches," and by implication cautioned all officers against using extra-legal means to support their case.

In short, times were changing. The questioning of certain police actions, whether justified or not on an individual basis, began the process of law enforcement professionalization that would continue throughout the 20th century to this day. Our analysis will now explore how this professionalization expressed itself in the technology, tactics and training of the force.

FORCE OLD AND NEW

Most officers went out onto the streets armed with a trusty revolver and, of course, the ever controversial nightstick. In a time of both civil unrest and of growing police accountability, the nightstick remained a particularly troublesome tool of law enforcement. As we have seen, New York police had trialed the banning of nightsticks in 1892 (except for use in civic emergencies), as an attempt to counter the growing reputation of the force as indiscriminate clubbers. Such restrictions, however, were significantly loosened under the leadership of commissioner Theodore Bingham, who led the NYPD from 1906 to 1909. Bingham was a disciplinarian by nature, and while he continued the reformist efforts to root out corruption and inefficiency in the police force, he also held the criminal community in utter distaste, and gave his officers more of a free reign to wield the club. In an article written following his time in office, Bingham argued:

> I told them [the police officers] that I would hold them responsible and they must do better work. I ordered them to cease paying any heed to political leaders. I advised them to use a nightstick on any leader, henchman, or heeler who interfered with them in the discharge of their duty, and promised that I would stand by them if any trouble came from that source.[102]

Bingham was not a solitary voice crying in the wilderness. The fairly merciless dispersal of protest marches, such as that made by socialist-backed unemployed workers in Union Square on March 28, 1908, inspired some searching questions, but the general unpopularity of the socialists plus the detonation of a bomb during the protest (intended for the police, but it killed a bystander instead)[103] quashed any serious outcry. Some individual incidents of beatings did, however, attract more backlash.

A typical story ran in the *New York Times* on May 6, 1907. It recounted how one William Casey, a restaurant broker, was awoken by the thumping sound of two men being clubbed by police officers on the street outside. Casey, moved to intervene, shouted down from his window, asking the officers to stop, and eventually went down into the street to see the condition of the men. When he stepped outside, there was one man left lying unconscious on the sidewalk. Casey attempted to get him to his feet. At that point, two officers returned and began beating Casey himself. Casey fled inside his house, but later in the evening three officers returned, literally smashed their way into his home, struck his wife on the hand with a club and ordered Casey to dress. Once fully clothed, Casey then received another substantial beating, and was dragged off to see the city magistrate. In front of the magistrates, the officers attempted to charge Casey with, in turn, felonious assault, simple assault, and disorderly conduct, but on each count the magistrate rejected the charges because of Casey's battered condition. Witnesses to the action also corroborated Casey's story.[104]

Such cases polluted relations between the public, the mayor's office, and Bingham, and led directly to Bingham's removal in 1909 (the event was more directly connected with the mistreatment of one young man, George Duffy, who was fairly systematically persecuted by the NYPD). When the mayor George Brinton McClellan was replaced by William Gaynor in November later that year, Gaynor took direct action against the widespread use of clubbing, only refraining from implementing the nightstick ban because of, ironically, an adverse reaction from the Press.[105] Gaynor implemented General Order No.7, a city ordinance designed to improve the reporting of clubbing incidents. It read as follows:

> Whenever complaint is made by a citizen for clubbing or assault against a member of the uniformed force, the Lieutenant at the desk will notify the Captain. If he is present, or in the absence of the Captain, the Lieutenant will hear the case at once and send a report of the same addressed to the Police Commissioner at headquarters before finishing his tour of duty, not regarding the hour of the day or night. Failing to comply with this order will be construed as a cause for dismissal. Captains of precincts will be held strictly accountable for the enforcement of this order.

Gaynor's ordinance was aimed at dissuasion through transparency. Surely a police officer would be reluctant to swing the club if the victim might then file a complaint guaranteed to make its way to the police commissioner. On top of this legislation, Gaynor passed a whole raft of other measures aimed at restricting police use of force. These included restrictions on the use of the club in handling street protests and similar forms of civil unrest. Such were important restrictions during a time when levels of civil and social protest were high, inspired by the familiar mix of poor working conditions for millions of workers, union agitation, and mass unemployment, plus the ingress of black workers into northern markets, prompting racial tensions. The rise of left-wing radicalism, often seen by the civic and federal authorities as the greatest of threats to the American way of life, not only brought police into conflict with protesting bodies of communists and socialists, but also put them at the frontline in the feverish hunt for socialist agitator groups.

As in the 19th century, the police handling of civil unrest could be muscular to say the least (see below), and there was adequate justification for wanting to control the excesses. Yet General Order No.7 brought about a steady public outcry in New York, especially as the order appeared to result in a significant rise in all forms of crime. One gang, the Car Barn gang of East Harlem, actively taunted the police and attacked officers under the protection of the new law, and hung up notices ordering police to stay out of their areas.[106] The backlash grew, with the city's Judge Joseph E. Corrigan the most prominent critic. Corrigan sent an open letter to the New York newspapers, explaining how the city was descending into ever greater criminality now that the police had to fight crime with one hand tied behind their backs. In his letter he listed the effects of Gaynor's legislation, and explained:

> The police force is demoralized and terrified. The men feel that they and not the criminals are the hunted, that (as many have told me) "if a man can keep out of trouble he is doing well," and that the only safe and sure way to do this is to "look the other way" when a crime is being committed.[107]

Although there was much political bitterness in the two camps – Gaynor accused Corrigan of being "vicious" and of deliberately massaging crime figures to support his arguments – there does seem to be some justification in his criticism. As we have seen, whatever the reality behind police use of force, officers were operating in a violent world. They were also on working-class wages, so the threat of losing their jobs through errant club use combined with the lack of any other non-lethal force technology put them in an unenviable state of anxiety whenever they walked the mean streets. A full-blown civic investigation into police powers and the supposed rise in crime resulted in a practical relaxation of General Order No.7, particularly in relation to policing of gangland territories, where it was accepted that the police had to be physically harder in their approach.

The clubbing debate illustrates a problem faced perennially by police departments to this day. On the one hand, the public is naturally disturbed by rising crime, and with an increased fear there follows demands for a more robust form of policing to stamp out the criminal elements. On the other hand, incidents of reported police brutality lead to calls for greater control over police use of force, and more liberal-minded policing. Yet it is one thing to call for more police restraint from a position of social safety, and quite another thing to exercise resultant policies in places where danger is real and present. This tension is reflected in the debates following General Order No.7. Steadily the power of the General Order was dissolved by subsequent mayors and police commissioners. Furthermore, improvements in police training and recruitment procedures apparently helped to reduce the number of complaints about excessive force when using clubs for a time, although concerns about the third degree tactics of the 1920s and 30s meant that public concern over police use of force never entirely dissipated.

While clubs remained a weapon of tradition, in the world of firearms there was much change. By the advent of the 20th century, bolt-action, magazine-fed rifles had become standard military issue, and in civilian markets were taking over from the lever-action rifles that dominated the second half of the 19th century. The bolt-action was reliable and relatively quick to operate, and the design could accommodate especially powerful cartridges for accurate long-range shooting. The bolt-action rifle in particular would provide the tool for the police marksmen, and the essential format of such weapons is little changed today when compared to rifles of 100 years ago.

The new kids on the block in terms of early 20th-century weaponry were semi-automatic and fully automatic firearms. While revolvers could fire a shot with every trigger pull, and the Gatling gun could spray out bullets by the hundreds, both relied upon manual power for the reloading process (in the Gatling's case, the turning of a handle). Automatic weapons used the physical forces generated on firing to perform the reloading process. Allied to magazine feed, this revolution meant that a single shooter could burn through cartridges at a dizzying rate. The first semi-automatic pistols were introduced in Germany in the late 1800s, and during the first two decades of the 20th century the design was perfected in weapons such as the M1911 Colt .45, still the bedrock design for many semi-auto handguns today.[108] The exploration of different methods of cycling the gun – gas, recoil, and blowback – led to the production of full-auto longarms: rifles, submachine guns, and machine guns.

The full-auto revolution transformed military firepower, as the opportunities to spray hundreds of bullets in a domestic law enforcement context were limited. Even in terms of handguns, the US police favored revolvers in most departments until well into the post-World War II period, with Colt automatics adopted by only a few isolated forces. Most police revolvers during the first half of the century were of .38 caliber and held six rounds, and so many police departments deemed the Colt's big, high-powered .45cal round and seven-round magazine capacity as "too dangerous for the rank and file."[109] Classic revolver types of the early decades of the century include Smith & Wesson's Model 10 and Model 1902 Military & Police Second Model, and Colt's Police Positive and Official Police. On the whole, these revolvers offered the most rudimentary personal firepower, especially as they were loaded with standard ball rounds, rather than the more effective hollow-point types used by most forces today.

Yet as our opening story in this chapter shows, there was some far more hefty firepower available to law enforcement agencies under special circumstances. Submachine guns (SMGs) emerged in the World War I period from Italy and Germany, and were quickly accepted into the military world as invaluable tools for close-range shooting. The rationale behind the submachine gun was that it fired a pistol-caliber round at full-auto speeds, the pistol round meaning that the range was short but the recoil of the rapid fire was controllable. The principle was quickly appreciated by global firearms designers, and was given life in the United States through General John T. Thompson, who designed arguably the most notorious firearm in criminal history.

The Thompson SMG first entered production in 1921, its official designation being the M1921. Alongside a later variation, the M1928, the Thompson became a notorious success, able to fire .45 slugs at rates of 700–1000rpm from either 20- or 30-round box magazines or 50- or 100-round drum magazines. Most Thompsons, including the M1 and M1A1 variants that gave sterling service in World War II, went into military hands, but the weapon was also available to both police and, initially, civilians, albeit with a hefty price tag. The crushing firepower of the Thompson soon led the US authorities to restrict civilian purchase of the weapons (by the end of the 1930s even private security agencies needed permission from the US Attorney General himself for the purchase of a Thompson). Yet it is ironic that an overwhelmingly military gun should be so remembered for its contribution, on both sides of the blue line, to the "war on crime" in the 1920s and 1930s, hence becoming a virtual icon of the Prohibition era. It acquired nicknames that resonate to this day, some with visceral reminders of what it could do to a human body: the "Tommy gun," the "Chicago piano," and "Chopper" – the last of these terms was a sensitive coining from the gangster world.

We mustn't overplay the Thompson's role – illegal Thompson use was actually extremely limited. Criminals of every age have always favored compact weapons, usually pistols that can be tucked unobtrusively into a coat or trouser pocket. The Thompson was neither compact nor discrete, so relatively small numbers were acquired by the gangsters for more extreme criminal tasks; most Thompsons in illegal circulation were obtained by raids on police station arsenals, or through deals with military personnel. Yet although the Thompson was not the chief gangster weapon by any means, its public prominence was assured by its use in some very famous hands, and in the most notorious killings of the gangland era. In 1929, henchmen of Al Capone used Thompsons to mow down seven members of the Bugs Moran gang in a Chicago garage, the bloody outpouring becoming known to history as the St Valentine's Day Massacre. Two of the SMGs used in the killings belonged to infamous hitman Fred "Killer" Burke; these were discovered by police in Burke's girlfriend's house, and ballistic tests revealed their connection to the massacre and to the killing of another gangster, Frankie Yale, in July 1928. The arms cache also contained rifles, pistols and shotguns, as well as armored vests (which were another favorite steal from police stations). Burke was eventually arrested, sentenced to life imprisonment for the murder of a police officer, and died of a heart attack in Michigan State Penitentiary on July 10, 1940.

Yet the most famous criminal exponent of the Tommy gun is arguably the legendary John Herbert Dillinger. Born on June 22, 1903, John Herbert Dillinger appears to have been born for trouble. His mother died when he was three years old, and the young John felt at odds with his stepmother when his father remarried six years later. He grew into a troubled, restless teenager, easily bored by conventional living and unable to hold down a steady job or a period in the US Navy – he deserted ship in Boston. Dillinger was headed for trouble, and he found it in the mid-1920s in Indianapolis. In partnership with another local villain, Ed Singleton, Dillinger attempted to rob a grocery store, during which he battered the shop owner with a heavy iron bolt, but was apprehended and spent the next eight and a half years banged up in Indiana State Prison. During the incarceration, an already turbulent character was warped even further, and once released he began a blistering criminal career in bank robbery – in association with a gang of criminals whom he had met in prison – that made him public enemy No.1 for the police. The media loved him. The published photographs showed a dark, menacing character who was nevertheless handsome and exciting to a depression-blanched society. His exploits gripped the nation, including several violent jail breaks and numerous stylish bank robberies. One robbery was conducted by Dillinger and his gang pretending to be film producers and actors, "rehearsing" a bank robbery in convincing fashion in front of a crowd of smiling customers. But along with Dillinger's cash acquisitions – he and his gang managed to steal over $300,000 between September 1933 and July 1934 – the death toll of officers, accomplices, and innocent bystanders was also mounting. Dillinger was a gun enthusiast, and during raids on police stations in Auburn, Indiana, and Peru, Indiana, in late 1933 he acquired significant numbers of Thompson guns, as well as rifles, revolvers, and bullet-proof vests. Ironically, it wasn't his theft of such an arsenal, nor the gang's shooting of several prison guards and law enforcement officers, that brought him to the attention of the FBI. During an escape from the county jail at Crown Point, Indiana, on March 3, 1934 (he was held in the jail charged with the murder of an East Chicago police officer), Dillinger stole the sheriff's car and drove it across the Indiana-Illinois state line, thus violating the National Motor Vehicle Theft Act. This was a federal offence, so now J. Edgar Hoover's boys were on the hunt for Dillinger.

It is interesting during this violent period to note how much the Thompson became a supporting actor in the whole drama. Dillinger was undoubtedly affectionate about the weapon, sometimes removing the shoulder stock to make it more discrete. In response, the police upgunned themselves, and the newspapers dwelt on the firepower equations developing between the police and the Dillinger gang. *The Daily Illini*, for example, carried the front page headline "Army of Officers Train Machine Guns On Roads over Midwest to Intercept Dillinger," following Dillinger's escape from Crown Point (during which, incidentally, Dillinger managed to grab two more Thompsons for his collection). Dillinger enjoyed posing with the Thompson for photographs, but he was not shy of using the weapon in earnest. On March 30, 1934, FBI agents cornered Dillinger and one of the gang, Homer van Meter, in some apartments in St Paul. Van Meter pulled a handgun while Dillinger sprayed the upper corridors with deafening full-auto fire, creating the cover to escape through a back door. Police officers later found a Thompson, two automatic rifles, one .38 Colt automatic pistol, and two bulletproof vests in the apartment. Dillinger was cornered several more times, but along with associates that now included the equally unbalanced Lester Joseph Gillis – better known as "Baby Face Nelson" – shot his way out of almost every trap.

An infamous shootout was unleashed on April 23, 1934, around the Little Bohemia Lodge holiday resort north of Rhinelander, Wisconsin. Dillinger and his gang decided to take a break at the lodge, terrorizing the lodge owners in the process. Nevertheless, the owner's wife managed to post a tip off to the authorities, and soon a heavily armed FBI task force was heading to Wisconsin. Like the Waco siege over 50 years later, the operation around Little Bohemia Lodge would stand as a black mark over FBI operational history. The lodge was surrounded under the cover of night, but events tumbled into disaster. Three innocent customers of the lodge exited and drove away in their car. The officers, thinking that the car contained gang members, opened up with everything they had, killing one of the men and seriously injuring the other two. With Dillinger now alerted by the sound of shots, the agents soon found themselves frantically curled up behind cover as Dillinger and others hammered at them with automatic fire. Two other agents and a local deputy went out to investigate a suspicious vehicle at a nearby cottage, and there found Baby Face Nelson with three hostages. Nelson fired a handgun, killing Special Agent W. Carter Baum and injuring the other agent.

They were pointless casualties – Dillinger and associates once again managed to slip through the net. The media had a field day reporting on the incident, and Hoover made changes to the leadership in the Dillinger hunt, appointing the rising star Special Agent Samuel A. Crowley to head the investigation. Finally, the law caught up with Dillinger, even as the rest of his gang started to fall. Following a tip-off from Anna Cumpanas (aka Anna Sage), a brothel madam in Gary, Indiana, on July 22, 1934, agents surrounded the Biograph Theater in Chicago, where Dillinger was watching the Clark Gable film *Manhattan Melodrama* with Sage and her girlfriend, Polly Hamilton. Crowley, in charge of the action, decided against entering the theater, naturally sensitive to the possibility of any civilian casualties following the Little Bohemia shootout. Instead he waited outside with his heavily armed officers.

At 10.30pm, Dillinger emerged, buoyant with the after-effects of the film and the promise of his female company. The FBI official report fills in what happened next:

> Upon identifying Dillinger, affiant Purvis gave the prearranged signal for the men to close in. Special Agents H. E. Hollis, Charles Winstead, Clarence Hurt, R. D. Brown and affiant Purvis immediately surrounded John Dillinger, all being stationed on the southeast side of the Biograph Theater. Officers Sopsic and Stretch of the East Chicago, Indiana Police Department had assumed a position at a point in a northwesterly direction from the theater, and at the time the signal was given Sergeant Zarkovich, who had been stationed at a point diagonally across the street from the Biograph Theater, ran across the street and notified officers Sopsic and Stretch, who had not seen the signal. Captain O'Neill and Officer Conroy of Captain O'Neill's squad had assumed roving positions during the entire covering of this matter. John Dillinger was seen to draw his gun, which was later found to be a .380 automatic pistol, from his right trousers pocket. He assumed a dodging, semi-crouching position and drew his gun from his pocket. At that time he was shot by Special Agents H. E. Hollis, C. O. Hurt and C. B. Winstead, who fired one shot each, except the last named, who fired three shots. Immediately after the shooting the above mentioned automatic pistol was taken from his hand and an ambulance called, inasmuch as it appeared he was not dead.[110]

But it was the end of Dillinger. He was pronounced dead at 10.50pm. Others would follow his path. Baby Face Nelson stayed on the run for several months, claiming the lives of more federal and local law enforcement officers. Like Dillinger, he was notorious for his use of automatic weapons, as one article from *The Daily Illini* reported on November 28, 1934:

> CHICAGO, Nov. 27. —The death-rattling machine gun of George (Baby Face) Nelson, Dillinger desperado and public enemy No. 1, late today took the life of another federal agent. A squad of agents from the command of Melvin H. Purvis, head of the Chicago division of the bureau of investigation, sought to trap Nelson, another man, and their woman companion, near suburban Barrington. Gangster guns blazed a tattoo of death and agent Herman K. Hollis, 26, fell mortally wounded. Samuel P. Cowley, chief assistant to Purvis, dropped critically hurt with bullets in his abdomen. Cowley and Hollis, long on the trail of Dillinger mobsmen, had been with their chief when John Dillinger and his elusive killers battered their bullet-slugged way through a troop of federal agents at the Little Bohemia resort in northern Wisconsin last April 22.

The deaths of Hollis and Cowley, two high-profile officers, were at least not in vain. On November 29, a tip-off led agents to Nelson's corpse lying in a ditch, punctured through with 17 gunshot wounds – he had been fatally wounded in the shootout with the agents the previous day.

Hollis and Cowley were not the only FBI officers to fall to heavy firepower in the early 1930s. The previous year had seen one of the most violent incidents in the Bureau's history – known bluntly as the Kansas City Massacre. On June 17, 1933, a unit of FBI agents and police officers were transporting criminal Frank "Jelly" Nash from Hot Springs, Arkansas, to the Leavenworth Federal Prison in Kansas. Nash was a good catch for the G-men.[111] Nash was a safe-blowing expert for the criminal underworld – the "Jelly" nickname was shorthand for nitroglycerine explosive – and his arrest in Hot Springs was a coup for the Department of Justice and a natural threat to the gangs with whom Nash had worked.

It was going be a tense trip for all concerned. Nash was first taken by train to Kansas City's Union Station, where he was transferred to waiting cars for a 30-mile drive to his destination. Along the route, everyone was vigilant, but the heavy presence of officers and agents was reassuring.

No-one, probably not even Nash, knew that there was an ambush waiting for them at the Kansas City railroad depot. Accounts of what happened became hopelessly confused, and the subsequent investigation into the massacre became a particularly troubled time in the Bureau's history. What is certain is that a number of gunmen, some armed with Thompson SMGs, opened fire on the officers and Nash as they were about to pull off in their cars. In a blistering hail of gunfire, three police officers, one Bureau agent, and Nash were killed, and two other agents were wounded.

Subsequent and historical investigation into the Kansas City Massacre revealed some question marks about FBI competency with firearms at this time. There is evidence to suggest that Nash, Agent Caffrey, and Officer Frank Hermanson were actually killed by inaccurate and panicked shooting from Agent Francis Lackey – these fatalities were the result of shotgun balls, whereas the attackers fired only .45 and .38 bullets.[112] Furthermore, many people have raised questions over the propriety of the investigation, and the subsequent conviction of gang member Adam Richetti, who took a trip to Missouri's brand new gas chamber on October 17, 1938. (One of the other men supposed to be involved in the massacre, Charles Floyd, was shot dead by Department of Justice men after being cornered on a farm.) Much of the evidence remains confused and controversial, but the incident did appear to galvanize the Department of Justice into formalizing its relationship to firearms. The following year the Department of

Justice gave its agents official sanction to carry firearms – before this point there was no firearms policy as such, only the improvisation of the officers – and to make arrests. The firearms bill was a critical step, for once an organization has authority to carry firearms, then it can begin the process of standardizing and implementing training regimes (see below).

Returning to the world of automatic weapons, however, note how in the newspaper cutting above the Thompson is labeled the "gangster gun." The Thompson was popularly perceived as an underworld weapon, and so the status of the gun, indeed any full-auto firearm, in law enforcement hands must have sent out some ambiguous messages. There was certainly an awareness of the power of automatic weapons to control public opinion and persuade good behavior. Numerous newspaper accounts from the 1920s–40s note instances where potentially riotous mobs were restrained by the menace of a machine gun mounted in an open upstairs window overlooking a street. In May 1922 Prohibition agents raided a cafe in New Jersey, looking for, and finding, a small quantity of illegal liquor. Just a few weeks earlier there had been a similar raid in the area, after which a certain Chief Enforcement Agent Con'e had stated that he would "clean up New Jersey City if I have to use machine guns." This statement took on new life with the cafe raid, as it just so happened that local residents spotted a US Army truck pass nearby, on which was mounted a machine gun. A *New York Times* article of the incident recounted how hundreds of now jittery residents believed that Con'e was good to his word, and had brought in some heavy firepower to sweep out the undesirables.[113] The truck was actually on its way to a nearby military barracks, but the power of the machine gun can lie not just in its firepower, but also in its presence. Thompson himself, following a demonstration of his SMG to officers in 1922, argued that the intense firepower offered by the gun had changed the equation of force on the streets:

> This weapon changes the odds which are now against the officers of the law, and gives them instead a decided advantage over the bandits. I think you will agree, after seeing this gun in action this afternoon, that any man will think twice before going up against one.[114]

Nevertheless, there are occasions when it seemed that the newly acquired heavy firepower was embraced with excessive enthusiasm. One lively article, again from the *New York Times*, recounts how an "airplane reserve" of the NYPD, kitted out with over a dozen aircraft, was specially tasked with apprehending private aviators who flew too low over the city, or who entertained its citizens with stunt flying. A report issued from the office of the Special Deputy Police Commissioner Rodman Wanamaker noted at the end:

> When our scout planes give chase to any lawless aviator, they will be speedy enough to keep up with him until he is forced to land, when the police plane also will land and put him under arrest. Police planes are equipped with machine guns, and all flying police officers are armed, but only in cases of extreme necessity will such force be used.[115]

The thought of what were effectively machine-gun armed fighter aircraft patrolling permanently over the city of New York would fill most New Yorkers with justifiable alarm, especially as the standards of training could be questionable. The passage begs the question as to the circumstances in which an officer might open up with a machine gun over a densely populated city at a lawless aviator, bearing in mind that even if the machine gun were not pointing directly downwards, the shower of bullets that missed the target would still retain lethality when they dropped to the ground.

Compared with today, when almost every shot fired by an officer has to be judged and accounted for, the law enforcement community of yesterday could be quite free with their automatic weapons at times. A classic example was the gunfight involved in the killing of Kate "Ma" Barker and her son, Fred Barker on January 16, 1935. Ma Barker gained a reputation as the matriarchal ruler of her four criminal sons, although her actual involvement in her sons' criminal enterprises – beyond simply giving support to children she loved – is questionable. On the date mentioned, 15 Department of Justice agents surrounded Ma and Fred in a cottage in Lake Weir, Florida. Shouted demands for the occupants' surrender were met with a blast of SMG fire, which in turn prompted the agents to open up with their own automatic weapons. Four hours later, the agents had poured some 1,500 rounds of ammunition into the house. Fred Barker was riddled with 14 bullets, and Ma Barker was dead from 1–3 rounds (accounts vary).

A clear impulse behind the purchase of SMGs for police departments was to achieve parity with criminal firepower, and this motivation emerges on several occasions to this day. Nor should we think that it was only the big city police departments or federal agencies who were investing in automatic firepower. The following excerpts are from the *Winona Republican-Herald* from 1934, the paper serving the town of Winona, Missouri, which during the 1930s had a population that scarcely cleared 20,000:

> Two bullet-proof vests and a Thompson sub-machine gun were purchased for the police department by the board of fire and police commissioners Wednesday night, and it was decided to get the department a new automobile. George W. Hoffman, secretary of the board, was instructed to advertise for bids on a car which will replace the light closed vehicle which has been used for traffic work for two years.

> The new police armament will arrive in 10 to 30 days, and will put Winona police on a par with criminals in equipment, said Chief of Police H. C. Riebau today. A faster car than any of the three now owned by the department is needed, he said... In addition to the new gun, Chief Riebau's men have an older model sub-machine gun, three shotguns and two automatic rifles...
>
> The sales must be approved by the department of justice, Bergland [the firearm's salesman] told the board, because of federal regulations designed to keep machine guns and bullet proof vests out of the hands of gangsters.
>
> The gun and vests are of the type sold by Bergland two weeks ago to the St. Paul police department, which bought four guns and eight vests with money raised by public subscription. The vests protect all vital spots except the head of the wearer.[116]

There are several elements to this quotation that have broader implications for our analysis here, as they are seen in numerous other police departments across the United States during this period. First, note how the purchase of the Thompson is allied to the purchase of bulletproof vests, there being the recognition that situations requiring heavy firepower are likely involve a higher risk of being shot oneself. Body armor was certainly crude at this stage, often consisting of little more than metal plates wrapped in leather or similar padding. A photograph from September 13, 1923, depicts a man firing a handgun bullet straight into the protected chest of an associate from a range of around 3 yards, while police officers stand on the sideline and watch (one a little nervously, given the possibility for ricochets).[117] By the 1930s, many police departments had stores of armor for major shootings or riots. Note also how body armor is included in the items that federal regulations were attempting to restrict. Gangsters were indeed utilizing body armor stolen in police raids, but they also manufactured their own out of bulky layers of cloth padding sufficient to arrest small-caliber handgun bullets. It was for this reason that the FBI later adopted the .357 Magnum handgun cartridge, which would easily cut through such protection.

The second point is that the automobile upgrade is actually integral to the expansion of force options, used to deliver armed officers quickly to wherever they are needed. Automobiles are, as we will explore later, part and parcel of the police continuum of force, and police vehicle pursuits are a leading cause of fatalities amongst both officers and suspects/bystanders. Yet automobiles were a necessity. The United States was becoming a massively motorized society, with 8,000 car registrations in 1900 compared to an astonishing 27 million by 1930 (bolstered by the 15 million Ford Model Ts produced between 1908 and 1927). With car ownership came car crime and misuse, and the police needed serviceable, powerful vehicles for policing the roads.

In the case of the NYPD, the number of officer deaths during vehicular pursuits rose by over 400 percent in 1920–29 when compared to 1910–19, and the death toll from vehicular assault, general motor accidents, and being struck by cars also leapt dramatically. The causes of death behind the NYPD figures, and those of the broader US law enforcement community, reveal police officers steadily adjusting to the dos and don'ts of vehicular policing. For example, on April 15, 1935, Patrolmen Burtiss Birkhoff of the Passaic PD, New Jersey, was chasing a young suspect on foot when he decided to commandeer a passing car. He ordered the driver to follow the youth, while Birkhoff rode externally on the running board. The driver, however, had to stop suddenly to avoid hitting the subject, catapulting Birkhoff from the vehicle, where he sustained fatal injuries. Doubtless riding on running boards quickly became a prohibited practice in that police department.

Yet despite these negatives, automobiles also provided faster response times to crimes and accidents. Once allied with two-way radio communications, which were more commonly adopted by police forces during the 1930s, there opened up the potential for truly coordinated, fast delivery of officers to trouble spots. Here is where the alliance with firearms came in. Although the idea of the Special Weapons and Tactics (SWAT) team was decades away, automobiles provided the means for what we would call "rapid armed response," especially when allied to souped-up firepower. During a police parade in Boston on October 12, 1920, the police department displayed its new "riot squad," which included a machine-gun squad with its automatic weapons actually mounted onto the vehicles, mimicking military armored cars. The previous January, New York's police under Police Commissioner Enright received approval to form a "police regiment of sharpshooters and four machine gun squads, to be equipped and prepared at all times for any form of riot duty and to combat revolutionary agitators or to meet with any similar emergency."[118] Police officers referred to the new units as the "Flying Artillery" on account of the use of powerful automobiles to transport the firepower around the city. The plan was for a "regiment" of 1,000 men – 600 men to be on normal patrol work at any one time, while the remaining 400 were kept on a reserve and ready status at various points throughout the city.

In this context, we now see how the police use of automatic weapons would be practically and socially distinguished from the applications of such guns in criminal hands. The "militarization" of deadly force, a term that has come to acquire a distinctly pejorative sense when used by many modern critics of the police, will be an important theme for the remainder of this book. In the context of the 1920s, military-style policing actually evoked a sense of discipline and regularity – controlled as opposed to sporadic, controversial force. The military connections in Enright's plan were extremely visible. The *New York Times* article quoted notes that 75 percent of the members of the new "regiment" (the word is a transparent militarization by itself) would have had training or combat experience in the US armed forces, particularly in the American Expeditionary Force (AEF) in France in World War I. (It is noted that there were at the time 1,500 ex-soldiers within the NYPD, and in many police forces today there is a high percentage of recruitment from ex-military personnel.)

Yet although automatic weapons were not uncommon in police use during the first half of the 20th century, if any money and time were going to be plowed into firearms training it had to be directed at the standard issue revolver, the weapon every officer carried and the one on which he, and also later she, would draw on as a first line of armed response. In short, all police needed firearms training.

PROFESSIONAL GUNHANDLING

In the history of US law enforcement, few individuals can have shown less professionalism, judgment, and responsibility with firearms than Deputy United States Marshal Richard J. Murphy. His story was told by a reporter of the *Winona Republican-Herald* in 1928, the tale delivered in a dead-pan style perfectly matched to the absurdity of the case. It is worth recounting in full:

> "You can't put me in jail," said Deputy United States Marshal Richard J. Murphy at the Warren Avenue police station last night. "I'm a government agent."
>
> But they put him in jail anyway, while the desk sergeant wrote the following items opposite Murphy's name: (1) creating a riot; (2) slugging a woman and a man; (3) shooting two bystanders; (4) biting a policeman.
>
> Murphy, in his automobile, was on his way to serve two warrants involving dry law violations. His car was held up by a stalled machine driven by Miss Marjorie Meeks, 17. Indignant at the delay, the marshal, according to Miss Meeks and others in her car, got out of his machine and struck her with a blackjack.
>
> A crowd that had gathered began muttering protests and Charles Herbert, a spectacled youth, was punched in the face by the marshal. This incensed the crowd and they began pressing in on Murphy who, witnesses said, drew a revolver and opened fire. Arthur Bandi was shot in the hip and Edward Tracy (who had just driven up and didn't know what the shooting was about) stopped a bullet with his left leg.
>
> Murphy arrested Bandi and started up with him to the Warren Avenue police station. Miss Meeks and the others followed to place complaints against the marshal.
>
> At the station Murphy was told he would have to remain while the affair was investigated. He thereupon drew his revolver again, informing the bluecoats they couldn't

> arrest him. It was during this imbroglio that one of Policeman Klick's fingers got caught between a pair of teeth, allegedly Murphy's.
>
> They locked him up.[119]

It is likely that Deputy Murphy would come out with a less than sparkling annual performance review, but his rather free and easy attitude to gunplay does raise a serious issue. As the century progressed, and a new desire for professionalism began to creep into the US police forces, it was increasingly recognized that an officer should not go out onto the street without adequate training in handgun technique. Roosevelt had introduced some short-lived elementary pistol training in New York way back in 1895. The content of the training, however, was extremely limited, consisting of little more than occasional trips to a pistol range where around ten cartridges were fired at a static target. By 1897, even such elementary training was often disregarded, and for the next 20 years most officers went onto the streets with little or no formal skill in their sidearm. Indeed, a survey in 1919 by the National Rifle Association (NRA) found that of all the police departments in the United States that policed towns with more than 25,000 people, no more than 12 (and probably much lower than that) had received any systematic firearms training.[120]

The deficiencies in the quality of handgun training were noted by many observant members of the public. Arthur Woods, a former police commissioner for New York City (1914–18), argued in his 1919 publication *Policeman and the Public* that "it will be found in some places that officers are taken on the force and turned out on the street to go about their duty armed with loaded revolvers, and yet with no training in the care or use of the weapon."[121] Woods expounded that in his opinion all officers should go through a systematic program of firearms training, beginning with basic sighting and squeeze trigger techniques and "not ending until he is proficient at snap-shooting without sighting."[122] To neglect such training, Woods argued, was a dereliction of duty on many levels:

> It is a really grave question whether policemen should be allowed to carry revolvers at all unless they qualify periodically, showing that they still know how to handle the weapon and can shoot straight enough not to be a menace in the street… It is a question further as to whether a police administration is not responsible, at least morally, for any harm that may be done with a revolver by an officer who has not been properly trained to handle and fire it. Unless he is trained and has passed satisfactory tests the administration knows, and should probably be held responsible for acting on the knowledge, that he is an unsafe man to be allowed to use a revolver.[123]

Woods expands the argument for pistol training from one of personal responsibility (in terms of the officer) to the corporate responsibility of the police department. Such may have fallen on many deaf ears during the 1920s and early 1930s, but an increasing number of departments were listening. An article in *The American Rifleman* in September 1923 noted that "A distinct trend has finally set toward the proper training of officers of the law in the one arm on which they can in final emergency depend for enforcement of the law. The surface has, as yet, been barely scratched, but the results beginning to show are most encouraging."[124] The article went on to note that several police departments around the country had begun to develop some level of pistol proficiency amongst their officers, whether through formal training at a pistol range, through officer affiliation with local shooting clubs, or through the establishment of their own shooting facilities for use by both officers and civilians. Police departments at Toledo, Philadelphia, and Detroit are highlighted for mention as "prominent figures on the Pistol Range at Perry" (Camp Perry, Ohio, a military base and firearms training center) and that "Last year a police high power rifle club was organized in New Orleans with a membership of over two hundred of the cities [sic] blue-coats." Other departments singled out include New Jersey, Hartford, and Boston.

An interesting spur to training was the development of national police shooting competitions, bolstered through the affiliation of many police departments with the NRA. These competitions spurred general officer competence in firearms; even if many officers didn't directly compete, there was doubtless some related benefit in belonging to a department that was renowned for its skill with firearms. A *Time* article of August 15, 1938, for example, looks back at how the marksmanship skill of Treasury officers was improved when Henry Morgenthau became Secretary. Noting that most of the 3,000 armed officers he commanded "were sorry pistol shots," Morgenthau implemented rolling pistol practice for the Customs Bureau, Alcohol Tax Unit, Bureau of Narcotics, White House Police, Bureau of the Mint, Secret Service, Bureau of Internal Revenue, Uniformed Force of the Secret Service, and even the Public Health Service.[125] The training was conducted by ex-military and US Coast Guard personnel, and the article noted that out of ten Treasury officers observed firing on the pistol range, nine of them drilled the bulls-eye. The Morgenthau Trophy for the best individual shot was implemented to inspire the officers, and competition does appear to have been fierce. The competition tests reflected the type of training – slow, aimed fire and rapid fire at distances of 15 and 25 yards, mostly with .38 revolvers using short 4in. barrels, but with an additional round utilizing .45 handguns with up to 10in. barrels.

The use of military personnel in the training of officers was often central to early police firearms instruction, but the policy was questionable. Although law enforcement units seem to mirror the military in the sense that they are uniformed, regimented bodies of officers authorized to carry firepower, military training carries entirely different standards of fire-control than those required by a more legally vulnerable police force. Doubtless, however, some elements of military training were useful, such as teaching officers the tactics of snap shooting – a skill of far greater practical use to an officer than the ability to plug a target accurately under controlled conditions.

Above all it was the civilian NRA that acted as a spur to the professionalization of pistol skills throughout the US law enforcement community. As early as 1925, the NRA opened a Police School that not only taught handgun, rifle, and shotgun shooting, but also trained officers as firearms instructors and provided some training in specialist policing such as riot control.[126] The NRA school, which also helped to promote the national competitions, was an important resource for officers looking to create some solid foundations for their shooting skills. Thousands of officers went through its doors between 1925 and 1941, at which point the retraction of federal funding at the outbreak of World War II ended its police-only courses until 1960.[127] The NRA course was undeniably useful, but its emphasis was squarely on controlled targetshooting, rather than the combat-realistic shooting we see attempted today. For example, NRA training generally taught officers to thumb-cock the hammer of the revolver before firing. This technique was appreciable in the context of slow, accurate shooting, but with the use of double-action revolvers it was largely irrelevant in training for engagements that could play out in the speed it took to snatch a breath and pull the trigger.

The theme of making training relevant will appear more extensively in later chapters, but some brief notes of context are important. While static targetshooting has its use, principally in teaching the student the fundamentals of firearms operation and trigger control, it has little correspondence with the way shots are actually taken in real-life encounters. On the streets, most shootings take place in a mental blur of a few seconds, or parts of a second, with the officer typically snap shooting his weapon without using the sights or adopting a formal shooting stance. Adrenaline levels are high, and the pressure to hit the target is extreme if the suspect is himself deploying a weapon. Effective training needs in some way to accommodate these realities, replicating as far as possible the actual dynamics of a lethal engagement so that the officer responds appropriately and instinctively when applying deadly force.

During the 1930s, the FBI made the first steps towards something approaching realism-based training, evolving into what became known as the Practical Pistol Course (PPC). The PPC was established by 1940 and was accessible to other law enforcement agencies through the FBI, not just the G-men. It did incorporate some of the more familiar, methodical shooting practices, such as firing aimed shots using thumb-cocking (although principally at longer range requiring a steadier shot), but there were more groundbreaking introductions, including:

- Much greater variety in shooting range, with targets engaged at ranges from 60 yards right down to 7 yards. The latter range, which tested ten shots in 25 seconds, was particularly useful, as most engagements occur within that distance.
- Reloading skills were honed, speeding up the time taken to refill a revolver's cylinders and therefore reducing the vulnerable interval in which an officer was effectively unarmed.
- Variety in postures. As well as testing the officers in a regular standing position, training was also given in prone, sitting, and kneeling firing positions, and in firing using the weak hand (important if the officer's main firing hand was injured, or if he had to shoot around cover on the non-firing hand side).
- Some training was given in shooting under low-light conditions, the conditions under which the bulk of deadly force engagements took place. Also, the officers were trained in snap-shooting without reference to the gun's sights.

The PPC was not the last word in realism-based training, but it was a major step in the right direction, and one that benefited the US law enforcement community at large. The FBI also developed a machine-gun course along similar lines. The following is the text from a poster describing the "FBI Machine Gun Course," dated to the 1940s:

> The Machine Gun Course is fired with the Thompson sub-machine gun on two bobber (Army E) targets placed two feet apart, alternating targets after each two shots or after each burst.
>
> 15 yard phase
> 1 clip of 10 rounds single fire from the hip level position in 8 seconds.
>
> 25 yard phase
> 1. 1 clip of 10 rounds single fire from the weak shoulder in 10 seconds. Load the weapon on the strong side; come to the ready position on the weak side. On the whistle, move weapon to the shoulder and commence firing.
> 2. 2 clips of 10 rounds each for 20 rounds in 25 seconds from strong shoulder. First clip in single fire and second clip in bursts from full automatic.
>
> 50 yard phase
> 1 clip of 10 rounds single fire from kneeling position in 15 seconds.

The machine-gun course here, like that of the PPC, seeks to replicate the full range of body dynamics that might be experienced in a real gunfight. Its aim was to impart complete physical unity between gun and shooter, thereby speeding up life-saving reaction times. Once police departments bought into the idea of systematically developing shooting skills, many invested heavily in constructing their own ranges – some expenditure figures range from $900 to around $18,000.[128] Most of the ranges were structured in a thoroughly conventional layout, consisting of human-shaped targets that could be adjusted for range, each target sitting at the end of a specific alley. It would take many more years and a lot more hard-won experience before training ranges adopted more urban authenticity and the modern "killing house" setup.

Although we might like to assume that the relationship between improved firearms training, accurate combat-shooting, and survivability would be obvious, the link is actually a little more tenuous than one might think. Research by Gregory Morrison and Bryan Vila has argued that there is actually little difference in hit statistics for armed engagements when comparing available data for 19th-century police officers and those of the late 1990s. We shall unpack this contention more in Chapter 5, but we have to acknowledge that even the improved firearms training of the 1930s and 1940s had its limitations. Nevertheless, one of the benefits of police training was that the public at least began to have a clear sense of the police as trained shooters, whether it be with a rifle or with a pistol. A *Daily Illini* article entitled "Bandits are Shot by Crack Gunmen" (February 1, 1936), for example, picks up on an Associated Press news story concerning a shootout between police and bank robbers in Los Angeles, in which the two criminals were shot dead. The article refers to the fact that the robbery takes place within a short distance of the local shooting range, then labels the police shooters as "crack gunmen" and "expert marksmen," clearly equating the range with the professionalism of the police, and the inadvisable choice of location for a bank robbery. Of course, the converse could be true, as the media would quickly jump on any instance of firearms incompetence with some glee. A *New York Times* article from August 1937, for example, recounts the tale of Patrolman Artollo Maskavich, seriously wounded by a gunshot to the stomach on the Elizabeth Police Department rifle range. Apparently Maskavich had thrown a helmet up into the air for a fellow officer, Patrolman Arthur Roggers, to shoot through with a rifle. Matters hadn't gone as planned, however, and Roggers ended up shooting Maskavich instead, in what was probably a clear violation of shooting range protocols.

The fact is that in the absence of firm data it is hard to assess the practical value of the new shooting regimes in street engagements. Nonetheless, the provision of genuine skill in handling a firearm would be hard to argue against, as would the confidence that such training might breed amongst both the police and public. In an age of expanding accountability, the law enforcement community had to be seen to control its tools of violence, both ethically and practically.

Such improvements took their place amongst a whole range of professionalizing measures that took place between 1930 and the end of World War II in 1945. Recruitment procedures were tightened, emphasizing the quality of the candidate's character and the capability of his intelligence for police service. Inter-agency cooperation and administrative centralization began to flourish, particularly in the implementation of the Uniform Crime Reports (UCRs), a system by which annual police department crime reports were submitted centrally to the FBI. The FBI's National Police Academy also supported the networking of information across state lines by drawing together officers from all over the country for training. Vila and Morris state that "To this day, the informal network of National Academy graduates, as they are known, is one of the most useful cross-jurisdictional law enforcement tools in the United States."[129]) At the same, the Supreme Court tightened its enforcement of constitutional rights. In three landmark cases, Brown et al. v. Mississippi (1936), Chambers et al. v. Florida (1940), and Ashcraft et al. v. Tennessee (1944), the Supreme Court ruled not only that physical and psychological violence was unacceptable in police interrogation techniques, but also that any confessions extracted by such means were inadmissible in court. To aid the police in their investigations, however, forensic techniques were increasingly coming into their own.

US law enforcement, therefore, was by the 1940s firmly on the road of professionalization, including its handling of deadly force. A prescient voice in this regard was NYPD's Police Commissioner Grover A. Whalen, who in 1930 issued a massive report on the crime situation in New York, which included a 33-page covering letter to the mayor noting how the trade of policing was to change:

> The complexities of the new social, scientific and mechanical age in which we live have sounded the death knell for the old-fashioned policeman. Special training is needed for the police officer to successfully cope with new police problems arising from the ever-increasing intricacies of traffic problems, social changes and new scientific and mechanical inventions.
>
> The higher education for the policeman is only in its infancy, but it is rapidly being developed ... in a few years police work will be placed on a par with the legal, medical and other higher professions. [130]

High hopes indeed for the time, but Whalen was largely correct in perceiving the professional shift in future policing, based on an expansion in education.

Yet we must not give the impression that law enforcement in the 1930s and 1940s stepped from darkness to light in one smooth movement. Many challenges faced the police, and none more so than the problem of how to deal with civil unrest.

STRONG ARM OF THE LAW

In an age that was frequently short on force training regarding individual assailants, the training provided for riot-control could be even worse. Questions over riot-handling also hung heavy over the military – the Regular Army and the National Guard – as it was both a federal and a state recourse should a civil disturbance stretch beyond the powers of local law enforcement. The reputation of the military in riot-handling was, to put it mildly, extremely poor at the beginning of the 20th century, mainly on account of its combative breaking of labor disputes in the late 19th century. The military's strike-breaking tactics produced the public perception that it was largely in the service of big business and anti-union government, and that its martial outlook expressed itself in unnecessary brutality in action.

To be fair, once military forces were called in to handle disputes, their position was awkward. A riot was neither outright war, for which the soldiers were purposely trained, nor simple unrest, as there was the potential for large numbers of casualties. It is not surprising, therefore, that military thinking on riot-control was muddled and had to evolve.

The roots of the problem stretch back to the Pullman Strike of 1894, a wildcat strike of 4,000 railroad workers of the Pullman Palace Car Company, who were naturally aggrieved at a 28 percent pay cut. Some 12,000 US troops were deployed to break the strike, principally of the Illinois National Guard, and in subsequent clashes 13 strikers were killed and 57 wounded. During the action, the US Army issued its General Order No. 23 on 9 July, which codified how it should handle "mob" situations tactically. From today's perspective, elements of the General Order make robust reading:

> A mob, forcibly resisting or obstructing the laws of the United States ... is a public enemy. It is purely a tactical question in what manner they [US soldiers] shall use the weapons with which they are armed – whether by the fire of musketry and artillery or by the use of the bayonet and saber, or by both, and at what stage of the operations each or either mode of attack shall be employed... They are not called upon to consider how great may be the losses inflicted upon the public enemy, except to make their blows so effective as to promptly suppress all resistance to lawful authority.[131]

Although other parts of the General Order did emphasize a mild quality of restraint, particularly in the early stages of a mob situation when the crowd was likely to contain a high percentage of innocent bystanders and observers, the graduated response to the unrest was one of escalating heavy force, including the use of snipers to pick off key troublemakers, in the same way as they would be employed in a combat zone to kill enemy officers.[132]

With the change of century, and the emergence of the Progressive era, the Army's position on riot-handling began to soften a little in theory, eliminating some of the harsher phrases from General Order No. 23, but there was actually little central guidance on how soldiers should handle civil unrest.[133] In lieu of central doctrine, several military officers produced their own manuals on riot control, some of the most influential being Henry A. Bellows' (Minnesota Home Guard) *A Manual for Local Defense* (1919) and *A Treatise on Riot Duty for the National Guard* (1920), and also *Troops on Riot Duty: A Manual for the Use of the Armed Forces of the United States* by Captain Richard Stockton (US Army) and Captain Saskett Dickson (New Jersey National Guard). These authors focused much of their attention on how to disperse gatherings without force, before they could degenerate into full-on riots, but acknowledged that military-level violence might be the ultimate recourse. Something of the confusing position of the soldiery comes through in Stockton and Dickson's book, which notes that:

> Troops on riot duty should keep in mind the fact that they are called upon to put down disorder, absolutely and promptly, *with as little force as possible*, but it should be remembered, also, that in the majority of cases the way to accomplish these ends is to use at once every particle of force necessary to stop all disorder.[134]

Striking the balance between minimal force and persuasive authority was not an easy task for either police or military. Eventually the government felt moved to step in with its own guidelines for the military with the catchily titled 1919 publication *Military Protection, United States Guards: The Use of Organized Bodies in the Defense of Property During Riots, Strikes, and Civil Disturbances*. The book had originally been intended specifically for the US Guards, a short-lived law enforcement body created in 1918 with a view to protecting against civil disorder, but its principles were applicable elsewhere. Borrowing heavily from existing manuals, *Military Protection* outlined the military's powers in a riot, emphasizing that troops had a de facto law enforcement role in any civil disturbance, but that when push came to shove, they could deal with a crowd using the military tactics and technology to hand. Laurie and Cole, quoting extensively from the guide, explain how this perspective related to the police use of firepower:

> Provisions for the use of lethal force were given as usual: troops should never be ordered on riot duty without an adequate supply of ball ammunition, for live ammunition was expected by rioters and "from the first, moral effect is obtained; it will not have to be used more than once, if not at all." Troops were ordered "never [to] fire over the heads of rioters. The aim should be low," to prevent casualties to innocent bystanders who are not involved in the disorder. "If anyone is hurt it should be the rioters." Soldiers were not to fear prosecution if rioters were killed, for "Most States provide that if it is not proven that the killing was through mere malice, wantonness, or cruelty, a soldier is not punishable for such an act."[135]

Laurie and Cole observe that the military on riot duty is fully readied for lethal violence, although with some consideration in weapons-handling to attempt to protect innocent bystanders. They also later note how the manual acknowledged that the military could use the full range of tools at its disposal for breaking up a riot, including bayonets, machine guns, nightsticks, and shotguns, in the case of the latter "preferably sawed off and loaded with No. 1 shot or buckshot."[136] This choice of ammunition is in itself interesting. The no. 1 shot or buckshot would consist of several balls, each roughly equivalent in diameter to a decent-sized pistol bullet. Fired at short-range from a sawn-off shotgun, the effect would be devastating, and would almost guarantee lethal results if directed into the rioter's torso. By contrast, a gun firing very small bird-shot pellets would have a limited lethality if fired from any sort of distance, although it would cause nasty localized injuries over a wide area (compared to large shot, small shot spreads into wider patterns when fired). The use of the shotgun in itself represents a miniature CoF, its effects ranging from minor injury through to almost certain death depending on the choice of ammunition according to the seriousness of the situation. And if matters became really critical, *Military Protection* also acknowledged that the military could roll out the artillery pieces if necessary.

Subsequent manuals did not deviate from this course: Major Cassius M. Dowell's 1925 manual *Military Aid to a Civil Power* noted that the military could employ tanks, combat aircraft, mortars, machine guns, and field artillery in suppressing riot situations, although in balance Dowell recognized that such tools lay at the extreme of riot policing, and that during more minor disturbances his troops might find mere civility an effective tool for preventing crowds getting out of control. By the 1920s, tear gas was another weapon in the US inventory, providing a non-lethal option for crowd dispersal.

As so often in this book, past policies look terrifyingly harsh to modern sensibilities. Note, however, that the thinking behind this lethal force policies was partly informed by expectations of massive, revolutionary disorders, such as had happened in Russia in 1917. The US military was preparing for complete social collapse, not just a nasty scuffle between the authorities and limited numbers of protesters. This did not stop the general public, however, being somewhat alarmed at some of the recommendations in official riot-control documents. The civil disturbance section of the US Army's *Basic Field Manual*, FM 27-15, not only gave extensive instruction on the applications of gas, but also reiterated the point that any available military weaponry and tactical thinking could be applied to civil unrest. Because this manual, unlike the previous publications, became available to the general public, it raised denunciations that the government was wielding the army in a tyrannical, undemocratic way, using a big stick to crush what might be legitimate labor dissent. The uproar led to the US Army withdrawing the field manual from public availability in 1936, and the following year it issued new regulations that reduced the role played by major weapons systems and combat tactics in civil unrest, putting more focus on the use of non-lethal technologies to disperse crowds. Such thinking would form the groundwork for the riot-control tactics of post-war law enforcement, which we will study in the next chapter.

The fact remains, also, that the military's apocalyptic force scenarios were mainly an exercise in worst-case scenario thinking, and crushing military firepower was never unleashed onto the American public during the first half of the century. Nevertheless, the tendency to project protesters into the role of "enemy" did result in serious bloodshed during this period.

There are so many bloody riots and civil disturbances in the United States during the first half of the 20th century that it is difficult to know where to start for judicious examples. A chilling place might be the Ludlow Massacre of 1914. The events began with a strike by Colorado mine workers affiliated to the United Mine Workers of America (UMWA). The conditions that the mine workers had endured for the last few decades were nothing short of criminal, with hideously poor standards of both pay and safety pushing relations between management and miners to absolute rock bottom. (Some 1,700 miners had died in Colorado mines in less than 20 years.) The Colorado Fuel & Iron Company (CF&I) had done its level best to suppress unionization, even deliberately employing a huge variety of ethnicities in its mines to prevent cross communication, but eventually the dam burst. The UMWA presented the company with a list of demands in 1913, demands rejected out of hand. Many hundreds of miners came out on strike, but were promptly evicted from their company-owned homes. Digging in, the striking miners erected a tent village, from which they harassed strike breakers and management in an attempt to force compliance.

Compliance was the last thing of the minds of CF&I executives. Instead they hired the Baldwin-Felts Detective Agency to smash the strike. The choice of Baldwin-Felts was no option for the faint hearted. Known for their violent tactics, they lived up to their reputation. Random shots were fired into the tent village, killing and injuring the strikers and forcing many to dig trench systems as protection. The "detectives" even drove around in a specially produced CF&I armored car, mounted with an M1895 Colt-Browning machine gun and lovingly referred to as the "Death Special." On October 17, 1913, the machine gun was used in earnest, spraying the tents and killing one man, plus wounding two children. By the end of the month, the state governor, Elias A. Ammons, had called up the National Guard and had also formed a militia force, primarily made up of mine guards and individuals strongly opposed to the miners' aims.

Still the miners did not give in, and the violence was starting to spiral. On March 10 the following year, the body of a foreign strike-breaker was discovered near the Forbes tents, and the commander of the National Guard, Guard Adjutant General John Chase, decided it was time to crush the various tent colonies and their strikers.

On April 20, the troops moved on the largest colony at Ludlow. They emplaced machine guns on high ground and, unnerved by the potential flanking responses of the miners, began firing. Stunned, the miners then returned fire with whatever weapons they had available, and the incident exploded into a combat-level firefight. The fighting lasted for 14 hours. Casualties amongst the miners would have been higher had a passing freight train not stopped near the camp and provided cover against the machine-gun fire while many miners and their families escaped. The camp's main organizer, Louis Tikas, went over to talk with the officer in charge, and instead was beaten over the head with a rifle butt then shot dead while still lying on the ground. Two other men were also killed under questionable circumstances; the National Guard also lost one man, as well as three company guards, and mercy was in short supply that day. The events reached an horrific crescendo when two women and 11 children all died after their tent, under which they were hiding in a pit, was set on fire by militiamen.

The killings at Ludlow prompted what virtually amounted to ten days of guerrilla warfare in Colorado, with armed miners and other workers attacking mine plants, and the National Guard responding with similar force. Over 60 people were killed in the fighting, which became known as the Colorado Coalfield War, and only the use of US Army forces eventually brought the situation under control.

The Ludlow Massacre is one of the worst incidents of civil violence in US history, and throws up two principal issues about the use of force at the time. The first is that the alliance between force and commercial interest was too paramount, especially as the militia was composed mainly of individuals with a definite interest in seeing the strike defeated. This issue was raised against none other than John D. Rockefeller, who owned the mine company, during cross examination before the Federal Commission on Industrial Relations in 1915. On May 21, Frank P. Walsh, the Commission chairman, started to question Rockefeller directly on the massacre:

> On April 18, five days before the Ludlow horror, you got a letter from Mr. Bowers [Lamont Bowers, the CF&I vice president] personally addressed to John D. Rockefeller Jr., in which he stated: "Another favorable feature of the strike situation is the organization of a military company of 100 volunteers at Trinidad next week; they are to be armed by the State and drilled by the military officers. Another squad has been organized at Walsenburg: they are independent of the militiamen and will be subject to orders of the Sheriff of the county. These volunteers will draw no pay from the State."[137]

Walsh went on to point out that the militia recruited to crush the strike included "Superintendents and foremen, the clerical force, physicians, storekeepers, mine guards and other residents of the coal camps," all in the employ of the mine. Such a partisan force hardly embodied impartiality, nor was it intended to, and the fact that they were not paid for their service also meant a consequent reduction in responsibility for the actions. Once such a force was armed, then the grievous implications of the situation expanded commensurately.

The other issue is that the use of force options seem to lack a clear sense of jurisdiction and central authority. The concept of US militia forces straddles a sometimes uneasy line between the federal and the domestic even today, and back then we see responsibility divided – probably "dispersed" would be a better word – between multiple parties. We have National Guard commanders (local and regional), militia leaders, local law enforcement, local personalities (it is easy to imagine that the "superintendents and foremen" had far greater leadership influence than the "storekeepers" and "mine guards"), the state governor, and the national leadership of the CF&I itself. Once the shooting started, therefore, each element of the strike-breaking force resorted to its own tactical agenda, tackling the situation only within the limits of its own restraint (weakened by the overall remit for crushing the strike) rather than operating under a sense of clear, cohesive guidelines.

Major incidents of civil unrest in the United States undoubtedly peaked during the 1930s, with a rapidly escalating death toll. During the infamous Bonus March in May 1932, some 10,000 cash-strapped World War I veterans and their families camped in good order around Washington DC in an attempt to prompt Congress into delivering a veteran's bonus pledged back in 1924. Congress voted against the bonus, and on July 27 Attorney General Mitchell ordered all the protesters removed from government property. This resulted in a riot, during which two protesters were shot dead. In consequence, President Hoover deployed federal troops under General Douglas MacArthur, who smashed the strike and wiped out the camp using cavalry charges, infantry maneuvers, and the use of six tanks. Huge numbers of people were wounded and two babies died, and the fact that the veterans had behaved in an orderly fashion for most of their protest drew intense public condemnation.

In a similar vein was the Memorial Day Massacre in Chicago, Illinois, on May 30, 1937. In a wearily familiar routine, a strike against the Republic Steel Company, organized by the Congress of Industrial Relations, descended into a lethally mounting tension. Members of the Chicago Police Department acted as protection to the strike-breakers, as did the plant's own hired guards, and levels of friction grew to a peak on Memorial Day, when 1,500 strikers marched on the plant. Events of the day are still confused, despite some elucidation by film provided from a Paramount Pictures film crew, present at the scene. What appears to have occurred is that the strikers, some carrying sticks and missiles at the ready, attempted to make a flanking maneuver around the police lines, which the police blocked. A violent shouting match between officers and strikers began, and some missiles were thrown into police lines, prompting a tear gas response and, from one officer, a revolver shot fired into the air. It was the cue for a massacre. Graphically illustrated by the film reel, the officers drew their pistols en masse and fired over 200 shots directly into the crowd, killing six people immediately and wounding four others who subsequently died. The officers then charged the crowd with drawn batons, resulting in dozens more seriously wounded. Sixteen police officers were also injured. What exactly happened that day isn't fully known, but the LaFollette Civil Liberties Committee subsequently established to review the events concluded, in the midst of general public outrage, that the police had both aggravated the situation by prohibiting many instances of legal, peaceful protest, and responded with clearly excessive force during the main riot.

As an aside, we should note that the firepower appropriated by the private armies of big business during the 1930s was quite alarming, and the very fact that major companies possessed their own arsenals at times of heightening industrial tension must have indicated something of a desire to use them. For example, in an article on the Memorial Day Massacre, Howard Fast notes that steel companies were "arming themselves for coming struggle."[138] He observes one order for weaponry delivered to Bethlehem Steel in September 1933:

12 blast type billies

100 blast type billies, cartridges

24 Jumbo CN grenades lot No. X820

24 military bouchons

48 1½" cal. projectile shells (CN)

24 1½" cal. short range shells (CN)

4 1½" cal. riot guns, style 201 sr. No. 337, 386, 390, 403

4 riot gun cases[139]

Fast also details another order to Youngstown Steel & Tube, which went to an even greater extreme in June 1934:

10 1½" cal. riot guns 201, $60 ea.

10 riot gun cases 211, $7.50 ea.

60 1½" cal. long range projectiles, $7.50 ea.

60 1½" cal. short range projectiles, $4.50 ea.

60 M-39 billies, std. barrel no disc, $22.50 ea.

600 M-39 billy cartridges, $1.50 ea.

200 grenades 106M, 10% disc., $12 ea.

These are substantial arsenals for civil companies. Indeed, after the Memorial Day Massacre, the LaFollette Civil Liberties Committee discovered that the Republic Steel Company and associated plants had spent a total on $40,000 of weapons and munitions, these including machine guns, rifles, shotguns, and tear gas. It was noted that Republic had greater stocks of weaponry than any law enforcement agency in the United States at that time.

The riots listed above are just two extreme examples of hundreds of such events that plagued the United States during this time. Trawling through newspaper archives shows many such riots descending into violence between protesters and police lines, while many others were quickly dispersed with a show of force, or sometimes simply through a conscientious police officer talking to the ringleaders.

The 1940s saw a reduction in the number of riots, as improved economic conditions, better workplace relations and the socially cohesive effects of World War II brought about a better mood. Yet as we shall see, riots and civil unrest remain forever a problem area of US policing. Without denying the horror and criminality of some police actions, there must also be a recognition of the difficulties they faced in dealing with civil unrest in the first half of the century. First, their actions were often motivated by a clear sense of purpose imposed by far higher authorities, stretching sometimes up to presidential level, and if modern psychology has proven anything, it is that large groups of people, police or not, will often give up their sense of personal responsibility for actions if a more influential body directs them on another course. Second, the response to civil unrest consisted not only of police, but also of a variety of private and military forces that all too easily dispersed any moral center in terms of response. Third, and something that must always be recognized, is simply that when confronted with hundreds of very angry, sometimes armed, protesters, police officers justifiably get scared, and people do not perform at their best under fear. Police officers were injured and killed during the riots of this period, and the fact that these casualties were far outnumbered by those of protesters does not diminish the anxiety of the individual officer for his well-being. Testimony of officers before the LaFollette Civil Liberties Committee often shows individuals responding to events within their own fearful tunnel vision, not deliberating on the overall quality of riot-response. For example:

> I heard some shots in the east ranks of the rioters. Then there was a shower of rocks and brick-bats. All of the marchers were armed with clubs or some kind of weapons. Some of them attacked me with clubs ... (Sergeant John J. Nugent)
>
> I was on the extreme right, next to Captain Mooney. The captain said for the strikers to stop and talk it over. One man had a meat hook. Suddenly another fellow jerked out a gun and fired it. Then everyone was fighting. I got hit with a brick ... (Patrolman John Crum)[140]

Regardless of how the final judgments evaluated such statements, the short, punchy sentence structure belies something of the panicked apprehension experienced by officers that day. All too often, we have police and military riot squads cast in the mold of vengeful automatons or bullies, only too willing to hack into striker's lines. While instances of brutality, some on a major scale, can and do exist, the fact remains that bad things were likely to happen when large bodies of emotionally fired people came into contact with nervous armed police, police who were often working under clear centralized orders to break up the crowd.

3

PROTEST AND PSYCHOPATHS 1945–79

From the moment they arrived on Los Angeles's 54th Street on May 17, 1974, it was obvious that these were no ordinary police officers. Clad in black uniforms and face masks, they moved with a tactical purpose that had more in common with an infantry rifle squad than a law enforcement agency. They were also similarly armed – AR-15 rifles, pump-action shotguns, .243 long rifles, AR-180 rifles, and automatic pistols in their hip holsters. Then again, they were not after regular suspects.

Formed in 1973, by the following year the Symbionese Liberation Army (SLA) was already headline-grabbing material. Created by Donald DeFreeze, aka "Marshal Cinque," the SLA perceived itself as a revolutionary guerrilla organization dedicated to the liberation of African-Americans from a repressive regime (although only one member of the group was actually black). Their rhetoric was the now familiar mix of explosive defiance mixed with formulaic left-wing ideology, but the authorities quickly had cause to take them very seriously. The group was committed to a violent, not a verbal, struggle, and its members spent much of their first year arming themselves and training to shoot on public shooting ranges. Then, on November 6, 1973, two SLA members assassinated school superintendent Dr Marcus Foster (an African-American himself) and his deputy Robert Blackburn as they left an Oakland School Board meeting. Their crime had been the policy of introducing identity cards into Oakland schools, a "fascist" step according to the SLA, plus cooperation with local law enforcement agencies and the intention of establishing a school system police unit. In the letter sent to the authorities, the SLA proclaimed that the two men had been killed on the authority of the "Court of the People," which found them "guilty of supporting and taking part in crimes committed against the children and the life of the people."[141]

The weapons used in the killings were a .380 pistol and a shotgun. In a chilling example of literal overkill, the pistol bullets had been packed with cyanide to guarantee their lethality.

Two men were eventually caught and convicted for the school murders, and the SLA began plotting its revenge. On February 4, 1974, they kidnapped Patty Hearst, the daughter of Randolph Apperson Hearst, newspaper magnate and chairman of the powerful Hearst Corporation. The kidnapping was accompanied by the usual letter, which not only threatened the execution of the hostage if the police attempted to rescue her, but also declared that: "This court hereby notifies the public and directs all combat units in the future to shoot to kill any civilian who attempts to witness or interfere with any operation conducted by the people's forces against the fascist state."[142]

Two months later, and in an extremely media-friendly turn of events, Hearst declared that she had actually joined the SLA, reinforcing the point on April 15 when she was photographed assisting in the bank robbery of a Hibernia Bank at 1450 Noriega Street in San Francisco. (Hearst was later arrested and convicted of this crime, but argued that she had been systematically brainwashed and abused by the group. She was released from prison after 22 months, her original seven-year sentence having been commuted by President Jimmy Carter, and she was later given a full pardon by President Bill Clinton.)

Patty Hearst's activities aside, on May 17 the Los Angeles Police Department (LAPD) finally had apparently solid information about the whereabouts of Hearst and the SLA principals. Several locations were pinpointed, including the actual location of the SLA cell – 1466 East 54th Street. On account of the seriousness of the threat – in the Patty Hearst letter, the SLA had again stated that they had "cyanide loaded weapons" – it was decided to deploy one of the newest tools in the LAPD's box: the SWAT team.

Formed a mere five years before, the SWAT was a rigorously selected, combat-trained unit of officers dedicated to tackling those situations beyond the capabilities, and firepower, of regular beat officers. The SWAT teams (two teams of eight men each, each team with a supervisor) quickly performed their first operational task, sealing off a perimeter around the suspect locations. The next step, according the official report after what followed, was to make an evacuation of nearby premises, then force the surrender of the SLA members in the two houses believed to hold them. In terms of the use of force at this stage, the report noted four main elements:

5. After the evacuation was accomplished, an announcement to surrender would be given to the suspects in 1466 East 54th Street and 1462 East 54th Street from the SWAT leader at the front.

6. If, after a reasonable time, no response was received from either house, tear gas would be used.
7. After tear gas was employed, additional announcements to surrender would be made and reasonable time given to effect the surrender.
8. LAPD SWAT units would fire their weapons only upon order of their supervisor or in self-defense. Emphasis was placed upon making an arrest with minimum force.[143]

By 4.20pm the perimeter had been established, and some initial evacuations began shortly afterwards. As the operation gathered momentum, more solid information came in that 1466 East 54th Street was the place where they should really focus their attentions. The officers quickly tightened their grip around that location. They had the right spot. Inside were DeFreeze plus the following SLA members: Nancy Ling Perry, Angela Atwood, Camilla Hall, Patricia Soltysik, and Willie Wolf, plus two other females and a male who, as it turned out, were not members of the SLA. An eight-year-old boy was also inside.

Now things were about to turn nasty. A SWAT officer, using a bullhorn, issued a demand for the immediate surrender of the occupants. Nothing. The demand was repeated, and this time the confused and scared little boy walked out of the house, and was scooped up into police lines. Shortly after, a black adult male appeared and walked over to the police, whom he told that the people inside the house weren't armed. The boy, once he had calmed down, flatly contradicted that line, stating not only that did the occupants all have guns, but that they had ammunition belts strapped across their chests, ready for action. The LAPD report now explains the thinking of the officer-in-charge, who:

> ... determined that the SLA members had the capability for barricading themselves indefinitely. Additionally, with darkness [it was 1744hrs when the first surrender demand was made], the danger of the armed occupants bursting from the location and spraying the area with automatic fire would become imminent. Because these hazards would increase with the passing of time and because of the danger this heavily-armed group presented to the neighborhood and to officers being positioned to contain them over an extended period of time, the SWAT Officer-in-Charge [OIC] decided to employ gas projectiles against the barricaded SLA members.[144]

At around 5.53pm, the first 509 CS Flite-rite tear gas projectiles smashed through the windows of the house and began pumping out their contents. The response was a hail of automatic fire. The situation soon whipped itself into a major gun battle, with the SLA members firing wildly out into the streets around them, while SWAT officers opened up with their AR-15s and shotguns. More tear gas canisters thumped into the house – gas masks had been found at other SLA locations, and the SWAT OIC intended to pump in enough gas to overwhelm the filters, should these members be similarly equipped. By 6.00pm, such was the volume of fire that officers had to send out for extra supplies of both small-arms ammunition and gas projectiles. The FBI provided additional support in the form of teams armed with M79 grenade launchers, used for launching additional tear gas rounds. Furthermore, in an attempt to match the volume of fire rippling in periodic bursts from the house, the OIC requested "four department automatic weapons," plus fragmentation grenades. The request for the former was accepted, the latter denied.

By 6.41pm, the house was beginning to catch fire. Given this extra spur to get out, one of the non-SLA females, Christine Johnson, exited the house and was taken into custody. Shortly after, the SWAT's automatic weapons turned up. The four weapons were an interesting choice. Two were full-auto M16 military rifles, as used by the US Army. The other two, however, were 9mm MP40 SMGs. These German weapons were World War II vintage guns, with an awkward layout for urban operations. Why these were on the SWAT weapons list is unusual, given the large variety of other weapons available on the market at the time, including the Heckler & Koch MP5 (which became the virtual standard in specialist unit SMGs), the Walther MPK, the Israeli Uzi and the Beretta Model 12. The choice of the MP40s smacks of a young organization with a limited budget, picking up whatever was on the market for the right price.

At 6.50pm, the house was ablaze with flames. At this point, Camilla Hall and Nancy Ling Perry attempted to make a break for it, still firing their weapons. Hall was shot dead as she emerged from a crawl hole at the side of the house, her body being dragged back inside the house by people still inside. Perry was killed in the open, as she fired a revolver towards one of the SWAT teams. Only eight minutes later, the roof of the house collapsed inwards, with noises of ammunition "cooking off" being heard, and the firing from the SLA house finally ceased.

All those who had remained inside the house were dead, having been killed by either the SWAT shooting, the fire, or suicide. Along with the bodies, the police investigators subsequently found a veritable arsenal of weaponry inside, which consisted of four M1 carbines (all converted to fire full-auto), two semi-automatic rifles (.30-06 and .244 calibers), six handguns, and seven shotguns, most with their barrels sawn off for close-quarters combat. A total of 4,247 rounds of ammunition were discovered, all but 475 being expended (although it was hard to determine which had been fired out of guns, and which had detonated in the fire). Add the collection of pipe bombs, and it was evident that the SLA did not intend to go down lightly.

Nor did the SWAT teams, for that matter. The final report acknowledged that "The prolonged gunfire at 1466 East 54th Street caused the barrel rifling of some of the weapons to completely wear out and the magazine springs to become unserviceable."[145] (This was not entirely on account of the SLA action, as the report also points out that officers had put 45,000 rounds through their weapons in previous training.)

The SWAT action on May 17, 1974, was not the first time that LAPD SWAT had blazed its way into the headlines. One of its first major operations was on December 8, 1969, when SWAT officers went to the city headquarters of the Black Panther movement in an attempt to serve a felony warrant. Like the SLA, the Black Panthers replied to surrender demands with shotgun and automatic weapon fire. In a five-hour gun battle, the two sides exchanged some 5,000 rounds of ammunition, although incredibly no-one was killed or even seriously injured. When the Black Panthers finally ran out of ammunition, they gave up. A big difference with the SLA incident was that much of it was filmed and televised. In the same way that the SAS became a household name following the televised breaking of the Iranian Embassy siege in London in 1980, the SWAT was now on the public map, most viewers being enthralled by its toughness, others being appalled. The SWAT team received 1,182 positive letters from the public, and 288 critical letters, with similar proportions of correspondence going to the *Los Angeles Times* and the *Herald Examiner*.[146] In the sincerest form of flattery, in 1975 ABC television started broadcasting a new drama entitled *SWAT*, produced by Aaron Spelling and Leonard Goldberg. This ran for only two seasons, and was eventually canceled over concerns about its violent content.

The birth of SWAT teams across the country will be a major focus of this chapter, for it signaled a landmark point in the militarization of police use of force, not only in terms of the SWAT team itself, but also percolating outwards into the wider police community. Note, however, that the term "militarization" will be neutral, not pejorative; I recognize that although police units must distinguish themselves from military forces, especially in terms of their far tighter rules of engagement, adopting a military-style approach to armed response is somewhat instinctive. The military, after all, trains its personnel to higher standards of controlled weapons-handling, especially as the forces are just as likely to find themselves on peacekeeping tours as on combat missions. Their investment in understanding fire-control is naturally of interest and benefit to law enforcement agencies, who can cherry-pick those aspects of training most suited to their needs.

THE WORLD TURNS

The period from the end of World War II to the end of the 1970s is one of the most politically and socially turbulent in US history, and it would be impossible to explore it in any great depth here. Some summary notes, however, will provide a context for what follows. One fact is particularly noteworthy. In 1949 fewer than 100 police officers (97) were killed in the line of duty. This would be the last time that annual officer fatality figures would remain below the century mark, and they showed that in many ways police work had been getting safer since the 1930s. Indeed, the single most lethal year for law enforcement officers was 1930, when 279 officers were killed.[147] Time and social changes altered the figures tremendously. The 1970s, however, according to the National Law Enforcement Officers Memorial, were the deadliest decade in police history, with 2,276 officers killed to make an average of 228 per year.

The social context for this alarming shift is, as we have noted, a complex one. Post-war America, unlike war-ravaged Europe, experienced an unprecedented surge in standards of living. The 1950s became the great age of American consumerism. By 1960 90 percent of US homes had televisions (in 1948 there were only 148,000 privately owned sets in the country), Gross National Product (GNP) surged from $284.6 billion to $502.6 billion in only 15 years (1945–60), much of middle-class America moved into the newly developed suburbs, their homes kitted out with the latest in white goods, and by 1955 there were over 67 million privately owned cars.

Lest we get carried away with such figures, however, we need the balance provided by the fact that there were still just under 40 million Americans living below the poverty line, of whom 11 million were African-Americans, 56 percent of the total number of African-Americans living in the country during the 1950s.[148] Indeed, race would become a salient issue for the next two decades, as the civil rights movement attempted to redress the gross inequities suffered by the black American community for well over 100 years. This movement would be just one of the factors that fed into the huge waves of social protest sweeping across America during the 1960s and 1970s. In addition to race issue protests, the burgeoning idealism and anti-militarism amongst America's emerging student classes fueled middle-class protest, often violent, on a scale never before seen in US society. Left-wing and eastern ideologies took pervasive hold amongst large swathes of US youth, all at a time when the government, spurred on by the more populous ranks of conservative America, entered into the vigorous anti-communist mindset of the Cold War era. The result was a society riven with radically opposed social and political agendas. Such a tension, plus the steadily rising unpopularity of the US war in Vietnam between 1965 and 1973, produced numerous radical groups hellbent on gaining compliance for their agenda through terrorism and direct action. Although the United States during the 1960s and 1970s did not suffer the hideous epidemic of terrorism experienced by Europe during the same period, there were still enough home-grown incidents and general anxiety to make terrorism a prevalent fear.

There was also a distinct shift in the nature of gang crime during this period. As we have seen, both rural and urban America have always had their violently minded gangs, so in a sense the post-war United States was little different. A significant shift, however, did occur in the African-American community. While black gangs of the 1950s were no innocents, they tended to focus more on disputes over the high-school pecking order or on minor territorial disputes over street corners or bars, and the use of impact weaponry and knives was limited, or even seen as cowardly.[149] During the 1960s, weaponry moved more to the fore. Handguns or sawn-off shotguns came to be the weapons of choice, and reluctance to use them a sign of weakness. Furthermore, the territorialism and aggression of the gangs was enhanced through new systems of self identification and expanded membership rolls. The most famous of the gangs to evolve was the Los Angeles "Crips," born when the FBI and LAPD shut down the Los Angeles chapter of the Black Panther Party (BPP) in the late 1960s and early 1970s.[150] The newly unemployed BPP members formed a fresh gang around its founder member, Raymond Washington. Ironically, although he was not shy about fighting, Washington was not a lover of using weapons to settle disputes. The genie was out of the bottle, however, and as the Crips grew prodigiously in Los Angeles so did violent gangs opposed to their territorial growth, most famously the group of local gangs that conglomerated into the Crips' arch-rivals, the Bloods. Gang units gathered around many of the new housing projects built during the 1960s and 1970s in Los Angeles, urban zones that soon became synonymous with violence and criminality. In this environment, Washington's original antipathy towards weaponry was smothered, and gun culture firmly established itself. Washington himself became a victim. On August 9, 1979, he was killed by a shot from a sawn-off shotgun fired from a passing car. The gang situation that he had started in Los Angeles laid the groundwork for the horrendous spread of violent gang culture through the United States during the 1980s, to which we shall turn in our next chapter. Gang criminality, including the resurgent activities of the Mafia, contributed to giving the 1960s and 1970s decades some of the highest crime figures ever witnessed in US history.

In short, the United States of the 1950s through the 1970s was a country whose radicalism, violence, and crime grew as fast as its prosperity, consumerism, and self-confidence. So where was the law enforcement community within this complex picture? The post-war law enforcement community was in many ways pursuing a continuation of the move to professionalism that had begun with people such as Vollmer. The difference was that during the 1950s to 1970s professionalism became more codified in nationally distributed books, guidelines, and programs. The ethical nature of policing was more recognized, and as such recruitment of the right sort of officer became paramount for many police departments. Such is noted in the following "Law Enforcement Code of Ethics," developed and published by the IACP in 1957. This formula, intended as a swearing-in statement by a new police officer, is still used in a slightly modified form even today:

> AS A LAW ENFORCEMENT OFFICER, my fundamental duty is to serve mankind; to safeguard lives and property; to protect the innocent against deception, the weak against oppression or intimidation, and the peaceful against violence or disorder; and to respect the Constitutional rights of all men to liberty, equality and justice.
>
> I WILL keep my private life unsullied as an example to all; maintain courageous calm in the face of danger, scorn or ridicule; develop self restraint; and be constantly mindful of the welfare of others. Honest in thought and deed in both my personal and official life, I will be exemplary in obeying the laws of the land and the regulations of my department. Whatever I see or hear of a confidential nature or that is confided to me in my official capacity will be kept ever secret unless revelation is necessary in the performance of my duty.
>
> I WILL never act officiously or permit personal feelings, prejudices, animosities or friendships to influence my decisions. With no compromise for crime and with relentless prosecution of criminals, I will enforce the law courteously and appropriately without fear or favor, malice or ill will, never employing unnecessary force or violence and never accepting gratuities.
>
> I RECOGNIZE the badge of my office as a symbol of public faith, and I accept it as a public trust to be held so long as I am true to the ethics of the police service. I will constantly strive to achieve these objectives and ideals, dedicating myself before God to my chosen profession of law enforcement.[151]

Such a lofty and inspiring commitment emphasizes the rectitude and impartiality of the officer, even in spite of the criminality he or she encounters on a daily basis. The statements about "unnecessary force" make it clear that force applications must be strictly matched to the situation, and never used on the basis of personal dislike of a suspect.

The motivating power behind the development of the Code of Ethics was Orlando Wilson, a landmark figure in the professionalization of postwar law enforcement. Wilson was a protégé of August Vollmer, under whom he had studied criminology at the University of Berkeley, California, during the 1920s. Wilson's highly academic mindset was balanced by plentiful practical work on the streets, first as a police officer with Berkeley PD. He was promoted quickly, however, and subsequent offices include Chief of Police in Fullerton PD (1925), Chief of Police Wichita PD (1928), colonel in the Military Police in Europe during World War II, and Superintendent of Police in Chicago PD from 1960 to 1967. Wilson also maintained his academic career, teaching at Harvard during the 1930s, working as director of the New England Officers' Training School, and becoming Professor of Police Administration at Berkeley in 1939, a position that led to his tenure as dean of Berkeley's School of Criminology between 1950 and 1960.

When Wilson began his career in policing, his education separated him from most of the officers, and this was a situation he sought to change throughout his police career. For Wilson, the character of the officers had to fuse with reforms in police practice and administration, the result being police departments free from the corruption, graft, and controversy that still plagued many departments in the post-war period (such as those he encountered when he stepped into his leadership role in Chicago). Wilson's most enduring legacy was the book *Police Administration*, published in 1950 and destined to become a landmark reference work for police leaders up and down the country. *Police Administration*, and Wilson's other publications, focused on the professionalization of every aspect of police work, from the hiring of police officers through to methods of improving response times to crime. He also acknowledged that policing was as much about crime prevention as about serving out jail time: "If society is to be effectively safeguarded against crime, the police must actively seek out and destroy delinquency-inducing influences in the community and assist in providing suitable treatment for the maladjusted."[152]

Wilson's work had a critical effect on policing throughout the United States. Note also that in 1961, Lois Lundell Higgins, director of the Crime Prevention Bureau of Illinois and president of the International Association of Women Police (IAWP), produced a volume entitled *Policewoman's Manual*. Although there had been some isolated and newsworthy incidents of women being hired as police officers back as far as the 1830s, the first truly official female hiring was that of Alice Stebbins Wells by the LAPD in 1910. In contemporary news reports, 'Stebbs' is treated in equal measure with respect, curiosity, and patronization, and *Good Housekeeping* acknowledged that, in terms of use of force, her place was very different to that of male officers:

> A star with lace ruffles is exactly what Mrs. Wells does not want. She wears no uniform, carries no weapon, and as often as possible keeps her star in her handbag. Measuring not

> much over five feet, she has no idea of using physical force in the discharge of her duties, which are no less varied than those of her brother officers, and often identical with them.[153]

No mention of a gun is made – indeed the issue of one to Stebbs is unlikely given that she does not even have a uniform, just a badge secreted away in her "handbag." Nonetheless, Stebbs made a critical first step in US policing, and by 1925 some 145 police departments had hired female officers. Most were employed in clearly distinct, less muscular, more empathetic, roles than their male counterparts, with specialties in handling incidents affecting juveniles, females, and families. Such was still largely evident in Higgins' manual of 1961; in her introduction she explains that female officers had managed to establish themselves in police work:

> ... not because they have tried to compete against men in work that always has been and will always be predominately [sic] a man's job. It is because they have brought to their work talents that are generally considered peculiarly feminine – an unusually highly developed interest in human relationships – and have accentuated, rather than subordinated, their femininity.[154]

In a modern climate of equality, these comments make the female officer appear professionally cornered by gender politics, and there was indeed much more work to be done to give female officers access to the full range of police vocations. Nonetheless, even today it is common for police departments to use female officers in certain roles, such as handling family disputes and dealing with young female offenders. At least by 1961 the female officer had received firearms, and the manual makes it clear that if no male officer is present to assist, the female officer must resort to her firearms or her training in unarmed defense to stop a dangerous subject.

Female officer use of force was, by the mid-1960s, also starting to hit the headlines. The articles are curious to read from the modern viewpoint. They are as much fascinated with what the officer is wearing as with the emergency of her situation, and always seem eager to emphasize her femininity, as if the use of force runs the risk of exposing harder undercurrents in the female psyche. And women were proving that they could indeed be tough. For example, on May 24, 1965, two female police officers, Marie Cirile and her partner Julia Tucker, were performing undercover surveillance on two men suspected of narcotics trafficking. Dressed in civilian clothing, with Cirile sporting a jaunty leopard-skin print hat (as the catalogue model-style photo in the *New York Times* illustrated) and Tucker in teenage clothes, the two officers followed the men – Thomas O'Neill and Harry Twyman – from a restaurant on 45th Street down to the nearby Duffy Square park. There they saw the two men perform a narcotics transaction, before heading back to the restaurant. When they emerged later, Cirile stepped forward and issued a challenge for the two men to submit. At that they turned and sprinted away at speed, perhaps emboldened by the incongruity of the arresting officer. Cirile drew her .32 revolver and fired a shot into the air, stopping the men in their tracks. Cornered like a city rat, O'Neill then whipped round and lunged at Cirile with a 5in. knife. Cirile responded by side-stepping the knife and shooting O'Neill in the hip, some witnesses stating that she enforced her intent by stating that she would "blow your head off" if he attempted another move. Both men came to their senses and were arrested for narcotics violations and assault. In a nice touch, the *New York Times* article on the encounter ends by noting that Cirile had made another pistol-point chase and arrest five years before in Manhattan, observing that "Five days later she went on maternity leave."[155]

Having noted the continuing professionalization of police, it is also important to recognize some of the lingering shadows over policing. The handling of race-related disturbances and continuing issues of corruption chained some police departments to elements of policing more at home in the 18th and 19th centuries than the 20th century.

The Knapp Commission of 1970–73 gave the issue of corruption a high public profile, as the NYPD came under a corruption investigation headed by lawyer Whitman Knapp. The commission was prompted by the allegations of corruption made by NYPD officers Frank Serpico and David Durk, who had taken their complaints to the media after finding no joy within the NYPD. Dozens of police officers took to the stand, and gave a sobering run of evidence about police involvement in underworld activities, including drug dealing, blackmailing suspects, and taking payoffs to ignore criminal activities. The final report, released on December 26, 1972, estimated around 50 percent of NYPD officers as having participated in corrupt activities. The summary also stated:

> Of course, not all policemen are corrupt. If we are to exclude such petty infractions as free meals, an appreciable number do not engage in any corrupt activities. Yet, with extremely rare exceptions, even those who themselves engage in no corrupt activities are involved in corruption in the sense that they take no steps to prevent what they know and suspect to be going on about them.[156]

The Knapp Commission prompted huge changes in NYPD practice and procedure in an attempt to clean up its act, including the creation of more effective internal affairs departments committed to investigating police corruption. New York was not the only city to come under the corruption spotlight – Chicago, Los Angeles, and others were also reviewed – and the visibility of such practices was increasing, aided by the spread of the television media.

Resistance by the officers of many police departments to the efforts of the black civil rights movement in the 1960s brought some of the ugliest episodes in the history of police law enforcement. In the state of Mississippi in 1960, for example, some 42 percent of the state's population was black, but only 2 percent were actually brave enough to exercise that right by registering to vote. Those who attempted to vote, or to push a civil rights agenda, often suffered brutality at the hands of police officers or groups condoned by police officers. Police departments throughout the state frequently had roots running into the Ku Klux Klan (KKK) or other racist movements. Officers very high up in the pay grade would openly declare anti-black attitudes, and Los Angeles became a hotbed for racial unrest and rioting throughout this period. On a smaller scale, in Neshoba County, Mississippi, for example, the KKK was allegedly in control of the sheriff's department from 1960 to 1972, headed by figures such as Sheriff Ethel Glen "Hop" Barnett and Deputy (later Sheriff) Lawrence Rainey. African-Americans in Neshoba effectively suffered a reign of terror during these years, and we find some of the most questionable applications of use of force. Rainey was particularly free with guns and clubs. He had killed a black man in his previous tenure in Philadelphia (Mississippi) PD following a traffic violation stop, and killed a black prisoner, Willie Nash, in May 1962 in Neshoba, the unfortunate Nash being shot several times while handcuffed and in police custody. In June 1964, the county became more nationally famous after three civil rights workers vanished and were subsequently discovered murdered, the FBI investigation alleging that Rainey, Cecil Price (Rainey's chief deputy), and Barnett had released the three workers, then pulled them over on the highway and had them murdered. For many people in the civil rights movement, the subsequent federal trial yielded unsatisfactory results, and only Price was convicted on lesser charges of infringing civil rights (there was no federal murder statute at this time). Barnett went on to secure a further tenure as sheriff, a position that he held until 1972.

The examples of use of force in racial control are legion in the post-war period, but this was the age in which the power of television was ever expanding. In April 1963, the world witnessed the police chief of Birmingham, Alabama – Eugene "Bull" O'Connor – unleash fire hoses, batons, and dogs upon crowds of peaceful protesters who were demonstrating against Birmingham's segregationist policies. The TV imagery gave the lie to the local police claims of self-protection, aided by choice audible statements by O'Connor that include: "I want to see the dogs work. Look at those niggers run."[157] The violence brought national and international condemnation, and although plenty more blood would be spilled it began the process through which America was federally desegregated. Police handling of race disturbances and civil rights protests was a seminal feature of law enforcement work during the period of this chapter, and one mired in regular controversy.

The effect of television on the police use of force, for good and ill, has been seismic. Violence witnessed is always more powerful than violence discussed, and the way that a TV news report is edited and presented can shape public perceptions. TV is by its very nature attracted to strong visual imagery, so scenes of police force were attractive to news agency chiefs from the moment that TV cameras became portable enough to transport between incidents. Regina G. Lawrence, author of *The Politics of Force*, a study of media representation of police use of force, notes several key distinctions between newspaper reporting and TV reporting, including the closer proximity of newspaper journalists to their police sources. Lawrence also notes that:

> ... local (and, with increasing frequency, national) television news often sacrifices discussion of public-policy issues for sensationalized and "human interest" news. Analyzing newspaper coverage captures a greater range of news coverage, from daily crime-beat reporting to serious, thematic coverage of policing problems.[158]

"Human interest" stories can undoubtedly make exciting and involving television, but they can be equally troublesome for a police commander, depending on the editorial judgment of the news producer. A five-second clip of a police officer striking a man with a baton can appear to be a clear demonstration of police violence, but denuded of context (other than what the voiceover tells us) we have little idea of the tensions and events that led up to such an action. Furthermore, for those not accustomed to violence, any physically violent action can appear shocking, and incites a judgment about the one who uses it.

We mustn't overstate the case of how much public perception of the police is shaped by the media. The behavior of a courteous officer personally encountered will typically leave a more lasting impression than the flashed images on the screen, which are competing with a world of other visually dramatic stories and incidents. Yet as we shall analyze in greater depth in the next chapter, in relation to the Rodney King incident, police actions captured on film can result in gross blanket judgments being applied to general police behavior.

During the 1950s and 1960s, there was a steadily expanding awareness amongst police chiefs that television was becoming a critical factor in the way the public perceived police actions, particularly violent ones. Trust between the media as a whole and the police was not high, the latter perceiving the former as intrinsically drawn towards stories involving use of force, fostering a particularly critical outlook of the police. An interesting footnote in James Wilson's *Varieties of Police Behavior* explains something about the way Chicago police judged their news coverage during the 1960s:

> In 1961, when the newspapers were very critical of corruption in the Chicago Police Department, 78.6 percent of the sergeants felt the newspapers were "too critical." But in 1965, when the newspapers were, on the whole, praising the police for their successful reformation, 65.3 percent of the sergeants *still* felt the newspapers were too critical. The police respond to newspaper coverage of particular cases as much or more than they do to generalized attitudes toward law enforcement.[159]

The last sentence here covers an important point, namely that the prominent coverage of one particular incident can have as much effect on the psychology of a police department as can the day-to-day encounters with the general public. Wilson also implies, in the context of the times, that once suspicion of the media's motives is established, then it is hard to shake off that suspicion, regardless of how the editorial policy changes. Wilson argues that amongst the rank and file officers, there is also a "great anger" that television cameras and newspaper photographers are constantly present, their recording of events putting the police under additional pressure not only in terms of their behavior, but also in their belief that, whatever they do, the presentation will be negative.[160]

An interesting case study in the relevance of television in particular, and a scene-setter for our later look at the handling of Vietnam War and civil rights protests, is the Democratic National Convention of 1968 in Chicago. The Convention couldn't have come at a worse time. Lyndon Johnson had pulled out of the presidential running, leaving Eugene McCarthy and Herbert Humphrey in the race, and the party was mired in a grossly unpopular war in Southeast Asia. Protests were expected, and the scale of force applied as preparation by Chicago mayor Richard J. Daley was extreme to say the least: 5,000 National Guardsmen, 5,500 Federal troops, more than 12,000 police. (Many Democrats had wanted the Convention moved to Miami rather than Chicago, on account of local industrial unrest and the increased possibility of demonstrations, and Daley was keen to ensure that nothing would disrupt proceedings.)

In total some 10,000 protesters gathered during the Convention, which ran from August 26–29, and matters quickly turned ugly under the lenses of the world's media. Violence began even prior to the Convention. On the 25th, police stormed protesters camping in Lincoln Park, using tear gas and batons to disperse them. Critically, this first "action" revealed that news reporters were targets for the police on account of their profession: 17 reporters were attacked on the 25th, including *Newsweek* reporter Hal

Bruno. Much worse was to come over the next few days. Regular clashes between the state forces and the protesters escalated in scale and violence. TV audiences worldwide were exposed to blood-splashed scenes of police beatings (many of them now revealed in full, glorious technicolor), the protesters, undoubtedly not all innocents, nevertheless looking very human and exposed in their light 1960s clothing when compared to the military or militaristic garb of their opponents. The treatment of the media as a literal "enemy" – 36 newsmen in total were injured during the disturbances – did not help the police in winning the battle of representation. In total, 1,100 people were injured during the riots, including over 150 police, and the world's media turned both on the town of Chicago and its bullish mayor, and on what it regarded as evidence of a "police state" mentality more akin to that behind the Iron Curtain.

The television representation of the Democratic National Convention was critical to the public outcry that followed, and Daley knew it. In an unusual attempt at editorial correction, the city of Chicago commissioned a one-hour television documentary showing its side of the story. The city administration was actually credited as the producer of the film, and the film was compiled from material from the Chicago PD, the Illinois National Guard, United Press International, and other news agencies.[161] The documentary understandably downplayed the footage of police wielding batons, and instead brought forward images and witnesses that attested to crowd provocation. This included shots of aggressive crowds chanting in front of police lines, missiles flying through the air into police lines, and a shot of weapons allegedly collected from the crowd after the riots, including petrol bombs, rocks, and other improvised missiles, a baseball bat with "Kill the Pigs" reflectively inscribed along its length, and a collection of knives. The documentary emphasized both the provocations of the crowds and the restraint of the police, and was shown on a total of 142 television stations, with 1,000 radio stations broadcasting an audio-only equivalent.

It is all too easy to dismiss the film as a piece of propaganda from Daley's office, which was much damaged by the whole incident. Indeed, the entire handling of the events around the Convention came in for some harsh judgments. The American Civil Liberties Union (ACLU), for example, denounced the film and argued that "There is an accumulated mass of eyewitness accounts and films which depict widespread police misconduct through the week of the convention."[162] In a trial the following year, eight police officers were indicted by a grand jury for civil rights offenses. Some aspects, however, require a little more consideration, and will merit a close look at the use of deadly force and police militarization during the 1960s and 1970s. First, it is worth bearing in mind that although many of the protesters had legitimate political grievances, the way they were presented offered genuine concern to the law enforcement units present, bearing in mind that they were guarding presidential candidates only six years after an actual president, John F. Kennedy, had been assassinated. The rhetoric of many of the groups involved, such as the Yippie International Party (YIP) and the National Mobilization Committee to End the War in Vietnam (MOBE, for short), was caustically aggressive, often imbued with utter disdain for any personnel relating to law enforcement or government. Much of the expletive-laced language was admittedly counter-cultural bravado, but delivered with vehemence from hundreds of mouths it must have been a fairly intimidating prospect for even the most hardened officer or soldier. When it was augmented by the odd missile, or a barrage of missiles, the likelihood of strong police reaction must have been dramatically increased, particularly once the crowd expressed a clear intention to march on the International Amphitheater in Chicago, the venue of the Convention. That there was provocation was acknowledged by the Walker Commission, headed by Daniel Walker (who later became the governor of Illinois) to investigate the events surrounding the Convention, but the police reaction was still classed as excessive:

> During the week of the Democratic National Convention, the Chicago police were the targets of mounting provocation by both word and act. It took the form of obscene epithets, and of rocks, sticks, bathroom tiles and even human feces hurled at police by demonstrators. Some of these acts had been planned; others were spontaneous or were themselves provoked by police action. Furthermore, the police had been put on edge by widely published threats of attempts to disrupt both the city and the Convention.
>
> That was the nature of the provocation. The nature of the response was unrestrained and indiscriminate police violence on many occasions, particularly at night.
>
> That violence was made all the more shocking by the fact that it was often inflicted upon persons who had broken no law, disobeyed no order, made no threat. These included peaceful demonstrators, onlookers, and large numbers of residents who were simply passing through, or happened to live in the areas where confrontations were occurring.
>
> Newsmen and photographers were singled out for assault, and their equipment deliberately damaged. Fundamental police training was ignored; and officers, when on the scene, were often unable to control their men. As one police officer put it: "What happened didn't have anything to do with police work."[163]

The Walker Report acknowledges that the police lines received missiles, and that some of these missiles were of a type to do potentially grievous damage. It also understands a police force "on edge," put there not only by the political pressure from the mayor's office, but also, it explains later, by the unhelpful cultural stereotyping of all the protestors as communist or anarchist in sympathies. The report, which included statements from 3,437 eyewitnesses, also based its analysis on 180 hours of film footage, an increasingly useful tool in the forensic box. Many of the eyewitness statements include harrowing testimony of outright, random brutality by the police against simple bystanders, much of it clearly beyond the realms of provocation. Yet one counterpoint made in the Daley film repeatedly was that "no one was killed." One officer shown in the film, Patrolman Gregory Kyritz, was seen stating "Every policeman there could have shot somebody, but nobody did."

Bearing in mind some of the other large-scale US riots of this time in which people were shot and killed, and accepting both the level of violence and the high levels of firepower available to the police over those days, the statement does merit some consideration. In part, the lack of a death toll may derive from the training implemented in the run-up to the convention. Not only had the police received several weeks of riot-control training, but they were also equipped with new tools for the job, including riot helmets and mace aerosols, plus updated radio communications to allow fast communications between units. Police patrols were heaviest in those places where trouble was expected.

In light of the near anarchy that subsequently exploded, we cannot say that the training paid off entirely. Yet the fact that no-one was shot suggests that the police and military units had at least some measure of restraint, if only because the toughness of the other force policies meant that guns could stay in holsters. Furthermore, the presence of the TV cameras was probably a strong disincentive to pulling the trigger, regardless of whether or not one felt justified doing so. The Convention riots changed the use of force landscape for riot situations in that television suddenly became an influence in terms of police behavior, and in terms of the judgments placed upon the police after the events. Daley's ineffective attempt to neutralize the furor with his own film at least shows that he understood the new media relation to force.

MILITARIZATION AND THE SWAT

The Watts riots changed everything. On Wednesday August 11, 1965, California Highway Patrol officer Lee Minkus pulled over one Marquette Fry, whose driving had been of suspect quality, in southcentral Los Angeles. Fry, who was with his brother in the car, subsequently failed a sobriety test, by which time an angry crowd was buzzing around the incident. Southcentral Los Angeles had some pleasant-looking neighborhoods, but it masked long-standing tensions between the district's principally African-American population and the police. The Fry pullover was about to become a catalyst for something far greater. As Minkus made his arrest, matters turned ugly, batons were drawn and swung, and an additional two arrests were made – Fry's mother and brother.

The simmering racial tension finally ignited, aided by a scalding summer heat wave that pushed everyone out onto the streets with feverish emotions. By the end of the day, Los Angeles was descending into a full-blown riot, and would stay there for four days.

At its height, it seems a gross understatement to describe what happened in Los Angeles as a riot, for it approached the scale of a minor civil war. Every conceivable missile, including petrol bombs, was hurled at the police, National Guard, and also the fire officers attempting to put out the conflagrations sweeping through the streets. (Over 600 buildings were either burned or looted.) Soon, hand-thrown missiles were not enough, and what started as clashes of muscle often degenerated into exchanges of firepower, the rioters firing opportunistic shots from windows and the police replying with their own volleys. Some 35,000 African-Americans poured onto the streets, and after four days of battling with around 16,000 law enforcement officers and National Guardsmen, 35 people were dead and more than 11,000 injured. The Commissioner's Report that followed the rioting, entitled *Violence in the City – An End or a Beginning?*, provided a breakdown of the causes of the fatalities as follows:

> The Coroner's jury ruled that twenty-six of the deaths were justifiable homicide, five were homicide and one was accidental. Of those ruled justifiable homicide, the jury found that death was caused in sixteen instances by officers of the Los Angeles Police Department and in seven instances by the National Guard.

Injury figures were explained as including: "90 Los Angeles police officers, 136 firemen, 10 National Guardsmen, 23 people from government agencies and 773 civilians." A total of 3,952 people were arrested, and the cost of the damage to the city was estimated at over $200 million. The bad blood generated by the Watts riots was obviously going to take a long time to work out of the system.

One LAPD field commander present throughout those chaotic days and nights acknowledges that nothing had prepared the police officers for dealing with events on this scale, even on the first day:

> We had no idea how to deal with this. There were seventy of us, eight hundred of them, maybe a thousand as the night wore on. We were constantly ducking bottles, rocks, knives, and Molotov cocktails. One officer was stabbed in the back. Guns were poked out of

> second-story windows, random shots fired. The rioters uprooted wooden bus-stop benches, pulling them out of their concrete bases and setting them on fire. Firemen could not get through – or wouldn't, terrified of being shot at. Two or three television mobile units were damaged, along with fifty to sixty vehicles. It was random chaos, in small disparate patches … Undermanned and overwhelmed, we responded cautiously. Guns were not be used unless an officer clearly felt his life was threatened. Arrests were not encouraged.[164]

In light of the eventual death toll, the officer's statements about the use of firearms are interesting. In actual fact, the bulk of the fatalities occurred on Friday night, when the violence and scale of the riots reached their peak. There was obviously by this stage a clear understanding, often absent in the first half of the 20th century, that deploying firearms and engendering deaths was actually a poor way to control a riot, especially in a neighborhood with widespread grievances and most likely plenty of firearms stored inside the homes. Furthermore, the account also acknowledges that there was little integration between riot tactics and the use of lethal force. At one point, the officer describes his command decision to line up LAPD officers at one end of a street, and Highway Patrol officers at the other, in hindsight acknowledging that "If any shooting had gone down, we would have been firing at one another. Somehow, this never entered our minds."[165] The lack of controlled firearms response became even more critically apparent once the snipers started shooting in earnest:

> Hundreds of sniper calls came into the 77th Street station. Someone would stick his head out of a darkened second-story window and fire once at a police officer. We had no organized response to snipers, so the police would shoot back indiscriminately. By the time I would arrive, everybody was blasting away. It was not easy to get them to stop. I remember the words I used most often: "*Cease fire!*" Or, "*Stop firing!*" I had a megaphone and I just kept yelling those words all night.[166]

The picture of officer response here is ethically and tactically confused. On the one hand, the officers are clearly and legitimately responding to a deadly force threat – being fired upon. On the other, it is evident that their tactical awareness is ill-formed and panicky, justifiably so in a situation more suited to the talents of combat soldiers in a war zone than to police officers patrolling a neighborhood.

The officer writing these accounts was none other than future LAPD Chief Daryl Gates, a powerful figure within the history of Los Angeles law enforcement, and indeed the policing of the nation. In the aftermath of the Watts riots, Gates was acknowledged as something of an expert on riot-control techniques, and traveled around the country delivering lectures on such to various law enforcement agencies. Yet Gates was preoccupied with a simple fact – the force response of officers could quickly reach limits in an epoch where riots, civil disorder, and heavily armed criminals could all generate firepower or tactical complexities beyond the capabilities of regular officers.

Sadly, the Watts riots were not an isolated incident at this time. In 1967, the death toll from major civil disturbances rose horribly. The Newark riots in New Jersey between July 12 and July 17 left 26 people dead and more than 700 injured, and riots during the same month in Detroit reached dizzying heights – 43 dead and 467 injured. In both incidents, the military (either National Guard or regular Army) was deployed, not without subsequent controversy. In the Detroit riots, for example, both the regular Army, in the form of troops from the 82nd Airborne Division, and the Michigan National Guard were deployed, yet the regular soldiers were responsible for only one death, while the National Guard accounted for 12. As the final report on the riots by Cyrus R. Vance, Special Assistant to the Secretary Of Defense, pointed out, very few of the National Guard were black, whereas the percentage in the Regular Army forces was much higher. He further observed that the standards of professionalism, and the leadership provided by the officers, were also deficient when compared to regular troops.

The final report on the Detroit riots contained some sage observations, and it is an important document in understanding the militarization of the police during the 1960s and 1970s. Vance's conclusions point to a confused command-and-control situation once multiple agencies were involved. Vance argues that local and state police should be quickly rationalized under a single commander, thus providing a more holistic and coherent force response. The military would then work in close cooperation with the unified police command.

An additional primary concern of the "Lessons Learned" section of the report is the rules of engagement for soldiery, rather than police officials. Part of the problem, Vance argues, is that the reporting of firearms incidents during a riot can be distorted by multiple voices, leading to an overeager employment of military units when the situation would actually be better contained by the police:

> In Detroit, the best immediately available indicator [of the riot conditions] was the log of incidents requiring police action which was maintained at police headquarters. This information was acquired by monitoring the police radio, cataloging transmissions by precinct, recording separately shooting incidents and total incidents, and producing a spot summary on a half-hourly basis.

> Such indicators, however, have serious deficiencies. First, it is necessary to have a "normal incident level" curve as a base of reference. If this is not available, there is the danger of a distorted picture of the riot activity. Second, in the case of sniping, a single incident may be reported 8 to 10 times or more by different sources who heard a shot fired, and it appears on the police log as multiple incidents. A warning shot, or the shooting out of a street light often may be reported as a sniping incident. Further study should be given to methods of culling out such distortions.[167]

Vance suggests that reported gunshots immediately act as a spur for force multiplication amongst the officers at the scene, including the use of soldiers to compensate for a perceived imbalance in firepower. While this observation may be valid, the shots nevertheless have to be seen in the context of the riot as a whole, and also in terms of preventative firepower – it is far better for police to have more firepower than is initially warranted on the street, than to discover that they have inadequate firepower later on during a critical firefight.

When it comes to the use of force, Vance sees clarity of purpose and force limitations as the main ingredients for future riot-control:

> Orders must be simple, direct and not subject to interpretation. Orders must be written or confirmed in writing as soon as possible. Certain orders should be issued in writing to every soldier, i.e., rules of engagement and the handling of civilians. Such orders could be printed on a small pocket-sized card. It would be most desirable if written orders were issued to all law enforcement personnel.[168]

Subsequent experience in military peacekeeping and law enforcement riot duty shows, however, that written rules of engagement, can only go so far. The critical factor in fire-control is the local commander's influence over his personnel (in the heat of a firefight the persuasive power of a small piece of cardboard tucked away in a pocket is limited) plus the levels of relevant training provided for the officers or soldiers. This is what Gates experienced during the Watts riots and in the Hoxsie shooting. Yet Vance was not entirely unrealistic about the conditions of a firefight and riot, and in the following passage, which addresses soldiers specifically, he explores the need for flexibility in applications of force on the ground:

> The general instruction with respect to civil disturbance rules of engagement and degrees of force described for the military commander as guidance in these areas requires clarification and change to provide more latitude and flexibility in their use. The general policy behind these

> instructions, which is to use the minimum force necessary to restore law and order, is proper and needs no revision or amplification. However, that portion of the letter of instruction issued to the Task Force Commander which prescribes the normal priorities to be used in the application of force should be studied with a view to provide the commander concerned with more flexibility, particularly with respect to the use of riot control chemical agents. The letter of instruction stipulates that normally the application of force will follow this priority:
>
> a. Unloaded rifles with bayonets fixed and sheathed.
>
> b Unloaded rifles with bare bayonets fixed.
>
> c. Riot control agent CS.
>
> d. Loaded rifles with bare bayonets fixed. It is believed that the use of riot control chemical agents should be permitted at any time at the discretion of the senior commander, who should have the authority to delegate its use as far down the chain of command as the company commander level. Further, it is suggested that there is one other degree of force which should be included in the priority listing above: Namely, unloaded rifles with bare bayonets fixed, with ammunition available on the person of the individual soldier, with a restriction that he may load his weapon and fire it only upon the authority from a commissioned officer. If this degree of force is prescribed, commanders must insure, through appropriate orientation, that their troops understand that there is considerable flexibility inherent in this instruction in that, where necessary in specific situations, officers may delegate in advance the authority to give orders to load and fire to senior noncommissioned officers. [169]

The strict stipulations about escalating force seem almost parodic, and one senses the absolute terror amongst officialdom towards the ultimate level of force – soldiers self-authorizing fire upon civilians. It is hard to see how without the strongest levels of officer control, the group of soldiers faced with a rapidly evolving and potentially terrifying riot situation could appreciate the qualitative distinction between "unloaded rifles with bayonets fixed and sheathed" and "unloaded rifles with bare bayonets fixed." Vance seems to sense the limitations in being too prescriptive, and argues that in certain circumstances the decision to open fire can be devolved to lower levels of rank, in his view "senior noncommissioned officers," although *in extremis* it is hard to see how the devolution would not go even further down to private ranks.

Vance's reflections upon the fire control of military forces in riot situations would become painfully apt as the 1960s merged into the 1970s. Above all, what happened on May 4, 1970, on Ohio's Kent State University campus placed a big question mark over whether military personnel, and particularly the National Guard, should be used in law enforcement situations at all.

The Kent State killings have burned their way into American consciousness, and some of the press photographs published from the event have since become visual landmarks of Vietnam-era America. The problems began on May 1, 1970, as student protests spread across the United States when details of US military involvement in Cambodia began to hit the news stands. At the Kent State campus, rioting began on May Day and on May 2 the Reserve Officers' Training Corps (ROTC) building on the campus was burned. Such defiance against federal property led to Governor James Rhodes mobilizing the National Guard, which by May 3 had deployed 1,000 troops. Purely on an ideological level, the mutual hostility between the soldiers and the student protesters was intense, and this friction found physical expression the following day.

The events of May 4 are still rather confusing to unpack, not least because the operating procedures of the National Guardsmen often seem hesitant and unclear. What is certain (according to a subsequent FBI report) is that after a period of rioting and attempts by the soldiers to disperse the crowd (including the use of tear gas), at one point a group of soldiers unleashed an 11-second burst of fire from their .30 M1 Garand rifles. Approximately 60 shots were fired, leaving four students dead and nine wounded.

The social and political fallout from the shootings convulsed US politics and divided social opinion. The big question hanging over the event was quite simply: Why did the Guardsmen open fire? The troops had certainly been the recipients of some rock-throwing, and it seems from subsequent investigations that the Guardsmen were buffeted by violent aggravation (some soldiers present argued that they heard firecrackers go off, and believed that this was gunfire), but not to the extent that warranted the shooting. A Department of Justice summary of the vast subsequent FBI report was skeptical about claims that the Guardsmen opened fire because they believed their lives were under threat:

> We have some reason to believe that the claim by the National Guard that their lives were endangered by the students was fabricated subsequent to the event. The apparent volunteering by some Guardsmen of the fact that their lives were not in danger gives rise to some suspicions. One usually does not mention what did not occur. Additionally, an unknown Guardsman, age 23, married, and a machinist by trade was interviewed by members of the Knight newspaper chain. He admitted that his life was not in danger and that he fired indiscriminately into the crowd. He further stated that the Guardsmen had gotten together after the shooting and decided to fabricate the story that they were in danger of serious bodily harm or death from the students. The published newspaper article

> … quoted the Guardsman as saying: "The guys have been saying that we got to get together and stick to the same story, that it was our lives or them, a matter of survival. I told them I would tell the truth and wouldn't get in trouble that way."[170]

Such an interpretation did not reflect well on the National Guard, and the FBI/Department of Justice tried to clarify whether simple inexperience or a lack of training in civil disturbance rules of engagement were to blame for the incident. Regarding the former, the Department of Justice summary declared:

> Each person who admitted firing into the crowd has some degree of experience in riot control. None are novices. Staff Sergeant Barry Morris has been in the Guard for 5 years, 3 months. He has received at least 60 hours in riot control training and has participated in three previous riots. James Pierce has spent 4 years, 9 months in the Guard. He has an unknown, but probably substantial, number of hours of riot control training and has participated in one previous riot. Lawrence Shafer has been in the Guard for 4 1/2 years. He has received 60 hours of riot control training and has participated in three previous riots. Ralph Zoller has been in the Guard for 4 years. He has received 60 hours of riot training and has participated in two previous riots. All are in G Troop. We do not know how much, if any, riot control training or experience William Herschler has.[171]

So if experience was not lacking amongst the men who opened fire, was there a lack of clarity regarding the rules of engagement? The investigations found, as we have just seen, that most of the National Guard personnel had received some riot-control training and related lectures. In these lectures, the rules of engagement were spelled out, but the possibilities for loose interpretation are apparent:

> Although we believe that the use of minimum force was covered in lectures, we have in our possession a copy of a briefing required to be read verbatim to all troops immediately prior to their employment in a civil disturbance. The orders which they receive are conflicting with regard to the use of weapons. The briefing provides as follows:
>
> "f. Weapons
>
> (2) Indiscriminate firing of weapons is forbidden. Only single aimed shots at confirmed targets will be employed.
>
> (c) Other. In any instance where human life is endangered by the forcible, violent actions of a rioter, or when rioters to whom the Riot Act (of Ohio) has been read cannot be dispersed by any other reasonable means, then shooting is justified."[172]

The provisions of point 2c contain a worrying ambiguity in terms of the rules of engagement. The briefing document does not seem to adequately clarify the distinctions between applying " single aimed shots" at "confirmed targets" and utilizing firepower for the more generalized purpose of riot dispersal. Within this confused context, the Department of Justice/FBI concluded that it was fairly impossible to say what ultimately provoked the shootings, one of the likeliest explanations simply being that one soldier opened fire, releasing a burst of contagious gunfire amongst nervous and harassed soldiers. (Note that Alan Canfora, one of the students wounded during the shootings, has recently claimed to have unearthed an audio recording that allegedly contains the voice of a National Guard commander giving a clear formal order to open fire upon the crowd "Right here!" "Get Set!" Point!" and "Fire!"[173]).

The lawsuits and recriminations ground on for many years. A federal grand jury indicted the Guardsmen in 1974, but all the charges were dismissed, although the ongoing controversy is much harder to dispel. Two clear points seem to emerge, however. First, although the distinction is often drawn between the heavily armed Guardsmen and the unarmed students, this is not the same as saying that the situation was without fear for the soldiers. One of the soldiers present that day, Mike Howley, told Lisa Daniel, a reporter for the *National Guard* magazine, in 2000 to "imagine driving into a city in this country and there's a glow of burning buildings on the skyline, that's how it was coming into Kent State."[174] Furthermore, Daniel explained how the soldiers had none of the protective gear, such as flak vests and shields, issued to modern riot-control units – their bodies were effectively naked against any missiles that were thrown at them. Yet although they were physically unprotected, the soldiers were issued with .30 M1 Garand rifles and bayonets, plus tear gas, meaning that once their non-lethal force options were exhausted, or perceived to be, they had fewer force options but lethal ones.

Daniel goes on to explain that for the National Guard, Kent State provided critical lessons in equipment and tactics:

> Following Kent State, the Army ordered hundreds of thousands of pieces of what is now standard riot gear: batons, flak vests, sideband radios, M3 and M5 chemical agent dispensers, shotguns, bullhorns, searchlights, floodlights and protective masks. With the disbursement of equipment, then Defense Secretary Melvin Laird said "Guardsmen must be placed in a posture where the psychological pressure to resort to deadly force, with its terrible consequences, can be resisted until such time as its use becomes absolutely necessary." From that point on, the National Guard has recognized civil disturbances as a critical mission, rather than a state and local distraction.[175]

The point that the Defense Secretary makes is a critical one, both for soldiers and for police officers. An officer or soldier armed with a multiplicity of force options is more likely to resort to a true escalation of force rather than jump straight to lethal force (although this is not to say that he or she will graduate the response systematically). Combined with better training, the use of force takes on more control, particularly under the guidance of experienced commanders. The Daniel article further explains that, according to Lieutenant Colonel Rick Patterson, a Washington National Guard spokesman, since Kent State the National Guard has worked with better coordination alongside regular law enforcement personnel, the latter relying on the former to provide a "show of force" that acts as a disincentive to rioters. The need for a close working relationship between police and soldiers amidst the smoke, cracked windows, and screams of a riot helps avoid the danger of more unilateral action from military forces, and probably gives National Guard troops the clear sense that they are involved in civilian and domestic policing, rather than entering a war zone.

So what about the US state and local police during this brittle time in American social relations? How did their use of force requirements change? What is interesting is that while the military was attempting to get its head around a more civilian style of use of force, the police were in essence heading in the opposite direction. Police departments around the country saw, quite simply, that the country was becoming more dangerous to police, and situations of social disorder or heavily armed opposition could soon stretch them beyond their own force response.

In his autobiography *Chief*, from which the Watts riots quotations above are taken, Gates also explains how an incident just a month after the Watts riots reinforced the impression that the police needed to transform their force options. LAPD officer Ron Mueller was sent to a house on Surry Street on a disturbance call. He arrived outside the house, knocked on the door, and waited. The door opened and the occupant, Jack Ray Hoxsie, simply opened the door and shot Mueller with a high-powered rifle. Mueller crawled away, badly wounded, just as another officer pulled up outside in his car. He too was shot and injured.

Two officers were now down, resulting in an all-units response that, in Gates' words, resulted in the house being surrounded by more than 50 officers by the time he arrived. He was greeted by a scene of utter chaos. Hoxsie was very well armed, and was going from window to window shooting at the police officers. They were responding with hails of ill-controlled bullets, and Gates suspected that when a third officer was shot the bullet might have come from police lines. Gates also noted that the officers were firing heavy slugs from their shotguns (instead of pellets), these being so powerful they were smashing through the walls of the wooden house and exiting through the roof. The building was so peppered with bullet holes that when tear gas canisters were fired inside they were ineffective – the gas leaked out through the hundreds of new apertures. Finally one brave officer, clad in rudimentary body armor, simply smashed into the house and shot the already wounded Hoxsie, who was taken to hospital. After the incident, Gates reflected, "we were going to have to devise another method for dealing with snipers or barricaded criminals other than our usual indiscriminate shooting."[176]

For Gates, the response to such incidents was to create the SWAT team units, a format that would be followed by almost every police department in the country over the next 30 years. We explore the foundations and operating methods of the SWAT in more detail shortly, but we should remind ourselves that the "militarization" of police force options was a general trend at this time. For example, a *New York Times* article, derived from an Associated Press (AP) story, in March 1968 reveals that "In city after city across America, the police are stockpiling armored vehicles, helicopters and high-powered rifles."[177] In their preparations for riot-response, the article goes on, police departments around the country were investing in pieces of kit that would look more familiar on a battlefield. In the case of Los Angeles, in which Gates was by this time deputy chief, one of the purchases up for consideration was a 20-ton bullet-proof armored personnel carrier that could be equipped with a .30cal machine gun and tear gas and smoke grenade launchers, the main question for the LAPD being whether they could afford its $35,000 cost. (The article notes that the Los Angeles sheriff's office opted for the cheaper alternative by buying an ex-US Army M8 armored car, and simply equipping it for civilian operations.) Detroit police force similarly invested in armored cars, the purchase informed by the grim light of recent experience. As well as purchasing five such vehicles, the department also ramped up its individual officer force options, the shopping basket including 25 sniper rifles, 500 semi-automatic carbines, 300 shotguns, 150,000 rounds of ammunition, 2,000 tear gas grenades, plus 1,200 gas masks. In a similar vein, the police of Tampa, Florida, had invested in 162 shotguns, 5 sniper rifles, and 25 auto/semi-auto rifles, while Monroe county (next to Detroit) had acquired not only a $50,000 riot-control truck, but also 100 rifles and 15,000 rounds of ammunition. Not all the purchases were physical force options, however. Also on the list of acquisitions are tools such as "binoculars," "walkie-talkies," and helicopters (five in the case of Chicago).

We mustn't overstate the military aspects of police policy, of course. At this time there was an equal if not greater emphasis developing upon more effective social policing and preventive work in the community. Yet there seems no doubt that the military was some form of inspiration in developing new force responses. In the same *New York Times* article mentioned, Major Eugene Olaff, a senior operations officer with the New Jersey State

Police, referred to the use of covert officers infiltrating militant organizations as a "military concept in attacking this problem." Such an approach is what Jerome H. Skolnick and James J. Fyfe have labeled the "war model" of policing – simply put, the criminal community is the "enemy" and the police are the allies. Skolnick and Fyfe note that military references litter the way the police discuss themselves:

> Military jargon shows up in virtually any discussion of the police. Police departments are "paramilitary," complete with "chains of command," "divisions," "platoons," "squads," and "details." In many places, patrol officers are "privates" or "troopers ." In virtually all places, officers report not to supervisors, middle managers, or executives, but to sergeants, lieutenants, captains, majors, and colonels. In police training academies, much attention is devoted to close order drill and military courtesy.[178]

Skolnick and Fyfe actually see the militarization of police as a fundamental problem, one that engenders instances of police brutality and excessive force, and which pulls away good street cops into more specialist and potentially violent firearms units. It seems, however, that accusations of police brutality existed even in times when the military model was weak, such as in the frontier towns policed by solitary marshals and sheriffs. Furthermore, the military model serves an important psychological function – it provides officers with a ready-made and understandable model for discipline and a strict chain of command. Buying military equipment, furthermore, is as much about survivability as unleashing force. Hence Daryl Gates, when commenting to reporters about the above-mentioned consideration of an armored personnel carrier, explained: "I realize how valuable it would have been in Watts, where we had nothing to protect us from sniper fire when we tried to rescue wounded officers."[179] The APC does not solely represent crushing force, it also represents the protection of the officers' own humanity.

We return now more squarely to Gates, and the creation of the SWAT teams, the ultimate expression of potential militaristic lethal force in US law enforcement. In Gates' autobiography, he notes how the incident at Surry Street prompted himself and a group of other officers to sit down and look at counterinsurgency warfare training and tactics, such as were being developed in Vietnam, and derive applications for police operations against hostile barricaded individuals. Steadily the specialist group expanded into a core of tactical experts, including officers John Nelson, Mike Hillman, Bob Smitson, Jeff Rogers, and Ron McCarthy. At an informal level, officers attended military training programs with the US Marines at Camp Pendleton, and Gates and his groups "brought in military people to teach them [the police officers] how to respond to sniper fire."[180]

In time, and under receptive chiefs such as Tom Reddin (1967–69), Gates was given permission to form his loose band of highly trained officers into a specialist unit, dedicated to tackling snipers and hostage takers. Eventually, the unit was given its famous label, Special Weapons and Tactics (SWAT), Gates being persuaded to adopt this label rather than his initial offering of Special Weapons Attack Teams, which was perceived as too aggressive. As a counterpoint to Fyfe and Skolnick's reservations about military-style policing, Gates notes that at first the SWAT officers were effectively shunned by regular police officers:

> For a long time they were *persona non grata*, even within the department. That SWAT operates like a quasi-militaristic operation offended some of the brass. I tried to explain the difference. Whereas the military will go in with bazookas and blow the place apart, SWAT's main objective *always* is to get everybody safely out. If anybody gets killed or injured, the operation's a failure, I steadfastly pointed out. To no avail.
>
> Banished from everyday police circles, we kept our training operations secret for years.[181]

Despite its marginalization, and underfunding that had it scrabbling around for the cheapest weapons on the market and making their own assault equipment, the SWAT team nevertheless trained itself to a high degree of proficiency in tactical assault, and on December 8, 1969, it was used on its first mission, the arrest of a Black Panther cell in southcentral Los Angeles.

The operation descended into exactly the type of mission that Gates wanted to avoid. The Black Panthers responded to the police knock on the door with hails of small-arms fire and grenades, and what was intended to be a slick takeover degenerated into a lengthy static firefight, with the SWAT and other assault officers pouring hundreds of rounds into the Panthers' fortified premises.

An interesting moment came towards the end of the action. Realizing that rifle firepower was actually inadequate against the Panthers' headquarters ("all it lacked was a moat"), Gates actually petitioned the US Marines at Camp Pendleton to supply his team with the grenade launcher. Requiring federal permission to do so, Gates convinced Mayor Sam Yorty to approach the Defense Department in Washington to gain approval for the transfer, which impressively he did. At the very last moment, however, the Panthers decided to surrender and the grenade launcher remained in a car parked nearby, a fact unknown to the media who were already creating something of a storm over allegations of police brutality.

The idea of SWAT may have been initially controversial, but it steadily caught on, and soon police departments around United States were marshaling their own equivalents. What provided the inspiration for them to do so is uncertain, although it may simply been the desire to keep up with developments elsewhere in the country. There were doubters, however. In an interview for the *New York Times* in July 1975, Dr Marvin E. Wolfgang, director of the Center for Studies of Criminology and Criminal Law at the University of Pennsylvania, hung a question mark over the rush to adopt the SWAT model:

> The thing that disturbs me about the trend ... is that police departments are adopting this policy before any evaluative research can be done on it. It is the kind of thing that quickly catches on in police departments because of the pressure to be up to date without any knowledge of exactly what they're getting into.[182]

Wolfgang's argument does hold some water. Exciting expertise or developments in law enforcement tend to radiate outwards across the nation steadily, and hence by 1975 around 500 police departments nationally had organized their own SWAT-style units, even amongst small-town departments with little obvious need for military-style force. By April of that year some 467 police departments had undergone SWAT training under an FBI program run at the Unites States Marine Corps (USMC) military base in Quantico, Virginia. The FBI had developed its own SWAT team units in 1973 following a rise in armed engagements and officer fatalities, with 1,500 special agents being put through the program in just two years. A keynote of the *Times* special report was that although the SWAT did have a defined purpose in big-city law enforcement – where the demographics and population density of the city made extreme incidents a greater likelihood – in smaller communities there was the danger that adopting the SWAT model was essentially a form of macho posturing. Nordheimer, the author of the report, looked at some placid, low-population suburbs of the San Francisco Bay area that had adopted SWAT teams armed with Uzi submachine guns, handguns fitted with silencers, and hunting knives strapped in holsters to their chests, with officials even looking into the dizzying possibility of purchasing a helicopter gunship. One suburb police chief resisted the SWAT team route. Chief Vic Cizanckas of Menlo Park was uneasy with this shift, believing that creating a force with heavy firepower simultaneously creates an eagerness to use it, even when it may not be justified. "There are some cops who want to solve all society's problems with an M-16," said Cizanckas. "Some of these men have lost perspective of their role in society and are playing mental games with firearms."[183]

In a nation with an evident enthusiasm for firearms and related gadgetry, there is undoubtedly some truth in Cizanckas' concerns. And yet, we must remember one salient fact about the 1970s, the decade in which most of the SWAT team development took place. The 1970s were by far the most dangerous decade in which to serve as a law enforcement officer. During the 1990s an average of 159 police officers were killed every year in the line of duty. Jump back two decades, and we find an average of 226 officers killed each year, with a peak of 275 in 1974. In total, 2,276 officers died during this decade, although these figures are of all causes, including accidents. To set the age in context with our own, note that between 1973 and 1976 there were 79,400 murders in the United States, with firearms accounting for an average of 66.1 percent of those murders. If we look at comparable data between 2003 and 2006 the percentage of murders committed by firearms is roughly the same, but the total number of deaths has fallen by 13,004.[184] In short, the 1970s were a dangerous time, and given the hike in officer fatalities it is hard to argue that the development of elite tactical forces was not necessary, regardless of the size of the police department. Note also that statisticians can only deal in the concrete data of fatalities and injuries; saying how many police officers' lives have been saved by the SWAT recourse is beyond anyone's knowledge. The fact remains that even today, the overwhelming majority of SWAT team incidents end without shots being fired. In this regard, the visual menace of the SWAT team, backed by the efforts of the hostage negotiation teams, can provide a hostile person with a very clear imperative to surrender, if he or she is still in possession of his faculties.

If we need a further illustration of why SWAT could justify its existence, we might point to the Austin Tower Sniper horror of 1966. On August 1, 1966, the deeply troubled soul that was Charles Whitman took the elevator up through the floors of the 32-storey main administrative building of the University of Texas in Austin. By this stage of events, Whitman had already murdered his wife and his mother, and was bent on one last act of horrific, inexplicable violence. Stored in a wooden crate – Whitman had circumvented security by posing as a research assistant with a delivery to make – was a forbidding arsenal: a 12-gauge sawn-off shotgun; two Remington hunting rifles, one fitted with a telescopic scope; an M1 carbine; and several hunting knives. The bright Texas day was about to become very dark indeed.

Eventually he reached the top floor of the building, at which point he had to climb three flights of stairs to reach the observation deck area. When he reached this point, he was met by the receptionist, Edna Townsley, whom he clubbed unconscious with a rifle butt and dragged behind a couch (she would later die). Remarkably, moments later a couple of sightseers descended into the reception area from the observation deck, and walked past Whitman and the bloodstained floor with nothing more than a hello – they believed that Whitman had been shooting pigeons. As soon as they'd gone, Whitman went up to the observation deck and barricaded the stairs behind him. Mentally and physically, he prepared for his last stand.

More victims soon appeared. Two families heading up to the observation deck were met by hails of fire – two people were killed on the stairs, and another two were critically injured and would end up with permanent disabilities. His blood up, Whitman now turned his attention outwards to the surrounding campus and city district. He put his hunting rifle to his shoulder, squinted down the scope, and began to shoot anyone who stayed long enough beneath his crosshairs.

The bizarre and extreme nature of the unfolding events meant that it took some time for police to gain the full picture, but once they did almost every available law enforcement officer in Austin raced to the campus. They began returning gunfire, but they were faced with the situation beyond anything they were trained for. Whitman was heavily armed, with superb fields of fire from his elevated vantage point. Once the return fire became too heavy, Whitman took advantage of the tower's robust waterspouts, using them as gunports so that he could shoot downwards from a protected position.

The body count was soon stacking up on the streets of Austin. Such was the frustration felt by police that they permitted armed civilians to join them in directing fire against the tower. Their role became invaluable, as was acknowledged by Texas Ranger Ramiro "Ray" Martinez, in his later autobiography *They call me Ranger Ray*:

> I was and am still upset that more recognition has not been given to the citizens who pulled out their hunting rifles and returned the sniper's fire. The City of Austin and the State of Texas should be forever thankful and grateful to them because of the many lives they saved that day. The sniper did a lot of damage when he could fire freely, but when the armed citizens began to return fire the sniper had to take cover.[185]

Martinez would be central to the final end of the shooting. He ascended the tower with Allen Crum, a military trained civilian, and two other officers, and began to pull away at the barricade that blocked the stairs up to the observation level. Whitman, hearing the noise, prepared for a face-off – he hunkered down in the northwest corner of the deck with his M1 carbine, waiting for the target to appear. Eventually Martinez and officer Houston McCoy, with conspicuous bravery, managed to access the observation deck, spotting Whitman in the opposite corner. Martinez leapt into the middle of the room and began firing at Whitman with his revolver. McCoy moved to the side with his shotgun, and saw his target – he hit Whitman with two shots, and Whitman fell to the floor. Taking no chances, the officers put more shots into Whitman as he lay on the ground. Whitman was dead, but he had taken with him 14 people and wounded 31 others.

The gross damage that a single, psychotically motivated individual could do was not lost on police departments around the United States, nor was the fact that there was no formalized procedure or tactical doctrine for dealing with such an incident. The deputization of civilians to add both firepower and, in some cases, military expertise highlighted to the police a concern that would be recurrent over subsequent decades – the fear of being "outgunned." The Austin shootings fed directly into the development of the SWAT teams in the United States. Those who chose not to follow this path, and they became increasingly fewer as the 1970s moved into the 1980s, ran the risk, however remote, that another Charles Whitman could appear in their communities.

TRAINED TO SURVIVE?

We have now discussed at some length the tactical elite of the US law enforcement community, but what of the regular beat officer? The SWAT teams were trained to deal with the anomalies of police work – the riot, crazed sniper, or hostage-rescue mission – but as we pointed out in our introduction, the vast majority of police time is spent in far more routine and mundane activities. Nevertheless, several incidents in the 1970s also shone the spotlight on the survivability and the deadly force handling of the regular police officer, few more so than the Newhall, California shooting of April 5, 1970.

This landmark incident began with one of the most common police procedures, a traffic stop. Admittedly in this case there was heightened tension about the stop, as two California Highway Patrol (CHP) officers, Walt Frago and Roger Gore, had just received a report that the occupants of the car had been seen brandishing a gun after an argument between two drivers. With the time approaching midnight, the two officers then spotted a suspect vehicle, a red Pontiac driven by one Bobby Davis, with his associate Jack Twinning in the passenger seat. The vehicles stopped close to one another, and the two officers stepped out to approach the vehicle, Gore heading for the driver-side, and Frago towards the passenger door. The two policemen were both carrying .357 revolvers, and Frago had a shotgun. Inside the suspect car, by contrast, was a far greater stash of firearms, including sawn-off shotguns, a Colt M1911 .45 handgun, revolvers, and rifles – the two men had actually been out in the desert testing firearms out for an intended robbery. Frago and Gore were walking into a death trap.

At first, it appeared as if Davis and Twinning would comply with the search demands. Davis disembarked, and walked to the rear of his vehicle where he was searched by Gore. Frago closed in on the passenger door, and it was at that point that Twinning burst from the door and opened fire with a Smith & Wesson Model 28 revolver. Frago went down with two fatal shots in his chest. Twinning then switched his fire to Gore, who pulled his revolver and returned the shots. At that point Davis managed to create some distance, draw a .38 revolver, and kill Gore on the spot.

A traffic stop had devolved into two fatal shootings in a matter of seconds, and was about to get worse. Another CHP cruiser pulled up on the scene, this one containing officers George Alleyn and James Pence. Seeing what had occurred, Alleyn and Pence immediately took cover behind their car doors and began firing, while the criminals blazed back with all their resources, plus the weapons that had been used by the dead officers. During this gun battle, problems in police weapons training and technology began to emerge. The frenzy of the engagement caused Alleyn to eject a live cartridge from his Remington 870 shotgun, reducing the number of rounds he had available to fire. Pence, after being hit in the chest and legs by .45 bullets, then struggled to reload his revolver manually cartridge by cartridge, as CHP officers were not equipped with speed-loading devices. Furthermore, the two beleaguered officers were simply outgunned by the well-equipped criminals, and both were tragically killed in the shootout. Note also that during the firefight, a passing civilian motorist, 31-year-old Gary Ness, showed unusual pluck by leaping out of his car, picking up the weapons of the fallen men, and adding to the firepower of the police officers. Ness actually managed to score a hit on Davis, who was injured in the chest by a fragment of a ricocheting bullet fired by Ness.

The Newhall incident eventually played itself out in the meaningless fashion so often seen in such terrible events. Twinning and Davis fled the scene and split up. Twinning would later shoot himself in a house 3 miles away, surrounded by police, and Davis was captured, and would be sent to prison for life. (He narrowly avoided a death sentence after the California Supreme Court ruled against it as a form of punishment in 1972.) For the CHP, and the broader law enforcement community, the somber post-shooting analysis began, however. Massad Ayoob, one of America's foremost authorities on deadly force engagements, has described the Newhall massacre as the moment when "the movement called Officer Survival was born."[186] This movement switched the focus of police training more squarely to using force to stay alive. The first lesson to emerge was essentially a new respect for a criminal. Popular tradition represented criminals as being poorly armed opportunists, and the police well-armed professionals. Newhall showed this to be a gross simplification; the fact was that the two Newhall shooters were both very well armed, far better armed, in fact, than the policemen who faced them, and could use their weapons with confidence. Note also that once the two criminals had split up, although one chose to go to his grave early, the other quickly surrendered after being surrounded in a parking lot by officers who were stacking up serious firepower.

Second, it became apparent that although CHP officers had conducted their basic firearms training with .38cal revolvers, the three officers who fired revolvers at Newhall were carrying .357 magnums, far more powerful handguns with different recoil and handling characteristics not adequately reflected in the training. Third, there was insufficient cumulative experience between the four officers who were killed – none of the officers had more than two years' experience in law enforcement, although a background as Vietnam veterans meant that three of the officers managed to return fire with commitment and intensity. The lack of a speed-loading device, however, was an awful deficit for officers clawing desperately for survival. Pence was killed during the process of reloading, as he struggled to fill the empty chambers of his gun one at a time, and all the while Twinning was moving in closer with his Colt .45 automatic. At the very moment when Pence dropped a cartridge into the last empty chamber and snapped the cylinder shut, Twinning was upon him. "Got you now!" he shouted, before mercilessly blasting Pence in the back of the head.[187] The last key lessons were procedural. The sequence of events during the traffic stop increased the vulnerability of the officers at the scene, from the way they approached the vehicle doors to Frago holding his shotgun "at port" – resting the stock on his hip with the barrel in the air – a poor position from which to deploy the weapon quickly.

The outcome of Newhall was a sequence of modifications to police procedure, both in the CHP and in the wider police force, which have undoubtedly saved dozens of officers' lives since they were put into place. The CHP itself standardized the firearms training around a more powerful .38 load, and also introduced speed loaders for all officers. Procedures for making both routine and felony traffic stops were tightened up. Today, officers learn to control traffic stops at every moment, including the place where the vehicles are stopped (stopping further back from a suspect vehicle gives the officer greater response time if the stop turns into an armed engagement), calling in the vehicle and suspect data before getting out to approach the suspect vehicle, putting one officer (if two officers are present at the scene) in a position of cover ready to engage while the other officer inspects the driver's documents, and calling for backup when there is the least suspicion of danger. The CHP actually used the word "Newhall" as an acronym for key points to remember during traffic stops, and this is used today throughout the United States as an aide memoire:

- N – Never approach a danger situation until you're adequately prepared and supported.

- E – Evaluate the offense and determine if you might just be dealing with something more dangerous than it looks.
- W – Wait for backup.
- H – Have a plan [in other words, don't just wade into a situation without planning every move].
- A – Always maintain the advantage over the opponent.
- L – Look for the unusual. [Ayoob notes: "The first two officers had reason to believe that the Pontiac contained one or more armed men, yet they ignored the warning and left their cover to approach them."]
- L – Leave the scene when in doubt.

If Newhall was a transitional event in the thinking about officer survivability in the use of deadly force, it was still just part of an explosion of official and professional analysis of police shootings that had begun in earnest by the late 1960s.

STUDYING DEADLY FORCE

In an age in which civil liberties became a prominent social philosophy, combined with an emergent anti-authoritarianism, it was inevitable that the police use of deadly force would come under increased scrutiny. Some of this scrutiny was, admittedly, of the most egregiously political variety, informed by the popular adoption of campus socialism. For example, in 1975 the Center for Research on Criminal Justice published the book *The Iron Fist and the Velvet Glove*, an overtly Marxist analysis of the US police community as an agent of class and race repression. Its take on the SWAT teams, for example, was far less charitable or wholesome than that taken by SWAT founders such as Gates:

> The actual behavior of SWAT seems to contradict its avowed purpose of employing restraint in curbing incidents of urban violence. Quite to the contrary, the net effect of SWAT's police-state tactics is to induce fear and outrage on the part of the community it purports to protect. The actions taken against the SLA and the Panthers seem designed less to minimize violence than to serve as a warning to anyone or any group that seriously challenges the forces of repression. The SWAT concept is an indication of the extent to which the police are willing and able to use the most brutally effective military tactics to ensure "order" at any cost in a time of social upheaval and mass discontent.[188]

Such analysis became commonplace during the 1960s and 1970s, and bred something of an animosity between the police community and academia. (Admittedly, those who took such positions had to perform some protracted class analysis to explain why working-class police officers were the tools for repressing thoroughly middle-class students.) Some officers even felt that this hostility made police more likely to use force against a protesting student crowd than many other social groups. A detective interviewed for the *New York Times* in July 1968, for example, spoke candidly: "Most cops I know will walk into the mouth of a cannon. But they're terrified of words. Don't forget, most cops don't have any education, they're inarticulate."[189] The detective goes on to say that this is one reason why, in his opinion, officers show more tolerance towards black Americans than they do towards students.

Yet alongside the frictions between police and the colleges, there was also a movement within law enforcement itself, and from related and more neutral organizations and individuals, to better understand the dynamics and realities of deadly force. This movement was spurred by various concerns and signs of the times. A deeper look into the use of deadly force was in many ways simply a natural progression of the professionalization of the police that had begun back in the Progressive era. By the 1960s and 1970s, major police departments nationwide were generally looking to rationalize all practices, bringing an element of controllability and understanding that would lead, hopefully, to better public relations and fewer civil actions against the police.

The initial major studies into police deadly force, and indeed even studies today, were hampered by the general lack of standardized and centrally collated information on police homicides and shootings. For decades, police departments had felt little motivation to zealously record every pulling of the trigger, and to make that information available to a public who might be potentially looking for scalps. Two sources of data were the FBI's Uniform Crime Reports, built upon police shooting data sporadically provided by police departments, and the Center for Health Statistics' *Vital Statistics*, with figures compiled from death certificates registered with state health authorities.[190] There were deficiencies in both these sources of information, however, and far better results were achieved by delving into the records of those police departments, aided by institutions such as the IACP, that did retain figures on the use of deadly force.[191]

Searching through the newspaper archives from the 1960s and 1970s, we get a sense of the stir these reports created. Geoffrey Alpert and Lorie Fridell state: "Police authority to use deadly force against citizens represents one of the most dramatic, most ominous powers of government."[192] Any anomalies or worrying patterns in these powers, therefore, were hot news for the media, and the headlines include "Albany to Study Curbs on Police

Gun Use," "Views on Police Shooting Rules Given," "US Agency Moves to Head Off Racial Conflicts Over Allegations of Police Misuse of Force," and "Deadly Force Study Dead-Ends."

Although space does not allow a full analysis of the mass of police shooting studies during the 1960s, 1970s, and into the 1980s, we can pick out some general themes and important data. First, overall there seemed to be a general nationwide decline in the number of police homicides in major US cities (populations of 250,000+), at least based on the available data collated from a mix of police department files and Uniform Crime Reports. One study suggested that in 1971, 353 individuals were shot dead by police, whereas by 1984 that figure had dropped to 172.[193]

Having said this, regardless of the numbers, the racial and social profile of those killed was often highlighted, if not as a cause for concern, then at least as a recognition that problems within certain communities predisposed them towards a head-on experience of police deadly force. In New York City, NYPD records obtained by the journalist David Burnham in 1973, covering the period from 1970 to 1973, indicated that three out of every five people shot dead by the police were African-Americans. Of the people shot dead by the police, 59 percent were black, 19 percent white and 12 percent Hispanic. The population densities for these groups in New York, by contrast, were 65 percent white, 19 percent black and 15 percent other.[194] With balance, Burnham also pointed out that these killing rates also roughly matched the arrest rates for violent crime for each specific community, suggesting a concentration of violent offences within the black community that makes the deadly force figures more comprehensible. Such a conclusion was not universal amongst the studies of this period, however. At least five studies highlighted similar disproportionate weighting towards blacks as the victims of police deadly force, with percentages ranging from 50 percent nationally through to nearly 80 percent in specific localities, depending on what numbers were crunched. Some argued that the greater likelihood of an African-American being shot by a police officer pointed to a clear racial bias in the police force, even if that bias was based upon expectations that a black opponent was more dangerous than a white one, rather than upon outright racism. Others took the position that police arrests in black neighborhoods did indeed expose the officer to more danger, leading to the officer reaching for his gun.

Marshall Meyer was one analyst who looked at what happened immediately prior to shootings, and explored whether this could explain the racial make-up of police shootings. His findings (his study was published in 1980), based on a study of LAPD officers between 1974 and 1978, are complex to interpret. Looking at black, white, and Hispanic opponents during police shootings, he did indeed find that black opponents were more likely to be perceived as reaching for weapons or disobeying a command to halt (leaving them open to the fleeing felon rule). In terms of actually using a weapon, however, or assaulting a police officer, the white and Hispanic victims proved to be more likely to do so.[195]

Interpreting such figures is a political and social minefield, and this is only the tip of the iceberg of studies of police violence during this period. Academics and officers scrutinized everything from the effects of time and locality on shootings, through to the percentage of hits scored out of the total numbers of shots fired by a police department. The latter investigations produced some particularly interesting figures, which Alpert and Fridell unpack here:

> Geller and Karales (1981) reported that 18 percent of the shots fired in Chicago during the period 1974–1978 hit a citizen; of those hit, 25 percent were killed. Fyfe (1978) reported a higher percentage of hits (31 percent) in New York City, as well as a higher percentage (33 percent) of hits resulting in death. Horvath (1987) collected statewide data from Michigan and reported that 32 percent of the shots fired hit a citizen and 35 of those incidents resulted in a fatality.[196]

Such figures gave a striking insight into not only the frequency of deadly force incidents, but also the ability of the officers in handling their firearms once they were pulled from their holsters. Other exposures of the world of deadly force found that a significant percentage of shootings (between 20 and 28 percent) actually occurred while officers were off duty, but still carrying their firearms. These figures were particularly telling, because they indicated that police officers were having to switch from a relaxed state of mind to the random terrors of an armed confrontation without the official system of preparation and backup around them. Few incidents better typify how desperate such a situation could become, while also providing some human balance to the world of data handling, than what occurred to Los Angeles Deputy Sheriff Gerald Douglas Slagle one Saturday in November 1979, as explained in a Los Angeles County District Attorney report.[197]

Enjoying off-duty time, Slagle headed down to the local Safeway store at around 7.00pm, accompanied by his three-year-old daughter, Jennifer. As every parent knows, few small children are capable of passing by the mechanized rides at the entrance to many stores, and Jennifer was no exception. Slagle lifted his child into the ride, and it was then that he noticed two men, pushing an empty trolley a bit too quickly into the market. Slagle was no doubt practiced in recognizing suspicious individuals, and he began following the men into the store, with Jennifer in tow. Then Slagle's fears materialized, as one man pulled a ski mask over his face and drew a revolver. Although he couldn't see the other man's hands, that suspect also had a firearm, later vaguely identified as a sawn-off longarm, such as a shotgun.

A FIGHT IN THE STREET.

A reasonably accurate depiction of a 19th-century gunfight. Note how the cowboys take aimed shots (shooting from the hip was not recommended) and the dangerous position of bystanders. (The Granger Collection/TopFoto)

Samuel Colt (1814–62) revolutionized America's relationship with firearms, giving the masses, including criminals and police, effective revolver handguns. (The Granger Collection/TopFoto)

Wild Bill Hickok (1837–76) was one of the United States' most famous early lawmen, his notoriety largely resting on his skill with a gun. (2001, Topham Picturepoint)

57 READE STREET, NEW YORK 263

SMITH & WESSON REVOLVERS
MILITARY AND POLICE

Model 1902, Hand Ejector, 6 Shot

Double action. solid frame, swing-out cylinder. Length of barrels, 4, 5 or 6½ inch. Blue or nickel finish. Rubber stocks. .32 caliber, for .32 W. C. F. cartridges. 38 caliber for .38 long Colt or S. & W. Special cartridges.
Price, $16.00

MODEL 1903.

Similar to Model 1902 but chambered for .32 S. & W. long C. F. cartridges. Blue or nickel finish. Rubber stocks. Length of barrels, 3¼, 4¼ or 6 inch. Price, $14.00.

Model 1905

Same as Model 1902 but shape of grip is different and is fitted with finely checked stocks. Blue or nickel finish. .32 calibre for .32 W. C. F. cartridges. .38 caliber, for .38 long Colt or S. & W. Special cartridges. Length of barrels, 4, 5 or 6½ inch.
Price, $17.00

Model 1908

Made on same pattern as Model 1905. Blue or nickel finish. .44 calibre for .44 S. & W. Special or .44 S. & W. Russian cartridges. Length of barrels, 4, 5, 6½ or 7½ inches. Price, $21.00.
With target sights, $22.50.

Model 1909

Frame and trigger guard in one piece. Barrel and sight in one. New locking device. Spiral springs. Safety rebounding block. Automatic extraction. Chambered for .38 S. & W. cartridges. 3¼ or 4 inch barrels, nickel or blue finish. Price, $14.00.

HAMMERLESS SAFETY REVOLVER.

This revolver, intended for pocket use, is so constructed that no external force can affect it, and the hammer cannot be operated except at the instant of deliberate firing. Made in blued or nickel finish, with automatic shell extractor and safety attachment.
.32 caliber, 2, 3, 3½ or 6 in. barrel, $14.00.
.38 calibre, 3¼. 4. 5, or 6 in. barrel... $15.00

)86754 SMITH & WESSON REVOLVERS.
redit: The Granger Collection, New York

Top right: The Smith & Wesson company began manufacturing and selling firearms in 1852, utilizing methods of mass production to produce huge volumes of handguns. (The Granger Collection/TopFoto) Top left: By the late 1800s, law enforcement was one of S&W's major markets, for which the company produced a dedicated range of revolvers. (World History Archive/TopFoto)

A late 19th-century print depicts city police arresting burglars. Three levels of force are in use – physical restraint, batons, and firearms, summing up the continuum of force available at the time. (Bettman/Corbis)

Top left: Gangster Clyde Barrow kneels beside his automobile, displaying his arsenal of revolvers, rifles, and pump-action shotguns. (Photo by Imagno/Getty Images)
Top right: A police officer practices his pistol marksmanship at the range – such was the limit of firearms training for many officers in the early–mid 20th century. (Photo by Carl Mydans/Getty Images)

An FBI agent tries out a Thompson submachine gun, which could fire at a full-auto rate of up to 1200rpm. Ironically, a major source of gangster 'Tommy guns' was robberies from police arsenals. (TopFoto)

Top left: Early experiments in police body armor, such as that seen here in the 1930s, involved medieval-style plate metal chest protectors. (General Photographic Agency/Getty Images)
Top right: Officers during the 1930s test out their associate's body armor by firing at point blank range into his chest, a test liable to endanger them as much as the target officer. (General Photographic Agency/Getty Images)

Riot control has always been a major challenge for police departments. While the 19th century often saw riots smashed by lethal force, during the 20th century there was an increasingly reliance upon non-lethal means, such as the fire hoses and tear gas seen here in this 1940s street disturbance. (Photo by Bob Landry/Getty Images)

US National Guard troops face a student protest during the 1960s. Note the limited range of force options at their disposal, with little between physical restraint and lethal force in the form of rifle fire. (Time Life Pictures/Getty Images)

The rough police handling of the protests outside the Democratic National Convention in August 1968 was a public relations disaster, and highlighted the need for more comprehensive training in riot control. (TopFoto)

Top left: Police officers practice on the range with M3 submachine guns, an example of how many police forces were keen to 'upgun' themselves during the post-war years. (Bettman/Corbis)
Top right: A modern SWAT team conducts urban assault training armed with Heckler & Koch MP5 submachine guns. The MP5 is popular within law enforcement for its ability to deliver automatic fire accurately and with controllable recoil. (TopFoto/Image Works)

Los Angeles, May 18, 1974. An LAPD policeman watches as the hideout of members of the Symbionese Liberation Army burns to the ground following a dramatic shootout with Los Angeles officers. The SLA incident was a high-visibility SWAT action. In total some 9,000 rounds of ammunition were discharged during the engagement, making it one of the largest police shootouts in history and igniting controversy about the paramilitary style of units such as SWAT. (Popperfoto/Getty Images)

State troopers brandish their weapons during the Watts Riots, August 1, 1965. Deployment of infantry and armored formations of the California National Guard was critical in bringing the riots under control. (Express/Getty Images)

An officer experiences the full force of the taser during a training exercise. The latest versions of the Taser induce complete muscular paralysis without affecting functions such as respiration, heartbeat, and bowel and bladder control. Such devices have added a important new stage in the continuum of force, providing an alternative in some situations to impact weapons and firearms.(Photo by Tony Savino/Corbis)

Modern police firearms training aims to improve marksmanship and weapons handling. It also uses video simulations to enhance the officer's use-of-force decision making and snap-shooting abilities. (Above: Photo by Anna Clopet/Corbis) (Left: Photo by David McNew/Getty Images)

US Army tanks from Fort Hood, Texas, patrol the perimeter of the Branch Davidian compound outside of Waco, Texas, in late March 1993 during the Branch Davidian standoff. The Waco siege saw the US federal authorities deploy the maximum deadly force resources, and the disastrous outcome of the siege reinforced a general public perception of an over-militarized operation. (TopFoto/Image Works)

Slagle, obviously intensely aware of his daughter's presence by his side, hung back. Although off-duty, he was still armed with his .38 service revolver, and burdened by the responsibility that came with his job, whether off-duty or not. He pushed Jennifer down behind the right wheel of a vehicle, drew his gun and waited. The two men emerged in urgent fashion from the store, heading directly towards Slagle's position. As they came close, Slagle advertised his presence – "Police, freeze!" The two men started, then went down the wrong path once more. The man with the longarm, later identified as Manuel Castillo Perez, screamed back at Slagle "Don't do it! Don't do it!" He then lifted his gun and fired once, Slagle snapping back with two shots, one of which struck Perez but didn't put him down. The two robbers split up, Perez moving across the parking lot while his associate managed to get away from the supermarket and into a getaway car. Meanwhile, Perez had moved across the lot in such as way as to negate the cover provided by the car. More shots were exchanged, and then the whole dynamics of the engagement changed, as explained in the District Attorney's report:

> Slagle glanced again at Jennifer and saw she was now down on the ground bleeding from a wound to her head. Slagle, believing his daughter was dead, stood up in disregard for his own safety and looked for Perez. He saw Perez in front of the store. Slagle fired his last two rounds at Perez, missing him, both rounds hitting the concrete exterior portion of the front of the market.[198]

Here the shootout ended, and Perez slipped away (he was later arrested). Jennifer was rushed to the local hospital with a serious gunshot wound to the head. She died at 7.53pm.

This horrifying and terribly sad incident illustrates the fact that police officers don't actually step out of danger once they sign off duty for the day. In fact, some studies of police shootings actually found that the higher rates of firearms discharge for African-American police officers was partly connected with the fact that such officers lived in more dangerous neighborhoods, where they were more likely to be involved in off-duty shootings.

All this new data opened a new window on the world of police shootings, and demonstrated that deadly force was not a simple "threat = response" equation, but a dynamic relationship between multiple psychological, social, procedural, and tactical elements, all leading to the final shot. For the police chiefs and the officers on the street, the studies brought changes. With the analysis throwing a more searching spotlight on police shooting practices, there came the threat of increased litigation against both individuals and entire local or state police departments.

THE FORCE CONTINUUM AND TRAINING

By 1978, the liability status of police officers had changed significantly. In 1961, the US Supreme Court heard the Monroe v. Pape case, which centered on the Chicago PD's highly aggressive interrogation of a black man suspected of murder. The result was that state and local law enforcement officers became personally liable for violations of constitutional civil rights. This legal shift was a critical one for the officers on the street, as police officers had been largely held above liability for constitutional offences. The power of the citizen to respond to such infringements was increased commensurately in 1978, when, after the Supreme Court considered Monell v. New York Department of Social Services, local municipal entities could be held responsible for officers' transgressions. Now more than ever, police departments sought systems and measures to protect themselves against ending up in court.

One consequence was that police departments began to develop the concept of the Force Continuum, or the Continuum of Force (an equally loaded phrase). We have already mentioned CoFs in earlier chapters, but it was during the 1970s that they took actual shape as guidance tools for police training. In essence, the CoF was implemented to provide officers with a sense of graduated choice in terms of their force responses. Police departments wanted officers to work through, at least from a training point of view, all the force options before selecting their guns.

The LAPD published one of the earliest CoFs, rendering it in the shape of a barometer with the mildest force options at the bottom but getting increasingly tough on the way up as the situation became "hotter". It was structured as follows:

Life endangering attack	Deadly force
Attack with dangerous weapons	Self-defense techniques
Bodily attack	Control holds
Aggressive resistance	Pain compliance
Passive resistance	Firm grip control
Cooperation compliance	Verbalization
SUSPECT'S ACTIONS	**OFFICER'S REACTIONS**

CoFs seemed to offer a useful way in which officers could understand appropriate levels of response to definite threats, yet taking the broader view many people have subsequently argued that CoFs create more problems than they solve. Reflecting on today's situation, John Peters and Michael Brave, writing for *Police and Security News*, note that:

> Today, there are more than 50 use-of-force ladders, circles, stair steps, wheels, and other uniquely shaped continuums used as visual training aids to assist officers in learning how much force to apply in a seemingly never-ending combination of situations. Many of these continuums are complex, ambiguous, confusing, and difficult to use, while others are deceptively simple and seemingly straightforward.[199]

Peters and Brave point out that there is no single, definitive CoF, as one might expect, but a variety of models each designed according to departmental policy or according to the philosophy of individual trainers. Proceeding from this fact, CoFs actually present two major problems to any police officer trying to implement one in real life. First, force situations often develop at a speed beyond cognitive thought (see Chapter 6) – it's very hard for an officer to think "Where does this situation lie on the Continuum of Force?" when someone close to him is reaching inside his jacket and pulling out what looks like a knife. Furthermore, the CoF is complicated by a multiplicity of factors. What if an opponent holding a gun is a juvenile, or a pregnant woman? The CoF could authorize lethal force in these circumstances, but the officer might feel it inappropriate because of the nature of the person standing before him. Also, during the sheer violence of an encounter, the officer may well transgress the CoF because of the split-second decisions that arise from strong emotions. In his book *City Police*, Jonathan Rubenstein quotes an officer who had to grapple with a man who had just stolen his gun. The violence of the encounter makes the precision of the CoF appear a little too clean:

> We were rolling around, you know, and he still had the gun and I was holding on to his hand so he couldn't shoot me. I was biting him on the face and kicking, my mouth was filling up with his blood and he was screaming. Then he gave up, I just stood there holding my gun and I really wanted to kill him. I did, but I just couldn't shoot. I smashed him with the butt.[200]

On a purely human level, the officer's final application of the gun butt is entirely understandable. Here was an assailant who just a few moments previously had been trying to put a bullet into the officer in a life-or-death struggle, yet once he finally complied no doubt expected to be treated with full attention to his human rights. Yet technically, once the fight was over the suspect threat drops well down the force continuum, and probably made the pistol whipping (a technique itself well off the CoF chart) a legal example of excessive force.

Here lies the doublebind of the CoF. While technically aiding an officer to make the right force decision, it could simply provide ammunition for prosecutors who pore over the fine gradations of response options outside of the sheer terrifying dynamics of the actual incident. A jury, for example, may think that when an officer arrives on scene at an incident he mechanically works his way up through the force ladder, whereas in actual fact he may be thrust straight into the higher levels of the CoF by the realities of the situation.[201]

An interesting angle on the CoF is presented by John Bostain, an instructor with the Federal Law Enforcement Training Center (FLETC) in Brunswick, Georgia. In interview with Jenna Solari, also of the FLETC, Bostain expresses a generally low opinion of the CoF model:

> Solari: So John, as a former officer and a current law enforcement trainer, what do you recommend we do with all the Use of Force Models and continuums that are out there?
>
> Bostain: Jenna, I get asked that question all of the time. In short, I think we should do away with them. That's what we've done here at FLETC. We have replaced the model with more legal training, which focuses on the Constitutional standard set forth by the United States Supreme Court. From the first week of training, FLETC students are exposed to Graham v. Connor and its requirements. [See the following chapter for more about Graham v. Connor.] After their initial legal training, the Constitutional standard is reinforced almost daily by our Firearms Division and Physical Techniques Division. The legal concepts are further reinforced through reality based training programs which include a use of force lab that focuses exclusively on use of force decision making skills. But, in my opinion, the most important thing we can do is focus on teaching students to articulate themselves in written reports that conform to the Constitutional standard. We have been conducting training like this for the past two years, and all of it has been without the use of a continuum.[202]

Bostain argues against the CoF on the basis that it is essentially unnecessary – constitutional standards provide the legal framework for force response, while, more importantly, rigorous training offers the practical tools for appropriate and split-second force judgments. Not everyone agrees, but returning to the 1960s and 1970s, we find that the training context for CoF is patchy and uncertain.

Police firearms training throughout the 1950s to the 1970s still hinged around highly traditional bullseye shooting, mixed with or dominated by elements from the FBI's Practical Pistol Course (PPC). Note that during this period no federally sanctioned standard for firearms training emerged, meaning that the quality and emphasis of the training varied wildly between states and local departments. Training courses were put together according to local practices, beliefs, and personalities. Nevertheless, the PPC was by far the most popular starting point for police training courses – a 1977 survey showed that nearly two-thirds of those police departments that responded to the survey used the PPC as their model for training, with only 11 percent still using the bullseye system as the primary method.[203] The need to switch to a more combat-oriented model of firearms training had emerged forcefully in the 1950s. Certain departments were prodded into further action partly by litigation. In New York, for example, the 1955 Meistinsky v. City of New York case developed when a police officer pulled his gun and attempted to shoot a hostage taker during a robbery. This bold move simply resulted in compounding someone's already bad day by hitting a nearby hostage (the aforementioned Meistinsky). Subsequent analysis of the event showed that the officer had not received proper training in firing his revolver double-action, resulting in his shots going off to the right of the intended point of aim.

Press reports focusing on the NYPD's quality of firearms handling waver between admiring reports of lethal dead-eye professionalism and hand-wringing over a perceived incompetence with guns. For example, the *New York Times* of June 22, 1957, excitedly reported on an NYPD trial conducted at New York State Maritime College at Fort Schuyler in the Bronx. The trial was designed to test whether the NYPD would adopt the FBI shooting model in its entirety, and 38 recruits, all destined to graduate within a week, were the guinea pigs. All but five of the officers had been trained in traditional "arm's length" target-shooting, firing a total of 280 rounds during their academy training. The remaining five officers had undergone FBI training, firing a total of 550 rounds in all manner of positions and techniques – prone, left-handed, rapid fire, firing from behind cover etc. From the trial, the 33 conventionally trained officers took an average score of 94 out of 100 shooting at static targets from their familiar standing posture. Then up stepped the five "top gun" equivalents, who promptly "managed to hit the torso of a human silhouette target with every one of forty rounds fired from three different positions from ranges of twenty yards down to two yards."[204] The top five shooters from the traditionally trained group were then put through the same combat course, at which they were described as "no match" for the more dynamic officers.

NYPD investment seems to have proceeded apace, for the very next year the *New York Times* covered a different story, revolving around the installation of one of the earliest varieties of firearms training simulators. The German-designed system consisted of a 16mm movie projector throwing films of criminal incidents onto a 5 x 8ft paper screen. The 20-second film clips focused as much on decision-making skills as on shooting technique – in one, a woman screams from an open window, before a man armed with a knife appears behind her (in this instance the officer is meant to refrain from shooting owing to the proximity of the third party). In another, a man runs into view, then turns and fires a revolver at the officer. Should the officer shoot, the film stops at the moment of detonation, and a red back light then shines clearly through the penetration hole on the paper screen, showing the bullet's point of impact. The officer in charge of the new machinery at the Police Academy, Captain William P. McCarthy – who at this point had recently referred to NYPD officers as some of the worst shots in the country – pointed out that the only problem for the police department was that there were 24,000 men on the police force, but it took around one hour for just 12 men to fire five bullets at the screen.[205]

What we see in the post-war decades is the steady movement towards pressure testing and "shoot/don't shoot" scenarios in firearms training. Simulators of varying sophistication spread amongst the larger police departments, as did the variety of shooting ranges (and the amount of money invested in them). The money sunk into firearms facilities became considerable in some departments – in October 1970 the LAPD received $250,000 in federal money to implement a new firearms training course using equipment "designed to place trainee officers in simulated stress conditions where they must make split-second decisions whether to shoot or to hold their fire."[206]

Yet the value of such training has been questioned by several leading researchers. Here Morrison and Vila argue that we should not look for any clear research-led or analytical model behind post-war law enforcement firearms training:

> Police handgun training was common by 1950, but the degree of its contribution to police gunfighting outcomes is open to question. Neither doctrinal, technical nor tactical developments were driven by research or program evaluation, but, rather, by trainers' various notions about good sense as constrained by resources. This has allowed departments throughout the twentieth century to offer a variety of approaches without usefully investigating their outcomes. Trainers' beliefs rest heavily on criteria rooted in their personal experiences as street officers, irregularly gathered anecdotal evidence and what they came to view as effective at the training range.[207]

Morrison and Vila are right to argue that there is much that is haphazard in the history of police training. They go on to illustrate their point partly through pointing out the inconsistencies of police firearms qualification (the standards each officer is required to meet before carrying a gun out onto the street) from place to place. Qualification became more the norm in the post-war period, but the "threshold scores" were not standardized nationally and officers who failed to qualify simply retook the test (often immediately) until they did, without extra training. Vila and Morrison also point to the woolly thinking behind some of the scoring systems – an NYPD requalification test, for example, allowed an officer to miss 25 percent of his or her shots without failure, even though missing with one in four shots in a real-life urban encounter was potentially catastrophic.

We will assess the value of firearms training more fully in the next chapter (particularly in terms of whether it results in improved results on the street), but here we should note that although such training did, and still does, contain anomalies and flaws, there did seem to be a general beneficial movement, at least in terms of officer awareness. What the 1960s and 1970s brought to a more self-conscious level was that most shootings were dynamic, close-range, fast-moving incidents for which traditional training had limited applications. Finding the first cause of this impetus is problematic, not least because elements such as the PPC predated World War II. In essence, a fusion of militarization, an increased liability environment, more academic scrutiny of lethal force, plus the snowballing attempts of police departments to professionalize every aspect of their service, all added to improved firearms handling. There was a definite self-consciousness now about the enormity of carrying guns in public. In 1972, for example, the NYPD developed a new set of guidelines for officers, tightening up the rules on when it was permissible to pull the trigger. Shooting at a fleeing felon was only permissible if the felon posed a direct danger to another officer or citizen, and officers were no longer allowed to shoot at moving vehicles nor to fire warning shots. In addition, any firearms discharge was to be investigated by a Firearms Discharge Review Board (FDRB), which would bring disciplinary action against any officer who took a shot outside the guidelines. At the same time, from 1970 the Firearms and Tactics Section of the NYPD also began an 11-year study into the dynamics of officer-involved shootings, gathering data from over 6,000 incidents. When the results were finally published, they provided a wealth of data that was of direct application in police training methods, including:

- In 90 percent of police fatalities in armed encounters the wounds were received at distances of under 15ft.
- The majority of incidents occurred under poor lighting conditions.
- In 90 percent of cases involving officer fatalities, firearms were the primary weapon, even though they accounted for only 60 percent of total armed attacks.
- Unauthorized holsters or fastenings were generally to blame for instances in which officers were either disarmed by their assailant or accidentally discharged their weapons.

- In 70 percent of shootings, the officers did not use the sights on the weapon.
- Cover was the element most likely to ensure survivability in an encounter.
- Double action was used in 90 percent of cases.[208]

All these findings, plus the tightened control of the FDRB, meant that there had to be an empirical improvement in firearms training in the NYPD, based on the actual practicalities of shootings. Thus while firearms training could be enormously variable, there was at least a general sense of evolution towards a practical, reality-grounded style of firearms training. The improvements, however, could not stop the controversies that followed.

4

TURF AND DRUGS, 1980–2001

On the morning of February 28, 1997, staff at the Bank of America on Laurel Canyon Boulevard, North Hollywood, slipped into their daily routine as usual. Customers filed in, coffee was made, phones rang. Yet outside the bank, under the bright California sunshine, a nightmare was in the making.

Two men – Larry Philips Jr. and Emil Matasareanu – sat outside in a white Chevrolet Celebrity, the phenobarbitals they had taken earlier flowing through their veins and going some way to steadying their nerves. Home-made body armor clad their torsos (constructed using freely purchased commercial body armor ballistic plates), and within the car was a potentially crushing arsenal of weaponry – a Romanian AKM-style rifle, Heckler & Koch HK41 and AR-15 rifles, two 9mm Beretta 92F pistols, and a .38 revolver. To fuel these weapons, they had over 3,000 rounds of ammunition, much of it of a specially purchased armor-piercing variety, with large-capacity drum magazines for some of the rifles. Philips and Matasareanu had the capability to wage a small war on the streets of North Hollywood, all for the sake of the $750,000 they expected to acquire that day.

At 9.17am, events began to accelerate. Philips and Matasareanu set the timers on their watches for eight minutes – the expected LAPD response time – picked up their weapons, exited the car, and walked through the doors of the bank. Even in these early stages of the bank raid, their plans had gone awry. Although they had a planned eight-minute window for the crime, they were actually spotted going into the bank by an LAPD cruiser patrol further down the street. The robbers' black balaclavas and heavy weaponry being a bit of a giveaway, the officers radioed in that a bank robbery was potentially in progress.

Inside the bank, the staff and approximately 30 customers went through a horrific descent from normality into abject fear and chaos. To underscore their seriousness, Philips and Matasareanu let off over 100 rounds into the fabric of the building, ensuring total compliance. In a matter of minutes the two men had netted just over $300,000 – a changed bank delivery schedule meant that the larger amount of cash was not yet in the branch. It was enough, however, for a morning's work, and guns at the ready they exited the bank doors. What met them was far from expected. Police cars had surrounded the bank, with dozens of officers at the ready. As if they hadn't attracted enough attention already, they also caught the attention of TV news helicopters that arrived on the scene shortly afterwards.

The two men's immediate response to being confronted was to open fire with everything they had. Here the police found themselves at an immediate disadvantage, despite their superior numbers. They were armed principally with 9mm and .38 handguns, plus some patrol shotguns, none of which were capable of punching through the body armor the two men were wearing. Television footage of the incident actually shows moments when Philips and Matasareanu literally walk casually under a hail of bullets, riding out the rounds that smack into their body armor. The police were hopelessly outgunned, the suspects' armor-piercing bullets slicing through the bodywork of the cars and through cinderblock walls that the officers were using as cover. Sergeant Dean Haynes, an officer present at the scene, graphically explained the effect of the opponents' firepower advantage: "I aimed my mighty Beretta at him and he just lit up my car. The whole car rocked. The tires were popping and glass and metal went flying. I felt an object go into my shoulder, and I saw that the three citizens were injured from rounds going through the car or skipping up off the ground."[209] Another officer, Martin Whitfield, who was seriously injured in the engagement, remembered hiding behind a tree and felt the tree shaking like a punch bag as bullets slammed into it.

Under the relentless fusillade of bullets, the police casualties started to mount, the police radio crackling with frequent shouts of "officer down." (In fact, the volume of radio traffic created a problem for effective police response, as there were so many calls of "officer down" that it was difficult to tell exactly how many officers had been shot and their precise locations.) The agonizing issue was that rescue missions for the downed officers were almost impossible to execute on account of the street being a virtual free-fire zone. Philips and Matasareanu seemed especially keen to try to finish off any individuals who were noticeably injured, so in the end officers resorted to firing their guns purely to distract the shooters' attention away to other targets. So outgunned were the police officers that at one point they were forced to requisition more powerful weapons and ammunition from a local gun store.

Eighteen minutes into the firefight, a SWAT team arrived with M16 rifles, and began to generate heavier firepower against Philips and Matasareanu, who doggedly refused to go down. Philips then broke away from the getaway car (which they had been using as cover), and moved off down Archwood Street at the end of Laurel Canyon Boulevard, firing with his AK-type rifle loaded with a 100-round drum magazine. The police, however, were starting to achieve their first meaningful hits. Philips's left hand was injured, and his automatic weapon jammed. He pulled out his Beretta handgun and continued firing, then was hit in the right hand. Doubtless realizing that death was closing in fast, Philips then picked up his handgun, jammed it under his chin, and killed himself with a single shot just as a police bullet split his spine.

Matasareanu, meanwhile, was also making a break. The getaway car was shot virtually to pieces by the police fire, but it worked sufficiently to get him away from the scene of the shooting. He eventually took over a truck, but that gave him no joy as the driver had knocked off the gas supply before fleeing. Matasareanu was by now seriously injured, and wounds to the lower legs brought him down. Finally, after a 40-minute gun battle, the police were able to close in on Matasareanu and apprehend him. He died of his wounds before an ambulance could arrive.

By the time the dust settled, 17 people were injured – thankfully the only people who died that day were the perpetrators themselves. The criminals had fired more than 1,100 rounds during the gun battle, and the police around 600. Although each was struck multiple times by bullets, Philips and Matasareanu were able to keep going, thanks to their body armor, until finally their wounds or own actions ended their lives.

NEW TOOLS

The North Hollywood shootout was an exceptional event, but for police departments up and down the country it was a clarion call for change, and built on the momentum for better weaponry noted in the previous chapter. What was clear was that the police during the shootout were outgunned pure and simple – two men were able to control a firefight with police officers for over 40 minutes by virtue of automatic, military-grade weaponry. During the 1980s and 1990s, many police departments up and down the country, particularly those involved with handling the black world of gang violence, were reporting increased uses of automatic weapons in crime – AK47s, Uzis, Mac 10s – and up to the time of the North Hollywood shooting, many regular police departments did not have the tools to respond. In essence, the police were now in an arms war with the criminal world.

We need some context for this moment in police history, beginning with a caution. We mustn't overemphasize the use of assault weapons in criminal acts.[210] The fact remains that criminals generally crave invisibility while they go about their business, and nothing robs you of visibility more than a bulky rifle or angular SMG. Some of the latter are, admittedly, highly compact, but still for most criminals their rippling bursts of fire bring more unwelcome attention than criminal advantage, hence the easily concealed and controlled handgun has always been the firearm of choice. Looking at figures from the 1980s and early 1990s, roughly 1 percent of firearms crimes were committed with assault weapons. In 1990 in California, for example, 36 of the 963 firearms used in homicides or aggravated assaults were assault weapon types, and in the same year Baltimore County reported seven murders using rifles and shotguns (of all types, not just assault weapons) out of a total of 305 homicides. In Miami, police seized 18,702 firearms from January 1, 1989 to December 31, 1993, of which 3.3 percent were assault weapons, and in New York in 1988, 80 "assault-type" firearms were part of the annual haul of 12,138 criminal firearms seized.[211]

Such figures illustrate how in the grand scheme of the annual US epidemic of firearms killings and crimes, assault weapons accounted for a relatively minor percentage. Furthermore, in his 1994 article "Rational Basis Analysis of 'Assault Weapon' Prohibition" (from which the above figures are quoted), David Kopel challenges the idea that automatic weapons were making life more dangerous for police officers:

> From 1975 to 1992, out of 1,534 police officers feloniously murdered in the United States, sixteen were killed with firearms defined as "assault weapons" by California law. The *Journal of California Law Enforcement* wrote: "It is interesting to note, in the current hysteria over semi-automatic and military look-alike weapons, that the most common weapon used in the decade to murder police officers was that of the .38 Special and the .357 Magnum revolver." The *Journal* found that "calibers which correspond to military-style shoulder weapons" accounted for 8% of total firearms used to murder police officers in California.
>
> The impression conveyed by some television programs is that shoot-outs between police and criminals involve steadily escalating amounts of fire-power. However, according to the New York City police department study of shootings at police in 1989, the average number of shots fired at the police per encounter was 2.55, and this number represented a decline from previous years.[212]

Kobel's arguments were common amongst the pro-firearms lobby during the late 1980s and 1990s, made in the context of increasing but largely ineffective attempts by the US government to control the proliferation of heavy firepower amongst its already well-armed citizenry. The 1968 Gun Control Act was one of the first major pieces of post-war legislation aimed at limiting both the types of firearm available, and the methods by which they could be purchased. The context of the legislation was an impressive acceleration in the volume of weapons imported into the United States. In 1955, for example, 67,000 handguns were imported into the United States for the civilian market. By 1966 that figure was around 500,000, and just two years later it had hit one million, and firearms crime was riding the swell of firearms production.[213] The 1968 Act brought in a raft of measures, including the prohibition of mail-order firearms and ammunition sales, proper licensing and record-keeping standards for gun traders, and the ban on interstate handguns sales. In terms of the type of weapons controlled, the Act banned 43 types of semi-auto assault rifle, prohibited the importation of foreign military surplus weapons, banned the sale and manufacture of new full-auto machine guns, and also prohibited the sale of conversion kits for adapting semi-auto firearms to fire in full-automatic modes. The Act essentially tried to shut down trade in weapons outside of "sporting" purposes – although as with many subsequent firearms acts, what constitutes a "sporting" weapon is open to elastic interpretation. This part of the Act was as much aimed at controlling the spread of "Saturday Night Special" revolvers – highly compact, cheap imported revolvers of no sporting and little self-defense value – as assault weapons.

The effect of the Act was ambiguous. The importation of weapons into US society undoubtedly fell – handgun importations alone dropped from 1,155,368 in 1968 to 349,252 the following year.[214] The BATF racked up more prosecutions for the importation of illegal types. And yet, the number of firearms crimes continued to rise, with a 40 percent climb between 1968 and 1973 and a 60 percent rise in handgun homicides. In reality, the Act had only a limited potential to affect gun crime, largely because the domestic production and sales market was so strong (domestic production of civilian handguns, for example, rose from 1,259,356 in 1968 to 1,367,300 in 1969), the numbers of firearms already in circulation were phenomenally high (up to 5 million second-hand firearms were traded in 1973), and because illegal firearm importers obviously had a poor respect for the law anyway. (For more details surrounding these figures, see the Zimring and Zawitz titles referred to in the Bibliography.)

The 1968 Act remained the dominant federal legislation governing firearms until the 1980s and 1990s (space here does not allow us to consider the many state acts that attempted to control firearms), when a handful of dire incidents switched governmental attention once more to the issue of assault weapons. On July 18, 1984, 41-year-old James Oliver Huberty marched into a McDonald's restaurant in San Ysidro, California, armed with a semi-automatic Uzi, a Browning handgun, and a 12-gauge shotgun, and massacred 21 people and wounded 15 others before being shot dead by a SWAT sniper. Five years later, on January 17, 1989, one Patrick Edward Purdy entered an elementary school in Stockton, California, with an AKS assault rifle. In a dreadful act of bloodletting, he killed five children and wounded 30 others before shooting himself. These, and a handful of other incidents, led directly to the 1994 Assault Weapons Ban (AWB). The AWB drew up a list of prohibited semi-auto assault weapons plus related large-capacity magazines, although the ban applied only to weapons manufactured beyond the Act date – those manufactured before were still permitted. Banned weapons included AK-type rifles, the Uzi SMG, the Colt AR-15, and the FN FAL, the models defined by certain "assault" characteristics, such as a pistol grip or a large-capacity magazine within the pistol grip itself (as in an Uzi or Mac 10). This application of characteristics, however, meant that the devil was in the detail:

> While it [the AWB] also banned "exact" or duplicate copies of the prohibited makes and models, the emphasis was on "exact." Shortening a gun's barrel by a few millimeters or "sporterizing" a rifle by removing its pistol grip and replacing it with a thumbhole in the stock, for example, was sufficient to transform a banned weapon into a legal substitute. On April 5, 1998, President Clinton signed an Executive order banning the imports of 58 foreign-made substitutes.[215]

In addition to this slippery handling of the AWB, there was also a mad rush in assault weapons production just ahead of the ban being enforced – of five categories of banned weapons, 204,000 were produced in 1994, compared to annual production of around 91,000 in the previous four years.[216]

Judging the level of success of the AWB in preventing firearms crime, and this relationship to the safety of police officers, has been a politically fraught and statistically complex exercise. Yet according to the US Department of Justice (from the previous source, p.9), gun murder rates in 1995 were over 10 percent below projections while "Murders of police by offenders armed with assault weapons declined from an estimated 16 percent of gun murders of police in 1994 and early 1995 to 0 percent in the latter half of 1995 and early 1996" (although it notes that the rarity of these incidents makes definitive judgment on the relationship between the AWB and police homicides problematic).

In the context of these figures, the 1980s and 1990s were important years for the use and perception of deadly force, not only in terms of refining the CoF, and for sharpening the understanding of deadly force dynamics, but also for transformations in the police arsenal. Two major movements occurred. First, the law enforcement community progressively and almost universally switched from revolvers to semi-auto handguns. Second, the numbers of military-grade longarms accessible to regular beat officers, and in the hands of the SWAT teams, increased dramatically, spurred by events such as the North Hollywood shooting described above.

Before exploring this further, it is worth noting that the budget is king in most police departments, and purchasing new firearms and their associated ammunition is a hideously expensive business. Wealth disparities exist between police departments as in wider societies, so there are many individual exceptions to the general rules that follow, with some departments lagging years behind, say, a wealthy suburban department on the edge of a major city. Although the general trends noted are valid, we should therefore remember that not every police department could buy into their benefits.

Taking the switch to pistols, the shift started to occur in earnest in the 1980s. (Some departments had switched to pistols far earlier. El Monte, California, for example, had adopted the Colt M1911 back in 1966, and the Illinois State Police had taken a Smith & Wesson model in 1967.) Pistols seemed to offer the perfect package for an officer – higher magazine capacity, fast reloading, more compact shape, improved usability. The shift was partly inspired by the US Army's wholesale adoption of the Beretta 9mm M92 as its standard side-arm in the early to mid-1980s. Indeed the Beretta became the leading brand to which police departments transferred, with 115 agencies having switched to it by 1983, and over 800 agencies by 1992.

Yet the major impetus was the perception that the ageing police six-shot revolvers, at least of the smaller calibers, were no longer up to the task in a new climate of violence. For the 1980s were truly the age of the gangs in the United States. By the beginning of the decade, the Crips and Bloods gangs of Los Angeles, plus various motorbike gangs and extremist groups, began a national expansion throughout the United States, spreading inter-gang violence, opportunistic theft and murder, and anti-police resistance as they went. African-American and Latino gangs became especially powerful and belligerent, fueled by the wave of crack cocaine that swept onto the narcotics market in the early 1980s and given a cultural status by the gangster rock music movement that spread out from southern California during the late 1980s and early 1990s. Amongst the complex social hierarchies of the gangs, the capacity for violence and being tooled up with a serious piece of firepower were routes to instant respect. AKs, Uzis, and Mac 10s were the weapons of choice where available, and large-caliber semi-auto handguns were virtually standard pieces of "protection."

The result was one of the darkest episodes of firearms-related violence in American history. In 1979, the total number of firearms homicides was 13,582. In 1980, that number leapt to 14,377, and the next 20 years brought some annual figures that bred alarm amongst both law enforcers and the increasingly threatened public – 15,025 in 1990, 16,376 in 1991, 17,083 in 1993 (the peak year).[217] Certain neighborhoods of big cities like New York, Los Angeles, Chicago, and Philadelphia became virtual war zones, the daily newspapers running ever more alarming stories of violence and chaos. It bred new phenomena, such as the drive-by shooting. Just a random scan over newspapers from the period alights on regular horrors. On July 22, 1991, for example, a four-year-old girl was killed and her pregnant mother, a 17-year-old boy, and another woman were wounded in Harlem by two men who sprayed the sidewalk with gunfire from a passing car. The same *New York Times* article noted that 99 children under 16 had been shot in the city between January and April 1991 alone. On November 24, 1991, the *Los Angeles Times* described a recent shooting in which two men in a yellow Mustang Maverick fired at random into a group of 20 men standing on the street, killing one and wounding six others, including a seven-year-old bystander. Nor were the victims limited to bystanders and gang members – police officers were also falling. In early September 1988, officer Daniel Pratt and partner Veronica DeLao were on patrol near Inglewood – an area of southcentral Los Angeles notorious for gang criminality – when they spotted a car suspected of being used in an earlier drive-by shooting. Inside the car were two men and two 17-year-old girls (one of the girls was the driver). The officers followed the car until it stopped, at which point they parked their own vehicle and prepared to approach the suspects. Yet even before they exited, the gang car suddenly spun a U-turn and raced towards the police car. The occupants fired a burst of automatic fire at the two officers, hitting Pratt in the face and killing him. LAPD Chief Daryl Gates, in a press conference at the time, spoke forcefully: "You have an officer, a young man like this, who was a member of the family, who also has a family, who has a child he will never see ... for young kids growing up without a father, because you've got no-good miserable sons of bitches out there that society continues to allow to roam the streets." Gates' words would resonate with many at the time and subsequently. The *Seattle Times*, for example, speaking about its own city five years later, observed:

> Thirty people have been murdered since June 1, and guns have been the dominant weapon – handguns, assault rifles, pistols and semi-automatics. But that's not news anymore. What is news is the degree of brutality and senselessness seen in these shootings. Gun slayings aren't limited to revenge by gangs; they include freeway fights, domestic disputes, jealous rages and drug deals gone bad.[218]

It was into this context of spiraling firearms violence that the police forces of United States decided to up-gun themselves. The most popular handgun models were from Beretta (as we have seen), Smith & Wesson, SiG Sauer, and Glock. The Glock in particular became, and remains, one of the most popular law-enforcement firearms in the United States alongside Beretta models, it being reliable, light, and with a magazine capacity of 15–18 rounds, depending on caliber and model.

While the rationale behind giving officers more firepower may have been clear in the context of the times, the switch to the automatics was not without raised eyebrows. The first level of controversy related to the inevitable period of adjustment from the mechanically simple revolver to the more complex semi-auto. The Glock in particular came in for some adverse publicity over a high accidental-discharge rate. All the Glock requires to disengage the safety and fire the weapon is a trigger pull (albeit a long one), unlike many other semi-auto pistols that have an external safety. In terms of its action, the Glock is useful for officers in that as soon as it is drawn from a holster it is ready to go, and the time taken to disengage an external safety mechanism could cost an officer his life in the blur of a gunfight. Yet the downside appeared to be that officers were initially more prone to shooting either themselves or others through accidental discharges. Over the ten years from the adoption of the Glock by the Washington DC Metropolitan PD in the late 1980s, there were a total of 120 accidental discharges, and in 1996 alone the city paid out over $1.4 million in costs related to these discharges. A special report into the phenomenon by the *Washington Post* listed many of the discharge incidents.[219] Some are darkly comical. One female officer was unloading her gun at home, when her husband accidentally bumped into her, resulting in the officer shooting herself in the foot. Another officer put a bullet through the floor of her own apartment, hitting the resident below in the leg. A large number of officers shot themselves in the thigh or leg while holstering or unholstering the gun. Other incidents are devoid of any sort of levity. On October 10, 1989, a police officer's two-year-old daughter was killed after she accidentally shot herself in the head with her father's pistol, one of several children shot with their parent's firearm. Guns went off several times during routine arrests or traffic stops, sometimes with fatal consequences.

The frequency of the discharges and the high profile of some cases gave the press a field day in reporting on apparent waywardness of the Glock. Yet many high-ranking police officers were also concerned. In 1991/92, for example, the Chicago PD actually voted against adopting the Glock, branding the weapon as too dangerous for general use (although they did authorize four other brands of semi-auto handgun for adoption).[220] The New York Police Commissioner Lee P. Brown and city mayor David N. Dinkins also opposed the Glock, but were overruled by the State Senate.[221] In reality, most of the problems with the Glock seemed to be due to much needed catch-up in the officer training program, rather than to any inherent flaw in the weapon design. The *Washington Post* investigation found that "75 percent of all DC officers involved in shootings during 1996 failed to comply with the retraining regulation. One officer waited so long to come to the range that firearms instructors found a spider nest growing inside his Glock."[222] On the plus side, in a firefight the Glock had the rapid-fire capacity required to put down an assailant in the least space of time, and those officers who did have to draw the gun in earnest were generally admiring of its performance.

Another objection more generally applied to the semi-auto class of handguns was that the increased magazine capacity could lead to unnecessary volumes of fire in deadly force incidents, increasing the risk to innocent bystanders in urban areas. This concern seemed borne out in an incident in December 1994, when a shootout with a gunman in Queens, New York, saw 18 officers fire a total of 247 shots that killed not only the gunman but also an innocent bystander. Furthermore, some engagements showed that officers themselves could be in more danger from errant shooting. On October 10, 1995, five policemen, all armed with semi-auto handguns, descended upon a grocery store in Alphabet City, Manhattan, in response to a 911 call reporting an armed robbery. There they ended up in a gunfight with three suspects on the cramped premises, in which one of the suspects was killed and an officer seriously wounded. The problem from the police point of view was that it appeared that only the police officers fired during the incident, meaning that police shots were responsible for the officer injury. In total 36 shots were fired, a substantial volume of fire for such a tight space.

News reports from across the United States around this time question whether the acquisition of pistols posed an irresistible temptation for officers to deliver more than the requisite firepower, and during the 1990s and early 2000s many police departments conducted retrospective studies to work out whether such was the case. In summary, there is a case to be made for a slight propensity to shoot more with semi-auto pistols. NYPD SOP-9 data, for example, shows that prior to 1993, the year in which the city's police force began to adopt pistols, the average number of shots fired per armed incident ranged between 3 and 3.9. From 1993 to 2000, however, the average shots ran between 3.6 and 5, and for five of those years they were above 4 shots per incident (although the figures don't necessarily relate to encounters with armed assailants; police in 1998, for example, fired 234 shots at dogs).[223]

Thomas Aveni of the Police Policy Studies Council (PPSC) notes that a Portland, Oregon, study in 1992 found that the average number of shots fired per incident went up from 2.6 in the days of the revolver to 4.6 with the adoption of a pistol. And yet, it seems that the hit ratio increased as well:

> From January 1, 1983 through January 5, 1990, Portland police reportedly struck adversaries with 24 rounds out of 67 fired (36 percent hit ratio). Firing semi-auto pistols

from July 21, 1984 through February 7, 1992, officers struck their adversaries with 19 rounds out of 44 that were fired (43 percent hit rate).[224]

In 1995 the NYPD, prompted by the adverse press over the store shooting, conducted a major two-month investigation into the apparent rise in volumes of fire. While they acknowledged that there was indeed a slight rise in the average shots fired per incident when compared with the days of the revolver, they also pointed out that the average number of shots fired by each officer armed with the 9mm weapons declined from .093 bullets in 1992 to .047 bullets in 1994, hinting at a steady familiarization with the new weapons.[225] The report acknowledged that more training was required to improve safe handling of the new semi-autos, but it also expressed interest in ammunition changes. At this point in time, the NYPD was using standard ball ammunition (i.e. jacketed, non-expanding rounds), and the report's authors speculated that switching to expanding ammunition types (ones that "mushroom" on impact) would not only reduce the risk of rounds penetrating through a suspect and hitting a bystander, but also improve the terminal performance of ammunition – they would cause more damage to the person they hit. (See Chapter 6 for more detailed explanations of ammunition performance.)

These early inklings that ammunition type was extremely important would steadily expand to become a major debate in law enforcement circles that still exists to this day. At first, the law enforcement community felt that the shift to the 9mm handgun balanced the criminal/police firepower. As one officer said in 1992: "Giving us the 9mm won't turn us into a bunch of John Waynes, but I think it will give us a little more confidence if we get into a gun battle."[226] As time wore on, however, perceptions changed. By 1995 several police departments around the country were claiming that the 9mm simply wasn't powerful enough (in terms of penetration and the size of the wound created) to take down an adrenaline- or drug-fueled assailant decisively, and as the decade wore on such views rapidly gained authority in the United States.

Earlier experience gained by the FBI was giving weight to this perception. On April 11, 1986, a team of eight FBI agents supported by officers of the Miami Metro-Dade PD was patrolling an area of southwest Miami, on the lookout for a suspicious vehicle. Tensions and expectations were running high. A series of extremely violent bank and armored car robberies in the area over the previous months had resulted in the death of one guard and the wounding of several others, and the officers were on the lookout for a black Chevrolet Monte Carlo with a Florida license plate. At around 9.30am, they spotted the vehicle. Inside were two men, William Russell Matix and Michael Platt, the hardened criminals that the FBI were looking for. Matix and Platt were former US Army soldiers: Matix had been a military policeman and Platt had served as a US Army Ranger. In the car with them was a small arsenal of weapons: a 12-gauge shotgun, a Remington Mini-14 .223 carbine, and two Smith & Wesson .357 Magnum revolvers. The combination of their military training, large array of weapons, and hardened characters was about to unleash a bloodbath on the streets of Miami.

The FBI team decided to pull over the car and make a felony arrest. Three FBI vehicles, occupied by special agents Benjamin Grogan/Gerald Dove, Richard Manauzzi/Gordan McNeill, and John Hanlon/Edmundo Mireles, rammed the Monte Carlo and forced it off the road. (Another FBI car containing two more officers was positioned at a distance.) The criminals' vehicle ended its journey against a tree, forced off the road in a hefty collision for all parties, but Platt (sitting in the passenger seat) was tough and well-motivated – he unleashed a volley of 13 shots from his Mini-14, followed by a blast from Matix's 12-gauge shotgun. The first casualties were taken. Special Agent Gordon McNeill was hit in the hand by a .223 round, and Mireles was struck in the forearm. The officers returned fire, and at this point Matix was probably hit in the right forearm.[227] Matix slumped back into the car, and was then hit by an FBI pistol round in the side of the head, rendering him unconscious before yet another bullet slammed into him, striking his neck and tumbling down into his chest. With massive injuries sustained, Matix's life began slowly ebbing away onto the floor of the car, although his resistance was not over yet. Platt exited the car gripping his Mini-14, and with terrifying fanaticism endured six bullet hits as he charged the police officers, attempting to take one of the FBI vehicles (his own car was trapped between two of the FBI cars). Making it to the vehicle, he then killed special agents Dove and Grogan and shot Special Agent Hanlon in the hand and pelvis.

By this stage of the firefight, two FBI agents were dead and three were seriously injured. Nor was the incident over. Matix had regained consciousness and crawled over to join Platt in the police cruiser. Now Mireles, one arm dangling uselessly, summoned incredible strength, cycling his pump action shotgun with one hand. He hit both men, stopping them from driving off but not totally incapacitating them. Platt, with extreme persistence, exited the vehicle and went over to near Mireles, whose shotgun was now empty. He fired three shots at the officer – mercifully all missed their target – and he returned to the car. Now Mireles struggled to his feet, pulled out his .357 revolver, and moved over to the car at close range. There he finished Platt and Matix, pumping bullets at close range into the two men and finally killing them.

The FBI was traumatized by the Miami shootout, and an intense self-analysis began into how two criminals were able to cause such bloodshed despite being outnumbered 4:1 in the immediate scene of the action. Critically, the two criminals, who were not fueled by drugs or alcohol, had been hit a total of 18 times, and the first bullet that hit Platt was essentially a fatal wound in itself. Yet the penetration and damage caused by the police bullets had not been sufficient for a decisive take down early on, plus those officers using .357 service revolvers had been hampered by slow reloading times. These factors led the FBI to adopt a wider range of auto handguns and also the powerful 10mm Auto Smith & Wesson 1076. The 10mm round certainly packed the requisite punch, but when fired it kicked like a mule and hence reduced the accuracy of rapid fire and made the gun hard to handle in less resilient hands. Consequently, the FBI gradually shifted to a less powerful .40 Smith & Wesson cartridge. During the 1990s, many police forces were also beginning the shift back to larger-caliber handguns, generally of .40 or .45 size, and the use of expanding ammunition became more commonplace. Although some police departments remained with revolvers, they became increasingly rare – almost all major city and town police departments switched to the semi-auto by the end of the 1990s.

Yet it wasn't only the issue of handguns that was transformed in the 1980s and 1990s. As we have seen throughout this book, a common police response to changing patterns in violence is to upgun, and the 1980s and 1990s were no exception. Hence as well as more advanced handguns, police departments often increased their quotas of rifles and assault rifles. Sometimes the requests for new firearms were rather questionable, and rightly came up against public scrutiny. According to the *New York Times*, in July 1989, the Chicago police chief Herbert Timm asked the city trustees for permission to purchase six Uzi submachine guns for the Winnetka suburb. The Uzi's ability to rattle through a 32-round box magazine in about three seconds, with limited accuracy, somehow told the city that this wasn't such a great idea, and the request was eventually refused.[228] Distributing more semi-auto rifles throughout the ranks of the police, however, was far less controversial. One of the findings of the FBI investigation into the Matix/Platt shooting was that carrying a greater diversity of firearms, including high-power rifles, would probably have given the FBI officers the firepower advantage in that engagement.

A key event to changing everything was the Bank of America shootout that opened this chapter. In the immediate wake of the incident, the Pentagon supplied the LAPD with 600 military surplus M16 rifles, these being distributed amongst regular police vehicle patrols. Miami followed suit shortly afterwards. In Phoenix, Arizona, police deputies were issued with M16 rifles in 1999, following a spate of officer fatalities, and bullet-proof glass was installed in all the patrol cars. Not every police department jumped on the bandwagon. We must always remember that re-equipping with new firearms and associated ammunition, plus creating the relevant training programs, is an extremely expensive business far beyond many police department budgets. Hence many police departments found the cost/benefit analysis pushing them towards rejecting standardized issue of rifles such as the M16, pointing to the fact that not every town and city suffered from the violence endemic to Los Angeles. Furthermore, the LAPD itself experienced some difficulties transferring its new arsenal into a street reality. A *Los Angeles Times* article from January 1998 noted that most of the M16 rifles donated to the LAPD remained locked in a storage vault on account of problems funding the necessary training for officers. There was also much debate about the best way to handle their deployment, with policy makers torn between controlling their use through specially authorized supervisors, or distributing them directly to the officers for immediate use. Another interesting element of the article is that the Police Commission had given officers permission to trade in their 9mm handguns for more potent .45 pistols, but take up of the switch was less than expected, probably because "officers are required to pay for the weapons."[229]

In the case of the SWAT teams, however, their more "elite" purview (although most US police departments are instinctively adverse to using the term "elite") meant that their active-duty arsenals were far more formidable than regular police units. By the late 1980s and early 1990s, most SWAT teams had SMGs as standard issue, the most popular model being the Heckler & Koch (H&K) MP5, but some also had Uzis. Rifles included the AR-16 (and its carbine version) and H&K G3, plus collections of sniper rifles such as the Remington Model 700 and Ruger 77. The MetroDade PD even had some scope-equipped crossbows for "special" jobs. Add all the tear gas launchers, stun grenades, and various other bits of kit, and a SWAT team thus armed, clad in black body armor with visored helmets, and deployed in armored vehicles, was doubtless a persuasive sight to any hostage-taker or drug dealer who was thinking about his resistance options.

Yet as in the 1960s and 1970s, there was a spreading concern that the police were in danger of becoming too militarized, their firepower and uniforms leading to a gung-ho mentality that didn't necessarily make the streets a safer place. Mistakes with firearms are always highly visible, and mistakes with heavy firepower are that much worse. The *St. Petersburg Times* from the 1990s, for example, provides some excellent Keystone Cops-type stories for the readers, which thankfully don't involve anybody getting hurt. In one incident in August 1995, an officer from the local Tactical Assault Team (TAC) left his MP5 SMG plus three loaded ammunition magazines on top of his cruiser when pulling out of the police station. Thirty minutes later he realized that the gun was missing, and had blown off the roof somewhere along the route. Naturally the police department was somewhat concerned to recover the weapon, and put up a $500 reward for its safe return.[230] Another, more hair-raising adventure from 1993 involved a SWAT team being called to restrain a suicidal man, described by the paper as the "avid and outstanding golfer" Jack Everett.

The incident, according to the journalist, ending in Everett giving officers the slip, resulting in a chase through Spring Hill with the officers firing Uzi SMGs and shotguns at him. The evasive Everett managed to escape the shots, and was finally brought to ground after he crashed his car during the chase. In this incident, the journalist laconically comments, "the Sheriff's Office may have found its lowest moment of 1993."[231]

Such incidents are doubtless exceptions to the professionalism of SWAT and TAC teams nationwide. Indeed the specialization of the SWAT, combined with their evidently military appearance and weaponry, created some further problems both in terms of public perception and within the ranks of the law enforcement community. One danger was clarified in an April 1993 FBI Law Enforcement Bulletin entitled "Rethinking SWAT":

> Besides the considerable financial commitment associated with maintaining SWAT units, there exists another more subtle, but potentially negative, cost to police agencies. As police managers know, the specialized training and status that certain units receive can inspire a welcome and very constructive sense of esprit de corps within those units. However, after several years of specialization, a destructive sense of institutional elitism can develop.
>
> Officers and supervisors in specialized units may lose a sense of identity with personnel in other sections of the department. If these views are allowed to persist, specialists begin to view patrol officers – the generalists – as second-class personnel. Even a perceived arrogance on the part of specialized units can lead to serious, and organizationally devastating, conflicts within agencies.
>
> Members of specialized units, such as SWAT teams, may also become so consumed by their narrowly focused missions that training in other areas becomes lax. This is not inevitable, but overspecialization can create a sense within SWAT units that the specific abilities they possess represent the best response to almost every situation. This sentiment runs counter to the evolving understanding that today's crime problems require a multifaceted approach from law enforcement.[232]

Tom Gabor here highlights the very American fear of elitism, and a justifiable sense that regular officers might see themselves as somehow second-class citizens compared to the drama and presence of the SWAT team. Yet from the SWAT team's perspective, we must also recognize that lethal force incidents remain rare, and there is always the danger that the SWAT skills are utilized in areas that could be handled perfectly well by regular officers, just to "exercise" the SWAT muscles.

For smaller departments, there is also the temptation to create a SWAT team where no reason warrants it. In the late 1990s, Peter Kraska, a professor of police studies at

Eastern Kentucky University, along with his colleague Victor Kappeler, published an influential study entitled "Militarizing American Police: The Rise and Normalization of Paramilitary Units."[233] What the study revealed was that while the general movement of policing in the United States was towards more community-based law enforcement, at the same time there was a dramatic increase both in the number of SWAT-type units around the country, and in the types of mission in which they were employed. In the 1980s, 60 percent of US law enforcement agencies serving cities of 50,000+ people (690 agencies) had SWAT units. By the 1990s, that figure had risen to 90 percent. Kraska showed that even small rural agencies in low-crime areas had SWAT units (65 percent in 1996). Furthermore, Kraska found that the applications of SWAT teams had risen tremendously, with their personnel, weaponry, and tactics being applied in serving high-risk warrants, making drugs busts, and performing roaming patrols as well their more traditional roles of hostage rescue and the apprehension/neutralizing of armed suspects. Kraska pointed out that SWAT team usage had increased 538 percent from 1980 to the time of the survey, with 75 percent of LAPD SWAT's work involved in high-risk warrants and drugs raids.

Both the press and the police began to question the validity of the SWAT model applied nationwide, with strong arguments made on both sides. On the against-SWAT side was the fact that the justification of small towns diverting limited resources into highly expensive response teams seemed questionable at best, and dangerous at worst. In an interview with the *Los Angeles Times*, Peter Kraska commented:

> The biggest problem in small towns is the SWAT team is extremely bored. You've got this neat unit with all this equipment and training, and nothing is happening. So you start using them in situations where they're not really needed, like routine search warrants. And pretty soon, you've got an ordinary situation turn deadly.[234]

Kraska argues that if you militarize a unit, then like soldiers that unit will experience a certain tension until their skills are expressed and proven. (Regular officers tend not to experience this problem, as they express their training every day in regular community and criminal policing.) Small communities, often blessed with quietness in terms of criminal activity, might therefore channel SWAT energies into areas that simply aren't appropriate.

An alarming example of a misapplied SWAT force comes from the town of Dinuba in San Joaquin Valley, which in 1997 had a population of 15,269 and its very own six-man Special Enforcement Team (SET). Dinuba was a respectably safe town, but some criminal spillover from nearby Fresno in the 1990s heightened tensions amongst police and residents, especially after a series of shootings in the neighborhood. The SET was established along SWAT lines, although by the police chief's own admission serious hostage or riot events would have been referred to the Tulare County Sheriff's department. Its principal specialty was in serving warrants.

On July 11, 1997, the SET team was called to apply a search warrant to the house of Ramon and Carmen Gallardo, two Dinuba residents whose son, Jesus, was suspected of being in possession of a sawn-off shotgun used in an attempted murder. At 7.00am the SET team went in, moving in fast through the open front door in full assault gear and with MP5s at the ready. Carmen was pushed forcefully onto the bed with the barrel of a gun in her back. In alarm, Ramon Gallardo grabbed for a folding knife, and was hit with a full-auto burst from the MP5. He died from 15 bullet wounds.

Although the Tulare County district attorney later proclaimed the shooting justified, in a civil case a jury awarded Carmen Gallardo $12.5 million, a crippling financial blow for the town. The case unpacked evidence that the SET team had had only three training sessions relevant to the mission,[235] and placed a large question mark over the very rationale for having such a force in a small community. Tom Gabor drew similar conclusions in his above-mentioned article:

> I do believe that many of the SWAT units maintained by individual police departments throughout the country could be disbanded without threatening law enforcement capabilities. In most cases, existing regional or county SWAT teams could fill any void created. Granted, in some areas, regional SWAT units will either have to be created or enhanced, but in the long run, this will prove more cost-effective than funding individual units.
>
> At the same time, the importance of maintaining regional SWAT capabilities cannot be overstated. Again, the Los Angeles County example applies. The county includes 47 municipal police departments and one sheriff's office (LASO). Each of the municipal departments has a mutual aid agreement with the sheriff's office, which maintains an extremely well-trained SWAT unit. Should an incident overwhelm a municipal agency's resources, the LASO SWAT team can be dispatched to help resolve the matter.[236]

Maintaining a SWAT-type unit is a luxury that many small police departments can't afford in terms of finance and training, and proper reliance on regional or county SWAT units can relieve them of the burden.

On the pro-SWAT side, the arguments justifiably centered on a dramatic increase in US violent crime, linked to an explosion in illegal drug trading, that necessitated a high-firepower rapid-response force. Major shootouts were admittedly a rarity, but they did happen from time to time, and having a SWAT team could mean that literally dozens of civilian or police lives were saved. Interestingly enough, after the Columbine High School massacre in April 1999, some authorities argued that regular officers should receive more of the weaponry and training available to SWAT, enhancing the ability to react to situations where every second of trigger-pulling time counts. Furthermore, the nationalization of gangs during the 1980s and 1990s meant that many previously sleepy suburban communities found themselves facing an overspill gang problem from the adjacent city, requiring force responses that might not have been necessary years previously. Often, the impetus behind creating a SWAT team came from a specific armed incident in which regular officers simply did not have the right tools, nor the right training for those tools, to deal satisfactorily with the threat while minimizing the danger to the public.

A more persuasive justification for the SWAT, however is the SWAT team's deterrent effect and its ability *not* to shoot. Modern, professional SWAT teams train just as hard in negotiation tactics and conflict resolution as they do in hard-hitting gun skills:

> Between 1988 and 1991, the Los Angeles County Sheriff's Office (LASO) responded to approximately 500 requests for SWAT assistance. Through the first 3 years, every incident – approximately 385 calls – resulted in a "talkout." SWAT members fired no shots, and no one was killed. In 1991, out of 115 calls, LASO SWAT exchanged gunfire with five subjects, killing four.
>
> During this 4-year period, negotiators settled 99 percent of the incidents without shots being fired. Even in the most violent year, 1991, LASO SWAT settled 96 percent of the incidents through negotiation. These statistics take on special significance considering that crime rates in Los Angeles County generally rank among the highest in the nation.[237]

This capacity to defuse situations is critical to the SWAT rationale. The modern SWAT team members whom I interviewed were without exception professional, courteous, and rightly proud of their martial skills, but they were equally insistent on their role in resolving conflicts through peaceful means. What seems important is that they are fully integrated into the wider police community, and fulfill enough policing roles to prevent both boredom and the deterioration of core skills. SWAT has certainly proved its usefulness, but the visible militarization it provides has to be treated cautiously lest it intimidate the very communities that it is meant to protect.

REDEFINING DEADLY FORCE

Deadly force incidents play out in rapid and chaotic ways, as we have seen throughout this book. The composure and presence of mind of an officer are tested to the limit in a compressed time frame. In many incidents, the relationship between threat and deadly force is clear, and it is worth reminding ourselves that not every shooting is controversial, nor do they all loom large in the headlines. Nevertheless, for the officer involved a shooting can change a normal day into intense life-changing drama. Carl Stincelli, a deputy sheriff in Sacramento, California, experienced this shift for himself in 1980, along with a trainee officer by his side. In an interview with the author, Carl recounted what happened after he received reports of a bank robbery:

> It was a day shift patrol, that's when most of the bank robberies occur of course, because banks aren't open at night a lot. I was assigned to the patrol division in our south area, which we call a "high target value area." There was a bank that was actually in the city limits, but where the city and county come right together we have jurisdiction in the whole county. But the Sacramento Police Department broadcast the bank robbery... [so that] available officers right there in the area could be on the lookout for this person. I had a brand new – this was his second ride – trainee (I was a training officer at the time), and this was his second day out in the squad car, right out of the academy. So we get the bank robbery call and I was literally right on top of it just kind of across the street. So I pull into the parking lot of this large shopping center where the bank is located, and as I pull into the driveway of the parking lot, there was a guy pulling out of the driveway. We were just getting the description that a black male in a black trench coat was the suspect, and just about simultaneously I lock eyes with this person I'm just driving past. And he sees me and just starts sweating bullets, and acting very nervous, because he knew I was pulling in there looking for him, probably ...
>
> So I whip a quick U-turn and get in behind him. He starts driving really slowly on the street, maybe ten miles under the speed limit to try to be very cautious, and I'm trying to have the radio update some more information so I could decide whether or not this was in fact my bad guy. I'm also talking to my trainee saying "This has got to be our bad guy, why don't you take the shotgun out of the shotgun rack." There's a special foot release that he has to do ... he takes the shotgun out and he puts it between his legs on the floor there. And I said to him "Jack a round into it," because we didn't keep a round in the chamber. So I'm kinda giving him instructions, while talking to my dispatcher, while driving.
>
> Then all of a sudden a light rain starts – this was in the winter time – and the light turned green for him and all of a sudden a pursuit was on. So we started the pursuit and we

> got some more information from the dispatch and I figure this was in fact my guy now, because he was running from me, on top of the look I got. We had a pursuit for maybe a half a mile and he then tried to negotiate a right-hand turn in the rain-slick street. He couldn't make the turn and crashed over the sidewalk into a small field. I pulled up to the kerb right behind him, maybe 20 feet away now, and we both, my partner and I, jumped out of the car, guns drawn. The bank robber steps out of the car with a gun in his hand. And we're yelling at him to keep his hands up and all that stuff, and he continued to just do whatever he wants. He starts to turn, I don't know whether it was to shoot me or to take off running, one of the two, but as he turned and wasn't dropping his gun I fired one round from my revolver, which at the time was a .357 Magnum ... That was a pretty big caliber. Not the .44 Magnum that "Dirty Harry" carried, but it was the biggest one we were allowed to carry on the street. It hit him ... I had a kinda side shot, looking at his profile, and I struck him in the left arm in the bicep area ... and it took four inches out of his humerus bone. He went immediately down – my partner did not shoot because he went down so fast ...[238]

The man Carl shot did not die. Nevertheless, Carl remembers that the procedural and administrative fallout from having discharged his weapon was intense, with multiple agencies making him account for his decision to fire. Although this episode seems transparent in terms of threat and proportionate response, in the eyes of the higher authorities any shooting has to be measured against its codified standards of deadly force.

The fact remains that legal concepts of what constitutes deadly force in United States have been shifting and malleable, particularly in the post-war era. As law enforcement agencies grew increasingly aware of liability issues, and as human rights organizations focused their gaze on protecting the public against alleged police brutality, the federal government was drawn into addressing that deceptively simple question: When is deadly force necessary?

The 1980s and 1990s witnessed several landmark pieces of deadly force legislation, tightening the rules on what constituted acceptable use of force while also attempting to appreciate the chaotic human dynamics involved in a split-second shoot/don't shoot incident. The first big change came in 1985, but harked back to an incident that occurred over ten years previously.

At around 10.45am on October 3, 1974, two Memphis, Tennessee, police officers, Elton Hymon and Leslie Wright, were called to an address in response to a "prowler inside" dispatch. Driving quickly to the scene, they arrived to find an agitated woman on the porch of her home, pointing to the house next door and saying she had heard breaking glass and had seen someone entering the house. Wright remained in the car to radio the dispatcher and say that they were on scene, while Hymon moved cautiously behind the house, peering into the darkness. The back door suddenly slammed, and across the darkened backyard ran teenager Edward Garner clutching his night's illicit takings – $10 and a purse. Hymon scanned his flashlight across the fleeing figure, ascertaining that he was in fact unarmed. Garner made it to the bottom of the perimeter 6ft-high chain link fence, and crouched down, preparing his next move. Hymon issued a short, sharp warning "Police! Halt!" Garner chose another option, and began climbing the fence. It would be the last major decision of his young life. Hymon, under the fleeing felon rule, was able to resort to firepower to stop Garner making his escape. The Tennessee state code clearly stated: "[i]f, after notice of the intention to arrest the defendant, he either flee or forcibly resist, the officer may use all the necessary means to effect the arrest." Hymon fired a single shot from his handgun, hitting Garner in the back of the neck and dropping him to the ground. The chase was over, and Garner's body began shutting down. He was rushed to hospital, but died on the operating table.

The killing of young Garner set in train a long legal process, as the father of the boy sought damages in the District Court, claiming that his son's constitutional rights had been violated. At district level, the court backed the police officer's actions, but the Court of Appeal reversed the decision and over a long period of time the case eventually worked its way up to the US Supreme Court.

The eventual decision went to the Supreme Court, where it took a distinctive turn. The Court measured the case against the constitutional standards of the Fourth Amendment, and found the fleeing felon rule wanting in several regards:

(a) Apprehension by the use of deadly force is a seizure subject to the Fourth Amendment's reasonableness requirement. To determine whether such a seizure is reasonable, the extent of the intrusion on the suspect's rights under that Amendment must be balanced against the governmental interests in effective law enforcement. This balancing process demonstrates that, notwithstanding probable cause to seize a suspect, an officer may not always do so by killing him. The use of deadly force to prevent the escape of all felony suspects, whatever the circumstances, is constitutionally unreasonable. (p. 471 U. S. 7-12).

(b) The Fourth Amendment, for purposes of this case, should not be construed in light of the common law rule allowing the use of whatever force is necessary to effect the arrest of a fleeing felon. Changes in the legal and technological context mean that that rule is distorted almost beyond recognition when literally applied. Whereas felonies were formerly capital crimes, few are now, or can be, and many crimes classified as

> misdemeanors, or nonexistent, at common law are now felonies. Also, the common law rule developed at a time when weapons were rudimentary. And, in light of the varied rules adopted in the States indicating a long-term movement away from the common law rule, particularly in the police departments themselves, that rule is a dubious indicium of the constitutionality of the Tennessee statute. There is no indication that holding a police practice such as that authorized by the statute unreasonable will severely hamper effective law enforcement. (p. 471 U. S. 12-20.)
>
> (c) While burglary is a serious crime, the officer in this case could not reasonably have believed that the suspect – young, slight, and unarmed – posed any threat. Nor does the fact that an unarmed suspect has broken into a dwelling at night automatically mean he is dangerous. (p. 471 U. S. 20-22)[239]

These judgments made several critical points. Most importantly, they held the fleeing felon rule as archaic, a relic of a former time when justice was harder and weapons were cruder. Edward Garner – "young, slight, and unarmed" – essentially died for $10 and a defiant nature. Hymon himself had operated under the rule of law, but the final judgment of the Supreme Court changed the nature of general police responsibility:

> The Tennessee statute is unconstitutional insofar as it authorizes the use of deadly force against, as in this case, an apparently unarmed, nondangerous fleeing suspect; such force may not be used unless necessary to prevent the escape and the officer has probable cause to believe that the suspect poses a significant threat of death or serious physical injury to the officer or others. (pp. 497 U. S. 7-22)[240]

From Tennessee v. Garner onwards, officers would have to demonstrate that shooting a fleeing individual was based on a definite and continuing threat to police or public – dropping someone simply for committing a felony and attempting to escape was no longer acceptable.

In one sense, Tennessee v. Garner changed little for the officer scuffing his boots on the street. Many police departments practiced the judgments of the Supreme Court anyway in their daily use of force policy – most police officers had little incentive to shoot petty criminals attempting to get away. Indeed, one of the motivations behind the Supreme Court decision was that certain major police departments had already demonstrated that restricting the use of deadly force could be effective. The NYPD had, alongside its formation of the Firearms Discharge Review Board, also established regulations in 1967 that limited deadly force to situations where the suspect posed a direct threat to the safety of police officers or the public, or to apprehending criminals with a known tendency to violence.[241] These two policies had led to a significant decrease in police homicides – 93 in 1971, 25 in 1976, 11 in 1985. These figures were also accompanied by a decline in officer fatalities, from 58 in 1971 down to numbers only just in double figures by the mid-1980s, proving the point that restricting the use of deadly force did not necessarily put officers at greater risk.

From a liability point of view, however, Tennessee v. Garner was highly significant and increased the burden of proof on police officers who had applied deadly force. From now on, if they shot anyone who was running they had to demonstrate that he was a continuing danger, not an easy thing to judge under immediate, dynamic circumstances or under the forensic spotlight of a court of law. One newspaper commentator, James Kilpatrick, put his finger on the pulse of many police officers:

> The nighttime arrest of a fleeing burgular is a nerve-tingling experience beyond the imagination of ivory-towered judges. Is the man armed? Has he just committed a rape or a murder in the course of the burglary? (An average of 280,000 such crimes are committed by burglars every year.) Is the escaping suspect a pathetic little 15-year-old boy or a career criminal with a record of violent crimes? O'Connor [a Supreme Court judge who questioned the Court's final voted decision] is right in protesting the majority's creation of "a constitutional right to unimpeded flight."[242]

Kilpatrick's argument taps into a perennial concern for police officers, namely that they will be judged for using deadly force in a court of law where the lawyers and jury have the luxury of sedate, reasoned judgment, a world apart from the "nerve-tingling" experience of meeting a potentially dangerous criminal in a dark city corner and having to make an instant decision.

Yet four years later, the Supreme Court further tightened up the rules of deadly force under Graham v. Connor. The case stemmed from an unpleasant incident in which a diabetic, about to go into a severe insulin reaction, was handled very roughly during a police traffic pullover. Graham's claims of excessive force were eventually upheld by the Supreme Court, and although this incident did not involve deadly force, the court established some criteria for judging whether force of all types is excessive or not:

- How serious was the offense that the offender was suspected of or had committed?
- Did the suspect pose a physical threat to the officer or some other person at the scene?
- Was the suspect resisting or attempting to flee?[243]

Graham v. Connor tightened up the way that courts and juries could judge use of force, and applied the standard of "objective reasonableness" to force actions. This standard cut both ways. On the one hand, it was clear that officers had to have some objective perception of danger to pull the trigger, while on the other hand it also acknowledged that the legal investigation had to focus on "the facts and circumstances confronting them [the officers]… judged from the perspective of a reasonable officer on the scene, rather than with the 20/20 vision of hindsight."[244] What was clear was that officers would be judged on how the suspect was behaving – i.e. what threat was perceived – at the time of the shooting.

In 1995, the federal government went even further in its attempts to define deadly force policy, this time applied specifically to nine federal law enforcement agencies but with clear implications for all law enforcement officers. The legislation was prompted by a series of questionable FBI shootings, but particularly by the killing of one Vicki Weaver in 1992. An FBI unit had surrounded the home of Vicki and Randall Weaver, the latter being a white supremacist whose son had been killed in a shootout with police the previous day, the shooting also resulting in the death of a US marshal. An FBI sniper shot through an open cabin door and killed Vicki on the spot as she clutched her infant daughter, and although no disciplinary action was brought against the sniper it was felt that the rules needed tightening. Here the resolution is quoted at length, as it provides a useful benchmark for some of the subsequent instances discussed in this chapter.

> I. Permissible Uses. Law enforcement officers and correctional officers of the Department of Justice may use deadly force only when necessary, that is, when the officer has a reasonable belief that the subject of such force poses an imminent danger of death or serious physical injury to the officer or to another person.
>
> A. Fleeing Felons. Deadly force may be used to prevent the escape of a fleeing subject if there is probable cause to believe: (1) the subject has committed a felony involving the infliction or threatened infliction of serious physical injury or death, and (2) the escape of the subject would pose an imminent danger of death or serious physical injury to the officer or to another person.
>
> B. Escaping Prisoners.
>
> 1. Unless force other than deadly force appears to be sufficient, deadly force may be used to prevent the escape of a prisoner committed to the custody of the Attorney General or the Bureau of Prisons: (a) if the prisoner is escaping from a secure institution or is escaping while in transit to or from a secure institution; or (b) if the prisoner is otherwise effecting his or her escape in a

manner that poses an imminent danger to the safety of other prisoners, staff, or the public (such as by attempting to ignite explosives).

2. The use of deadly force is not permitted if the subject is in a non-secure facility or a facility under the control of the Immigration and Naturalization Service, and (a) has not used or threatened the use of force likely to cause serious physical injury in his or her escape attempt, and (b) has not otherwise manifested an imminent threat of death or serious physical injury to the officer or community.

3. The use of deadly force is not permitted if the subject is in transit to or from a non-secure facility and is not accompanied by persons who are in transit to or from a secure facility and the subject (a) has not used or threatened the use of force likely to cause serious physical injury in his or her escape attempt, and (b) has not otherwise manifested an imminent threat of death or serious physical injury to the officer or community.

4. After an escape from the facility or vehicle and its immediate environs has been effected, officers attempting to apprehend the escaped prisoner may not use deadly force unless such force would otherwise be authorized in accordance with this policy.

C. Prison Unrest. Deadly force may be used to maintain or restore control of a prison or correctional institution when the officer reasonably believes that the intended subject of the deadly force is participating in a disturbance in a manner that threatens the safety of other inmates, prison staff, or other persons. The use of deadly force would be unreasonable and thus not permitted to quell a disturbance when force other than deadly force reasonably appears sufficient.

II. Non-Deadly Force. If other force than deadly force reasonably appears to be sufficient to accomplish an arrest or otherwise accomplish the law enforcement purpose, deadly force is not necessary.

III. Verbal Warning. If feasible and if to do so would not increase the danger to the officer or others, a verbal warning to submit to the authority of the officer shall be given prior to the use of deadly force.

IV. Warning Shots. Warning shots are not permitted outside of the prison context. In the prison context, warning shots may be fired within or in the immediate environs of a secure facility if there is no apparent danger to innocent persons: (a) if reasonably necessary to deter or prevent the subject from escaping from a secure facility; or (b) if reasonably necessary to deter or prevent the subject's use of deadly force or force likely to cause grievous bodily harm.

V. Vehicles.

A. Weapons may not be fired solely to disable moving vehicles

B. Weapons may be fired at the driver or other occupant of a moving motor vehicle only when:

1. The officer has a reasonable belief that the subject poses an imminent danger of death or serious physical injury to the officer or another; and

2. The public safety benefits of using such force outweigh the risks to the safety of the officer or other persons.

VI. Vicious Animals. Deadly force may be directed against dogs or other vicious animals when necessary in self-defense or defense of others.

VII. Rights of Third Parties. Nothing in this policy and the attached commentary is intended to create or does create an enforceable legal right or private right of action.[245]

The upshot of all this combined legislation was that police were now operating in a far more rigorous force environment. Combined with the fact that by the end of the 1990s many officers were armed with an array of less lethal force options (see the next chapter for a full discussion of these), the legal situation facing police officers was a complex one. FBI Law Enforcement Bulletins published following the Reno document are replete with case studies working out the limits of liability. One document by John Hall from April 1996 provides a broad range of force scenarios, and discusses each case in terms of the application of deadly force. The following sample provides a clear insight into how federal agents were now obliged to reason their actions:

Relevant Factor: The subject possesses a weapon, or is attempting to gain access to a weapon, under circumstances indicating an intention to use it against the agents or others.

Scenario: Agents approach a residence during the day to arrest a bank robbery subject who threatened bank personnel with a handgun during the robbery. Before the agents are able to fully establish a perimeter, a person matching the description of the subject bursts from the back door of the residence with what appears to be a pistol in his hand and runs through the backyard toward adjacent homes.

Agents shout, "FBI! Stop! Or we'll shoot!" Ignoring the commands, the subject continues to run. An agent fires a shot from a distance of about 15 yards, striking the subject in the back.

Discussion: The use of deadly force is permitted.

Necessity: The agent has probable cause to believe that the subject, who has armed himself with a firearm, has done so to resist arrest and poses an imminent danger to the

> agents in the immediate vicinity. The subject ignored commands to stop. There is no safe alternative to the use of deadly force to avert the danger.
>
> As long as the fleeing, armed subject remains within gunshot range of the agents, he has the ability to turn and fire on them before they can effectively respond by taking cover or returning fire. Attempting to pursue an armed subject increases that danger. In addition, the subject poses an imminent danger to those agents who are trying to form the perimeter and whom the subject is likely to encounter as he continues his flight.
>
> In deciding whether to use deadly force in this scenario, agents also should consider that the suspect is fleeing in a neighborhood setting. Accordingly, agents should assess whether its use creates a danger to third parties that outweighs the likely benefits.[246]

Bearing in mind a raft of deadly force legislation that came into being during the 1980s and 1990s, it's worth asking whether there is any tangible effect of such legislation at the street level. Looking at Tennessee v. Garner specifically, US Department of Justice figures showed that 108 fleeing felon police homicides were committed in 1976, but by 2000 that figure had dropped to an almost negligible 15.[247] In terms of police homicide figures in all circumstances, the following data from the FBI/Department of Justice shows the crude figures for 1976 to 1998:

1976	415
1977	311
1978	313
1979	442
1980	457
1981	381
1982	376
1983	406
1984	332
1985	321
1986	298
1987	296
1988	339
1989	362
1990	379
1991	359
1992	414

1993	453
1994	459
1995	382
1996	355
1997	361
1998	367[248]

The figures take a little unpacking. The overall trend seems to fluctuate in a fairly tight band, although it is noticeable that the figures drop to their lowest point in the immediate aftermath of Tennessee v. Garner. They also decline in the aftermath of the federal legislation in 1995, at least compared to the terrible three years that preceded that event. Overall there appears to be little predictable overall decline, but rather a series of peaks and troughs. However, bear in mind that "from 1976 to 1998, the US population age 13 or older grew by about 47 million people and the size of the police force in the United States grew by over 200,000 officers."[249] Factoring this data into the equation, we find that in terms of the rates of police homicide per 1 million of the population, the rate declined from 2.49 in 1976 to 1.69 in 1998. Lest we think that these figures could be explained by society generally cleaning itself up, crime rate data proves emphatically otherwise (and helps explain some of the spikes in police shootings in the 1990s). Looking at 1980, in that year the US experienced 1,344,520 violent crimes (including 23,040 murders). In 1994, the highest year for police homicides in the data above, the number of murders stayed roughly the same but violent crimes had reached 1,857,670. Rapes had gone from 82,990 to 102,220 and aggravated assaults from 672,650 to 1,113,180.

US society was clearly going through a rough patch in terms of its ethics and order. Yet despite this shift, police officer fatalities were actually declining. The following are the numbers of US law enforcement officers killed in the 1976 to 1998 period:

1976	111
1977	93
1978	93
1979	106
1980	104
1981	91
1982	92
1983	80

1984	72
1985	78
1986	66
1987	74
1988	78
1989	66
1990	66
1991	71
1992	64
1993	70
1994	79
1995	74
1996	61
1997	70
1998	61[250]

Held against the above-mentioned rise in police numbers during this period (200,000), it is clear that officer survivability was increasing, aided by better training and tactics and also by the wider distribution of body armor amongst officers. Of course, the streets still remained a dangerous place to be for officers, particularly those whose work took them directly into potential lines of fire. For the Department of Justice report from which the above statistics are taken, participating US police departments submitted short case studies on typical deadly force incidents. Most have an official and controlled tone, but some of the stories hint at the utter panicked defense of life faced by officers when circumstances turn against them, such as this episode from the NYPD:

> On Monday, April 8, 1996, two New York City police officers were conducting an undercover "buy and bust" drug operation in the Bronx. As one officer approached a group of males to purchase the drugs, he overheard several of the males arguing. During the argument a gun was mentioned. The officer turned back to relay this information to his partner. As the two officers conferred, one officer observed one of the male suspects brandish a gun and fire two bullets at another person in the group. The officers drew their firearms and sought cover behind a telephone pole. One officer identified himself as a police officer and ordered the suspect to drop his weapon. The gunman, standing 25 feet away, turned toward the officers and began firing his 9 mm semi-automatic pistol at them. Both officers returned fire. During the course of the gun battle, the officers exhausted

> their ammunition supply. The perpetrator, with his gun in hand, then began to advance toward the officers. With no bullets remaining in their pistols, one officer retrieved his off-duty revolver and fired one shot at the advancing gunman, causing him to stagger and collapse to the ground, where he succumbed to his wounds.[251]

The following, and rather more eerie, incident, came from Oklahoma City:

> At approximately 12:37a.m. on Friday, August 6, 1996, several Oklahoma City Police Department officers were attempting to locate an armed subject who was reported to be en route to his girlfriend's residence. Information about the suspect had been announced in a general broadcast over the police radio. The suspect had been recently released from the Oklahoma State penitentiary. Initially, officers did not have an address but after searching phone records from the enhanced 911 system, dispatchers were able to find an address for the subject's girlfriend. While on the phone with someone at the girlfriend's residence, a female dispatcher heard what she thought were three gunshots. When responding officers arrived at the apartment, the first responding officer knocked on the front door without a response. Officers were able to peer inside the apartment through a window near the front door. From the window the officers observed what appeared to be blood spattered on the walls and a person lying on the floor. The officers kicked open the apartment's front door. The first officer to enter confirmed a body on the floor. The officer stepped over the body in the hallway and moved toward a bedroom where he observed the body of another female also on the floor. A small child was sitting on the shoulder of the dead female, looking at the officer. Another child was nearby. As the officer began to move into the bedroom, a voice from the bedroom warned the officer that if he came in he would be shot. The only light in the bedroom was that of a television. The officer observed the silhouette of a man holding a handgun. The officer immediately retreated to a nearby bathroom. The officers identified themselves and ordered the suspect to drop his weapon. When the gunman changed locations inside the bedroom, the officer attempted to verbally coax the children out of the bedroom. From inside the bedroom and out of sight of the officer, the suspect announced he was going to push the two children out through the bedroom door. As the suspect came into view of the officer in the bathroom, the officer could see that the suspect was still armed with a handgun. The suspect moved and was standing directly over the body of the dead female. He began to raise his weapon and then pointed it in the direction of the officer in the bathroom. The officer responded by firing two rounds from his .45 caliber service weapon. Both rounds struck the suspect, killing him. The deceased suspect had just committed three homicides.[252]

A final illustration from this report, from Philadelphia, illustrates the value of bullet-proof vests for officers:

> On Friday, November 15, 1996, at approximately 8:51 a.m., a Philadelphia police officer at a school crossing was approached by a 29-year-old male in a car. The man asked for directions. The officer noticed a gun in the suspect's vehicle. While the officer was investigating the incident, the suspect pulled out another gun and shot at the officer, striking him one time in the chest. The officer returned fire, striking the suspect several times in the chest and neck. Both officer and suspect were taken to a local hospital. Because the officer had been wearing a bulletproof vest, he was not seriously injured and was soon released. The suspect was pronounced dead at 9:20 a.m.[253]

These case studies are, despite the modern era, every bit as visceral and terrifying and the cowtown and gangster shootouts of earlier times. They prove that, although legislation changed, the second-by-second dynamics of deadly force remain forever the same. In the rest of this chapter, we will look at some of the other landmark deadly force incidents of the 1990s. As we shall see, they demonstrate how, the moment a gun is pulled, officers put at risk both their lives and their careers.

LIGHT AND SHADOW

February 4, 1999, 4.00am. Four plain clothes officers of the NYPD Street Crime Unit (SCU) were on patrol in the Bronx, on the lookout for the regular trouble that punctuated the dark hours of the city. (The officers were Kenneth Boss and Sean Carroll up front, with Ed McMellon and Richard Murphy in the back.) They spotted someone. A man loitered in a doorway, looking up and down the street, then into the vestibule of the building he stood in. When he spotted the officers it seemed that he was trying to shrink away from their attention, movements that naturally had the opposite effect. They reversed the car, and all four men stepped out, fixing their eyes onto the nervous-looking figure. McMellon produced his badge: "New York City Police. May we have a word with you please?" In response, the suspect began backing himself into the vestibule slowly, reaching for the door handle with his left hand while rummaging around in his right pocket. "Stop! Show me your hands!" McMellon and Carroll shouted, with clear force. Now the suspect was making the officers nervous. In low-light conditions, any suspect who is not complying with instructions and is obviously trying to pull something from his pocket sends officers into instant anxiety and hyper-vigilance. His hand started to emerge from the pocket, clutching something black and shiny.

The ratcheting tension finally broke in a few seconds of dreadful violence. Carroll, fearing for McMellon, who was closest to the suspect, screamed "Gun! He's got a gun!" McMellon started and drew his own pistol, and as the suspect, his own adrenaline exploding, began to move faster, the two men opened fire. McMellon staggered back as he fired his handgun, and tumbled down the steps, but to the other officers it appeared as if he had been shot. (In the street lighting conditions and with the flashes of guns going off, Carroll later testified that he believed he saw flashes coming from the suspect's gun hand.) The other two officers now started firing, working on the fundamental deadly force rule that you keep shooting until the threat is down and no longer posing any challenge. The suspect was now crumpling to the floor in his own blood, downed in a hail of 41 bullets, of which 19 hit home. When his body hit the floor, the firing stopped, the whip-crack noise of the pistol shots dying in the crisp winter air.

Carroll approached the suspect while Boss and Murphy checked out McMellon – he was entirely unhurt, having simply fallen down the steps in the chaos of the shootout. Carroll bent down over the man and opened the "gun" hand – to find a black leather wallet. In later court testimony, Carroll wept as he recounted the incident, saying repeatedly: "Where's the fucking gun! Where's the fucking gun!" He then noticed that the suspect was still breathing and moving a little, but Carroll was reluctant to perform cardiopulmonary resuscitation (CPR) on account of the victim's chest wounds. The suspect, Amadou Diallo, a 22-year-old immigrant from Guinea, then died in front of them.

The killing of Amadou Diallo brought a hurricane of political protest, and cries of racial brutality against the NYPD from many sectors. Political cartoons depicted NYPD officers as nothing more than racist, gun-crazed sociopaths who could kill with impunity. Even aside from the vitriol, there did indeed appear to be a case to answer – 41 shots had been fired at an unarmed man. In January 2000, all four officers were brought to trial, and the opening statement for the prosecution by Eric Warner of the District Attorney's Office summed up widespread sentiments:

> MR. WARNER: Thank you, Judge. Good morning, ladies and gentlemen of the jury, your Honor, defense counsel.
>
> In the 1990s in Bronx County, in Albany County, or anywhere else a human being should have been able to stand in the vestibule of his own home and not be shot to death, especially when those doing the shooting are police officers sworn to protect innocent people. When these four defendants, Kenneth Boss, Sean Carroll, Edward McMellon, and Richard Murphy killed Ahmed Diallo in a hail of 41 bullets in the early morning hours of February 4, 1999, at his home at 1157 Wheeler Avenue in the Bronx, Ahmed – he was also

> called Amadou – was just 22 years old. He was five feet six inches tall and he weighed 150 pounds. Physically, he was not an imposing man.
>
> And he lived a very simple life. Amadou lived with two roommates, apartment 1R, on the first floor of a two-story building at 1157 Wheeler. He worked 10- to 12-hour days, six days a week, sold videotapes and things like that from a table directly in front of a convenience store in lower Manhattan. He had the consent of the owner to do that. On February 3, 1999, at about 10:30 p.m., just hours before he was killed, Amadou left the store. He took the subway and he arrived in the Bronx shortly before midnight. Shortly after that he arrived at his apartment, where he spoke with his roommate, one of his roommates, about their utility bill.
>
> Less than an hour later, Amadou Diallo would be dead. Less than an hour later, he would be standing in the cold, clear night air in the vestibule of his home, unarmed, minding his own business and doing nothing wrong.[254]

Testimony against police officers, such as that above, typically contrasts the innocence and vulnerability of the victim with the power and perceived excess of officer actions, and for a police defense team the burden is to educate the jury as to the realities of a deadly force incident – only if this occurs can they make up their minds as to whether the shooting was justified or not.

In the case of the four officers who shot Amadou Diallo, the court found in their favor after a three-week trial. Diallo's killing was horrific and deeply sad, but the "objective reasonableness" criteria described above could be proven. The officers were dealing with a non-compliant subject. (Diallo actually had limited grasp of English, and was also involved in selling illegal bootlegged tapes, hence he might have been extra nervous of the police.) The black nylon wallet, in the low light conditions, appeared to be a gun, especially as it seemed that Diallo thrust out the wallet at arm's length. The officers fired 41 times because that was what it took to put him down (remembering that not all the bullets struck home). They were also issued with regular 9mm ball ammunition, an ammunition type that has a poor takedown power, but even the best ammunition cannot ensure a swift negation of a threat unless a truly critical point of the body is hit. (See Chapter 6.) In Massad Ayoob's analysis of the Diallo shooting, he also points to an incident in which a gun-wielding drug addict in Cook County, Illinois, was shot 33 times by officers but still managed to remain standing while reloading his gun. Only two powerful shotgun slugs finally brought him down.[255] The court case also showed the officers to be no monsters, but rather men who were mentally damaged by the events of that night.

The Amadou Diallo shooting was a street investigation gone horribly wrong. We now turn to an entirely contrasting event, one that generated equal if not greater controversy and which carried a far higher death toll – by the end of the situation four law enforcement officers were dead and 16 wounded, and over 80 civilians were also killed.

The handling of the Branch Davidian siege in Waco, Texas, in February 1993 has been one of the most analyzed events in modern US law enforcement, although this is not to say that all questions have been answered. Space here does not allow for a full-depth exploration of this traumatic event – entire books have attempted to plumb the depths of the events. Yet we can look at one particular aspect of the mission – the extent to which it became militarized – and through that revisit our spotlight on the militarization of law enforcement.

By February 1993, the federal authorities, and in particular the ATF, were increasingly concerned about the activities of the Branch Davidian Seventh Day Adventist Church at its headquarters at Mount Carmel, to the northeast of Waco, Texas. Headed by the charismatic but unpredictable David Koresh (real name Vernon Wayne Howell), the Church members had gathered at Mount Carmel under the expectations that the Second Coming was imminent. The members felt that this event might attract some unwelcome attention, and to that end began stockpiling an intimidating arsenal of weaponry. This effort came to the attention of the ATF in May 1992, after a United Parcel Service (UPS) delivery broke open in transit, revealing firearms plus inert grenade casings and quantities of black powder. UPS informed the ATF and the latter agency began tracking the cult's weapons acquisitions. The investigation, opened by Special Agent Davey Aguilera of the Austin ATF office and later much criticized in government reports, began to be increasingly concerned by what it found:

> Tracing UPS invoices, Aguilera learned that more than $43,000 worth of firearms (including AR-15 semiautomatics), firearms parts (including AR-15 lower receivers), grenade hulls, and black powder had been shipped to the Davidians' storage facility. One of Koresh's neighbors, who had served in an Army artillery unit, told Aguilera that he had frequently heard the sound of automatic weapons fire – including .50-caliber fire – coming from the Davidian residence. Aguilera also learned that in November, a deputy sheriff had heard a loud explosion at the Davidian residence which produced a cloud of grey smoke. Through interviews with former cult members, Aguilera learned of numerous allegations that Koresh had had sexual relations with girls younger than 16 years of age. These allegations would later feature prominently in Aguilera's affidavit in support of the search and arrest warrants.[256]

The prospect of a little-understood cult arming itself to the teeth with semi- and full-auto weapons, plus explosive devices, could not be ignored, and as well as reporting their findings to the broader federal authorities, the ATF prepared to make a decisive move. The problem was, Koresh and his followers were entirely aware that they were being observed, and quickly rumbled ATF attempts at undercover operations. Furthermore, subsequent investigations found that much of the evidence used to elicit the final search warrant was questionable. Most of the Branch Davidian weaponry was legally purchased, and the kits that the ATF claimed were bought by the Branch Davidians to convert semi-auto firearms to full-auto were actually legal spare parts kits. (Full-auto conversion kits are actually fully regulated as if they were full-auto firearms.) Furthermore, at an early stage in the investigation Koresh had invited ATF agents into his property to inspect the compliance of his weaponry, an opportunity that for reasons unknown the ATF did not take up. Yet paranoia on both sides of the divide was mounting, and the ATF secured their search warrant.

On February 28, 1993, the ATF went into action. Subsequent congressional hearings criticized the ATF on the grounds that "planning for a military style raid began more than 2 months before undercover and infiltration efforts even began," and that the range of options for defusing tensions was limited on account of the "ATF's propensity to engage in aggressive law enforcement." The fact was that the ATF pulled together 75 armed Special Response Team (SRT) agents to raid the compound utilizing flash-bang stun grenades and personal weaponry, with Texas National Guard helicopters brought in to provide a distraction (although initially the National Guard was told that the helicopters were purely for observation and command-and-control). This was no "softly, softly" approach. To scale up the tension further, the Branch Davidians knew the raid was coming after a reporter, aware of the forthcoming action, asked for directions to the compound from a UPS driver, who happened to be Koresh's brother-in-law. Koresh also unmasked an undercover ATF agent in his midst and, in a state of deep agitation, he ordered the women and children to hide and the men to take up arms and find cover. Combined with poor planning (there was no central, written raid plan) and the fact that the various teams involved had trained together for only three days before the raid, a disaster was in the making.

The raid involved two parties of agents, delivered at speed to the door on cattle trailers pulled by pick-up vans. When they dismounted, they attempted forced entries at various parts of the building, rather than opting for the "knock and announce" federal rule on delivering search warrants. The mission collapsed from the outset, as one agent, ATF Special Agent John Henry Williams, testified afterwards:

> As we approached the front door, David Koresh came to the front door dressed in black cammo fatigues. As he closed the door, before we reached the door, one agent reached the door, and at that point that is when the doors erupted with gunfire coming from inside. It was 10 seconds or more before we even fired back.[257]

From this point on, the raid dissolved into a terrifying gun battle, with the ATF agents outgunned by the individuals inside the compound and with little tactical response plan to provide a clean extraction. The gun battle lasted from 9.45am to 11.30am, and was brought to a close only by the ATF running low on ammunition and the local sheriff brokering a ceasefire. Four ATF agents had been killed and 16 wounded, and on the Branch Davidian side there were six dead and an unknown number of wounded. The ATF were back where they started, but now had a serious death toll on their hands.

With the killing of so many federal officers, the FBI took over command of the operation, headed now by Jeff Jamar of the FBI's San Antonio office. The FBI brought with them enormous resources, the hundreds of personnel including negotiators, tactical assault teams, surveillance specialists, forensic psychologists, explosive experts, and commanders. They locked the compound down under a siege that would remain in place for the next 51 days.

Yet the FBI personnel were not the only ones present. A contingent of 31 Texas Rangers were also initially deployed, with a principal responsibility for processing the crime scene along with the ATF and Attorney's Office. According to a subsequent investigation, the Texas Rangers were made to feel far from welcome by the FBI team:

> Captain Byrnes [the Rangers' commander] reported that the Rangers' relationship with the FBI command post deteriorated rapidly. Numerous Rangers complained to him that SAC Jamar and others in the command post had treated them rudely. The Rangers eventually pulled out of what they considered a hostile atmosphere.
>
> Captain Byrnes recounted a specific event in which the FBI's failure to cooperate may have impeded the search of the crime scene. On the afternoon of February 28, Michael Schroeder, a Branch Davidian, was killed while he and others attempted to penetrate the ATF perimeter on the north end of the property. Jamar initially allowed the Rangers to recover Schroeder's body and perform a limited crime-scene analysis. Later, the Rangers asked to be allowed to complete the crime-scene search by casting footprints and gathering other evidence. Jamar refused the request, and did not allow them back onto the crime scene for ten days. By then, rain had severely eroded the footprints they had hoped to process. After this incident, the Rangers had little or no contact with the FBI for the next

> three to four weeks. On occasions when they did meet with Jamar, they were forced to wait for extended periods of time, and often left without ever having seen Jamar.[258]

One group that did stay around was the National Guard. They had to, because the FBI requested the use of a wide range of military vehicles as possible assault tools. Although the vehicles had their main weapons systems removed to comply with the strictures of posse comitatus, they still constituted a rather alarming escalation of the force requirements. The final list included two Bel UH-1 helicopters, nine Bradley infantry combat vehicles (ICVs), two M1A1 Abrams tanks, and one tank retrieval vehicle. Furthermore, also present as "observers" at the siege were a good number of military personnel from the Special Forces community.

The problem with the FBI's accretion of force, as every military strategist knows, is that the more that force is built up the greater the propensity to use it. There was doubtless a substantial threat inside the compound, as the deaths of four agents had proven, but it did seem apparent from the negotiators' efforts that the Branch Davidians were not hell-bent on killing law enforcement officers. Nineteen children were released, and Koresh sent out a video showing that everyone else was there of their own accord (although many children remained). Furthermore, as the siege dragged on the FBI began applying psychological warfare techniques – playing deafening, distorted music through amplifiers throughout the night, cutting off utilities supplies, crushing and removing the Branch Davidian cars using the military vehicles. A congressional report noted a division beginning to emerge in the perceptions of the FBI personnel:

> In the case of Waco, the negotiators felt that the negotiating and tactical components of the FBI's strategy were more often contradictory than complementary. The negotiators' goal was to establish a rapport with the Branch Davidians in order to win their trust. As part of this effort, negotiators emphasized to Branch Davidians the "dignity" and fair treatment the group would receive upon its exit from the compound. By contrast, the negotiators felt that the efforts of the tactical personnel were directed toward intimidation and harassment. In the negotiators' judgment, those aggressive tactics undermined their own attempts to gain Koresh's trust as a prelude to a peaceful surrender.
>
> In particular, some of the negotiators objected to: (1) the loud music, noise, and chants used as "psychological warfare;" (2) the shut-off of electricity to the compound on March 12 shortly after two people exited the compound; and (3) the removal of automobiles from the compound on March 21 after seven people exited the compound. All of these actions were viewed by the negotiators as counter-productive to their efforts. The electricity shut-

> off and the removal of cars were seen as particularly unwarranted since these actions in effect "punished" Koresh for permitting the departure of compound members.[259]

One side or the other would have to win out – negotiation or force? Finally, the latter was chosen. With some FBI authorities fearing that the Branch Davidians might be about to commit a mass suicide, on April 12 the Bureau presented a plan to the US Attorney General, Janet Reno, for ending the siege. The plan essentially revolved around using the armored vehicles to close up to the compound and then either shoot or pump CS gas into the building, forcing the people inside (including 23 children) out of the building where they could be arrested. If the people inside weren't flushed out by the gas, the plan contained the final, chilling idea that "if all subjects failed to surrender after 48 hours of tear gas, then a CEV [combat engineer vehicle] with a modified blade will commence a systematic opening up/ disassembly of the structure until all subjects are located." Not surprisingly, the plan also made proposals for how it might handle an unexpectedly large number of casualties.

The plan was finally approved after much angst, and was put into action on April 19. CEVs went in at 5.55am, punched holes in the outer walls and began pumping in tear gas. FBI officials spoke with the Branch Davidians inside, and told them that this was not an assault and that they would not enter the building. For those inside, already sleep deprived, anxious, and with heightened eschatological sensibilities, the actions would have doubtless fitted the perfect description of an assault.

Despite being cautioned against firing on the CEVs, bullets from the Branch Davidians soon started zinging off the armor plate. In response, the FBI sent in the Bradley vehicles to fire Ferret rounds – munitions canisters filled with CS – into the building. Those Branch Davidians who weren't fighting back were sheltering in a cinder block room inside the building, some using gas masks to keep breathing normally. Up to 380 Ferret rounds penetrated the building in total. Gradually the building became a choking, and in many locations structurally unsound, place of refuge for the Branch Davidians.

Worse was to come. Just after noon, three separate fires ignited inside the building, and the smoke and flames gradually spread until the whole structure was a raging inferno. The FBI had no fire crews on standby, having initially rejected those resources as vulnerable to small-arms fire. The fire ultimately engulfed the compound, and brought the Waco siege to an end by killing all but nine of the people left inside. In total 80 people died inside the building, including the 23 children.

The legal and political fallout from the Waco siege was seismic. The threatening nature of the Branch Davidians was not disputed – over 300 firearms and hundreds of thousands of rounds of ammunition were found in the ashen remains – but the competence and details of the operation were harshly questioned. Much debate centered on the reasons behind the fire. Initially, both the FBI and the Attorney General denied that any munitions used against the compound were pyrotechnic in nature, and asserted that the fire was started internally. The latter belief still remains highly plausible, but in 1999 the Attorney General was finally forced to admit that military-style CS-dispensing munitions with pyrotechnic qualities were in fact used "in limited numbers," and that a previous FBI crime lab report had had the page that referred to these munitions removed before subsequent investigations.[260] These munitions might not have been responsible for the fires, but they did show that the FBI had limited its presentations of that day, a fact that gave further room for various conspiracy theories about the siege to thrive and spread.

Ultimately, the Waco siege might well be a perfect example of when militarism does indeed become a problem when bolted onto law enforcement. FBI sources interviewed for *Newsweek* by Daniel Klaidman and Michael Isikoff stated that for many of the FBI's tactical teams, the siege provided "an opportunity to put their expertise to use, and to break out some new weaponry."[261] The siege became, in effect, a monster too big to stop or control, although there is no denying that bringing the crisis to an end by negotiation alone was proving to be a tough objective after 51 days.

Yet there was one example from the 1990s when an overt recourse to military support in a domestic setting did not result in uncontrollable violence, at least on the part of the military. We have already seen many of the problems that occur when military forces are applied to civil disturbances, and in 1992 Los Angeles saw the necessity for one of the largest peacetime deployments of National Guard forces since the end of World War II. On March 3, 1991, the 32-year-old African-American "Rodney" Glen King, intoxicated on alcohol and marijuana, was pulled over by police following a high-speed car chase. In the confrontation that followed, King was tasered twice, both applications failing to bring him down, after which he was hit a total of 56 times with batons by several officers, 27 officers being present at the incident. The whole episode was captured on camera, however, by a civilian nearby, who then passed her video tape over to the news networks.

For the public here seemed to be an undeniable case of excessive force, and the four principal officers involved in the assault were charged and brought before a court. On April 29, 1992, the court found three officers not guilty of the charges and was unable to reach a decision over the fourth officer. Even President George H.W. Bush was shocked at the outcome, but nothing prepared America for the severity of the social response. Following the verdict, six days (April 29–May 4) of rioting spread throughout Los Angeles in scenes more akin to a war zone than to a sophisticated urban zone in a peacetime nation.

By the time the rioting subsided, 53 people had been killed and over 2,000 injured, mostly through the actions of rioters turning on each other or criminals taking the opportunity to settle scores. (Remember that at this time there were an estimated 100,000 gang members active in Los Angeles County.) For example, the Korean-American citizens of Koreatown actually formed themselves into armed defense groups to protect their stores, resulting in street battles with similarly armed looters. Some 1,100 buildings were destroyed through arson and the total repair bill ran close to $1 billion.

Such was the scale of the rioting that shortly after 9:00pm on April 29, the office for the governor of California requested the deployment of 2,000 soldiers of the California Army National Guard (CANG). By the time the riots drew into their last days, more than 10,000 CANG troops and 3,500 regular soldiers (2,000 regular army and 1,500 Marines) had been mobilized on the streets of Los Angeles.

Taking some of the blood-washed precedents already studied in this book, the deployment of such a hefty force, bristling with all the paraphernalia of war, onto the streets of a major city could have been the prelude to another landmark massacre. Furthermore, in cases of civil disturbances, special lock plates were meant to be installed that rendered the CANG M16 rifles incapable of full-auto fire. In the case of the Los Angeles riots, however, there simply was not time to have these installed. The CANG troops also had little civil disturbance training and no riot shields or batons – their CoF essentially consisted of three levels: visual presence, verbalization, and then potentially devastating firepower.

Yet by this stage in history there was an acute sensitivity to the implications of using the military in civil disturbances, and the military trod lightly. Tasking orders were centralized in the Los Angeles County Emergency Operations Center (EOC), although the military units found themselves barraged by ill-formed requests for assistance, mainly because the LAPD had been bolstered by multiple other law enforcement agencies in the attempt to quash the riots. Nevertheless, the CANG and then the regular forces spread out through the city, and were critical in bringing eventual order by implementing a dusk-to-dawn curfew. Incredibly, the CANG, the formation deployed during the worst of the riots, fired only 20 rounds in total.[262] Two people were killed by CANG troopers, compared to eight by regular law enforcement officers. For example, during one shooting, a gang member had stood before CANG troops and issued a challenge that he would return later and kill them. This did not worry the National Guardsmen unduly – the riots were a time of vitriolic language – but this time the individual was determined to press home his claims. He returned after the curfew, behind the wheel of his car. He drove directly at the Guardsmen at speed, attempting to hit them, and on his first pass hit one Guardsman, although he was not seriously injured. The suspect swung the car around for a second attempt. This time, however, the safeties had come off on the M16s. Ten rounds were fired at the car tires, an extremely difficult target area that brought no success. In a few seconds it became apparent that this individual required more decisive action, and one bullet in the shoulder and two through the head finally brought the car to a stop.

Law enforcement officers and the CANG had essentially quenched the worst of the riots by the time that regular forces arrived (plus the rioters were running out of steam), but on May 1 the president ordered the CANG federalized – i.e. brought under the control of the regular forces. For many in the CANG, this was initially a slap in the face that dented morale,[263] although retaining CANG commanders at high levels of operational control helped to restore pride somewhat. In terms of the use of force, one notable aspect of the federalization order was the attempt to create stricter deployment of arms onto the streets, as Lieutenant Colonel Christopher Schnaubelt pointed out in the military magazine *Parameters* in 1997:

> The single most contentious issue following federalization, however, was the designation of arming orders. An attachment to the rules of engagement, arming orders prescribed the readiness condition of individual weapons during the crisis. The arming orders specified six individual readiness postures ranging from AO-1 – rifle at sling arms, bayonet in its scabbard, magazine in the ammunition pouch, and chamber empty – to the highest level, AO-6. In this posture, each soldier's rifle was to be at port arms, bayonet fixed, magazine in the weapon, and a round in the chamber. In actuality, even at the highest levels of arming order, soldiers kept their bayonets on their belts because the bayonets were both useless during the riots and dangerous to oneself and to other soldiers. The controversy concerned whether soldiers should routinely keep a magazine in their weapons, which constituted an AO-5 arming order.[264]

The arming orders harked back to earlier attempts to frame civil disturbance force doctrine, but Schnaubelt goes on to note that they were widely ignored, especially by the CANG, whose soldiers tended to keep a magazine in the weapon at all times. Such disobedience is not surprising, as the CANG troopers had experienced the full intensity of the riots, and were doubtless unwilling to face a fluid riot situation without an instant firepower response. Yet the fact that the military firepower never seriously slipped out of control is indeed a testimony that times had changed. Major General (Ret.) James Delk of the CANG saw the key reason for this residing on the shoulders of the NCOs:

> If there is a secret to our success in Los Angeles, it is probably our young noncommissioned officers. We have been powering down for years in a consistent program involving at least the last four division commanders. This powering down was not designed for civil disturbances, but merely part of what the 40th Infantry Division considers battle focus. For instance, all noncommissioned officers in tactical operations centers throughout the division are expected to be able to brief. The payoff came during the riots. For example, one young sergeant with five other soldiers was responsible for an entire shopping center in Compton. Night after night, he and his soldiers exhibited unprecedented professionalism and restraint in spite of stress, fatigue and great provocation. Such soldiers were the real secret of success in Los Angeles, and we are extremely proud of them. [265]

Although the old adage "Guns don't kill people, people kill people" tends to be used today in a somewhat facile manner, Delk's observation about the benefits of giving NCOs more localized authority does prove an important point in this context. Although the CANG was armed with full-auto weapons, disregarded federalized arming orders, and were faced with violent assault, they generally maintained restraint throughout, the product of improved professionalism and a better sense of what they were there to do. Such is the goal of any use of force policy, civilian or military.

5
NEW WORLD ORDER?

This individual was emotionally disturbed. We had received a call that he had cut the house up, the curtains and different things. It was the summer months, he was in the kitchen, which is not a good place to be if you're going to get into a scuffle because there're sharp things in kitchens – knives and different things like that. Well when I first walked into the kitchen, what happened was he was wearing a parka and it was almost 98 degrees outside, so you know something's wrong right off the bat. Something's not quite right. So we try to verbalize and talk and say "Hey, why don't you take the jacket off?" because obviously you want to know what's under the jacket. Well as I entered the kitchen he ended up taking one hand and inserting it into the sleeve of the left hand side of the jacket. His hand disappeared, which instinctively told me that something bad was about to happen. I knew that. As soon as he reached up his sleeve I started to gain distance... I started to back up. My backup officer behind me saw what was going on and knocked some relatives out of the way, to keep them away from me. So he had my back, I was fine, I was in a good situation.

All the training now was kicking in. At that point I was drawing my service weapon because he was drawing something out of his sleeve and I didn't know what it was. But my SiG was coming out of the holster, I drew down [took aim] on the individual and immediately went to commands "Drop the knife! Drop the knife! Drop the knife!" when I saw the knife. So I was creating distance, which would give me reaction time, while my backup had my back cleared, so I knew that nobody was going to jump me from the back or do anything they shouldn't... The individual drew the knife then ran out the back door ... out of sight for me.

Then you go right back into a [different] scenario... at this point I had my SiG on top and my taser underneath – I had my taser in my hand, which I had carried into the situation. You want to use the least amount of force that you can use. If I can retire from this service without having to shoot anyone, that's great. I don't have a desire to hurt anybody, but I'm not going to allow anybody to kill me, hurt me … I'm going to do what I need to do, how I've been trained to do, and do it properly.

Well at that point I began what's called "plying the door" – I don't know where this guy is, he's just shot out the door. My major concern at that point is: OK, I just got a guy who went out back, he's armed with a knife … I'm starting to take slices out the door from where I can see … I want to make damn well sure what's on the far side before I take any step outside … I really don't care to get cut. Well right in the middle of that, another individual comes running in the door, and it turned out not to be the individual who had just pulled a knife. It was a relative. So the first thing that I do is glimpse at the individual's hands so I recognize that this isn't my target – there's nothing in the hands. All he's doing is fleeing right beside me, and I let him clear me… That was a moment in which I had to make a split-second decision – shoot/don't shoot, and that goes back to the shoot/don't shoot training. I had been put in [training] scenarios long before this ever happened and from the training I recognized that the first thing you look for is nothing in the hands… I'm safe right now, but I can take this guy down if I have to, if he comes in my direction, but it was evident that he just wanted to get away. Turned out that he saw the other guy run out with the knife and he wanted nothing else to do with that…

I get around far enough and I see this [the individual with the knife] on the deck, and he's holding in an offensive position. He's waving it at me like "C'mon, I'm ready for you!" OK, now I've got target lock, and I start to close the actual distance between him and me so I can get into taser range, because that's the first choice … if I can get him with the taser I'm not going to have to squeeze that trigger [of the SiG] … I got out and he was kinda bouncing back and forth, and we had two shots in our earlier [model] taser. The first – one dart hit and the other dart hit the deck siderail, so that didn't take effect. I ended up deploying the second one – that hit his parka and another [dart] hit him. It was enough that it caused him a problem, so he closed on me a little bit and at that point it was a question of shoot/don't shoot? Again you go back to that, and I had taken all the slack out of the trigger on my handgun because if he was going to try to move that knife he was not going to make it, he was not going to get to me. Luckily, the taser bit enough to the extent that he threw the knife down … I relaxed my grip on the handgun, holstered my handgun at that point, got it out of the way, and locked and secured it so that it was safe for me to approach the suspect. I had the taser trigger down and finally when I got close to him I kicked the knife off the deck so only he and I were on the deck. I dropped the taser to my side and I took him down – we had Cap-Stun, it was a [tear] gas that we used, because he was still struggling … I utilized that to gain control of him … so now it was a hand-to-hand situation; we had de-escalated from a deadly force scenario to a use-of-force scenario, but

> it was all hands on. I was able to get him in custody and nobody was injured... I went home that night and he went to whatever facility was necessary.[266]

This dramatic story, courtesy of Second Lieutenant Dan Courtney of the Fairfax County Police, illustrates perfectly a fundamental change that has occurred in law enforcement over the last 20 years. At one point Dan has two weapons in his hands – his firearm and his taser.[267] The decision he had to make was which trigger to pull – one trigger could send the suspect to the floor, the other could send him to the morgue. Complicating the equation was that the wrong decision could have resulted in either Dan's serious injury or death (or that of a third party), or the unnecessary death of the suspect. In this instance, the professionalism of the officer and the effectiveness of the taser meant that the situation resolved itself in the best way possible.

This chapter will bring our history of police use of force up to date, looking at the period from around 2000 to the present day. Much remains the same, as we shall see, but the pressures upon police have continued to sharpen, and the use of force spectrum has become ever more complex.

LESS LETHAL

Over recent decades the US law enforcement community has witnessed the steady, progressive introduction of "non-lethal" or "less lethal" technologies into its use of force arsenal. The two terms are applied to the same weapons – tear gas, rubber bullets, bean bag rounds, taser – but with different degrees of confidence. "Non-lethal" suggests that they never kill, while "less lethal" acknowledges that, on rare occasions, they can and do. Such is the root of their controversy.

Less lethal technologies have been around in one shape or another since the 1920s and 30s, principally in the form of tear gas. Yet tear gas was generally deployed as a non-standard weapon for quashing civil disturbances, rather than an issue piece of kit that hangs on the belt of the officer. That situation changed in the 1980s and 1990s, as police departments around the country began to snap up man-portable less lethal technologies to provide alternatives to using firearms or batons. The ideal was that aggressive and violent subjects could be controlled without seriously harming them, ensuring that the police could protect themselves while also reducing their exposure to criminal or civil liability. Experiments with arming police officers with mace canisters began back in the 1960s, with mixed results. Police in Pittsburgh, for example, received mace back in 1965, but the program was wrapped up ten years later on account of problems controlling the dispersion of the irritant spray. On several occasions, blowback from the mace container left the officers wincing on the floor while the assailants hot-footed their escape. It was also found that spraying intoxicated or enraged individuals with mace often simply made the individual even madder, rather than incapacitating him or her.

An improved alternative to mace was sought, and the late 1980s and early 1990s saw the introduction of pepper sprays, principally the Cap-Stun product designed to deliver a blast of organic Oleoresin Capsicum (basically an extract of chillis). (Pepper sprays were actually introduced into the US postal service during the early 1980s to see off angry dogs.) Directed at the face of an assailant, the pepper spray produces uncontrollable coughing and scalding eye watering, plus a loss of body motor control (through the pain) and an intense burning sensation on the skin, all of which can immobilize even the most passionate individual.

The idea caught on. The FBI switched from mace to Cap-Stun in 1989, and within a year more than 1,000 police agencies had followed suit. In fact, here were the roots of controversy. The FBI officer who conducted the first pepper spray assessment studies, FBI Special Agent Thomas W.W. Ward, became the product's most vocal promoter. In 1996, however, Ward was forced to admit that he had accepted $57,000 from the spray's manufacturer, which was actually owned by his wife. None of this looked good, and indeed Ward ultimately served two months in prison and three years' probation.

Yet pepper spray was still promoted as an effective weapon, despite growing concerns that it was actually a prime cause of significant numbers of fatalities. The FBI, as leader of the pepper spray movement, obviously became concerned by such cases during the late 1990s, as the February 1997 Law Enforcement Bulletin made clear:

> Unfortunately, as the use of pepper spray increased, so, too, grew the list of injuries reported and the number of cases in which the aerosol agent failed to subdue offenders. On July 11, 1993, an officer from the Concord, North Carolina, Police Department sprayed a 24-year-old male charged with disorderly conduct. After being sprayed, the subject complained of respiratory difficulty and then collapsed. Officers drove the man to the police station where he was found to be unresponsive. He was pronounced dead a short time later. After the autopsy, the medical examiner issued the following statement: "In my opinion, the cause of death in this case is asphyxia due to bronchospasm precipitated by inhalation of pepper spray."
>
> Just 3 months later, a 34-year-old man died of cardiac arrest after officers subdued him with pepper spray. In January 1994, a 37-year-old man being committed for psychiatric care by his family became violent. When police officers arrived, they chose to use pepper

> spray to subdue the subject rather than using more aggressive control measures. The subject died a short time later at an area hospital.
>
> As a result of these incidents, many departments collected cans of pepper spray and banned use of the product that they had so optimistically distributed to their officers just a short time earlier. Such a reaction may cross the line into overreaction. There is nothing necessarily wrong with pepper spray; nor was its use in these three incidents necessarily inappropriate. The problem lies in the fact that departments bought the product under false assumptions and allowed it to be used under unrealistic expectations.[268]

The point about "false assumptions" is critical. No single less lethal technology is a panacea, a faultless way to control out-of-control people. The problem with pepper spray, and one that remains to this day, is that it interferes with breathing as part of its *modus operandi*, and that is rarely something to be recommended. Most deaths associated with pepper spray usage appear to be caused by the pepper spray aggravating some other condition or state, such as asthma or the suspect being placed in a restraint position in which they find it difficult to breathe (death from this latter cause is referred to as "positional asphyxia.")

In 2003, by which time the most US police officers were wearing pepper spray on their belts, the US Department of Justice got to grips with the issue in a report entitled "The Effectiveness and Safety of Pepper Spray." The report consists of two parts. The first uses the records of three North Carolina police departments to assess how the introduction of pepper sprays in 1993 affected 1) the numbers of police officers injured in assaults; 2) the numbers of injuries to suspects through police use of force; and 3) the numbers of excessive force complaints against the police. The second part features an analysis of 73 deaths in custody following the use of pepper spray, then judges the degree to which the pepper spray was responsible for the fatalities.

In the North Carolina study, the three departments assessed were (with dates in which they introduced pepper sprays): North Carolina State Highway Patrol (SHP; January 1993), Charlotte-Mecklenburg (CMPD; April 1993), and Winston-Salem (WSPD; January 1995). The rates of officer injuries did indeed make a general decline after the introduction of pepper sprays, although in some cases a decline had already begun before the sprays arrived. In the case of the SHP, however, 87 officers were injured on duty in 1992, whereas in 1993 only 58 injuries were recorded, and the figures have remained generally low ever since.[269] (The report points out that similar studies in Baltimore County also found drops in the number of assaults on police following the introduction of pepper sprays.) In CMPD and SHP, the numbers of suspect injuries also declined with the introduction of pepper spray, suggesting that it provided officers with improved mid-range force procedures compared to whacking someone with a baton.

Regarding the data relating to in-custody deaths following the use of pepper spray, the study (conducted at the University of Texas, Southwestern Medical Center) found that in the 63 cases fit for study, the pepper spray appeared to be a primary contributor to fatality in two cases, one involving an asthmatic and the other involving someone who suffered bronchial spasms as the result of inhaling significant quantities of the spray. However, in both cases there were other factors that could have contributed to the fatality. The bronchial victim mentioned, for example, was obese and was handcuffed with his hands behind his back and placed face-down on the floor when being transported. This restraint position is a common denominator in many positional asphyxiation cases:

> When a subject is made to lie face down, hands cuffed behind, pressure on the abdomen forces the abdominal contents up against the diaphragm, making it harder to breathe. This situation is exacerbated when the subject is obese. Weights applied to the back, such as an arresting officer placing his weight on the subject's shoulder-blade area, also interfere with a suspect's ability to breathe (in one case reported in this study, a sofa was placed on the subject to help control him).[270]

The dangers of positional asphyxiation illustrate how any use of force by police, however seemingly removed from deadly means, can carry with it lethal consequences if aggravated by other factors, such as the health or mental state of the victim. The Department of Justice report admitted that all the data it presented relating to pepper spray use is open to interpretation, and doubtless the controversy about it will reignite following the next, inevitable death. Yet the point of less lethal technologies is not to guarantee entirely that someone will not die, but rather to provide a more positive option than pumping them full of bullets or delivering hefty blows with a baton. Essentially, police officers do not want to use any degree of force – the decision to do so is largely in the hands of the suspect, at least if the officers are true professionals.

From pepper spray we now turn to another controversial less lethal technology, one that has inspired even greater media frenzies. At the time of writing, the conducted energy device (CED), better known by the name of its most popular manufacturer, Taser, is riding high in the headlines once again, following a particularly distressing case.

On October 2, 2008, NYPD officer Lieutenant Michael Pigott rose early on his 46th birthday and slipped quietly out of the house, taking with him a photograph of his wife and children. He drove over to his former command station in Brooklyn, went inside, and took a 9mm Glock handgun from an officer's locker. He then shot himself, leaving a suicide note nearby.[271]

The source of Pigott's despair was an incident that occurred on September 24, 2008. Iman Morales, an individual suffering from schizophrenia and bipolar disorder, had been confronted by police following a disturbance, and was chased through the apartment block. Stark naked, Morales climbed out of a fourth floor window using the fire escape, and stood on the security gate container over the front doors, 10ft above the ground. There he kept police officers at bay, waving an 8ft-long fluorescent light bulb as an improvised weapon. The impasse went on for some time before Pigott, the officer in charge, ordered one of his officers to deploy a taser on Morales. This the officer did, and the electric charge flowed into the suspect. Morales was locked rigid by the 5,000 volts of current, and he fell headfirst onto the sidewalk below, where he sustained fatal injuries. Pigott was under investigation following the incident, having ordered the taser deployed at a figure occupying an elevated position, in breach of departmental guidelines. The burden of the man's death, and the possible consequences for Pigott's career, were obviously too much for the officer to bear.

Two points emerge from this sad episode. The first is the general issue of officer suicide. Make no mistake, officer suicide is a serious problem that is only now just emerging into the light. The head of the National Police Suicide Foundation in Maryland, Robert E. Douglas Jr, notes that police suicides run at the rate of one every 19 or 20 hours, making fatalities from suicide more than double the number of officers violently killed in the line of duty.[272] While about 11 out of every 100,000 Americans will commit suicide, amongst police officers the rate starts at 18 per 100,000, and some experts think that the actual figures could be double or even treble that number. (The CHP lost an average of one officer every month during an eight-month period in 2006.[273]) The cause of the high rates of suicide is not hard to see if you start to dig deeper into the issue. Policing is a high-stress job in which police officers often see, and occasionally are required to do, dreadful things. Divorce rates amongst the ranks of the police are high – possibly as high as 75 percent – precipitated by long, unsocial hours and the tension brought home from the job. Stress levels are kept constantly high, and in September 2008 research from the University at Buffalo highlighted some of the insidious effects this was having. Officers over 40 had a much greater chance of suffering a heart attack, high cholesterol, or high blood pressure when compared to the rest of the population. Some 23 percent of male officers and 25 percent of female officers had suicidal thoughts (the civilian average is around 13.5 percent), all of this aggravated by constant exposure to human misery and the disrupted circadian rhythms that resulted from night shifts.[274] The police culture has been traditionally poor at encouraging traumatized officers to talk about their experiences and to seek professional counseling where necessary, these seen as clashing with the macho ethos. Some agencies have responded better than others to this crisis. A Los Angeles sheriff's anti-suicide program, launched in 2001, reduced the number of suicides to just two out of 9,000 officers between 2002 and 2007.[275] More work remains to be done if this dark corner of policing is to be eradicated.

The second point about the Morales incident, and turning back to our study of CEDs, is that although tasers and their ilk are used hundreds of times each year in the United States with no serious consequences for the suspects, incidents such as the Morales death put them back on the map with civil rights and anti-CED organizations. For many such organizations, the CED is tantamount to torture, bringing what they see as the ghastly electro-practices of some foreign police states into the United States. In 2006, Amnesty International released a report condemning taser use for its violation of human rights and its possibly fatal effects:

> Since June 2001, more than 150 people have died in the USA after being shocked by a taser. Of those deaths, 85 have occurred in the USA since Amnesty International released its report (in November 2004) calling for a suspension on the use and transfer of these weapons. Amnesty International raised its concerns in its previous report that the number of taser-related deaths had been rising each year. There were three deaths reported in 2001, 13 in 2002, 17 in 2003 and 48 in 2004. In 2005 there were 61 taser-related deaths, and by the mid February 2006 there have already been 10 deaths.[276]

The report argues that CEDs could precipitate cardiac or respiratory arrest in medically vulnerable patients, especially if they were shocked multiple times. One of its examples is that of 21-year-old Patrick Lee, from Nashville, Tennessee. Having been thrown out of a night club for disruptive behavior on September 22, 2005 (he had been taking LSD and marijuana), Lee stripped naked outside and was confronted by police officers. Lee resisted arrest forcibly, and as a result the officers deployed their tasers, shocking him 19 times in total. At this point, officers noted that Lee was having trouble breathing, and requested an ambulance. Two days later he died. The autopsy found that it was not the drugs he had taken that were responsible for his death, but rather a state of "excited delirium" (more about that term shortly), exacerbated by the tasering.[277] Amnesty International points to numerous other instances where individuals have experienced cardiac arrest following taser incidents. Another problem that Amnesty International associates with taser use is that, in its opinion, many police departments place taser use too low on the CoF, and consequently officers are more inclined to use them either casually or excessively when other force methods are more appropriate.

Before addressing these concerns, it is worth reminding ourselves what a CED actually does, specifically the taser. Tasers were invented during the late 1960s and early 1970s, but took a long period of refinement before they slipped into widespread police issue during the 1990s. The first major commercial model was the Air Taser 34000, but several failures during tests and actual street use (such as in the Rodney King incident) led to the development of two improved versions, the M26 and the X26. (Both these later models were configured like firearms, with pistol grips and proper triggers, while the earlier model was simply a box shape.) We'll take a closer look at the X26, to see the most recent version.

To operate the X26, a cartridge is locked onto the open front of the gun. This cartridge contains two small but extremely sharp metal probes, these connected to wires that are linked to a battery power pack contained in the grip. To fire the X26, the safety is moved to the fire position, and on doing this a laser beam is projected from an emitter beneath the front of the gun to the target. The operator then pulls the trigger, and the two darts are fired by gas propulsion, the wires unraveling behind them in flight. The prongs stick into the target, then the X26 delivers a 50,000-volt charge down the wires, the two prongs making an electrical circuit. Whereas the first generation of taser only produced pain compliance, the M26 and X26 induce "neuromuscular incapacitation" (NMI) – the subject goes completely rigid, all the major body muscles locked into complete spasm, although breathing and heart muscles still function. Even if the prongs don't punch through skin, they can still deliver their electrical load through thick clothing. The initial electrical burst lasts for five seconds, but the officer can then deliver subsequent bursts by flicking the safety switch up and down. During incapacitation, officers can handle and handcuff the suspect as long as they don't place their hands directly on the line between the two prongs (which would add them to the electrical circuit). Furthermore, the X26 can also be used as a direct-contact weapon, cattle-prod style – when the cartridge is removed the exposed electrical conduct nodes can be pressed directly against a hostile individual and deliver a jolting spark. Prong removal is performed by the officers on site using a special sterilized medical kit provided with the taser, although if the prongs are lodged in the breasts (of a female suspect), genital areas or eyes, then the suspect is taken to hospital.

It is hard for civilians to appreciate how the taser is appreciated by many law enforcement personnel. As the opening narrative of this chapter illustrates, the taser provides an officer with the option of taking down a potentially or actually violent individual without resorting to firepower. Indeed, given the instant incapacitation achieved by the latest generations of tasers, it is arguable that tasers have the advantage over firearms even in life or death situations, given the frequently unpredictable results of conventional bullets. A senior officer of the Springfield, Missouri, PD wrote in 2004 that "In my opinion, the Taser is the single most important police device ever invented. We have only scratched the surface of Taser capability and the long term positive impact it will have on accomplishing the police mission with reduced potential for death and injury."[278] The only downside is the taser's limited range (up to 35ft, but practical ranges are generally about half that) and its one-shot cartridges, but as a glimpse of the future, Taser has recently introduced the XREP. The XREP packs all the punch of the X26 into a single shell that can be fired from a smoothbore shotgun and has a range of up to 65ft (the electrical charge is initiated wirelessly).

On the issue of the taser's safety, in June 2008 the Department of Justice issued an interim report entitled *Study of Deaths Following Electro Muscular Disruption*. The report brought together broad expertise from across the medical and law enforcement communities, and came to a very definite conclusion about the safety of CEDs:

> Although exposure to CED is not risk free, there is no conclusive medical evidence within the state of current research that indicates a high risk of serious injury or death from the direct effects of CED exposure. Field experience with CED use indicates that exposure is safe in the vast majority of cases.
>
> Therefore, law enforcement need not refrain from deploying CEDs, provided the devices are used in accordance with accepted national guidelines.[279]

The report goes on to state that "there is currently no medical evidence that CEDs pose a significant risk for induced cardiac dysrhythmia when deployed reasonably," and that although hyperventilation can occur following the electrical charge "there is no medical evidence of lasting changes in respiratory function in human subjects following exposure to CED."[280] A key cause in many of those cases where death has followed the use of a CED is "excited delirium," here explained by the report:

> *Excited delirium* is one of several terms that describe a syndrome characterized by psychosis and agitation and may be caused by several underlying conditions. It is frequently associated with combativeness and elevated body temperature. In some of these cases, the individual is medically unstable and in a rapidly declining state that has a high risk of mortality in the short term even with medical intervention or in the absence of CED deployment or other types of subdual.

> Excited delirium that requires subdual carries with it a high risk of death, regardless of the method of subdual. Current human research suggests that the use of CED is not a life threatening stressor in cases of excited delirium beyond the generalized stress of the underlying condition or appropriate subdual.[281]

Overall, the Department of Justice report acknowledges that any use of force carries with it mortal risks, hence the police generally use the term "less lethal" rather than "non-lethal." This caution can be applied to any force tool, from batons through to relatively new weapons such as the "bean bag round" – a non-bursting bag of shot fired from a shotgun that hits the suspect with all the force of a boxer's fist, but which causes no penetrative injury. For police officers, the taser and other less lethal technologies are critical tools in handling social violence without hiking up the body count.

Nevertheless, some police departments are treading warily. In October 2008 in San Antonio, Texas, Police Chief William McManus prohibited officers from using tasers against known drug addicts and stipulated that no more than one officer at a time could taser the suspect.[282] At the same time, use of the taser has increased exponentially in many agencies. In Orange Country, Florida, for example, in 2001 chemical agents were used in 41.9 percent of force deployments and tasers in 43.4 percent. By 2003, however, chemical agent usage had dropped to 7.76 percent while had taser usage ascended to 77.63 percent.[283] After the Sean Bell shooting in 2006 (see Chapter 6), a RAND Corporation study of deadly force in the NYPD actually recommended the increased training in and distribution of tasers to reduce the number of civilian deaths in force encounters, a view that would sit awkwardly with Amnesty International's findings.[284]

The fact remains that the law enforcement community is operating in an increasingly litigious society with few compunctions about taking a police officer to court. Between 1984 and 2000, the rates of litigation brought against the police in the United States rose between 21 and 40 percent, depending on the court and jurisdiction.[285] And here we encounter another problem with the use of less lethal weapons. With their introduction, the police CoF has become more complicated. Now, an officer must prove not only that a dangerous suspect was a direct threat to his or her well-being, but also that that choice of force option was entirely warranted, and that another force option was not viable or possible under the circumstances.

This situation is just one of the modern minefields through which police officers step. A good example provided by Thomas Aveni in interview was that of seven officers called to apprehend a disturbed individual. All seven officers deployed their tasers, and no single individual managed to embed both prongs of the taser shot into the suspect, resulting in an ineffective incapacitation. The situation was resolved when a police cycle patrol officer simply jumped off his bike and wrestled the suspect to the ground. In this case, there is the suggestion that having more options within the CoF could make actually make officers resort to technology when more old-fashioned forms of policing could suffice.

TRAINING AT THE NEXT LEVEL

It was another of those incidents that stirs a society often jaded from gun crime. On February 24, 2005, one David Hernandez Arroyo Sr marched towards the steps of the Smith County Courthouse in Tyler, Texas. Engaged in a bitter child support battle with his ex-wife (they had been married 22 years), Maribel Estrada, Arroyo meant deadly business – he was wearing body armor and was carrying a semi-auto MAK-90 rifle, similar to an AK-47. Seeing his wife and son, David Hernandez Arroyo Jr, walking towards the courthouse, Arroyo approached them on the court steps, his fury building. Once he was close, he opened up with his rifle, the shots cracking across the town square. Life ended in an instant for Maribel, hit in the head by a 7.62mm round, and Arroyo Jr also went down, his leg smashed by the high-velocity round. Unfortunately, Arroyo's energy for vengeance wasn't spent. Police officers around the courthouse drew their pistols and began to fire at him; he returned in kind with volleys of shots that were soon dropping officers from serious injuries, and smashing up the glass front of the courthouse.

At this point, a local civilian, Mark Allen Wilson, attempted to bring the shootout to an end. Wilson had a concealed firearm permit, and was carrying a Colt .45 automatic pistol. With Arroyo distracted as he slugged it out with the police officers, Wilson moved up close and put a .45 round right into Arroyo's torso. Unfortunately, Arroyo's body armor meant that the bullet did little more than make the gunman stagger, and he turned on Wilson, who was now taking cover behind a vehicle. Another .45 round hit Arroyo to no decisive effect. Arroyo opened up on Wilson, the full-metal jacket (FMJ) bullets easily capable of penetrating the vehicle bodywork. Wilson fell forward onto the floor. Arroyo covered the distance and blasted the life out of Wilson with a ripple of shots at point blank range.

The situation was tumbling out of control for the police. The imbalance in firepower was somewhat corrected by the arrival of Sergeant Rusty Jacks, who brought with him an AR-15-type rifle and, in a display of guts, actually rode spread-eagled on the hood of a police cruiser in an attempt to catch up with Arroyo, who was now attempting to make his getaway. With 116 spent shell cases littering the vicinity of the courthouse, Arroyo had jumped into his truck and sped off, with the police in fast pursuit.

The chase soon moved from the streets of Tyler onto the freeway, the shrieks of police sirens being punctuated by the occasional shot from both police and suspect. It was critical that Arroyo's flight was brought to a halt, so Deputy Sheriff John Smith rammed the truck, firing at Arroyo out of his window at the same time. Arroyo did indeed stop his truck, but only to get out and fire at Smith, who sped away to safety. But Arroyo had made a fatal error – he had stopped, and police shooters now had their opportunity. As he moved back to get into the truck, Jacks was out of his vehicle and targeting him. Jacks pumped out five quick shots, and just as Arroyo swung his leg into his truck, one of them went straight into the back of his head, killing him instantly.

The Tyler Courthouse shooting was an exceptional event, but one that police departments spend more and more time training for. The episodic and truly dreadful school shootings that have occurred in recent times – particularly those at Columbine in April 1999 and Virginia Tech in April 2007 – and the Washington beltway sniper attacks seem to show that such training is entirely warranted. Yet as we shall see, some researchers and specialists have begun to question the broader relevance of this training for dealing with what is known as the "active shooter."

Police firearms training has undoubtedly reached a high degree of sophistication. At the well-equipped Fairfax County (Virginia) training facility, for example, which I had the pleasure to visit, almost every tactical scenario was catered for. A specially constructed shooting house – a mock-up building used to enact tactical scenarios – allows students to practice forced or contested entries against instructors or other students posing as suspects, the use of painful "simunitions" in real weapons, plus the large body of critical instructors and students watching from galleries above, providing the adrenaline rush that is vital to effective training. Another area is devoted to rifle and shotgun shooting against a thoroughly bullet-riddled car, simulating a violent traffic stop. In the scenario I witnessed, one officer put down rifle fire on the mannequins around the car, while another officer made a flanking maneuver around the car to shoot at it with his pistol from another angle. In the video-simulation room, hundreds of tactical scenarios could be projected onto the screen, requiring the officers to make dynamic shoot/don't shoot decisions. To inject some motivation, a compressed air BB gun hovered menacingly over the screen – the instructor running the video could aim and fire this at the students, providing a stinging reminder that they had been too slow or had not taken sufficient cover. The screen could even play the scenarios in a low-light mode, with a simulated flashlight throwing a patch of light up onto the screen.

The breadth of training is excellent and shows how far law enforcement has come since the early days of sending a few dozen rounds into a static target then calling the officer trained. Furthermore, modern police officers can now boost their expertise through the dozens of privately offered deadly force training programs being run throughout the United States. These high-energy programs are often run by former SWAT or even ex-military personnel, and they tend to focus on active-shooter scenarios or on devolving the tactical skills of SWAT down to the street-level officer.

There is a problem, or at least a potential problem, however. Does this "trickle-down" of SWAT training increase the likelihood that officers will resort to inappropriate tactics in regular street policing, using deadly force when other types of force would be appropriate? The fact is that for most officers, the bulk of deadly force encounters occur as unexpected developments of banal policing situations, not the choreographed tactics used in a planned SWAT operation. For example, a total of 575 police officers were feloniously killed between 1996 and 2005. The primary situation in which these fatalities occurred were "Arrest situations" (147 fatalities), "Ambush situations" (102), "Traffic pursuits/stops" (102) and "Disturbance calls" (95).[286] "Tactical situations," by contrast, resulted in just 19 officer fatalities, yet may be presented in some training programs as the goal for which every officer must prepare. In other words, fatalities are more likely to occur during a normal day's policing than in an extreme shootout situation, so if shooting training is skewed towards the latter, then it could leave big gaps in an officer's judgment when faced with a situation that unexpectedly unfolds in front of him. Either he could be too quick to shoot (over 40 percent of people shot by police are unarmed), or the emphasis on using the gun could lead to basic procedural oversights that put the officer unnecessarily in the line of fire.

Thomas Aveni of the Police Policy Studies Council has highlighted this problem in several compelling articles. He asks:

> Is a patrol officer trained in quasi-SWAT tactics "better prepared" for a self-initiated [as opposed to tactically planned] confrontation of an armed felony-in-progress? Probably – if his/her firearms and tactical training has adequately instilled competency in essential skills. However, problems arise if officers have only been taught to use a "hammer" and everything he/she encounters begins looking like a "nail."[287]

To illustrate the issue, Aveni describes an actual incident in which officers were called to arrest a man who was known not to have a firearm and who had no history of being aggressive (he had never been arrested before). One officer nonetheless went in to the arrest with his gun drawn and aimed at the suspect's chest, SWAT-style, and apparently stumbled and discharged the weapon, killing the suspect. Aveni goes on to note that the "muzzle-heavy" approach to weapons-handling and law enforcement's "most highly specialized tactics and techniques" need a "firewall" between them and standard police practice if unnecessary casualties are to be avoided.[288] Furthermore, an emphasis on rapid deployment of the firearm, and the ability to take quick shots, means that "We're seeing grossly inadequate muzzle and trigger-finger discipline in officers."[289]

In an interview with the author, Aveni noted that there was an increasing problem in the United States with officers wanting to train more in aggressive forms of policing – the "ninja effect" – particularly in the heightened state of emotion generated in the aftermath of the 9/11 attacks. Furthermore, the problem with many of the private training courses, Aveni argues, is that they achieve popularity by marketing themselves with extreme militaristic or SWAT-style imagery – posters of wrestling with vomit-covered drunks, a much more likely but still potentially serious scenario for officers on the street – wouldn't quite carry the same impact:

> So, in an attempt to distinguish themselves from the pack, competing training companies feel compelled to "out-SWAT" each other. How often do you see police training marketed with imagery of trainees in black BDUs [Battle Dress Uniforms], Kevlar helmets and bloused combat boots? Or, perhaps more tellingly, how often don't you see police training marketed with a SWAT motif?[290]

The problem with this type of mindset is that it can conceivably predispose some officers to think more in terms of how they deploy their weapons than of how to avoid deploying them in the first place. Furthermore, as the fatality statistics above demonstrated, the primary causes of officer fatalities are not those high-risk situations that occur once in a lifetime, but the day-to-day grind of regular policing:

> Beyond the marketing imagery lies the real problem. We know, from even a casual perusal of annual Uniform Crime Reports (UCR) and Law Enforcement Officers Killed and Assaulted (LEOKA) publications, that we're losing officers to similar mistakes that we've always lost officers to. Much of that has to do with the basic nature of policing, which doesn't change much. We're duty-bound to take some risks and place ourselves in some predicaments that we'd rather not be in. But, when we look critically at what we see the vast majority of commercial trainers impressing upon officers, we're likely to see aggressive, proactive techniques geared heavily toward active-shooter scenarios. This should come as no surprise, since many of the most influential commercial trainers have DOD backgrounds – and little if any legitimate police experience.[291]

Aveni argues that bearing in the mind the relatively few man hours police departments spend on shooting training (4–16 hours per annum), the training should spend much less time "shooting at paper and steel" and far more on developing situational awareness using video simulations, role playing (with pain-inducing munitions to inject more realism), and survival awareness. For "The speed we are encouraging on paper and steel seldom (if ever) translates into lives saved but frequently seems to contribute to a plethora of avoidable errors."[292]

Gregory Morrison extends the argument that police training has become somewhat disconnected from reality – indeed, he feels that it has never been effectively connected to the true experience of street-level policing:

> My biggest problem with police training today, is that we still do not systematically evaluate the officer-involved shootings from the standpoint of informing our programs. Officer-involved shootings are investigated for administrative and possible criminal charges, so it's an investigation to find out whether the officer violated a policy. A lot of the information that could be gleaned from shootings either isn't provided to police trainers, or they won't allow them access to it ... So we are still doing a lot of guessing about what works. What happens is we end up depending primarily on sort of anecdotal information and what individual instructors who are responsible for these programs thinks make common sense – which is why programs are all over the place.[293]

Morrison and Aveni both make critical observations as we approach the end of our historical analysis here. If we were to make a broad summary, it seems that the general movement of police training in the 20th century has been towards professionalizing instruction through better understanding of tactical realities, and the use of improved training technologies such as video simulation. However, we might say that the process of professionalization has gone too far, mainly through the increased militarization of some training programs. Instead of absorbing all the lessons from academic research (and Aveni, himself a long-time police officer, hints that the police community tended to be resistant towards academic work), much police training has become geared to high-order armed incidents or the proficient use of firepower, whereas actually these are not necessarily the things that keep average officers alive. Aveni is clear about the direction in which training should now go:

> Once your trainees have acquired basic marksmanship skills, get them away from live-fire as much as possible. It restricts the number of core judgment competencies that you can

> address safely. Live-fire limits your creativity in terms of trainee interactions with target mediums. Pop-up, turning and moving 3-D targets are nice, but they fail to adequately address the most vexing problems officers routinely face on the street. Live-fire almost always restricts your angles of fire – even if you have an expensive, 360 degree "shoot-house." The more realism you try to inject into live-fire training, the more you'll find yourself cursed by safety constraints.[294]

What Aveni is recommending is not a turn away from live-fire training, nor a rejection of preparation for the active shooting, but rather a deep familiarization with all the street scenarios that occur on a daily basis. Aveni also argues that low-light training should form a large part of any training program, since as many as 75 percent of all felonious assaults against police occur during evening and night tours of duty; in addition, about two-thirds of all officers feloniously slain in the line of duty are victimized during evening and night shifts. Combined with genuinely realistic programs, stretching the nerves and decision-making skills of the officers, this shift may well reduce the numbers of inevitable controversial shootings, although the psychological constants of deadly force engagements mean that these will never be entirely eradicated.

The problem involved with putting the new paradigm into action is a deep-seated cultural and emotional attraction to the tactical aspects of firearms training. Some of the blame must lie at the door of Hollywood and television, which undoubtedly glamorizes the cop who uses his guns to settle a problem. The "Dirty Harry" sequence of films in the 1970s and later movies such as the *Die Hard* and *Lethal Weapon* series, plus modern masterpieces such as *LAPD SWAT*, depict police for whom tactical skills and unbelievable gun handling are the apogee of policing, the talents that really get things done. The films also show killing someone as having remarkably few consequences for the police officer. In reality, when an officer shoots someone his gun is taken away and he is typically placed on administrative leave, both humbling experiences, although not ones that translate well to the big screen. We might say that such illusions are ironed out when the officer goes through police training, or starts to experience life on the street, but such representations of police officers are so all-pervasive that they surely have an impact on perceptions. A limited number of studies has shown that fictional cops do exert some level of influence over real officer behavior, from simple use of TV phrases through to adoption of ethical outlooks and even tactics.[295] Until society at large ceases to glamorize the "way of the gun" (which admittedly seems unlikely), then law enforcement must continue to focus its efforts on educating officers on the reality of gun use and the responsibility that comes with carrying a firearm.

Such are the negatives. On the positive side, what we can say is that most police are still largely better trained today than their counterparts of 20 or 30 years ago, with improved skills in gun handling when such becomes necessary. Yet bearing in mind what we have said above, the US law enforcement community has to watch out for any unwelcome trends. The numbers of people killed in justifiable homicides show a general upward climb since 2000. According to FBI figures, in 2000 law enforcement officers committed 309 justifiable homicides, reaching 437 in 2004. The numbers dropped back down again in 2005 to 341, but over the subsequent two years began to rise once more, to 391 in 2007. We have to be careful with such figures, as justifiable homicides peak and trough like waves throughout history. Rather than say that police officers are becoming more likely to shoot – and we must bear in mind that these shootings have been deemed as "justifiable" – the challenge for the future is ensuring that use of force training and expectations are plugged directly into the realities of an officer's vocation, and not thrown out of balance by excessive preparation for the active shooter.

NEW THREATS/OLD THREATS

In terms of officer safety, the 2000s give both new hopes and new concerns. The general trend over the last four decades is that policing has become safer, particularly in terms of the numbers of officers feloniously killed. Compare, for example, these six comparative years, three from the 1970s and three from the 2000s, and the numbers of officers killed in each year:

1973	134
1974	132
1975	129
2003	52
2004	57
2005	55[296]

The improvement is striking, brought about by a combination of better procedures and training (despite the issues noted above), plus the turn away from some of the truly unwholesome criminal trends of the 1970s. And yet, policing remains dangerous work, and figures released around the time of writing show that there is no cause for complacency. Indeed, in 2007 there was a 30 percent climb in officer fatalities (188 total fatalities) on duty when compared to 2006 (153 officers), with the number succumbing to hostile gunfire rising to 65. Yet one of the biggest causes of the fatality rise were automobile accidents, which numbered 36 in 2006 but rose to 47 in 2007.

Automobile accidents incurred during vehicular pursuits are a major cause of death of police officers – and suspects and civilians – each and every year, and deserve a brief consideration in a book on use of force. Indeed, the application of vehicles often forms part of department CoFs – most police officers are now trained to use their vehicles in a variety of offensive maneuvers, such as pushing a fleeing car off the road by ramming it in a (hopefully) controlled manner. There has long been the recognition, however, that whenever an officer flicks on his blue lights and puts his right foot down, he or she is entering a very dangerous phase. Back in the 1970s and 80s, various police departments conducted studies into pursuit, and the numbers gave some alarming insights into the unpredictability of high-speed chases. In the early 1980s, for example, the CHP studied the outcomes of vehicular pursuits over a six-month period. It found that in 683 pursuits, 198 ended in accidents, with 99 resulting in injuries and 7 resulting in deaths. A three-year study (1985–1987) in Dade County, Florida, saw the figures break down as follows: 952 pursuits analyzed; 364 pursuits resulted in accidents; 160 pursuits resulted in injuries; 7 pursuits resulted in deaths. (See Alpert and Fridell, *Police Vehicles and Firearms*, pp.101–03, for more details.) Similar figures emerged throughout the 1990s, leading the US Congress to implement the National Police Pursuit Policy Act of 1998. This act not only attempted to provide motorists with incentives not to flee the police (three years' minimum mandatory prison sentence), but also introduced guidelines about how officers should receive adequate pursuit training and how departments should implement proper pursuit data recording.

Despite such legislation, the problem in fact seems to be getting worse, not surprisingly given the massive increase in vehicular traffic in the United States over the past two decades. In 2004, the journal *Injury Prevention* published an article entitled "Motor Vehicle Crash Deaths Related to Police Pursuits in the United States." Its core results revealed a frightening death toll on US roads through vehicle chases:

> There were 260–325 police pursuits ending in a fatality annually in the United States for a total of 2654 crashes involving 3965 vehicles and 3146 fatalities during the nine year study period. Of the 3146 fatalities, 1088 deaths were of people not in the fleeing vehicle and 2055 to people in the fleeing vehicle. Altogether 102 (3.2%) of the fatalities were non-motorists, 40 were police officers, 946 (30.1%) were occupants of vehicles uninvolved in the police pursuit, and three were unknown. Most of the innocent deaths were motor vehicle occupants, with 102 being either pedestrians or bicyclists.[297]

These are sobering figures, and illustrate the critical need for a well-reasoned pursuit policy amongst police departments. The balance of any pursuit hangs on the question: "Does the perceived benefit of chasing and apprehending the suspect outweigh the risk posed to the suspect, public, and officers involved?" It is not an easy question to answer, and the policy changes according to the department involved.

The complexities of whether to begin a pursuit in the first place are illustrated by the following excerpt from the Pine Bluff (Arkansas) Police Department guideline document "Police Vehicle – Pursuit Driving":

> A. INITIATING THE PURSUIT
>
> 1. The decision to initiate pursuit must be based on the pursuing officer's conclusion that the immediate danger to the public created by the pursuit is less than the immediate or potential danger to the public should the suspect remain at large.
>
> 2. Any law enforcement officer in an authorized emergency vehicle may initiate a vehicular pursuit when ALL of the following criteria are met:
>
> a) The suspect exhibits the intention to avoid arrest by using a vehicle to flee apprehension for an alleged felony or misdemeanor offense; or
>
> b) The suspect operating the vehicle refuses to stop at the direction of the officer; and
>
> c) The suspect, if allowed to flee, could present a danger to human life or cause serious injury.
>
> 3. The pursuing officer shall consider the following factors in determining whether to initiate pursuit:
>
> a) The performance capabilities of the pursuit vehicle;
>
> b) The condition of the road surface upon which the pursuit is being conducted;
>
> c) The amount of vehicular and pedestrian traffic in the area; and
>
> d) Weather conditions.[298]

Note that this is just a sample pursuit policy from the many that exist across the United States (although most will follow similar principles). Yet the effects of changes in policy can have a dramatic effect on the streets. A Department of Justice study found that when the Metro-Dade (Miami) Police Department adopted a more restrictive policy in 1992, limiting pursuits to "violent felonies" only, the numbers of pursuits declined by a prodigious 82 percent in 1993. Conversely, in 1993 Omaha, Nebraska, made its pursuit policy more permissive, and the outcome was that pursuits leapt by more than 600 percent in the following year.[299]

Pursuit policies must wrestle with the fact that vehicle chases are high-emotion incidents, and during them officers must monitor both themselves and fellow drivers for the "red mist" of anger descending upon them, clouding judgment and increasing the risk of an accident. In fact, the vehicular death of officers competes with and sometimes beats gunfire as one of the most common causes of officer deaths. For at high speeds, the fatalities can occur in the blink of an eye. For example, on May 15, 2004, Patrolman Timothy Shane Miller, a 27-year-old officer with the Tabor City Police Department, North Carolina, was out on his first shift as a law enforcement officer, the passenger in a patrol car driven by another officer. Six hours into the shift, Miller found himself in a high-speed pursuit of another vehicle along NC 904. The patrol car moved out to overtake a slow-moving vehicle and smashed into an oncoming vehicle. Miller was killed, bringing a very promising career as a law enforcement officer to an end even as it began. The driving officer was injured, as were five people in the other vehicle.

Such tragedies illustrate how danger surrounds officers even when firearms are safely holstered. Furthermore, the life of a police officer also brings some heart-rending complexities when it comes to making judgments about deadly force. For example, since the 1980s the phenomenon known as "suicide by cop" (SBC) has entered into widespread use. This sad phenomenon involves an individual performing actions that deliberately provoke the police into opening fire, the suspect's apparent intention being to end his or her own life through the actions of the officers. The reasons for this mode of death are multiple, as Rebecca Stincelli, a expert on the phenomenon and author of the aptly titled *Suicide by Cop – Victims From Both Sides of the Badge*, explained in an interview. Reasons for going down the SBC route range from a belief that an insurance company won't pay out upon suicide, as opposed to killing by a third party, through to devout anti-suicidal Catholicism.

A particularly painful recent example of SBC occurred on July 22, 2008. Jason Aiello, a retired NYPD sergeant, was confronted by police outside his Staten Island home, Aiello having stood in the street screaming and waving a gun around. Officers surrounded Aiello, who was still holding the gun, and repeatedly gave the command that he drop the weapon. After the third issue of the command, time ran out for Aiello, as he put the officers at an unacceptable level of risk. He was shot in the head and died. Officers at the time reflected that as a former police officer Aiello would have understood the implications of his actions clearly, and felt that this was a clear example of SBC.[300]

In another example from the same month, but this time in Florida, 44-year-old Dallas Dwayne Carter felt that life had simply become too hard to endure. This unfortunate man was unemployed through disability (he had received two replacement hips), plus had to look after his two sons aged 13 and 8 while struggling with $6,000 of debt. Late one night, Carter put his sons to bed, then wrote a suicide note. His next action, as he descended further into despair, was to make a 911 call and inform police that he had a gun and that his boys were safe inside in bed. (His suicide note included the name and address of the boys' mother.) Police and a trained negotiator were soon on the scene. Initial attempts to reason with Carter via a bullhorn were unsuccessful – in response he began firing rounds across the street with a .40 handgun and a .30 rifle. Just over half an hour after he had made the call to police, Dallas Carter was brought down in a hail of gunfire, and was declared dead at the scene.

Such incidents are uniquely traumatic for officers involved. Gary Bush, a former officer of the South Charleston PD, was involved in a suicide by cop incident on December 23, 1994. Here is his vivid and harrowing account of the shooting:

> A call comes at 10:25pm and Dee is still finishing her paper work. I take the call so she can finish up in time for the Christmas party at 11:00pm. It amazes me how fate comes in and knocks the breath out of you. Robbie and I take the call and I remark on the way that we are going to have to arrest this guy and we will be late for the party. When we arrive at Kinder St, a white male in his thirties exits the house and states that his uncle has been pointing a gun at him and his family all night and threatening to kill the whole family and himself. He states that he is drunk and has gone to the garage apartment in the back. Rob and I walk down the alley towards the garage and a man comes up behind us and says that the guy in the apartment is his cousin and maybe he can talk to him. I stated that he had a gun and as soon as we secured the scene he could talk to him. We go to the door and I stand on the left side while Rob stands on the right. We take our guns out and I knock on the door with my left hand. At this time I notice that the door has a latch not a door knob. The door is pushed to but not closed. I knock again with my left hand and again get no answer. I then pushed the door open and step inside. The room is well lit and rectangular in size. There is a bed at the end of the room perpendicular to the rectangle. The uncle is laying down with his head towards the left side of the room. As I step further into the room, he sits up on the bed with his feet on the floor. He stares at me for a couple of seconds and I am about to speak when he reaches to his right. As he reaches, I notice on the left side of the bed there is a rifle. He picks up the rifle and I remember thinking I can't believe he is doing this. He grabs the rifle and I bring my gun up and start to back out of

> the room. He starts to swing the rifle towards me and I tell him drop the gun, drop the gun, drop the gun. He swings the rifle almost to his shoulder and I fire one shot. I didn't hear any thing but I recall the shock I felt as the gun went off. I backed out of the doorway and stood to the left as Rob was again on the right. I did a quick peek into the room and remember feeling that the last thing I wanted to do was go back into that room. I reentered the room with my gun trained on Mr Knuckles. He was still on the bed leaning to the right on his right elbow. The rifle was still in his right hand with his finger still on the trigger. As I approached him I again told him to drop the gun, drop the gun. I soon got close enough to grab the rifle and I handed it to Rob and told him to clear it. I handcuffed Mr Knuckles and flipped him back over so he was facing me. I wondered if I had hit him and looked at Rob and asked him if I had hit him. Rob said he didn't know. I stared at his chest and stomach and could not see any wound. I remember feeling relieved that I had shot at this man and missed him. The threat was over and nobody got hurt. I started flipping through his layers of clothing and still couldn't see anything. I got down to his tee shirt and saw a small hole just below his chest close to the middle. I turned to Rob and told him to holler at headquarters. Tell them that shots have been fired, suspect down, we need back up, first responders and paramedics. At this time the man in the alley started yelling to let him come into the room and pray with Frankie. I knew from training that when you are in charge of a crime scene you are not to let anyone into the area. I also knew that Mr Knuckles was hit in a bad spot and there was a good chance that he would die. I told Rob to search him. He did and stated that he was clear. I told Rob to let him in. I took the handcuffs off Mr Knuckles and held his left hand while his cousin held his right hand. We prayed. After we said amen, I told his cousin to leave. Mr Knuckles then looked at me and said "why did you shoot me?" "I told you to drop the gun." "I wouldn't have shot you!" How was I supposed to know that?
>
> The man I killed that night pointed an unloaded 30.06 at my partner and I. Why? Who knows! I do know that there is hell on earth and I have been there. The great part is that through this nightmare I have met some extraordinary people who truly care about police officers and the struggles we face. I thank these people, officers and civilians alike, for their love and support. God bless![301]

The psychological effect on Gary of these events was profound, and he subsequently had to leave police service owing to the effects of post-traumatic stress disorder (PTSD). In an interview with the author, he noted that there was virtually no support for coping with the aftermath of killing. In the immediate aftermath of the shooting, he was prohibited from talking to anyone, there was no critical incident debrief, and peer support was largely drowned out in a culture that either looked down upon or misunderstood psychological issues. The result was a psychological problem that ran unchecked, although today Gary utilizes his experience by educating officers (and authors) about the emotions that might follow any police homicide. SBC appears especially cruel to police officers as it is only after the event that they realize the person was suicidal rather than homicidal, and such brings a high degree of guilt. For the media, the treatment can be less sympathetic towards officers, as Rebecca Stincelli points out: "You know, when people kill themselves in other ways, nobody blames the rope, or the pills, or the gas, but they certainly blame the police officer because that's a human being."[302] Such treatment largely stems from misperceptions about the power of a knife relative to a gun (see Chapter 6), but also from the contrast between the visually powerful officers and the vulnerable mental disorder of the suspect. Yet the fact remains that the suspect was intent on actions that would force his or her shooting, actions that without the benefit of hindsight clearly endanger the lives of others.

SBC is just one example of the ethical complexities faced by police officers when they draw their guns in earnest. One lesson of the historical chapters of this book is that deadly force does not take place in a vacuum – violence is always conducted within the policies, perceptions, and disorders of the day. At the same time, we must be cautious against over-using historical explanations for specific events. While many police homicides do reflect identifiable trends, the fact remains that each officer had to make a decision whether to pull the trigger or not based on the specific threat confronting him or her. Sometimes that decision was justified, and other times it was not. Yet as deadly force situations are chaotic, random, and emotionally electrifying situations, it is now worth a final exploration of what unites them all.

6
REALITIES

In the early hours of November 25, 2006, Sean Bell's world was his bachelor party. The party was thumping at the Kalua Club strip joint in Queens, New York, a sultry venue in which the 23-year-old former electrician could unwind before his wedding to Nicole Paultre, with whom he already had a young daughter.

Yet night clubbers were not the only people out that night. Both the neighborhood and the participants had received their share of interest from the police. The Kalua Club was under investigation by New York undercover detectives for alleged prostitution activities. Bell himself had been arrested three times previously: twice for drug dealing and once for illegal firearms possession. Two of his friends out with him that night, Joseph Guzman and Trent Benefield, also had arrests for firearms possession. As midnight ticked by, little did Bell and his associates suspect that their paths would soon collide with the police once more, but with much more violent consequences.

At 11.30pm the previous night, Lieutenant Gary Napoli of the NYPD had briefed an eight-man Club Enforcement Team at the 7th Precinct Station in Manhattan. The unit's objectives for the night included a prostitution bust at the Kalua Club, in which two undercover officers would be operating, with a third undercover cop observing activities from outside. In case of an arrest, other officers waited outside the club as backup, in three vehicles. They were prepared for a long night.

Shortly before 4.00am, things began to warm up. A group of men – Bell and his friends – were seen arguing with another man outside the club. Police vigilance went up a notch. As the group broke away, Guzman was, according to subsequent testimony, heard to say "Yo, get my gun, get my gun." Two undercover officers, one armed, one unarmed, watched the argument, and became anxious. The armed officer spoke to Lieutenant Napoli on a cell phone and advised "Getting hot on Liverpool [the incident had now moved on to Liverpool Street] for real, I think there's a gun." Events from this point on become more clouded.

(Note also that some witnesses later testified that no such argument had occurred, and at no point did they hear Guzman say anything about a gun.) What is certain is that the police began to move in to apprehend the group of men, who got into a Nissan Altima car parked on the street. The police approached the vehicle, guns drawn. While officers stated that they clearly identified themselves and ordered the men out of the vehicle, other witnesses contend that no such identification was issued; whatever the case, as five officers began surrounding the vehicle, the car accelerated away, striking a minivan up the road. The night was now shattered by whipcrack reports of handgun fire from five officers. In total – much to the interest of the press and the legal system in the aftermath – 50 shots were unleashed. The volumes of fire delivered varied tremendously between officers. One officer pulled the trigger just once, while officer Michael Oliver fired a full 31 rounds, making a reload of his handgun during the shooting. The car was utterly riddled, and all three men were hit. Guzman was shot 19 times and Benefield three times, although they would survive the shooting. Bell was not so lucky. Struck four times in vital zones, he became a police homicide.

The shots died instantly, but the controversy and anger over the shooting burned considerably longer. Mass street protests were made, and the Reverend Al Sharpton became a figurehead for the uproar, appearing on *Larry King Live* with Nicole Paultre to declaim police tactics and procedures. The mayor of New York, Michael Bloomberg, also stamped a question mark over the officers' behavior, stating at a City Hall summit: "It sounds to me like excessive force was used… I can tell you that it is to me unacceptable or inexplicable how you can have 50-odd shots fired." Concern centered on how so many shots had been fired when NYPD procedures stipulated that officers should pause after firing three shots to evaluate the situation, and also should never fire on a moving vehicle owing to the danger it presented to bystanders. (Bullets struck another car, a house, and some also flew through parts of the Port Jamaica Air Train station, where they nearly hit a civilian and two station patrolmen.) The five officers involved in the shooting were stripped of their weapons and sent on administrative leave while the incident was being investigated. For three of the detectives, criminal proceedings followed: two of the detectives faced charges of first- and second-degree manslaughter, first- and second-degree felony assault, and reckless endangerment, while a third faced charges of reckless endangerment. After a heated trail, however, the three men were acquitted on all charges on April 25, 2008, a ruling that prompted huge, although non-violent, protests on the streets of Manhattan and Brooklyn.

The Sean Bell shooting, as with so many shootings that have racial implications (the shooting of African Americans awakens grim historical memories), will forever remain a divisive incident. Our purpose here, however, is not to wade into this ethical and procedural quagmire, nor to open up a re-evaluation of a court case that involved over 100 witnesses, many of whom brought conflicting recollections of how events unfolded that tragic night. What we will do in this chapter, after the prolonged historical analysis of earlier chapters, is to give the use of force its full and proper context. For despite the mass of media coverage surrounding police shootings, the public and many within the legal profession still remain largely uninformed about the true dynamics of a lethal force incident. For example, in his closing remarks during the Sean Bell trial, prosecutor Charles Testagrossa reflected on officer Michael Oliver's discharge of his gun 31 times: "Thirty-one shots, thirty-one separate pulls of the trigger... Thirty-one separate decisions to use deadly force. Thirty-one opportunities to pause and reassess whether continuing firing was necessary."[303] Regardless of whether the total number of shots fired was excessive, Testagrossa's assessment that each shot was encapsulated within its own act of decision is, as we shall see, critically flawed. Police are familiar with this misjudgment and with countless others, such as why officers didn't shoot a gun out of an assailant's hands, or why they didn't shoot him in the legs to put him down. Here we will explore in more detail what really occurs psychologically and practically when an officer has to draw his gun and fire. Although this examination does not justify every police shooting – we have seen a wealth of questionable shootings throughout this book – it should make us less quick to judge officers who have to make life-or-death choices in a few chaotic, traumatic seconds.

GUNS

We should begin with the tools of their trade, the firearms with which officers are issued. The word "issued" is deliberately selected here. Many officers I spoke to during my research went out on patrol with firearms in which they had limited confidence, in terms of either operation or caliber, so we shouldn't imagine that as soon as an officer puts on a gun he feels omnipotent. (In discussions with officers, those who had previous military service often seemed the most critical of what they felt were inadequate weapons, having dismissed their illusions about firepower in the military.) Nevertheless, there is no doubt that the officer's relationship with his or her firearm can be a psychologically complex one. Peter Scharf and Arnold Binder in their excellent work from the 1980s entitled *The Badge and the Bullet – Police Use of Deadly Force*, explore this relationship in some depth. They note how much the firearm is part of the officer's identification, worn like a badge to state his or her profession in the same way that a hard hat might identify a construction worker or a briefcase might distinguish a banker. For some officers, Scharf and Binder note, this instrument is worn simply as a tool, with little implication for the officer except as an extra weight on the belt or one more item that provides procedural concerns. Yet on the flip side, the authors found that many officers regarded their firearms as clear expressions of power and potential force. One officer interviewed spoke of his handgun with brutal clarity:

> I carry it wherever I go. It's always near me when I sleep. I take it to court and to the gym. I always know where I can get it. I know a guy in this department who got robbed when he was getting diapers for his kid. Not me. Any motherfucker comes at me, he gets this [his gun] up his asshole.[304]

The authors go on to portray a cultural love of firearms amongst the police that can be slightly unnerving at times. The more powerful the firearm, the greater the affection in which it is held. There are two elements about Scharf and Binder's analysis that should be borne in mind. First, officers are bound to have a dependent relationship upon a firearm as it could be the very tool that keeps them alive in a dangerous job. Any sort of equipment with that much significance will undoubtedly have a deeper mental resonance than, say, the departmental flip-chart pad or the standard police notebook. Scharf and Binder's book also possibly reflects a slightly older mentality, reflective of the more lenient times of the 1970s and early 1980s, both times of peaks in gang crime and urban violence. In my interviews with police in liability-heavy 2008, it would be hard to imagine any officer so explicitly promoting the violent power of his firearm, although there is an undoubted light in the eyes of any young cop who is issued his first firearm. Furthermore, as a policeman becomes more seasoned, and experiences either violence first-hand or the fact that his gun remains mostly sheathed, attitudes typically change. Scharf and Binder note one officer's comments: "When I got on [joined the force], I got into the .357 this, waste that motherfucker that, all that shit. Now it's stupid, like a bunch of kids playing cowboy."[305]

Much of the back room talk about firearms is undoubtedly fueled with bravado. Yet there certainly remains a sense that any person's relationship with a gun needs to be tamed and controlled through training, particularly in males. An enlightening study in the psychological relationship between men and guns came from psychologists at Knox College in Galesburg, Illinois. Thirty male students were enlisted in the study. Each had his testosterone levels ascertained through saliva samples, after which they were seated at a table on which was one item – either the board game "Mousetrap" or a large handgun.

The students then spent the next 15 minutes handling the item, and writing down instructions for assembly and disassembly. Once the 15 minutes were up, the students were then retested for their testosterone levels. Surprise, surprise, those students who had been handling the firearm had much higher levels of testosterone than those with "Mousetrap." Building on these results, the psychologists then asked each student to prepare a drink for another student, consisting of a glass of water and quantities of "Frank's Red Hot Sauce." The amount of sauce added by the student to the glass was voluntary, but after the concoction was prepared (the students did this out of sight) it was then analyzed for chilli sauce content. Those students who had been handling the firearm – i.e. those who had inflated testosterone levels – added around three times more hot sauce than those who played with the board game. Judging the levels of sauce added to be indicative of an "aggressive" attitude (the desire to inflict more discomfort on a third party), the psychologists' conclusion ran as follows:

> The present results demonstrated that males who interacted with a gun showed a greater increase in testosterone levels and more aggressive behavior than did males who interacted with a children's toy. Mediational analyses suggested that part of the reason that guns increase aggression is that they cause increases in testosterone levels.[306]

Such experiments are not a failsafe way of judging human responses to handling firearms. Context matters greatly: the experience of the student left alone with the handgun is likely to be very different from a police officer candidate in training, who has to follow numerous safety and procedural rules regarding the firearm or risk failing his or her training course, or an officer who knows that discharging his weapon could take away both another life and his career. Nonetheless, such experiments do carry implications for police officer selection and training, as it will be undoubtedly true that new officers will experience some level of personality "expansion" when they go out into public carrying an exposed and loaded firearm. Yet whether or not this occurs is perhaps beside the point. As with soldiers in action, a police officer *needs* a certain amount of aggression to handle a violent situation; a desiccated, computer-like mentality is impossible when someone is drawing a gun on you.

What is critical is that the aggression is controlled, kept flowing in the right direction, and that is where good training comes in. The balance between aggression and professionalism is perfectly exemplified by one of the dozens of policemen interviewed by Mark Baker for his book *Cops – Their Lives in Their Own Words*, recommended reading for insight into police psychology:

> Walking down the street in that uniform and seeing blue-haired old matrons turn to look at you like, "Thank God, you're here," is really a wonderful feeling. It's like Dodge City and you're the sheriff. This street is mine and ain't nobody going to fuck with it. That's a great and professional feeling. You've done something, you're important. Up until then in your life you may have done absolutely nothing. Now all of a sudden, at the ripe old age of twenty-one, there's a whole lot of people looking at you to protect them from the madhouse around them. That's a wonderful thing.

The mix of pride yet a potentially violent energy towards criminals is readily apparent here, and both sides of the personality feed off each other. In this type of mindset, the gun becomes energized as part of the war against criminal elements, and the protection of the vulnerable.

We will focus the initial part of our study on the weapon issued to almost every officer, the simple handgun. Understanding the capabilities and limitations of this weapon is vital to the correct interpretation of the vast bulk of officer-related shootings, as the handgun is the most common weapon drawn. In modern use, the type of handgun that has become almost universal is the semi-automatic, magazine-fed pistol, typically in 9mm, .40, or (less commonly) .45 calibers. Classic types adopted by police forces include the Glock 17, SiG-Sauer P226, Smith & Wesson Military and Police, and the Beretta 92. As we have seen, the semi-automatic handgun offered several key advantages over the revolver as it bumped the latter out of use during the 1980s and 90s. Its principal advantage was magazine capacity. Typically, a modern police handgun will have a magazine capacity of between 12 and 15 rounds, at least doubling the revolver's maximum six rounds. The reloading process itself is also faster: most officers will carry two or three spare magazines on their belts, and in proficient hands these can be swapped in one or two seconds.

The outcome is the ability to deliver considerable firepower from a handheld holster weapon. During the Sean Bell trial, firearms expert Alexander Jason tested the speed with which 31 rounds could be fired from a SiG-Sauer weapon. Including the mid-point reload, the 31 rounds were discharged in 12.5 seconds, with a 15-round magazine dispensed in just 4.5 seconds. Note, however, that Jason trialed a weapon with a fairly heavy trigger pull, and noted that a gun with a lighter trigger pull could fire faster. Some handguns could quite comfortably empty a magazine in under four seconds.

The devastation such firepower could wreak if it hit someone would be catastrophic, but here is the rub about handguns – it is actually quite hard to hit a target with one, even at close range. This is important – handguns are actually one of the least effective weapons in the firearms family. In any firearm, it is the barrel that imparts stability to the bullet in flight. Roughly speaking, the longer the barrel the better the stability of the bullet, and hence its accuracy over range.[307] This is why police marksmen use rifles with barrels typically in the region of 22–28in. Furthermore, rifles have the advantage of a very stable hold, with the marksmen applying four points of contact to the weapon – the stock in the shoulder, the cheek against the cheek rest, the trigger hand around the rear grip, and the front hand supporting the fore-end (this front hand can be replaced by an external support, such as wall or sandbag). Handguns, by contrast, have a relatively unstable support system – the user has to support the weight of the firearm at the furthest point from his body's center of gravity – and extremely short barrels, usually measuring from 2.5in. up to 8in., with police weapons being more around the 4in. mark.

As a consequence of these dimensions, the practical combat range of a handgun will be in the region of 50ft at most, but frequently much less than that. At first this might not seem like a problem. Annual reports from the US Department of Justice show that most police engagements take place under 21ft range, with some interesting variables. Engagements by police in the confines of New York City generally take place at about 10ft, while those of officers from sheriffs' departments, highway patrol, and border patrol units often exceeded 21ft and extended up to 65ft, although the last group of officers tends to rely more on longarms.

On this basis, the practical range of a handgun and the actual range at which handgun engagements occur seem to work quite well with each other, but this perspective applies only to the static, measured shooting of the range. In a real-life, dynamic, and adrenaline-soaked deadly force encounter, the handgun will be in a state of rapid motion and the shots will be taken at frantic pace, often without clear reference to the gun sights. A shift of only 1–2in. from the centerline of aim will translate into a shift of 2–4ft at typical ranges – a crucial fact considering that a human torso is typically less than 2ft wide and will be moving, presenting itself in shifting angular profiles during a shootout. (Remember that the fugitive will, in most cases, actively seek to avoid getting shot.)

We gain first-rate insight into the inherent inaccuracies of police shootouts using the invaluable SOP#9 series of documents from the NYPD. Thomas Aveni, wading through many of these documents for the Police Policy Studies Council, disinterred some astonishing statistics that challenge our notions of police deadly force. In one exercise in data collection, Aveni reviewed shooting incidents recorded by the SOP#9 between 1988 and 2001, looking particularly at the number of shots fired during "shooting incidents"[308] and the number of those shots that actually struck the adversary. In the first year of the study, 1988, there were 251 recorded shooting incidents in which a total of 540 shots were fired by officers at suspects. Of those 540 shots, just 100 actually hit home, a hit rate of 18.5 percent. Move into the mid-1990s, by which time automatic handguns had been introduced (see Chapter 5), and the statistics show some variations. In 1995, for example, there were 345 shooting incidents, yielding some 1,245 shots fired at suspects. In this case, 255 shots struck the target – 20.5 percent. Yet in 1999, of the 367 shots fired at suspects in 389 shooting incidents, just 58 bullets went where they were intended, 14.9 percent. What these figures showed was just what a high proportion of shots fired missed their targets. Data from other police departments shows similar results. To complete the picture for the NYPD, now note that 94 percent of the engagements between 1994 and 2000 took place at distances within 15 yards; 69 percent of all the shootings occurred within just 2 yards, effectively point blank range.[309]

In the Miami Metro Dade Police Department from 1988–94, the use of automatic handguns also increased the rates of miss – revolvers had a miss rate of 65 percent, while semi-automatics had a miss rate of 75 percent.[310]

All this data presents a curious picture to those who are unfamiliar either with the psychological realities of a gunfight or with firearms. It shows that although the vast majority of officer-involved shootings take place at extreme close range – often within the length of the officer's own arm – the majority of the shots fired will miss their target. Why is this so? Aren't these figures an alarming indictment of police firearms training? Should we dispense with the handgun as a standard issue weapon?

For all these questions, the answer in most cases is an emphatic no. First, we must address the value of a handgun. The primary reason that officers are issued with a handgun as standard is not its qualities as a weapon, but its portability and public acceptability. In short, handguns are easy to carry and don't look too threatening. In terms of portability, a handgun is conveniently handled in a side holster, leaving the officer's hands free to do all those things officers do in regular police work – take down notes, wrestle with fugitives in non-lethal scenarios, drive a car, and use a baton. If the officer had a rifle, either he would have both his hands occupied with the weapon, or he would have to labor under his beat with 8–12lb of metal and wood slung around his shoulders. The primary quality of the handgun, therefore, is that it realizes and makes practical the possibility of an armed police force. Such is not to say that handguns are inferior weapons; properly used within their understood limits, and with correct technique, they are excellent tools for the job, giving the officer a recourse to deadly force but without interfering with the daily run of police duties. For the point of view of public perception, furthermore, handguns are the least threatening face of deadly force, slotted away almost out of sight in a holster. High-powered rifles and shotguns unavoidably have military connotations and emphasize lethality in their very appearance; the gun literally stands in between the public and the officer. In the military, handguns tend to be assigned to purely backup use, something to resort to when all else fails. In the civilian world, they are the most low-profile face of firepower.

Having said this, there are obviously extreme situations, as we have seen, when handguns simply aren't up to the job. Recognizing this, US police forces put in place systems so that officers and units can escalate firepower rapidly when needed. This means having rapid access to rifles and shotguns, and, in the case of specialist units such as hostage-rescue teams, SMGs.

The virtues of the rifle are its power, accuracy, and reach. In terms of power, rifles generally pack a much larger volume of propellant into their cartridges than handguns, which combined with the longer barrel (more conducive to burning up propellant efficiently) translates into far greater velocities when compared to pistols. Velocity, as we shall see, generally equals penetration, and penetration (combined with good bullet design) results in a better takedown of the perpetrator, and the ability to punch through light cover. Accuracy in a properly zeroed rifle is also impressive. A police marksman armed with a modern sniper weapon, typified by a heavy barrel, high-precision mechanism, and telescopic sight system, should be able to put a bullet in the center chest of an opponent at 600 yards and beyond. A regular officer armed with, say, an M16 rifle or a Remington Police Patrol Rifle, should be shooting accurately out to 200 yards purely with the factory-fitted iron sights. The distances noted here also emphasize the rifle's third virtue – reach, or the ability to hit an opponent at a relatively safe distance.

Yet police engagements are not typically about long-distance firefights. Most take place in urban settings, apart from the odd engagement along the southern borders of the United States or firefights in remote rural areas. We have already seen how the vast majority of engagements take place at very close range, but some more up-to-date figures help clarify the issue. In 2006 NYPD officers fired 540 shots in a total of 126 incidents. The figures from NYPD's *Firearms Discharge Report* paint an interesting picture about combat ranges for police officers:

Distance between officer and target	Number of shots fired
0–2 yards	252
3–7 yards	95
8–15 yards	40
16–25 yards	7
Over 25 yards	30
Not stated	116[311]

If we take out the omissions of the "Not stated" column, we are left with 424 shots about which we have range information. A full 252 of those shots were fired at under 2 yards, after which the numbers tail off dramatically. Only 1.7 percent of the shots were taken at 16–25 yards, although there is a somewhat confusing lift to 30 shots in the 25 yards+ category. Nor is this lift explained by the officers resorting to longarms such as rifles. In fact, the weapons used in the shootings are almost exclusively handguns, except for one recourse to an Ithaca 37 shotgun and three uses of what is referred to as a "non-standard weapon."[312] (For reference, and to give us a useful insight into the firearms composition of a typical US police force, the available weapons listed are: revolvers, semi-auto pistols, Ithaca 37 shotgun, Colt M4, H&K MP5, Ruger Mini-14, M24 rifle, Non-standard weapon.) The dip at 16–25 yards might be explained by the target occupying a no-man's land in what the officer considers a viable range – if the perpetrator moves from a close range to a longer range, the officer might see 16–25 yards as the point at which he moves out of viable shooting distance. Yet if the perpetrator is first seen at over 25 yards, and the surroundings allow, the officer might be more inclined to release an opportunistic shot.

The important point here is that rifles and shotguns are rarely used in police work, and for good reason. Most gunfights occur unplanned and end in seconds, so the handgun is usually the only available and immediately accessible firearm. Rifles and shotguns come into play, as we have seen, either when the gunfight is prolonged or the officers outgunned, or when the unit makes a planned assault in which longarms are considered appropriate (such as hostage rescue). With rifle weapons, officers have to be especially cautious about overflight and penetration. To take the former, a 5.56mm round fired from an M4 carbine will quite happily continue a lethal flight for over a mile if it misses its target. The penetration of a rifle bullet also needs consideration. A single bullet from an M16 rifle will punch through a 3/8in mild steel door, and at close range will slice through a human torso and retain its lethality for some distance afterwards. These factors mean that rifles have to be treated with considerable respect by officers, especially when using them in confined streets or in buildings where rooms are partitioned by thin and easily punctured wallboard.

An SMG is a very different animal, and hence they are exclusively the preserve of special units such as SWAT. An SMG is a useful tool in hostage rescue work in particular. It fires pistol ammunition so the recoil and therefore the accuracy is controllable in close- to medium-range shooting, and while the long barrel of the weapon gives this ammunition better velocity, range, and accuracy when compared to a simple handgun, there remains less danger of over-penetration than when using a rifle. Some units are also authorized to use their SMGs in full-auto mode when necessary, although the courage needed to flick the switch to such a mode in a civilian context must be considerable. The advantage of a full-auto burst, however, is that it can take down a perpetrator decisively in seconds with a single trigger pull.

Shotguns are far more common secondary weapons for police officers, and receive much more airing in public. Many patrol cars now carry shotguns fixed into a lockable mount between the driver and passenger seats. Pressing a button disengages the lock and gives the officer quick access to the weapon. The great virtue of the shotgun in police work lies not so much within the gun itself, but in the versatility of the ammunition types that it can fire. Shotguns can take less lethal options such as rubber shot, beanbag rounds, and CS/irritant shells, plus lock-smashing breaching rounds, or heavy-duty slugs designed to punch their way through automobile bodies. The typical load, however, is 00 buckshot, a heavy grade of buckshot in which each ball is roughly equivalent to a 9mm handgun round.

Shotguns are strictly close-quarters weaponry – maximum range is about 100 yards with the 00 buckshot – but they have two primary values. First, because shotguns fire a spread of shot (albeit over a fairly tight circle) rather than a single bullet it means that a single shot carries with it multiple chances of a hit, reducing the need for precision accuracy. Having said this, at the typical combat distances noted above, the spread of shot will only be a few inches at most, so we are not talking about the blunderbuss-style blasts often portrayed by Hollywood movies. If someone is hit, however – and here we move on to the second value of the shotgun – they are likely to go down very quickly from multiple strikes causing massive concentrated tissue damage. On the down side, the fact that multiple pellets are fired means that some of the pattern can fly outside the target area, posing a danger to bystanders. For this reason, officers are trained to use a shotgun with as much consideration for accuracy as with any other firearm.

In some police departments across the United States, however, the writing may be on the wall for the shotgun. While it has undoubted virtues as a close-range decider, the shotgun comes in a poor second when compared to many of the powerful assault-type weapons that have flooded the country over the past 30 years. Using standard ammunition, shotguns pellets also deliver poor penetration through physical structures, not good if your assailant is firing from behind cover or is wearing body armor. Consequently, police departments are increasingly supplementing shotguns with assault rifles/carbines that can punch through cover and can match the criminals' own firepower. A report by Jim Adams in the Minneapolis *Star Tribune* in March 2008, entitled , "Police gunning to equal criminals' firepower with assault rifles," pointed to the increased acceptance amongst local officers that handguns and shotguns simply weren't adequate in many deadly force situations. Adams quotes Dave Bellows, chief deputy sheriff in Dakota County, who states that "The change from shotguns to [assault] rifles is becoming more common throughout law enforcement because law enforcement is getting outgunned by crooks." Other police forces are following a similar route, although the general policy seems to be to replace shotguns with assault rifles in some, but not all, patrol cars to provide a greater mix of rapid response firepower.

The shift from shotguns to rifles will not be without its complexities or controversies. A key issue for police departments is the need to modify training. While shotguns have typically been general issue weapons – meaning that any officer can handle them – rifles need to be handled with much greater respect, owing primarily to the increased risk of "collateral damage" from bullets that have a killing range of over a mile. There is also a major jump in expertise required – controlling and understanding a semi-auto handgun with a 15-round magazine is a different matter from using a high-powered, gas-operated assault rifle with a 30-round magazine. Some police departments have tackled the issue by acquiring weapons that make cross-training that much easier. The Remington firearms company, for example, has made a series of patrol rifles that are based directly on its popular Model 870 pump-action shotgun. While the pump-action mechanism is somewhat unorthodox for a rifle, the patrol rifle does mean that officers trained in the shotgun can easily switch to the rifle, reducing training times and lessening the risk of bad publicity from an officer unleashing semi-auto rifle fire from a large-capacity box magazine.

There is another area of firearms technology that requires our consideration – ammunition. We are not wandering into abstruse areas of ballistics here. The choice of ammunition fired from police weapons can and does have an impact on the evolution of a gunfight, and the choice of ammunition type has produced some vitriolic arguments amongst law enforcement and civilian agencies. Before we can understand ammunition, however, we need to get to grips with the reality of what happens when someone is hit by a bullet.

TAKEDOWN

Almost every movie of a police shootout includes the following depiction of violence: good guy shoots bad guy, bad guy instantly drops dead. This representation is bolstered by a general Hollywood veneration for the gun – firearms are shown as all-powerful death-dealers (think Dirty Harry with his iconic .44 Smith & Wesson revolver, "the most powerful handgun in the world"). The problem – and it's a problem for police officers, not for the general public – is that people rarely drop down dead instantly having been hit by a bullet, or several bullets for that matter.

First we must answer a simple question – what happens when someone is shot?[313] When a bullet hits someone, it does its damage by two mechanisms. The first mechanism is termed the "permanent cavity," and this basically consists of the flesh that is destroyed by the crushing and tearing effect of the bullet itself. The permanent cavity can vary tremendously in terms of damage effect, according to multiple factors. A bullet might strike bone on its passage into the body, causing it to tumble and follow an irregular path through the victim. Different bullets also have different effects. A standard copper-jacketed ball round, such as the military commonly uses in its rifles, might cut a very straight, narrow permanent cavity, although as it decelerates in the human body it might yaw around its axis to widen the cavity out. Expanding, or hollow-point, ammunition works by "mushrooming" or "petaling" outwards when it strikes its target, thus forming a wider, rougher frontal service that creates a wider permanent cavity, although the trade-off is that such bullets decelerate more quickly than a ball rounds, meaning that their penetration isn't as great.

Associated with the permanent cavity is what is termed the "temporary cavity." If any phenomenon has caused such harsh argument in the tight world of wound ballistics science, it is hard to think of a better example than the temporary cavity. The temporary cavity is a displacement of tissue caused by the "splash" effect of the bullet impacting upon the tissue; the cavity can be many times larger than the diameter of the round, but subsides once the bullet has expended its energy in the target. During the 1960s and 1970s, a mythology built up around small-caliber, high-velocity rounds such as that fired from the 5.56mm M16 (this has a muzzle velocity of around 945m/sec – 3,100ft/sec). The belief grew that they caused hugely destructive physical effects by virtue of an enormous temporary cavity, one that would literally cause large parts of the body to explode. Later research has shown that while the temporary cavity was a factor in some of the extreme wound patterns, it was only by virtue of the fact that the high velocities caused that bullet to fragment on impact: each fragment formed its own permanent cavity, and the temporary cavity then united these paths into one wound. (By contrast, note that the non-fragmenting ammunition usually fired by an AK-47 creates regular, slender wound patterns, even though the bullets are delivering well-sized temporary cavities at supersonic speed.) Nevertheless, the damage was done, and the temporary cavity was treated by some as the Holy Grail of ammunition design, equated with "knock-down" power.[314]

The reality is that the temporary cavity can do some damage to inelastic body structures such as the bowel, liver, spine or inside the cranium, but the general rule is that when it comes to significant wounds, it is the permanent cavity that is the real decider. We need to hold this rule in mind for the following analysis.

There are three main ways in which someone will succumb (i.e. lapse into submission, unconsciousness, paralysis, or death) from bullets. First, there are psychological factors at play. Even if a bullet strike is not physiologically decisive, the victim might respond to the recognition that he or she is shot by collapsing to the floor and surrendering all thoughts of resistance. This is a typical line of response. The commonly held, and wildly inaccurate, notion that to be shot means that you are going to die results in many people simply dropping on the spot. Such a psychological response is useful to the officer, as it usually indicates that the person is giving up his resistance and requires no more shots. Yet this is not always the case. Sometimes individuals might fall down, then experience a surge of adrenaline that powers them to their feet once again, there to maintain resistance. Individuals who are high on drink or drugs are also particularly unreceptive to recognizing their own condition, or even comprehending that they have been shot. An officer interviewed by David Klinger provides evidence for this outcome. The officer was called out for a burglary report, but the situation degenerated into a horrific situation where a fellow officer ("Mike") was held at gunpoint in a wood, the perpetrator having got hold of his gun. Mike suddenly managed to grab the perpetrator's revolver and hand, and as these two men wrestled, the other officer ran in at speed with his gun drawn: "When I got there, I stuck my gun into what I thought was the center of his stomach and pulled the trigger. It was like an instantaneous reaction. I ran there so fast that we had a collision. Boom, I got there, my gun went off, and we all fell to the ground like a bunch of bowling pins." Despite having just been shot in the torso, the man nevertheless kept resisting, meaning that the officers were required to force the man into a position where he finally stopped struggling and gave himself up to be handcuffed. It was at this point that the officer who took the shot started to unpack the realities of the incident:

> Once we got the cuffs on, it dawned on me that the guy was still alive. I could see a big, powerful powder burn on his shirt, so I raised it up. He was an obese guy, and I could see two holes on his big belly, an entry wound and an exit wound. There was a little bit of blood coming out of the holes, but I really couldn't tell how bad he was hurt. It turns out the gunshot wasn't that bad at all. The round had gone in at an angle on one side of his belly, traveled between the dermis of the skin and the peritoneum, and went out the other side. It never entered his abdominal cavity, so it was basically just a superficial wound. All I knew is that he was still alive and that sort of shocked me, given the fact that I'd just put a contact shot into his gut.[315]

The surprise of this officer is palpable as he struggles to reconcile what he always believed about the effects of gunshot wounds with the evidence standing and breathing before him.

Even though the perpetrator had received a gunshot directly to the stomach (although it was not a fatal wound) he still had enough psychological momentum to keep his resistance up for a further period of time. The lesson to emerge from this and many other incidents, is never to assume that just because a person has been hit by a bullet he is going down.

From psychological responses to being hit, we turn to physiological responses. First, the bullet could hit the central nervous system directly, striking the brain or the upper spinal cord. This is usually the only situation in which someone will drop into instant unconsciousness. Such a result is a comparative rarity – the head is a small target to hit and bullets have to cope with the thick wall of the skull, and the upper spine is protected behind dense masses of tissue and a shield of ribs. The second way bullets have their bodily effect is by causing a massive loss of blood volume, this leading to the onset of circulatory shock and ultimate unconsciousness. The truly important point about this process is that it takes time, time in which a perpetrator can continue to function and resist if his or her motivation is high enough. Adults can maintain sufficient blood pressure to keep operating with a 20–25 percent reduction in blood volume. Thus even a catastrophic injury will leave a window of opportunity, as researchers Urey Patrick and John Hall explain in their book *In Defense of Self and Others ...*:

> Assuming that the thoracic artery is severed (the largest artery), it will take almost five seconds at a minimum for a 20 percent blood loss to occur in an average-sized male. But:
>
> Most wounds will not bleed at this rate because:
>
> 1) bullets usually do not transect (completely sever) blood vessels;
> 2) as blood pressure falls, the bleeding slows;
> 3) surrounding tissue acts as a barrier to blood loss;
> 4) the bullet may only penetrate smaller blood vessel;
> 5) bullets can disrupt tissue without hitting any major blood vessel resulting in a slow ooze rather than rapid breathing; and
> 6) the above mentioned physiological compensatory mechanisms.
>
> This analysis does not account for oxygen contained in the blood already in the brain. Even in cases where the heart stops beating and blood flow to the brain ceases, there is enough residual oxygen in the brain to support willful, voluntary action for 10 to 15 seconds.[316]

The time it takes for a person to hit the ground is critical knowledge if someone is to have a mature understanding of the dynamics of a deadly force encounter. The fact remains that as long as the perpetrator is standing and functioning, then he or she remains a threat, regardless of whether he is armed with a gun, a knife, or a table leg. To prove the point, we need only think back to the Matix/Platt incident described in Chapter 4. In the forensic analysis of the incident by Dr W. French Anderson, we see clearly how one of the first bullets that hit Platt was the terminal shot, but not in the short term:

> As Platt crawled through the passenger side window, one of Dove's 9mm bullets hit his right upper arm, just above the inside crook of the elbow. According to Dr. Anderson, the bullet passed under the bone, through the deltoid, triceps and teres major muscles, and severed the brachial arteries and veins. The bullet exited the inner side of his upper arm near the armpit, penetrated his chest between the fifth and sixth ribs, and passed almost completely through the right lung before stopping. The bullet came to a rest about an inch short of penetrating the wall of the heart. At autopsy, Platt's right lung was completely collapsed and his chest cavity contained 1300 ml of blood, suggesting damage to the main blood vessels of the right lung. Dr. Anderson believes that Platt's first wound (right upper arm/chest wound B) was unsurvivable, and was the primary injury responsible for Platt's death.[317]

From this study, it is clear that Platt took a major hit to the torso, the sort of impact that would usually have a Hollywood bad guy crumple to the floor in an unresponsive pile. Nevertheless, he was able to keep going on his rampage for some considerable time, at a terrible cost.

We need to tackle another myth – the one in which the recipient of a bullet is hurled to the floor by the force of bullet impact. This is the myth of "energy transfer," and is supported by neither physics nor experience. The energy of an outgoing bullet is essentially equal, at least at the muzzle, to the recoil imparted on the shooter's hand or shoulder, recoil that does not knock over the shooter unless he or she is standing in some ludicrously unstable position. A world authority on wound ballistics, Martin Fackler MD, proved this hypothesis in the most dramatic way – a brave scientist allowed himself to be shot in the chest by a full-power 7.62mm (.308 Win) rifle round while wearing body armor. Fackler noted that "He is not knocked backwards perceptibly; he repeats it while balancing on one foot with similar results."[318]

So if there is no guarantee that a person will go down immediately having been hit by a bullet, and the power of the bullet itself will not knock the person to the floor, how does this affect police tactical deployment of firearms? Almost all law enforcement firearms training courses (non-sniper courses, that is) work on a simple principle – put as many shots as necessary into the center mass (the torso) of the perpetrator until he or she is down and is no longer a threat. As no individual handgun bullet, of whatever caliber, can reliably ensure a takedown, the multiple-round strikes accelerate the overall volume of blood loss, increase the perpetrator's physiological shock, and give him less opportunity to respond with his own deadly force. Head shots are another option, but are difficult to achieve in a fast-moving engagement against a highly mobile target. Nevertheless, most officers are taught head shots as an option if the head is the only target that presents itself.

The "shoot to stop" policy, as it is known, is a breeding ground for much public resentment and incomprehension following a deadly force incident in which a citizen dies. Two common questions asked by the public and prosecutors are: "Why did the officer have to shoot him so many times?" and "Why didn't the officer shoot him in the arm or the leg instead?" Both questions are, in most modern circumstances, fundamentally misguided. Officers shoot multiple times because a) they cannot put a figure on the number of bullets required to stop someone prosecuting violent actions (as the data above illustrated, it could take 10–15 seconds to put someone down even if their heart has stopped); and b) the torso presents the best chance of a significant hit.

Note also that a suspect need not be armed with a knife to require multi-shot takedown. Table legs, iron bars, samurai swords, pointed umbrellas, chairs – officers have been confronted with almost every conceivable hand-held weapon. One issue that needs to be laid to rest, however, is that of the perceived advantage of a gun over a knife. The lethality of a knife must not be underestimated. It requires no loading, reloading, or firing procedure, can produce lethal injuries with every single thrust, retraction, and slash, and is often better than bullets at generating injuries producing critical blood loss. Patrick and Hall make note of tests done at the Firearms Training Unit (FTU), and the FBI Academy in Quantico, Virginia, where a rubber-knife armed instructor would charge and attack a fellow officer, armed with a blank-firing pistol, from a variety of ranges:

> Beyond a distance of 21 feet, the agent with the handgun had time to evade the initial attack and shoot, if the gun were already in hand. Inside 21 feet, most of the agents could still fire a shot by the time the attacker reached them with the knife, as the attacker concurrently was able to stab or slash the agent. The harsh reality in such circumstance is that unless the shot happens to hit the attacker in the central nervous system, the attack will succeed … At closer ranges, the attack was successful before the agent could raise his weapon and fire a shot. When the agent started from a holstered position, he was successfully stabbed/slashed every time when the attack commenced inside 21 feet.[319]

Such tests demonstrate that knives should never take second place to guns in a notional scale-of-force. In a video seen by the author, four Brazilian police officers – all armed with guns – surrounded a deranged assailant armed with a kitchen knife. The knife-wielding man subsequently managed to wound three of the four officers before he was finally brought to ground by gunfire.

The realities of lethal dynamics have, in most cases, yet to transfer themselves into the public and media domain. Take the following exchange on the WLKY News Channel 32 from 2003. The context for the interchange was the shooting of one James Taylor, 50, in Louisville, Kentucky, by officers, a shooting during which the perpetrator was hit 11 times:

> Boel: Detectives say they tried to stop him with their hands and feet, but they say Taylor, who was under the influence of cocaine and alcohol, backed Detective Michael O'Neil into a corner. O'Neil fired 12 shots, hitting Taylor 11 times.
>
> State Police Training Academy Director Greg Howard: "Someone asked me, 'Is there anytime that a person is not totally secure, even if in handcuffs?' Absolutely, yes there (is)."
>
> Boel: "The head of training at the State Police Academy says, as hard as it is for some people to believe, shooting a handcuffed man 11 times may be appropriate. Because handcuffed suspects have stolen cars or hurt people before."
>
> Howard: "We teach them to shoot until the threat is stopped. Sometimes the first round you shoot at a person might actually be a wound that might kill them, but they can continue on and do damage."
>
> Boel: "So you should keep shooting until the person stops, or goes away?"
>
> Howard: "Possibly."
>
> Eastern Kentucky Dean of the College of Justice and Safety, Dr. Gary Cordner: "The public expects police officers to be able to keep somebody in custody and control them when they're handcuffed without having to shoot them."
>
> Boel: "The Dean of the College of Justice and Safety at Eastern Kentucky University says LPD now faces a heavy burden, to show why Taylor had to be shot."
>
> Cordner: "I think many people in the police field feel the same way that many people in Louisville do, that it seems improbable, that it doesn't seem right that police would have to shoot someone who's handcuffed."
>
> Boel: "Saying, 'enough is enough,' state Rep. Tom Riner has introduced a bill to establish new standards for the use of lethal force, including limiting officers to two shots, and only allowing them to shoot if they're under fire.
>
> Riner, D-Louisville: "Many people have the idea that if someone uses a firearm in a law enforcement situation, they'll try to wound you, they will not try to kill. But the state manuals say when you shoot, you shoot to body mass, you shoot to kill and release every round in the gun."

Former police chief William Carcara: "To limit police officers to two shots is just ludicrous."

Boel: "As you might expect, police hate the idea. But it's interesting to note that until the mid 1980s, trainers like Sgt. Mel Allen of LPD taught recruits to take two shots and then pause."

LPD Sgt. Mel Allen: "Problem is, we conditioned officers into thinking that would solve the problem, when it didn't, we had officers getting injured."

Fraternal Order of Police President David James: "Most shootings are over in less than five seconds, so to take two shots and wait to see what happens while you're waiting to get shot at is not smart."

Allen: "The medical community has taught us that if a person has the mindset, you can actually shoot someone in the heart, and they can continue to be a viable threat for 10 to 15 seconds, and we all know what can happen in that amount of time in that close proximity."

Boel: "No Louisville police officers have been indicted for any criminal wrongdoing in any of the 44 shootings we examined. But the city of Louisville has paid out large sums of money, hundreds of thousands of dollars just last year, to people who sued over police conduct."[320]

The shooting of the handcuffed individual is clearly an act that takes some explaining. Yet also embedded within the debate is incredulity – a general disbelief that someone can be shot with one or two bullets and yet still present a danger to officers and the public for a significant duration of time. The return to a "double-tap" principle advocated by Riner reflects the "shoot-reflect-shoot-reflect" pattern often expected by the public, but the officers correctly argue against the plausibility of such a policy. Occasionally legislators and activists will also propose that police should only open fire if they are fired upon. Such a position is tactically ludicrous. Often the person who fires first is the person who wins the firefight, so pushing police officers into that position of mortal exposure would be unacceptable.

AMMUNITION AND ARGUMENTS

Ammunition and the caliber of weapons are two powerful topics amongst the US law enforcement world, and not only amongst those with an arcane fascination with the minutiae of ballistics and firearms. During a recent field visit to a US police department, I found that many officers equipped with 9mm handguns suffered from serious concerns about the efficacy of their weapons, and yearned for heavier calibers such as .40 or .45. The root of their concerns was both a nagging doubt that the 9mm rounds had sufficient penetrative power against physical structures such as car windshields (which often shred and deflect bullets upon impact) and the fear that an armed assailant might take longer to hit the floor when hit by 9mm rounds as opposed to the larger calibers.

In one sense, the debate about ammunition detracts from a central fact that any ammunition can kill efficiently if it hits the opponent in the right place. Dave Spaulding, a former law enforcement officer and writer on firearms engagements, noted after his research into 200 real-life shooting engagements: "Truly, the most important thing in all this is where you hit your opponent. I have spoken with a little old lady who severed the aorta of a home invader with a FMJ .32 [a small, non-expanding round] while, at the same time, talking to a police officer that could not stop a knife-wielding assailant with five rounds of .45 ACP hollow-point [a large-caliber expanding combat round]."[321] A further example comes from South Carolina in November 1992. Highway patrolman Mark Coates was in an armed confrontation with a large, 300lb adult male. Coates managed to put four rounds of .357 Magnum straight into the assailant's torso. The .357 Magnum round is widely regarded for its undoubted power, but in this case the assailant kept functioning. He returned fire with a single bullet from a .22 mini revolver; the .22 is a round generally reserved for light, short-range target-shooting and hunting vermin. The single bullet penetrated Coates' left upper arm and went into his chest through the armhole of his bullet-proof vest (Coates had already been shot twice in the vest during an earlier struggle with the assailant), there to deliver a fatal wound.[322] So the fact remains that where someone is shot is ultimately more important that what they are shot with. Yet this is far from saying that caliber and ammunition does not matter. The chances of a quick takedown are dramatically improved with effective ammunition and a gun of the appropriate caliber.

Handgun ammunition selection criteria has been a vehement topic of law enforcement debate – naturally so considering the ubiquity of handguns in police use. So what is the base criteria for an effective handgun round? Essentially, a sound law enforcement handgun round should combine good penetration with the capacity to create as large a permanent cavity as possible. Regarding the former, an FBI report of 1989 concluded the following:

> It is essential to bear in mind that the single most critical factor remains penetration. While penetration up to 18 inches is preferable, a handgun bullet MUST reliably penetrate 12 inches of soft body tissue at a minimum, regardless of whether it expands or not. IF THE BULLET DOES NOT RELIABLY PENETRATE TO THESE DEPTHS, IT IS NOT AN EFFECTIVE BULLET FOR LAW ENFORCEMENT USE.[323]

A 12in. depth of penetration ensures that however the target is presented the bullet will usually go through to hit vital organs in the torso. Remember that in firearms engagements a bullet may well strike a non-vital part of the body – often an arm – before going on to enter the torso, hence a decent depth of penetration is required.

Now we factor in expansion. While the military is prohibited from using expanding ammunition by international conventions, the police operate under no such restrictions. This might raise eyebrows, but a closer look shows that the policy is based on common sense. Expanding ammunition, as we have seen, balloons out on impact to create a wide frontal area and therefore a larger permanent cavity. Expansion provides other benefits for law enforcement officers apart from its terminal effect. As it expands the bullet slows more quickly, thereby reducing its risk of going straight through the perpetrator and striking an innocent bystander beyond. The expansion also, usually, ensures that the bullet's effect is kept within the target's body – a bullet that goes straight through might sound horrendous, but it is actually expending much of its energy flying through and beyond the target, and will often leave a neat, uncomplicated hole in the process.

Lighter expanding bullets will slow more quickly than heavier ones, therefore reducing the depth of penetration. Heavier bullets carry more mass and momentum, and will retain useful penetration depths even as they expand. The result is that many of the law enforcement agencies in the United States have opted for calibers with a "4" in them – .40 or .45. The .40 in particular is becoming the cartridge of choice in many instances. It delivers greater punch than the standard 9mm round (a .40 Smith & Wesson, 180-grain hollow point penetrates about 16in. into ballistic gelatin), and creates a larger permanent cavity with the right bullet head, but also has less recoil than the thumping .45. Less recoil means it takes less time to recover the point of aim between shots, thereby permitting more accurate rapid fire, which as we have seen is extremely important to the shoot-to-stop tactics necessary to take someone down.

To complicate the picture, however, note that police officers come in all shapes and sizes, and so do their hands and shooting abilities, and the one-size-fits all policy may not always be appropriate. One advantage of the 9mm is that it is a very controllable round in terms of recoil making it a "faster" gun – the shooter can recover his point of aim more quickly between each shot, so he can put more onto the target in a given space of time. There will doubtless be occasions when that advantage is preferred to a gun offering a heavy caliber, but a bucking, slow shooting experience. On the basis of wound ballistics alone, however, it would seem that most policy makers are gravitating towards the .40, although the economics of replacing hundreds of firearms often prevents that conceptual shift becoming a reality for officers on the street.

UNDER PRESSURE

The fact that people often don't go down immediately after being shot is, in many ways, at the root of the public misunderstanding of the use of deadly force. For we now turn to the actual dynamics of deadly force incidents from the officer's point of view. In doing so we will add a further layer in explaining some of the seeming excesses and incongruities of police behavior in gunfights, and why subsequent lines of psychological and legal inquiry may be unfair.

We'll start with a real incident, that experienced by Major Mike LoMonaco of the Fairfax County SWAT team in 1986. In what follows, note how the officer is continually called upon to manage fast-unfolding chaos:

> We go after a guy… It's 1986, an area in McClean… Two patrol officers and the mental health people go down to serve a mental detention warrant. The guy was supposed to be a nice guy, he wasn't meant to be armed, he never had a gun or anything … until they go down there, knock on the door and are met by gunfire coming through the door. The guy, as it turned out, was armed with a shotgun and a .357 [handgun]. He fires somewhere between 50 and 60 rounds during the whole incident. He fired at negotiators with bullhorns, he fired rounds through police cruisers and everything…
>
> They call us [the SWAT team]. We'd been up probably 24 hours already serving high-risk warrants with the Feds that morning. We go down there. We do surround, go ahead and evacuate the people in the apartment [below] – he's in the top level. We try negotiating with the guy; everything that we could possibly do we do it… A team that was going to try to breach the door went up the stairs and they were met by gunfire and retreated down to the next level.
>
> Probably over the course of two or three hours, the guy fires outside, the guy fires inside. The guy next to me was hit in the vest, I was hit in the wrist – not real bad, it was like a glorified cigarette burn. We didn't have shields and stuff at the time; we didn't know until later when it got light and the incident was over that we had about five, six, seven rounds right over the tops of our heads that the guy was firing through the open doors. 'Cause we were trying to contain the guy because there were still people who weren't evacuated and if we left he had access to the whole top floor. We fired gas inside to try to get the guy out – again, unless we have to we try escalating our force level. We tried firing our gas in but the guy has his bathtub filled with water and was breathing through a fish filter with charcoal…
>
> We gave our snipers the green light, but they really didn't have a target to see what happened… I guess it's about 4 or 4.30 in the morning. In the meantime we are still trying

> to call the house – doesn't work, and the negotiators with a bullhorn around the corner are met with gunfire as soon as they go round there. The guy doesn't want to listen to anything. And then, about 4.30 in the morning, the guy comes out, and we think he's carrying a box, and he has the shotgun and everything else with him and he's coming toward us. So I fired three times and I dropped him. He goes to the hospital, he dies. What the box turned out to be is a 8" x 11" piece of granite which was wrapped in brown paper that was addressed to Nancy Reagan. The guy was a mental case. He thought that if he died Iran would fall and he'd be married in the White House...
>
> We tried everything we do to get the guy out, and in some instances there's just no chance.[324]

SWAT shootings, as we have seen, tend to be somewhat different from the spur-of-the-moment engagements experienced by most patrol cops. SWAT teams respond to specific threats that have already been identified and possibly contained, and the application of deadly force has a "planned" aspect to it, in the sense that deadly force is an expected possibility and weapons are readied for that eventuality. Yet even so, Mike LoMonaco was faced with a continually evolving chaos. There was frequent, life-threatening gunfire; officers were attempting to evacuate nearby civilians; the perpetrator was actively resisting non-lethal force options with some considerable ingenuity; the man finally emerged holding what could have been an explosive device. The fact that the "bomb" turned out to be a lump of granite does not figure in the lethal force equation – officers can only go on what unfolds directly in front of them, not on the subsequent findings unearthed by inquests and investigations.

On this basis, LoMonaco's final assertion that "in some instances there's just no chance" is perfectly warranted, yet all too often comments of this kind are treated harshly by the world outside of law enforcement. In a 1984 article on deadly force, for example, William Waegel argued that justifications for police shootings have become "routinized," the explanations for deadly force being part of a general culture aimed at the "deflection of responsibility":

> Conduct becomes explainable by locating it within such a routine account. When an officer explains a shooting by saying, "It happened so fast" or "I didn't have a choice," further explanation may not be required. Colleagues can fill in and flesh out the account using background understandings about the nature of policing and the use of force. What Rubenstein (1973) has called "cop's rules" – informal, subcultural understandings about acceptable methods of handling persons and situations – provide a common context of interpretation.

> Routine ways of accounting for a shooting centered on deflecting responsibility to the conduct of the person shot or to special circumstances at the scene. Grounds for shooting were commonly expressed in terms of the theme, "It was him or me." This justification was applicable to a wide range of situations, and was explicit and implicit in accounts of incidents whenever the victim was armed.[325]

This overview of police justifications suggests that police accounts of deadly force incidents work through a semi-formalized system of explanations, and that those explanations may be used whether or not they entirely fit the facts of the case. While it is true that these explanations are indeed common, I would argue that this is more to do with the realities of deadly engagements than with attempts to justify actions to a police investigation or the public. Much work in the realms of deadly force psychology has been undertaken over the last 20 years, and this research has changed the face of how we understand life and death traumas in law enforcement.

Let's first look at the justification "it all happened so fast." This is true in many deadly force encounters for two reasons. First, shootings usually do occur within a few seconds, and second, we have to look at how the officer's psychological state during the shooting affects recollection after the shooting. In terms of the duration of actual shooting, the length of time in which the overall incident unfolds varies hugely, but the window in which the officer must decide to take a shot is typically a matter of a fraction of a second. An officer may draw his gun on a suspect, but will usually refrain from pulling the trigger until a clear signal is given that the suspect intends to deploy a weapon. I was introduced to this reality, albeit in an extremely safe environment, during a visit to Fairfax County Police headquarters Firearms Training Center, during which I was put through some training simulations on a video simulator.

One scenario unfolded as follows. A "call" came in that there was a man behaving aggressively in an office building, having just been told that he was being laid off work. I was given a rapid-fire description of the male, then faced the video scene, gun drawn, as the scenario played out in front of me. The suspect appeared, framed in an office doorway. He was verbally confrontational, but as yet there was no obvious sign of a weapon. There was lots of movement in the scenario – snatched glimpses of portions of the suspect's body in the doorway – but so far no distinct physical threat. Then a gun appeared in the suspect's hand, still pointed at the ground. Instinctively I took the shot and dropped the suspect, before turning back for analysis from the expert firearms officers around me. They agreed that the shot was justified, but what struck me was the miniscule window in which the decision to shoot was made. My heightened state of alertness actually made the final shoot decision harder, as you have to make an important decision at speed while excited. And this was only a simulator, with nothing approaching the levels of sheer fear and tension of a real shooting.

It is hard to grasp for us in the civilian world how quickly a law enforcement situation can go from normality to horror in a few ticks of the second hand of a watch. One who discovered that reality was State Trooper Steven Stone of Tyler, Texas, during the nighttime hours of March 22, 2006. Stone had pulled over an SUV for speeding 7 miles east of Tyler on Highway 31, the vehicle containing two male suspects. The driver, Ramon Ramos, stepped out to present his driving license, but left his door open by the side of a busy highway. Stone stepped forward to close the door, and as he looked inside spotted an open bottle of alcohol, triggering alarm bells. A pat down of the driver revealed a bag of drugs in his coat, and more: "When I was placing the handcuffs on Ramos I noticed a pistol magazine in his pocket, and at that same time the passenger door flew open on the truck and I knew that things were fixed to get bad."[326] He was unfortunately right. The second man, Francisco Saucedo, stepped out of the door, his body angled suspiciously into the interior, as if hiding or extracting something. Stone screamed at him to "Stay in the car" and pulled his gun to enforce the message. Suddenly Ramos, his hands not yet bound, twisted around with a handgun and shot Stone, who fell backwards to the side of the road. Both Ramos and Saucedo, devoid of mercy, completely emptied their handguns at the helpless officer, letting off more than 25 rounds as Stone screamed with pain and fear on the ground. Miraculously he survived, thanks in part to his bullet-proof vest. In his court testimony, Stone gave a sobering reflection on the experience of being on the receiving end of deadly force, remembering two specific impressions: "One, I wanted them to stop shooting, and to me in my mind every round they fired was hitting me and I was going to die." When asked by CBS News how he had survived the shooting, Stone replied:

> I wish I could tell you, sir. It's by the grace of God that I'm here and have the ability to talk to you. After that first shot, my vision goes black. I didn't know I had fallen or was rolling down the embankment or anything. I didn't get my vision back 'till I was already down in the embankment, and I – at that time, I was looking up at them firing down on me.[327]

After delivering their fusillade, Ramos and Saucedo then jumped back into their vehicle and sped off. Their vehicle was later spotted, and so began a winding fast vehicle pursuit by police officers. During the pursuit the two men unleashed a further 75–100 rounds at officers, before coming to a stop after hitting another vehicle that had broken down by the side of the round. The two men were arrested, and inside the car police discovered a Norinco SKS assault rifle and three handguns.[328]

Stone's experience occurred in a hideously compressed timeline. Measured against the digital clock on the video footage from the police car, a period of roughly four seconds elapsed from the moment the passenger door opened to the moment that Ramos took his first shot. Note that this is not saying that Stone had four seconds in which to decide whether to pull the trigger himself. The actual exposure of a threatening firearm takes place in a fraction of a second, and terminates instantly in the first shot being fired. Above everything, police training teaches officers to focus all their attention on a suspect's hands, basing their split-second decision about whether to shoot or not on what is contained within the hands and what the hands are doing. Note that many criminals are instinctively aware of this, hence both Ramos and Saucedo conceal their firearms until the last possible moment. The judgment on the part of the police officer has to be near instantaneous, yet can have graver consequences either way than almost any decision we can take in civilian life.

A more scientific analysis has been conducted into police response times at shootings by the Police Policy Studies Council (PPSC). Thomas Aveni conducted an analysis of 307 officers under simulated engagement conditions, and assessed the factors that led an officer to take a shot or not. The groundwork of the test was as follows.[329] Using a interactive training video system, the officers were confronted with a series of scenarios played out by actors in and around a furniture store. The officers were "sent" to the store on the basis of one of a) a robbery in progress; b) a burglar alarm going off; and c) a possible mugging in progress. Each scenario was played out with a different outcome: "a suspect who intends to surrender empty handed, a suspect who intends to surrender with a non-weapon object (cell phone, flashlight, police ID wallet) in hand, and a subject determined to shoot."[330] The test was performed in low-light conditions. This is a vital consideration to which we shall return – those officers who have to make life or death decisions often have to do so in varying degrees of darkness, further reducing the levels of information they receive to make their decision.

At the scene, the officers faced the suspect, but were confronted with an individual with his back to the officer, the hands held at waist level but out of sight. Such is a nightmare scenario for an officer, and the "threat ambiguity" (to use Aveni's phrase) was increased by the suspect glancing over his shoulder, as if acquiring some preparatory targeting information. Then, all of a sudden, the suspect turned toward the officer, the hands kept low until the last second, when they moved up.

The turn point was the critical moment of decision for each officer in the test. If the suspect was deploying a gun, he or she had to act within a fraction of a second to save his or her own life. If the suspect had nothing but a mobile phone in his hand, then the officer could be heading for a murder charge, or at least severe psychological and vocational outcomes. The results found that 38 percent of the officers participating shot unarmed subjects. Furthermore, 92 percent of the unarmed subjects shot were actually in a surrender position (hands held above the waists, palms exposed, fingers upwards) when they were struck by the first shots.

How did the PPSC account for such disconcerting findings? An initial conclusion – and one of ambiguous comfort – is that the racial profile of the suspect and of the officer had no bearing on whether the shot was taken or not, assaulting the commonly held idea that you are more likely to be shot merely for being an ethnic minority than if you are a Caucasian. Second, of the scenarios presented the officers were most likely to shoot during the robbery in progress, principally because they drew their guns in advance of entering the building, whereas in the other two scenarios they were less likely to take preemptive action. Even more significant, however, was the "acting quotient" of the suspect – the vigor and conviction with which the actor portrayed his role – and the speed with which events occurred. Aveni explains the former quality:

> They [the most convincing actors] performed with unchoreographed nuances. That is, they made moves with vigorous intensity and speed, versus tepidly. They kept their hands low, rather than high. They tended to crouch partially or fully as they turned instead of remaining upright, and they fully or partially clenched their hands, rather than keeping them open... A suspect's intensity has much to do with whether an officer felt compelled to pull the trigger before the circumstances became manifest. It became one of the most reliable predictors of whether a person got shot.[331]

The nature of a suspect's behavior is critical as a pre-emptive factor in a shooting. Yet the study found that even when suspects moved without vigor, the speed of movement allowed almost no time for the officer to ascertain what was in the subject's hands:

> As the hands typically swung through an arc of 4–5 feet, the officers' eye movement inevitably lagged behind, so that the action was perceived "as a blur or a smear of motion. Judgment about what, if anything, the suspects held could not be made with certainty until the hand movement stopped. When a suspect had a gun, that was too late." With an officer behind the reactionary curve, Aveni says, "the lag time can allow the suspect to fire one or more shots before the officer can shoot back." Indeed, in the study armed suspects were able to shoot first 61% of the time. From a critical juncture in a scenario, an officer typically had "1/3 of a second or less" to decide whether to use deadly force or risk being shot, Aveni claims.[332]

Further research into the time it takes for a suspect to deploy and fire a gun clarifies the point that action before a suspect takes a shot is always preferred to reaction after the shot is fired. Dr Bill Lewinski (now Chief Executive Officer of the FSRC) headed research in which civilian subjects – mostly undergraduate students with no firearms training – were given a sequence of movements to make with a Smith & Wesson .22 revolver loaded with blanks. The 11 different movements represented common means by which suspects deployed real firearms, and the movements were timed from the moment they were initiated up to the discharge of the gun. The following are some of the results, and they leave little doubt as to the speed with which deadly force encounters occur. All the times are given in fractions of a second:

1. Action:

 Suspect sat in a vehicle, in the driver's position, with gun stored next to right thigh. Draws gun across body and fires through the driver's window.

Average time: 25/100ths; Min time: 9/100ths

2. Action:

 Gun held in pants waistband. Draws the gun and fires from a position with the firing hand tucked against the waist (known as a "combat tuck").

Average time: 23/100ths; Min time: 9/100ths

3. Action:

 Subject running. Points gun backwards while running and discharges a shot.

 Times taken from discharge of the gun through the point where the weapon was no longer aimed at the officer (the "drop off" point) up until the gun hand returned to an aimed firing position (the "square back" position).

Average time: 14/100ths; Min time: 0/100ths

4. Action:

 Subject stands facing the officer. Draws the gun from a concealed position behind the right thigh and fires while performing a 180-degree turn to run away.

Average time: 54/100ths; Min time: 37/100ths[333]

The compressed space in which the officer has to make his deadly force decision, a space so short as to be effectively beyond the timescale of rational thought, is something often omitted in legal or media considerations of police shootings. Dr Bill Lewinski and Dr Bill Hudson note that "we must remember that officers in this country are currently charged with homicide for being less than half of a second out of policy or out of what a prosecutor deems appropriate. Less than one half of a second too late on stopping a trigger pull."

This claim is elucidated through the Tempe Study, Lewinski and Hudson's analysis of reaction times in 102 officers at the Tempe, Arizona Police Department. The reaction times were measured in terms of the time it took for officers to pull the trigger of a time-measuring training gun in response to stimulus generated by a light or sequence of lights. For the simplest reaction test – pulling the trigger in response to a light coming on – the average trigger pull was 31/100ths of a second.[334] Note that of this time, 25/100ths was taken up by mental processing, and only 6/100ths by the actual mechanical process of pulling the trigger back. This in itself leads to an important conclusion: once an officer starts to pull the trigger there is little he can do to stop the gun firing, even if there is a flitting change in circumstance as the trigger is being pulled. Furthermore, thinking back to the test of suspect shooting times, it becomes clear that a motivated subject can often deploy a firearm and shoot it faster than many officers can actually process the visual information before them and get off their own shot, even with the gun drawn. Yet the authors of the study raise an important point about the value of the basic test:

> … officers in lethal encounters are seldom doing one thing. Just like drivers, many are multi-tasking and working with a varied degree of split attention. They are moving, pointing, ducking, seeking cover, shooting, processing, reacting emotionally etc. The question that was researched is – does multi-tasking affect the officer's reaction time, both in the starting of the trigger pull reaction as well as the termination of the trigger pull reaction?[335]

To explore this question, the officers were faced with a new test. When the light came on, they had to pull the trigger of the gun as many times as possible, but then stop immediately the light went off. In essence the officer in this task was engaged in basic multitasking – focusing on the lights and on the mechanical action of pulling the gun trigger as fast as possible. For the bulk of the officers (68 percent), stopping trigger pull took between 1/10th and 6/10ths of a second, during which time some officers fired additional shots in the process of stopping. Furthermore, these tests, although invaluable assessments of reaction times, do not duplicate the massive emotional and causal effects of a real life or death shooting, in which the multitasking demands are, as listed in the quotation above, hugely complex and demanding.

The implications of this type of analysis, and of other similar studies, are persuasively presented by Patrick and Hall:

> … if we assume that the target being shot no longer merits shooting, then the shooter must first recognize and identify that fact and decide to stop shooting (decision time). The nerve

> impulses must travel from the brain to the gun hand and direct the gun hand to stop pulling the trigger. The gun hand must stop pulling the trigger. Typically a decision/response sequence can take almost 0.5 to 1.0 second to complete in ideal circumstances. Thus the shooting previously decided upon can be *continuing* during the decision/response time and the cessation of shooting will lag behind the recognition that cessation is necessary. This explains why law enforcement officers firing multiple shots in deadly force confrontations can shoot their adversary as or after he falls, or in seemingly other inappropriate ways, and not be aware of it.[336]

The "other inappropriate ways" can include shots delivered to the suspect's back. These might be caused by the suspect twisting during the shooting, or actually presenting his back to the officer as part of his own shooting stance. Either way, we now have an important gathering of elements here. First, handguns in particular are difficult to shoot accurately, therefore the officer must shoot at the largest part of the target – the center mass of the torso – if he is to achieve significant hits. Second, people rarely collapse on the spot from a single bullet, and they can prosecute deadly force actions for many seconds even with fatal wounds. Therefore the officer needs to fire as many rounds into the suspect as are required to put him down. Third, the speed in which a suspect can pull a gun and deliver a potentially fatal shot at an officer can be faster than the officer's own mental processing and gun speed, especially if the officer has his gun holstered. Therefore, it is ridiculous in most cases to criticize an officer for shooting first – the officer has to take pre-emptive action if the suspect's behavior warrants it. Finally, once an officer is shooting, there is an inevitable lag in stopping shooting, often explaining seemingly dubious wound patterns on the suspect.

Another factor to evaluate in the volume of fire put out by officers is what has been labeled "contagious gunfire." This term, and the synonymous "contagious shooting," gained currency during the 1990s and refers to what some argue is the predilection for one officer to start shooting if another officer begins to engage a suspect. The result, so the theory goes, is a "mass reflexive response" in which the individuals effectively renege on the responsibility to control their own firepower and collectively produce an overkilling hail of bullets. Edward Mamet, a former police captain who had specific responsibilities for investigating police shootings, and is now an independent consultant, argues that regarding contagious shootings we must take into account the differences between the revolver and automatic pistol eras:

> My experience, which goes back to 1959 when I was first appointed to the Police Department, was that there were always contagious shootings. However, it was limited by

> the number of rounds a police officer could fire. For example, we were required to have six in the revolver and 12 extra rounds on our belts, so even if you had a situation of contagious shooting there was only so many bullets that could be fired, and then you had to reload by hand, which took time. Today the officers carry 9mm semi-automatics with 16 rounds ... so they can let off 16 shots in a matter of seconds and then quickly reload... So you have a situation where the number of shots by the same officer has increased more than triple.[337]

The Sean Bell incident already described produced a furious round of media exploration of contagious shooting. *The Village Voice* expressed incredulity at the pattern of shooting responses developing within the NYPD:

> The harsh reality: In 2005, New York City police officers fired 616 bullets, about 30 percent more than the 477 annual average from 1999 to 2004. In just one incident last year, police fired 77 shots before winging a gunman who was returning fire outside the Taft Houses in East Harlem. Including the Bell incident, NYPD cops have fired 483 shots this year, putting them on pace for fewer than last year but still about 12 percent more than the 477 average.
>
> But here's the oddest number of all: In New York City between 1999 and 2005, major crime has plummeted by some 60,000 complaints, about 48 percent. Also, the number of police-involved shooting incidents has actually been lower, by about eight per year, during that time period.
>
> In other words, police have been getting into fewer shootouts but firing more once it's on.[338]

The idea of contagious shooting has gained widespread currency amongst both the media and some law enforcement specialists, and in early 2007 the RAND corporation began a $500,000 commissioned study into the contagious shooting phenomenon within the NYPD. The report's eventual findings were hampered by a lack of source data on such shootings, but the authors of the report did make a spread of recommendations, including increasing the tactical reliance on less lethal weaponry such as tasers and in training officers more specifically to the possible dangers of contagious fire.[339]

Not everyone, however, buys into the idea of contagious shooting. From the street level, many police officers argue that the tunnel-vision state each officer goes into during a shooting often means that he or she is literally unaware of what other people are doing, firing or not. Carl Stincelli, whose account of shooting a bank robber we featured in

Chapter 4, explains this phenomenon from his experience:

> I'll say usually most of the time, a lot of the time, if there is a deadly threat and there're two officers they both fire, and if there're five officers they all fire. You get tunnel vision, and you have an auditory block, which I experienced – I did not hear my gun go off but I of course felt it and saw it... I remember squeezing the trigger, and I remember the recoil, and I remember forcing my barrel back down to try to obtain a sight picture and squeeze off a second round if he was there and I needed to, but as I forced my gun hand down he wasn't there, and as I kept going down I could see him on the ground. And of course all that went in slow motion, kind of, where you can see and think about a lot of stuff in a very short period of time, and that's probably the adrenaline factor. And I don't remember if my partner shot or not because of my auditory block – that's pretty common...
>
> All they [officers] know is that there's danger to everybody, and deadly force is authorized. You don't hear the other people do their shooting, but you're taking care of what you know to be the threat... And you could not of course count on – as a matter of fact it was a good job I didn't rely on my partner shooting, because he was a trainee and if I was counting on him to really shoot, then I'm leaving myself open, because I don't know whether he is going to shoot.

Stincelli's account implies that each officer in an incident might fire not because proximate officers do so, but because he or she is in a mental bubble focused on his or her own survival. Other conditions also back up his perspective. Thomas Aveni found that those shootings that involved high numbers of rounds fired by multiple officers often took place within the context of prolonged engagements between a suspect and large metropolitan police departments – there are simply more guns at the scene than in cases of individual shootings. Furthermore, low light conditions were a common denominator. Darkness brings uncertainty and uncertainty increases fear, and the increased volume of fire produced by multiple officers can serve as a compensation for the uncertainty when lives are at risk:

> In specific terms, low light conditions contribute to situational ambiguity by obscuring the following critical issues; The nature of the threat, The origin of the threat, The identity of the threat, The persistence of the threat. As a consequence, often when one officer fires in a multiple officer scenario, it tends to create a compelling influence on other officers before facts and circumstances may have been independently identified by all parties involved. This isn't likely the result of a contagion – it's more accurately portrayed as a manifestation

> of the uncertainty highlighted above. Under low light conditions, even after a threat has been neutralized by police gunfire, there often exists residual uncertainty about whether the threat has ceased. This is often reflected in the "over-flow" effect of additional rounds being fired after a threat has been neutralized.[340]

Aveni's points about low-light shooting are critical to any judgment we pass upon police shootings. In other articles he has also pointed to the fact that a full 75 percent of incidents in which a police officers shoots an unarmed suspect occur in low-light conditions.[341] Such conditions degrade optical performance, and even with powerful illumination from flashlights or car headlights there is still a major problem in evaluating contrast between shapes – such as a gun held against dark clothing.[342] If no, or inadequate, illumination is available, then reliance upon naked eyesight is problematic. At night, peripheral vision is heightened while central vision is degraded, meaning that looking directly at a darkened suspect will actually cause his silhouette to degrade and blur. None of this is good for an officer or group of officers responding to a serious threat, when adrenaline levels are jacked up and life may be in the balance. If the suspect does not comply with verbal commands, and there are movements suggestive of an imminent armed threat, then the officer's only recourse may well be to open fire. Furthermore, as shooting accuracy is degraded at night (low-light conditions provoke a natural tendency to shoot high) then an increased volume of fire may be the only solution to ensure sufficient takedown hits.

FEAR FACTORS

There is one final element we must consider when assessing how police officers behave when confronted with a deadly challenge. It is an element that, if not understood, will warp court proceedings and can even lead officers to appear as unreliable, shifty witnesses. This element is, quite simply, fear. Hollywood has here done us a disservice. Cops from Clint Eastwood's "Dirty Harry" Callaghan through to Bruce Willis' John McClane have traditionally been depicted with steel in their hands and in their minds. Even under blistering volleys of automatic fire, the jaw remains bravely square and the actions are clear and decisive. Alas, the reality is all too different. In research for another publication, I spoke to an Iraq war veteran who had been involved in numerous violent engagements. While prolonged combat exposure built up a steely veneer, he acknowledged that the first times in combat were the same for everyone: "No matter how tough you are, I guarantee that the first time someone starts shooting at you the response is the same: you crap your pants and try to dig yourself into the smallest hole possible."

This unwholesome image of stress response applies equally to the world of law enforcement, perhaps even more so. A soldier goes out into a combat theater mentally primed for action, with loaded weapons held ready and tactical procedures in place. A police officer, by contrast, will enter his day's work certainly alert, but generally not expecting that the day will transform itself into a life or death struggle. Should that occur, the descent from normality to trauma is rapid and frightening.

Training, as we have seen in previous chapters, does pay dividends in terms of officer survivability and response in an armed engagement. Yet regardless of the level of officer training, the "fight or flight" stress response will kick in just the same. A Technical Memorandum on Use-of-Force Training issued by the Florida Department of Law Enforcement in 2004 provides full details of the physiological effects that officers will experience should they be faced with a "potentially violent encounter." They form an alarming list in the context of someone who is meant to be taking critical responsibility for his or her actions:

PHYSIOLOGICAL CHANGES

- Increased heart rate
- Increased respiration
- Vascular flow moves away from the extremities (The body pulls the blood away from the arms and legs into the torso. This keeps it near our organs in case of emergency. This also protects the arms and legs (our weapons) from losing too much blood during the battle, in the event they are damaged. Since the blood has been pulled into the torso there is less blood in the extremities and the capillaries are contracted, restricting the available blood flow.)
- Auditory exclusion (hearing is diminished)
- Loss of fine motor skills at a heart rate of 115 beats per minute
- Loss of complex motor skills at a heart rate of 145 beats per minute
- Gross motor skills are enhanced as working heart rate exceeds 150 beats per minute
- Increase in strength (For a short period of time.)
- Increase in speed (For a short period of time.)
- Heart rate will sometimes spike during a violent encounter to well over 200 beats per minute

VISUAL PERFORMANCE CHANGES

- Binocular vision is dominant (Both eyes remain open. Very difficult to close just one eye.)

- Loss of peripheral vision and depth perception (Tunnel vision.)
- Loss of near vision (This is one reason that most officers involved in shootings never see the sights of their firearms. Physiologically it is nearly impossible to focus.)

COGNITIVE FUNCTIONS

- The cognitive brain, the part that logically thinks and plans, begins to shut down at 145 beats per minute.
- Horizontal decision making is inhibited (The more choices we have the slower we are to make a decision.)
- Reaction time increases (This may be because of too much stimuli to process quickly or because of denial that a violent encounter is actually happening.)[343]

Transfer the list of symptoms here into a deadly force encounter, and some extremely serious implications float to the surface. At the very moment when, theoretically, an officer needs to be physically dexterous, level headed, aware of his surroundings, and able to use the sights of his gun, the exact opposite is typically happening. Such is not an argument against police being allowed to deliver lethal force. Good training is a proven way to limit the deleterious effects of shooting stress; as we have seen, proper training should inculcate decent threat assessment and gun handling as an automatic feature of the police response. Yet there is no denying that officers will still undergo a dramatic mental transformation during the shooting event.

The realities of the stress response are hard to understand through rational explanation, but something of their nature comes through in police radio communications of deadly force incidents. The following is a period of radio traffic following a dramatic incident in Cincinnati on February 2, 1998. Officer Kathleen S. Conway was shot four times in her patrol car by an assailant, who pushed the severely injured officer over into the passenger seat, and drove off. Conway, however, turned the tables by pulling her revolver and shooting the man dead. The subsequent radio communications show the obvious trauma of an injured officer, but also the effect of the stress response upon all those drawn into the incident:

Conway: Help! Help! I need assistance! I'm shot in the car! Help, I'm shot!

Female Officer: Where do you need it?

Conway: Help! I need help!

Male officer: 1238 Elm, I believe. 1030 I believe I heard shots fired there.

Conway: [screams]

Female officer: Location ... 1212, what's your location?

Male officer: 1080, we got a location?

Female officer: Negative … Officer needs assistance, District 1, unknown location … 12th and Elm. Officer needs assistance, 12th and Elm. Possibly shots fired.

Male officer: 1080 35, 12th and Elm, do not see them.

Male officer: 1240, play the tape back.

Female officer: 1212, what's your location?

Conway: Distress? I've been involved in a shooting on Central Parkway north of Liberty. I need some help.

Male officer: 1080, I copy that. Check on her safety.

Female officer: 1212, are you hurt?

Conway: That's affirmative.

Male officer: 1080, I'll be there in 5 seconds. Blocking it off with four cars.

Female officer: Attention all cars, all departments. An officer has been injured. Possible shooting offense at 12th and Central Parkway. Repeating, Cincinnati officer needs assistance at 12th and Central Parkway. A possible shooting offense. The officer reporting she is injured. Approach with caution.

Male officer: [Unintelligible] … She's at Liberty and, uh, Elm. 1240, 1240, no more cars.

Female officer: 1240, are you on the scene?

Male officer: A … crash (unintelligible) let me talk.

Female officer: Go ahead.

Male officer: We're at about, uh, just about north of Central Parkway. We've got a couple rescue units. We've got an officer in the car shot. [sirens in the background]

Female officer: OK, uh, you need to go slower. Where are you?

Male officer: [Unintelligible] … We're at the corner of Central Parkway, just north of . . .

Female officer: OK, Parkway north of what?

Male officer: North of West Liberty Street.

Female officer: You got any other cars with you?

Male officer: I need a rescue unit. I need a rescue unit!

Female officer: Attention all cars, all departments. No additional officers are to respond. Reference the officer shot on Central Parkway just north of Liberty. Repeat: no other units are to respond on the assistance. 1240, 1240 go ahead.

1240: I will take care of it on the scene here. We have the perimeter secure. We need a fire company to expedite.

Female officer: Fire company is responding … other units.

Male officer: Other units to transmit at this point. I'm also going to need the what-do-you-call-it list?

> Female officer: I need if you can give us a call to know the condition right now also.
>
> Male officer: I'll give you one in two minutes.
>
> Male officer: We've got the address right. 1627 Central Parkway.
>
> Female officer: Copy 1627 Central.
>
> Male officer: Car 15 responding.

The harried conversation here is a good example of how all involved in a shooting participate in its stress. Procedures are still followed in reporting, but the elements of panic, unintelligibility, and confusion creep in as the urgency of the situation clashes with the mental changes of the fight or flight response. In some cases following shootings, officers have discovered themselves to be soaked with urine generated by the sheer fear of the encounter.

The psychological and physiological responses to traumatic incidents are not only relevant during the incident itself. Their relevance carries over into the aftermath of the shooting incident, and as we have seen, can dog the rest of an officer's life.

CONCLUSION
JUDGMENT

If one point is clear from this book, it is that the use of deadly force always has consequences – social, legal, professional. We must also acknowledge the personal impact on the officer. While he or she may have mentally accepted the possibility that joining the police could result in having to shoot someone, the living reality of experiencing it is a totally different matter.

Following a shooting, an officer will frequently find himself in a disorientating world. From purely a mental point of view, many officers who have been involved in shootings will often report the full gamut of post-traumatic stress disorder (PTSD) conditions: depression, loss of appetite, obsessively replaying the event, nightmares, physical tremors, guilt, nausea etc. These symptoms can extend for weeks and months, sometimes years, during which time the officer will also have to cope with the procedural and legal fallout from the incident.

In the aftermath of a use of force incident, the officer in question will be temporarily suspended from duties pending an investigation, and civil and criminal proceedings may be enacted. (Until the review is complete, the officer will usually be separated from other officers who participated in the shooting.) Within his own police department, the officer will have to submit a Use of Force report and will typically go before an assessment board to explain his actions. The district attorney will also examine the report and circumstances of the shooting, as might other state or city public bodies if the post-shooting procedure is so configured.

While this is occurring, the civilian processes of judgment are usually swinging into life. The officer may have to cope with lurid headlines in the press about the incident, often bolstered by activities of freshly created support groups for the victim, or the genuine distress of relatives appearing on television. Civil or criminal law suits can be filed by the family, and it is here that the gap between actual experience during the shooting and the forensic analysis in the courtroom can seem so at odds. Think back to the list of physiological and mental conditions outlined in the previous chapter, those experienced by most officers during a deadly force incident. While a shooting is taking place, a number of distortions in perception occur on account of these conditions, distortions that have major implications for the officer's future accounts of the shooting. Based on analysis conducted by David Klinger, auditory distortions – typically expressed as diminished awareness of sounds, or that single sounds are amplified – occur in about 95 percent of cases. Some 51 percent of officers reported tunnel vision – the brain responds to the threat by focusing purely on it, to the exclusion of peripheral events. Finally, as the brain switches away from cognitive thinking and increases reaction time, the experience of time distorts dramatically. Fifty-six percent of the officers studied reported time going into slow motion, while 23 percent felt time speeded up.[344]

The upshot of these distortions, which often work in combination with one another, is that the officer will often lose a clear sensory and temporal appreciation of his surroundings, creating blanks in subsequent memory recall of the events in question. Charles Remsberg here quotes Bill Lewinski on the oddities of recall, and their implications, following a shooting:

> After a shooting, an officer is often ordered to "tell us everything that happened from start to finish and don't leave anything out." If he says he can't remember some things, he's perceived to by lying because "people don't forget really significant, emotional events." Dr. Lewinski explained that "it's true they don't forget, but they will not remember everything. There is memory loss in 100 percent of shootings. Legitimately, officers may not recall 90 percent of what happened and they do not remember an event as continuous action. They tend to remember in chunks – specific, brief memories, fragmentary images." He cited an Arizona officer he recently defended successfully who shot and killed a woman trying to run him down with her car. The officer remembered only three elements of the entire episode: the determined look on the suspect's face, an image of her front tire quickly turning toward him and her upper body as a target. The "current neurophysiological model of how the human brain works is directly opposite to the legal model" which expects full and accurate recall. The more an officer is pressured to remember information missing from his memory, the more likely he is to "fill in the blanks" with what seems logical or right.[345]

The partial nature of memory following a shooting can create a world of problems for the officer. On the court stand, his attempts to explain chaotic events can seem at best confused or at worst incompetent, or his subsequent attempts to reconstruct events for the courtroom can lead to the appearance of perjury, if the events don't stack up against more leisurely gathered evidence of timelines, witnesses etc. Increasingly officers are being trained in methods of handling this clash of expectations. The key point is that officers only state what they can clearly remember, particularly in terms of the specific catalysts behind the deployment of deadly force. These catalysts could be the movement of the suspect's hands and his non-compliance or use of a weapon prior to the shooting, plus the reports of other officers involved in the incident. It takes a strong officer to keep his composure under close cross-examination, when the prosecutor might be pushing for second by second details of the incident, while the officer recounts the event from a perspective shaped by different mental forces.

The appearance of guilt on the part of the officer can also be compounded by the police department's insurance company pushing for a settlement rather than take the case through court, this decision often being made on hard economics rather than the merits or otherwise of the officer's case. From the media and relative's points of view, however, the drive to settle can be seen as a tactical admission of guilt, though this is often far from the case.

Should a police shooting actually go to court, however, the chances are that the officer will be acquitted. Court cases tend to throw up the full picture behind the suspect's behavior, at which point the officer's shooting is seen in its broader perspective. The very low percentage of successful prosecutions against police has flagged up interest amongst the media and human rights organizations, with some passion. An editorial in the *Chicago Tribune* in 2007 captures the flavor:

> There is also no place for cops who are prone to shooting people who pose no threat or could be handled by other means. In the eyes of the Police Department, though, that type of cop doesn't exist here. In the last decade, more than 100 people have been killed by Chicago cops and 250 others have been injured, but in more than 99 percent of the cases – including 12 incidents during which a civilian was shot in the back – the shootings were held to be justified.[346]

The fact that so many officers are exonerated by courts is not as suspicious as these figures imply. With the presentation of actual evidence, and the use of expert witnesses who can explain the pressures under which officers must decide to take a shot, it is found that most officers have acted reasonably or in good faith, and in the service of the community. Nonetheless, the passage through court can be a trying one for the officer. A moving exposure of the psychological complexity of the aftermath of a deadly force incident is given by one officer in Mark Baker's *Cops:*

> "Did he fire at you?" they ask. They love to ask that question. "How many shots did the suspect fire at you before you shot him?" Like you're supposed to give the guy a couple of freebies to make for a better sense of fair play. Bullshit.
>
> The headline in the next day's paper was, "Buckshot Shooting Cop Critically Injures Youth in Robbery Try." I was the fucking bad guy. This guy got a raw deal, but he managed to survive this terrible assault by law enforcement.
>
> He didn't die, so that made it easier. I had to go up into the hospital one time while he was there to talk to an officer who was guarding him at the hospital. He was fucked up and I felt bad. I didn't go around telling anybody that, but I did feel bad.
>
> Believe it or not they rolled the guy into the courtroom in a wheelchair and he pled not guilty. I get up on the stand. This guy has got a wife and a baby that I didn't know about. They're sitting in the spectator seats of the courtroom. I had to testify that I was the one that shot him. I could see her looking at me. He's going bye-bye into prison in a wheelchair. We're going through all the formalities of the sentencing and the wife jumped up and started calling me a motherfucker. She almost got locked up for contempt. Unpleasant.
>
> I almost felt, one time, like going up and saying that I was sorry that it happened that way and that he got fucked up so bad, but I never did. For one thing, he wanted to kill me. I could tell when he got shot and he still went for that shotgun. I said, "Fuck it. He didn't care about nobody. He didn't care about that pharmacist or the girl. He didn't care about me certainly."[347]

Police officers such as this officer are in a fraught position regarding deadly force. Many officers have commented on how the public is quick to mourn for an officer killed in the line of duty, but is also equally quick to condemn when an officer uses positive action to stay this side of the grave.

Police move through a dangerous world, and unlike most of us they face a realistic, albeit rare, chance of violence whenever they step out of their front doors for another day's work. Of course, as we have seen in this book, there have been many occasions in history when officers have overstepped the mark, sometimes to a criminal degree. In the modern world, however, with all its accountability and liability, those extreme cases are the rare exception. Ultimately, for those of us who are shielded by the police, regardless of the imperfections in any system, we should be slow to judge.

* * *

Throughout this book, we have seen a slow, often grindingly slow, advance in the understanding, techniques, and teaching of deadly force techniques in the law enforcement agencies of the United States. While in the second half of the 19th century deadly force, indeed any use of force, was a loosely governed phenomenon largely controlled by the personal restraint of the individual officer, the turn of the century brought a new direction with an emergent emphasis on broad police professionalization. As a movement, if it can be termed such, professionalization affected all areas of police operations, including firearms training. Yet as we have seen, even though some degree of formalized firearms instruction crept onto the training agenda of many police departments (although far from all), there was still a high degree of mismatch between the type of training actually required to prepare officers for street encounters, and the type of training they received. Yet all seeds take time to grow, and it was in the second half of the 20th century, under the more intense glare of media attention, academic scrutiny, and racial/civil rights controversies, that the US law enforcement community began programs of force training that were squared more directly to street realities. These programs have been constantly tweaked and improved to the present day, often in response to the lessons derived from specific tragedies or post-shooting investigations.

We have undoubtedly come a long way. A 19th-century rural marshal likely went into harm's way with no more deadly force training than that imparted to him by a father, relation, or friend, supplemented by whatever personal practice he had put in. By contrast, the modern officer, serving in a reasonably well-funded agency, will likely benefit from training technologies such as shoot/don't shoot video simulations, shooting-house role-playing games using simunitions for added realism, a solid bedrock of safety and tactical training, and access to numerous privately funded firearms training courses.

There is no denying that the steady professionalization of firearms and force training has brought benefits in the overall reduction of officers killed and the numbers of innocents downed by police fire. And yet, there is no escaping the fact that officers and civilians will continue to die in police engagements, regardless of the introduction of less lethal technologies – the United States remains, after all, a place with relatively high levels of violent armed crime. Equally doubtless is the fact that officers will make mistakes that hit the headlines in block capitals and exclamation marks. The fact is that regardless of the type of training applied, there are certain psychological constants involved in a deadly force encounter, and they will always limit the degree of control over outcomes. A modern, highly trained police officer facing death is just as scared as a 19th-century sheriff confronting the same. The problems of making a profound life decision – whether to shoot someone – in a fraction of a second are never entirely eradicated by training, no matter its degree of sophistication. Deadly force will always be part chaos and random consequences, and this is one reason why it often clashes with public sensibilities. In the civilian world, we can become conditioned to the neatness of TV or Hollywood shootings, whereas in the real world shootings are mentally frantic and physically unpredictable, and should always be judged on the basis of such.

What is critical for officers is what occurs during the lead up to the shooting. In Chapter 6 I raised concerns about the modern emphasis on active-shooter scenarios, particularly in private training courses, which might create an excessively warrior-like mentality in some officers. The focus on high-level tactics may well obscure some of the more mundane but potentially life-saving (for the officer and the suspect) procedures that take place before a gun is drawn. Training has to strike a balance in order to develop an officer who constantly thinks about how to *prevent* armed engagements, yet who can also handle a weapon with confidence and controlled aggression should it be required.

Here lies the future challenge of law enforcement training, particularly in a tense atmosphere of potential terrorist attack, horribly regular school shootings, and the persistent threat of the active shooter. Working out the future evolution of force training is complicated, not least by the fact that contrasting funding situations in the huge number of agencies across the United States mean that not every department progresses at the same rate or with the same technologies. The political, legal, and social fallout from police shootings remains as high as ever, and it is likely that less lethal technologies will take an ever-increasing center ground in force policy. In the very long term, it may well be that taser-like weapons will emerge that have all the range, accuracy, and ammunition capacity of regular firearms, plus the guaranteed takedown effects that so often elude the regular bullet. Microwave and sonic weapons might control entire riots in the flick of a switch, rather than require masses of adrenalin-fueled police and civilians locking horns.

Such developments are a long way off, and will be expensive. Until then, officers will continue to walk the streets with firearms little different to those developed a hundred years ago. On very rare occasions, they may well have to draw those weapons and kill or seriously injure another human being. Having done so, they must live with a situation from which most of us in the civilian world, thankfully, are shielded.

NOTES

INTRODUCTION

1. Extract quoted in Sven Crongeyer, *Six Gun Sound – The Early History of the Los Angeles County Sheriff's Department* (Fresno, CA, Linden Publishing, 2006), p.20.
2. www.camemorial.org. Vu Ngyuen was one of six California officers killed in 2007, the majority during high-speed car chase accidents.
3. National Law Enforcement Officers Memorial Fund official website at: http://www.nleimf.org/TheMemorial/Facts/history.htm
4. Source of data: Officer Down Memorial Page Inc.: http://www.odmp.org/year.php?year=2007 and http://www.odmp.org/year.php?year=2008
5. David Klinger, *Into the Kill Zones – A Cop's Eye View of Deadly Force* (San Francisco, CA, Jossey-Bass, 2004), p.11.
6. Mark Baker, *Cops – Their Lives in Their Own Words* (New York, Simon & Schuster, 1985), p.145.
7. For more on the nightwatchmen, and on the history of policing in the United States in general, see Bryan Vila and Cynthia Morris (eds), *The Role of Police in American Society: A Documentary History* (Westport, CT, Greenwood Press, 1999), pp.3–14.
8. Benjamin Franklin, *Memoirs* (Philadelphia, PA, 1788).
9. From George P. Rawick (ed.), *The American Slave: A Composite Autobiography*, vol. 9 (Westport, CT, Greenwood Press, 1979), pp.3460–61.
10. Vila and Morris, *The Role of Police*, p.16.
11. *Norfolk Argus* (October 12, 1860).
12. Patrick Henry and J. Elliot, *Debates in the Several State Conventions 45*, 2nd ed. (Philadelphia, PA, 1836).
13. "An Act to establish the Judicial Courts of the United States," in Statutes at Large, Session 1, Chapter XX, Section 27 (September 24, 1789).
14. Note that in 1870 the US Marshals Service came under the jurisdiction of the newly created Department of Justice, with the Attorney General overseeing its activities.
15. Roger D. McGrath, "A Violent Birth: Disorder, Crime and Law Enforcement, 1849–1890," in *California History* (Winter 2003).

16. Richard Maxwell Brown, *No Duty to Retreat: Violence and Values in American History and Society* (New York, Oxford University Press, 1991), p.131.
17. *New York Times* (December 19, 1857).
18. Vila and Morris, *The Role of Police*, p.35.
19. James F. Richardson, *The New York Police: Colonial Times to 1901* (New York, Oxford University Press, 1970), pp. 45–46.
20. *Brooklyn Daily Eagle* (June 7, 1865).

CHAPTER 1

21. Michael A. Bellesiles, "The Origins of Gun Culture in the United States, 1760–1865", in Jan E. Dizard et al. (eds), *Guns in America – A Reader* (New York, New York University Press, 1999), pp.17–46 (p.19).
22. Ibid, p.21.
23. *Quincy Daily Whig* (August 18, 1906).
24. Bellesiles "The Origins of Gun Culture", p.36.
25. Roger D. McGrath, *Gunfighters, Highwaymen, & Vigilantes – Violence on the Frontier* (Berkeley and Los Angeles, CA, University of California Press, 1984), p.255.
26. Chris McNab (ed.), *Gunfighters – The Outlaws and their Weapons* (San Diego, CA, Thunder Bay Press, 2005), p.340.
27. McNab, *Gunfighters*, p.346.
28. Leon Claire Metz, *The Shooters – A Gallery of Notorious Gunmen from the American West* (New York, Berkley Books, 1996), p.130.
29. Bill O'Neal, *The Pimlico Encyclopedia of Western Gunfighters* (London, Pimlico, 1998).
30. Ibid.
31. Ibid, pp.49–50.
32. To provide an idea of the volume of cattle concentrated in Abilene, over three million head of cattle were transported out east from the town between 1867 and 1870 alone.
33. *The Kansas Daily Commonwealth* (August 15, 1871).
34. McNab, pp.300–01.
35. Joseph G. Rosa, in McNab, *Gunfighters*, p.276.
36. "KANSAS; The Shooting Affray at Topeka A Private Citizen Kills a Deputy United States Marshal History of the Parties," *New York Times* (April 22, 1860).
37. Pat Garrett, *The Authentic Life of Billy the Kid* (1884).
38. Leon Claire Metz, *The Encyclopedia of Lawmen, Outlaws, and Gunfighters* (New York, Checkmark Books, 2003), p.156.
39. Ella Davidson, interviewed as part of the WPA Project in 1938.
40. Joel H. Garner and Christopher D. Maxwell, "Measuring the Amount of Force Used By and Against the Police in Six Jurisdictions", National Criminal Justice Reference Service: http://www.ncjrs.gov/pdffiles/nij/176330-2.pdf#page=13
41. "A Day Of Fighting In Chicago," *New York Times* (July 17, 1877).

42. Joe Zentner, "Western Gunslinger Myths": www/desertusa.com/mag05/jul/myths.html
43. *New York Times* (August 22, 1880).
44. "Egbert Kills Five People," *Adams County Union*, May 7, 1896.
45. Metz, *Encyclopedia*, p.234.
46. David J. Cook, *Hands Up! or Twenty Years of Detective Life in the Mountains and on the Plains* (1882); quoted in J. G. Rosa, *The Gunfighter: Man or Myth?* (Norman, OK, and London, University of Oklahoma Press, 1969), pp.58–59.
47. "Eugene Bunch Killed," *New York Times*, August 23, 1892.
48. Pennsylvania Historical and Museum Commission, "The Lattimer Massacre": http://www/phmc.state.pa.us/ppet/lattimer/page2.asp?secid=31
49. Ibid.
50. Ibid.
51. Handbook of Texas Online: http://www.tshaonline.org/handbook/online/articles/LL/fla80.html
52. "Court Proceedings on the CLEAR FORK! Judge Lynch Presiding," *Frontier Echo* (May 12, 1876).
53. Charles M. Robinson III, *American Frontier Lawmen 1850–1930* (Oxford, UK, Osprey Publishing, 2005), p.12.
54. For further details of the Courthouse Riot, see Ohio History Central website at: www.ohiohistorycentral.org/entry.php?rec=488
55. Texas Department of Public Safety: http://www.txdps.state.tx.us/director_staff/texas_rangers/#HistoricalDevelopment
56. N. A. Jennings, *Texas Ranger* (1882).
57. Robert M. Utley, *Lone Star Justice: The First Century of the Texas Rangers* (New York, Oxford University Press, 2002), p.164.
58. Ibid, pp.162–63.
59. Ibid, p.166.
60. John R. Brinkerhoff, "The Posse Comitatus Act and Homeland Security" (February 2002): www.homelandsecurity.org/journal.Articles/brinkerhofffpossecomitatus.htm
61. Ibid.
62. Marilynn S. Johnson, *Street Justice – A History of Police Violence in New York City* (Boston, MA, Beacon Press, 2003), p.17.
63. Samuel Gompers, *Seventy Years of Life and Labor* (E.P. Dutton & Company, 1925), pp. 32–34.
64. Johnson, *Street Justice*, pp.18–21.
65. *Brooklyn Daily Eagle* (October 23, 1892).
66. *Report and Proceedings of the Senate Committee Appointed to Investigate the Police Department of the City of New York* (1895).
67. Johnson, *Street Justice*, pp.55–56.
68. John J. Hickey, *Our Police Guardians* (New York, 1925) p.70. For a more in-depth analysis of the New York police and baton use, see Johnson, *Street Justice*, pp.87–100.

69. Johnson, *Street Justice*, p.90.
70. Ibid, p.91.
71. John C. Schneider, *Detroit and the Problem of Order, 1830–1880: A Geography of Crime, Riot, and Policing* (Lincoln, NE, University of Nebraska Press, 1980), p.118.
72. Ibid, pp.117–18.
73. *Brooklyn Daily Eagle* (September 6, 1893).
74. "Seymour Had Three Revolvers," *Brooklyn Daily Eagle* (February 3, 1895).
75. David I. Caplan, "Even Deadly Force: Fully Justifiable Homicide Vs. Barely Excusable Homicide," Second Amendment Foundation online: www.saf.org/JFPP12ch1.htm
76. *New York Times* (November 18, 1858). Quoted in Paul Chevigny, *Edge of the Knife – Police Violence in the Americas* (New York, The New York Press, 1995), p.127.
77. "An Escaping Prisoner Shot by Policeman," *Brooklyn Daily Eagle* (October 11, 1869).
78. Jeffrey S. Adler, "Shoot to Kill: The Use of Deadly Force by the Chicago Police, 1875–1920," *Journal of Interdisciplinary History*, XXXVIII (Autumn 2007), pp.233–54; p.236.
79. Ibid, p.237.
80. Ibid, p.241.
81. Ibid, p.243.
82. Ibid, p.246.
83. Illinois vs. August Spies et al. trial transcript no. 1, volume 1 (July 19, 1886) pp.238–40; text available from Chicago Historical Society, Haymarket Affair Digital Collection: www.chicagohistory.org/hadc/transcript/volumei/201-250/1231-249.htm

CHAPTER 2

84. "Chicago Has Real War," *New York Times* (May 27, 1900).
85. Source: Officer Down Memorial Page Inc.: http://www.odmp.org/
86. Johnson, *Street Justice*, p.81.
87. As an interesting aside, McLaughlin later gained a retrial for the murder, but while awaiting the retrial was charged with assaulting a reporter, James P. Robbins, with his baton, a clear sign that relations between the press and police were fairly antagonistic.
88. Johnson, *Street Justice*, p.82.
89. For a deeper analysis of the origins of the term, see Jerome H. Skolnick and James J. Fyfe, *Above the Law – Police and the Excessive use of Force* (New York, Simon & Schuster, 1993), pp.43–44.
90. From Ernest Jerome Hopkins, *Our Lawless Police: A Study of the Unlawful Enforcement of the Law* (New York, Viking, 1931; reprint De Capo, 1972) pp.191–92; see also Skolnick and Fyfe, *Above the Law*, p.44.
91. Johnson, *Street Justice*, p.134.
92. Ibid, p.136.
93. Adler, "Shoot to Kill," p.250.
94. Ibid, pp.243–44. Adler references the quotations as follows: for Gleason *Chicago Tribune*

(January 16, 1915); *Chicago Tribune* (September 14, 1918); for officials, *Chicago Times-Herald* (December 23, 1900); *Chicago Tribune* (August 24, 1907); *Chicago Record-Herald* (August 24, 1907; and *Chicago Tribune* (December 26, 1920).

95. Adler "Shoot to Kill", p.246.
96. Ibid, p.252.
97. "Tavern Owner Slain in Beer Syndicate War," *Chicago Tribune* (August 11, 1932).
98. August Vollmer, "The Policeman as a Social Worker," in *International Association of Chiefs of Police: Proceedings 26th Convention (*April 14–16, 1919).
99. "The Finest of the Finest," *Time* (February 18, 1966).
100. Richard Sylvester, "A History of the 'Sweat Box' and 'Third Degree,'" in *International Association of Chiefs of Police: Seventeenth Annual Session* (May 10–13, 1910).
101. Ibid.
102. Theodore Bingham, "Why I was removed," *Van Norden's Magazine* (September 1909).
103. Ibid, p.94.
104. "Casey Got a Clubbing," *New York Times* (May 6, 1907).
105. Johnson, *Street Justice*, p.101.
106. Ibid, p.103.
107. Joseph E. Corrigan, March 22, 1911.
108. A semi-automatic firearm is defined as one that requires a single trigger pull for each shot fired, the weapon reloading itself between shots. A full-auto weapon is one that will keep firing for as long as the trigger is depressed.
109. Massad Ayoob, "Guns 50th Police," *Guns Magazine* (Jan 2005).
110. Affidavit of Special Agent In Charge M. H. Purvis and S. P. Cowley, Sworn to Division of Investigation, Department of Justice, Chicago, Illinois, on July 28, 1934. FBI file 62-29777-1-24.
111. "G-men" was, and remains, a term used for FBI agents, and was supposedly coined by George "Machine Gun" Kelly who apparently shouted "Don't shoot, G-men" when being arrested by Department of Investigation (DOI) agents in September 1933.
112. Robert Unger, *Union Station Massacre: The Original Sin of J. Edgar Hoover's FBI* (Riverside, NJ, Andrew McMeel, 1997).
113. "Machine Gun Awes Liquor Raid Crowds," *New York Times* (May 6, 1922).
114. From a speech delivered by Thompson in Hackensack, NJ, on May 10, 1922.
115. Report issued by Special Deputy Police Commissioner Rodman Wanamaker (July 22, 1922). "Six Police Patrol Over City All Day," *New York Times* (July 23, 1922).
116. "2 Bullet Proof Vests, Gun Bought For Police Force," *Winona Republican-Herald* (May 24, 1934).
117. Library of Congress, Prints and Photographs Division, npcc.46874.
118. "Enright to Form Regiment," *New York Times* (January 29, 1920).
119. "Federal Agent Gets Too Free With Gun; Police Lock Him Up," *Winona Republican-Herald* (August 15, 1928).
120. Gregory B. Morrison and Bryan J. Vila, "Police Handgun Qualification: Practical Measure

or Aimless Activity?" *Policing: An International Journal of Police Strategies & Management*, vol. 21, no.3 (1993) pp.510–33; p.515.

121. Arthur Woods, *Policeman and the Public* (New Haven, CT, Yale University Press, 1919) p.159.

122. Ibid.

123. Ibid, pp.159–60.

124. "Adding Policemen to the List of Those Who Know How to Shoot," *The American Rifleman*, 71, no.7 (September 1, 1923), p.14.

125. "Dead-Eye Henry," *Time* (August 15, 1938).

126. Morrison and Vila, "Police Handgun Qualification," p.516.

127. Ibid, p.516.

128. Ann Arbor Police Department, "Ann Arbor's Outdoor Range": http://www.aadl.org/aapd/outdoorrange

129. Vila and Morris, *Role of Police*, p.133.

130. Police Commissioner Grover A. Whalen, 1930.

131. General Order no.23 (July 9, 1894).

132. For one of the most substantial treatments of the US government use of federal troops in social unrest, see Clayton D. Laurie and Ronald H. Cole, *The Role of Federal Military Forces in Civil Disturbances 1877–1945* (Darby, PA, Diane Publishing, 1999).

133. Ibid, pp.346–47.

134. Quoted in Kristian Williams, *Our Enemies in Blue: Police and Power in America* (Soft Skull Press, 2003), p.211.

135. Laurie and Cole, *Role of Federal Military Forces*, p.349.

136. Ibid, p.350.

137. Testimony before the Federal Commission on Industrial Relations, May 21, 1915.

138. Howard Fast, "Memorial Day Massacre," at: http://www.trussel.com/hf/memorial.htm

139. Ibid.

140. Testimony before the LaFollette Civil Liberties Committee, June 19, 1937.

CHAPTER 3

141. Text from *Symbionese Liberation Army – A Study Prepared for the Use of the Committee on Internal Security, House of Representatives, Ninety-Third Congress, Second Session* (Washington DC, US Government Printing Office, February 18, 1974), p.2.

142. Symbionese Liberation Army, Communique #3, February 4, 1974.

143. Los Angeles Police Department, *The Symbionese Liberation Army in Los Angeles* (July 19, 1974) p.31.

144. Ibid, p.44.

145. Ibid, p.96.

146. Ibid, p.137.

147. Data from National Law Enforcement Officers Memorial website:

www.nleomf.org/TheMemorial/Facts/impdates.htm

148. Carole Bryan Jones, *Twentieth Century USA* (McGraw Hill, 2005).

149. Detective Wayne Caffey, Los Angeles County Sheriff's Office, "Crips and Bloods," at http://www.nagia.org/Gang%20Articles/Crips%20and%Bloods.pdf; p.2

150. Ibid, pp.1–2.

151. International Association of Chiefs of Police, 1957.

152. Orlando W. Wilson, *Police Administration* (New York, McGraw Hill, 1950), p.4.

153. Bertha H. Smith, "The Policewoman," *Good Housekeeping*, 52 (February 1911), pp.296–98; p.296.

154. Lois Lundell Higgins, *Policewoman's Manual* (Springfield, IL, Charles C. Thomas, 1961), p.xi.

155. David S. Broder, "Policewoman Shoots Suspect on 45th St.," *New York Times* (May 25, 1965)

156. Commission to Investigate Allegations of Police Corruption, *The Knapp Commission Report on Police Corruption* (New York, George Braziller, 1973), p.3.

157. Byran Jones, *Twentieth Century USA*, p.162.

158. Regina G. Lawrence, *The Politics of Force* (Berkeley, CA, University of California Press, 2000), p.11.

159. James Q. Wilson, *Varieties of Police Behavior* (Harvard University Press, 1978), p.81.

160. Ibid, pp.80–81.

161. Donald Janson, "Daly's TV Film Shows Convention Week Clashes," *New York Times* (September 16, 1968).

162. ACLU, Illinois Branch statement, "A Fault of Reason" (1968).

163. Daniel Walker, *Rights in Conflict: The Violent Confrontation of Demonstrators and Police in the Parks and Streets of Chicago During the Week of the Democratic National Convention of 1968* National Commission on the Causes and Prevention of Violence, (released December 1, 1968) Summary.

164. Daryl F. Gates, with Diane K. Shah, *Chief – My Life in the LAPD* (New York, Bantam Books, 1992), p.91.

165. Ibid, p.102.

166. Ibid, p.102.

167. Cyrus R. Vance, *Final Report of Cyrus R. Vance, Special Assistant to the Secretary of Defense Concerning the Detroit Riots July 23 through August 2, 1967* (1968): http://www.lbjlib.utexas.edu/johnson/archives.hom/oralhistory.hom/Vance-C/DetroitReport.asp#LL

168. Ibid.

169. Ibid.

170. Department of Justice, Civil Rights Division, Summary of FBI reports into Kent State (July 1970): http://www.may4archive.org/appendices.shtml#FBI

171. Ibid.

172. Ibid.

173. See Mike Nizza, "An Order to Fire at Kent State?" *New York Times* (May 2, 2007):

http://thelede.blogs.nytimes.com/2007/05/02/an-order-to-fire-at-kent-state/?scp=1-b&sq=kent+state&st=nyt

174. Lisa Daniel, "Lessons Applied," *National Guard* (May 2000).

175. Ibid.

176. Gates, *Chief*, p.109.

177. "Police Stockpiling Weapons for Riots," *New York Times* (March 2, 1968).

178. Skolnick and Fyfe, *Above the Law*, p.113.

179. See note 177.

180. Gates, *Chief*, p.110.

181. Ibid, p.115.

182. Jon Nordheimer, "Tough Elite Police Units Useful but Controversial," *New York Times* (July 14, 1975).

183. Ibid.

184. Data from US Department of Justice, Bureau of Justice Statistics: "Percent of Murders, Robberies and Aggravated Assaults in which Firearms were Used, 1973 to 2006" (data revised January 25, 2008).

185. Ramiro "Ray" Martinez, *They call me Ranger Ray* (New Braunfels, TX, Rio Bravo Publishing, 2004).

186. Massad Ayoob, "Lessons of the Newhall Massacre," *Association News* (March 2001), p.6.

187. Ibid, p.8.

188. Center for Research on Criminal Justice, *The Iron Fist and the Velvet Glove – An Analysis of the U.S. Police* (Berkeley, California, 1975), p.97.

189. David Burnham, "Police Violence: A Changing Pattern," *New York Times* (July 7, 1968).

190. See Geoffrey P. Alpert and Lorie A. Fridell, *Police Vehicles and Firearms – Instruments of Deadly Force* (Prospect Heights, Illinois, Waveland Press, 1992), p.36.

191. Ibid, pp.36–37.

192. Ibid, p.36.

193. Lawrence W. Sherman et al., *Citizens Killed by Big City Police, 1970–84* (Washington DC, Crime Control Institute, 1986), p.20.

194. David Burnham, "3 of 5 Slain by Police Here Are Black, Same as the Arrest Rate," *New York Times* (August 26, 1973).

195. Marshall W. Meyer, "Police Shootings at Minorities: The Case of Los Angeles," The Annals of the American Academy of Political and Social Science, Vol. 452, No. 1 (1980) pp.98–110.

196. Alpert and Fridell, *Police Vehicles and Firearms*, p.37. The studies to which the authors refer are: William A. Geller and Kevin J. Karales, *Split-Second Decisions: Shootings of and by Chicago Police* (Chicago, IL, Chicago Law Enforcement Study Group, 1981); James Fyfe, "Shots Fired: Examination of New York City Police Firearms Discharges" (unpublished dissertation, State University of New York, 1978); Frank Horvath, "The Police Use of Deadly Force: A Description of Selected Characteristics of Intrastate Incidents," *Journal of Police Science and Administration*, 15 (1987), pp.226–38.

197. For a reproduction of the report, see Peter Scharf and Arnold Binder, *The Badge and the Bullet – Police Use of Deadly Force* (New York, Praeger Publishing, 1983), pp.78–79.

198. Ibid, p.79.

199. John G. Peters Jr. and Michael A. Brave, "Force Continuums: Are they Still Needed?" *Police and Security News*, 22:1 (January/February 2006), p.2.

200. Jonathan Rubenstein, *City Police* (New York, Farrar, Straus and Giroux, 1973), p.330.

201. See Peters and Brave, "Force Continuums," p.3.

202. Jenna Solari and John Bostain, "Use of Force Continuum (podcast transcript)," Federal Law Enforcement Training Center, Department of Homeland Security website: http://www.fletc.gov/training/programs/legal-division/podcasts/hot-issues-podcasts/hot-issues-transcripts/use-of-force-continuum-podcast-transcript.html

203. Morrison and Vila, "Police Handgun Qualification," p.519.

204. Michael James, "Dead-Eye Police in Pistol Test Prove Value of F.B.I. training," *New York Times* (June 22, 1967).

205. Michael James, "New Range Shows Police Weak In Shooting at Moving Targets," *New York Times* (February 5, 1958).

206. "Police Get $250,000 Arms Training Grant," *Los Angeles Times* (October 10, 1970)

207. Morrison and Vila, "Police Handgun Qualification," p.520.

208. The Virginia Police and Deputy Sheriffs, "NYPD SOP 9 – Analysis of Police Combat": www.virginiacops.org/Articles/Shooting/Combat.htm

CHAPTER 4

209. Nancy J. Rigg, "Shoot-out in North Hollywood – Command and Communications": http://www.9-1-1magazine.com/magazine/1997/0997/features/rigg.html

210. By "assault weapons" we mean semi-automatic or full automatic military-style rifles and submachine guns designed purely for combat usage rather than sporting applications

211. Figures from David B. Kopel, "Rational Basis Analysis of 'Assault Weapon' Prohibition," *Journal of Contemporary Law*, 20 (1994), pp.381–417: pp.407–10.

212. Ibid, pp.410–11.

213. Franklin E. Zimring, "Firearms and Federal Law: The Gun Control Act Of 1968," *Journal of Legal Studies*, 4 (1975), pp.134–200: p.143.

214. US Bureau of the Census, Foreign Trade Division, FT246 U.S. Imports for Consumption 1964–73.

215. Jeffrey A. Roth and Christopher S. Koper, "Impacts of the 1994 Assault Weapons Ban: 1994–96," *National Institute of Justice – Research in Brief* (March 1999), p.2.

216. Ibid, p.5.

217. Source: US Department of Justice, Bureau of Justice Statistics.

218. Linda Keene, "With A Gun, Anger Becomes Deadly – Seattle's Sad Summer Of Killings Blamed On Dominance Of Firearms," *Seattle Times* (September 24, 1993).

219. Deadly Force Special Report, *Washington Post* (November 18, 1998):

http://www.washingtonpost.com/wp-srv/local/longterm/dcpolice/deadlyforce/police4_list.htm

220. Jane Fritsch, "Gun of Choice for Police Officers runs into Fierce Opposition," *New York Times* (May 31, 1992).
221. Ibid.
222. Ibid.
223. Thomas Aveni, "Officer-Involved Shootings: What We Don't Know Has Hurt Us," Police Policy Studies Council Document, p.5. Available online at: http://www.theppsc.org/Staff_Views/Aveni/OIS.pdf
224. Ibid, p.5.
225. Clifford Krauss, "Police Plan More Training in 9-mm. Gun," *New York Times* (June 5, 1995)
226. Jane Fritsch, "Gun of Choice for Police Officers Runs Into Fierce Opposition," *New York Times* (May 31, 1992).
227. See W. French Anderson MD, *Forensic Analysis of the April 11, 1986, FBI Firefight* (1996) for one of the most detailed analyses of this incident. Also refer to the Firearms Tactical Institute website at: http://www.firearmstactical.com/briefs7.htm
228. "Chicago Suburb Turns Down Submachine Guns for Police," *New York Times* (July 20, 1989).
229. Matt Lait, "LAPD Has Yet to Deploy Assault Rifles It Urgently Requested," *Los Angeles Times* (January 16, 1998).
230. "Gun," *St. Petersburg Times* (August 15, 1995).
231. "Odd," *St. Petersburg Times* (December 28, 1993).
232. Tom Gabor, "Rethinking SWAT – Police Special Weapons and Tactics," FBI Law Enforcement Bulletin (April 1993).
233. Peter B. Kraska and Victor E. Kappeler, "Militarizing American Police: The Rise and Normalization of Paramilitary Units," *Social Problems*, vol. 44, no. 1 (February 1997).
234. Mark Araz, "Small Farm Town's SWAT Team Leaves Costly Legacy," *Los Angeles Times* (April 5, 1999).
235. Ibid.
236. Gabor, "Rethinking SWAT".
237. Ibid.
238. Interview with Carl Stincelli (October 27, 2008).
239. Tennessee v. Garner, 471 US 1 (1985).
240. Ibid.
241. Johnson, *Street Justice*, p.278.
242. James Kilpatrick, "Supreme Court decision in Garner case too rigid," *Columbia Missourian* (April 8, 1985).
243. Randy Riders, "Graham v. Connor: Gauging Excessive Force," Officer.com: http://officer.com/web/online/Investigation/Graham-v-Connor/18$40765
244. Graham v. Connor, 490 US 386 (1989)
245. US Department of Justice, Resolution 14b, Policy Statement "Use of Deadly Force."

Accessed through US Department of Justice website: http://www.usdoj.gov/ag/readingroom/resoluton14b.htm

246. John C. Hall, "FBI Training on the New Federal Deadly Force Policy," *FBI Law Enforcement Bulletin* (April 1996).

247. US Department of Justice, "Justifiable Homicides by Police and Citizens, 1976–2005": http://www.ojp.usdoj.gov/bjs/homicde/d_justifyreason.htm

248. FBI database, *Supplementary Homicide Reports*. Quoted in Jodi M. Brown and Patrick A. Langan, *Policing and Homicide, 1976-98: Justifiable Homicide by Police, Police Officers Murdered by Felons* (US Department of Justice, Office of Justice Programs, Bureau of Justice Statistics, March 2001) p.3.

249. Ibid, p.1.

250. Ibid, p.21 (Source: FBI, *Law Enforcement Officers Killed and Assaulted*.)

251. Ibid, p.16.

252. Ibid, p.17.

253. Ibid, p.17.

254. The People Of The State Of New York v. Kenneth Boss, Sean Carroll, Edward McMellon, and Richard Murphy, Albany County Courthouse (February 2, 2000).

255. Massad Ayoob, "Hallway Firefight: The Amadou Diallo Shooting," *American Handgunner* (November 2000).

256. Report House of Representatives 104th Congress, 2nd Session, Union Calendar no. 395, August 2, 1996. Investigation into the Activities of Federal Law Enforcement Agencies toward the Branch Davidians; Thirteenth Report by the Committee on Government Reform and Oversight, Section IIb.

257. Ibid, Section IVb.

258. US Department of Justice, "Report to the Deputy Attorney General on the Events at Waco, Texas, February 28 to April 19, 1993" (October 8, 1993) Section VIII/A.

259. Ibid, Section III/C.

260. Daniel Klaidman and Michael Isikoff, "A Fire That Won't Die," *Newsweek* (September 20, 1999).

261. Ibid.

262. See Major General (Ret.) James D. Delk, "Military Operations in Los Angeles, 1992," California State Military Department, The California Military Museum: www.militarymuseum.org/HistoryKingMilOps.html; previously published in *Military Review* (September 1992).

263. Ibid.

264. Lieutenant Colonel Christopher M. Schnaubelt, "Lessons in Command and Control from the Los Angeles Riots," California State Military Department, The California Military Museum: www.militarymuseum.org/LARiots1.html; previously published in *Parameters* (Summer 1997), pp.88–109.

265. Delk, "Military Operations".

CHAPTER 5

266. Interview with Second Lieutenant Dan Courtney, July 13, 2008.
267. Note that "Taser" is actually a brand name for conducted energy device made by Taser International. Such is the ubiquity of the company's devices, however, that "taser" has in many ways become a generic term, as it is used here.
268. Samuel D. Faulkner and Larry P. Danaher, "Controlling Subjects: Realistic Training vs. Magic Bullets," *FBI Law Enforcement Bulletin* (February 1997).
269. National Institute of Justice, "The Effectiveness and Safety of Pepper Spray," (Washington DC, US Department of Justice, April 2003), pp.2–7.
270. Ibid, pp.8–9.
271. Rocco Parascandola, "New York Police Officer Commits Suicide Over Taser Incident," *Los Angeles Times* (October 3, 2008).
272. Alison Leigh Cowan, "Suicide Bigger Threat for Police than Criminals," *New York Times* (April 8, 2008).
273. John Ritter, "Suicide Rates Jolt Police Culture," *USA Today* (February 8, 2007).
274. See University at Buffalo: www.buffalo.edu/news/9660
275. Ritter, "Suicide Rates".
276. Amnesty International, *Amnesty International's continuing concerns about taser use* (2006): http://amnestyusa.org/document.php?lang=e&id=ENGAMR510302006
277. Ibid.
278. Major Steve James, "TASER Today: Controversy, Credibility and Control Considerations," Policeone.com (May 14, 2005): http://policeone.com/police-products/less-lethal.taser/articles/100546-TASER-today-controversy-credibility-control-considerations
279. National Institute of Justice, *Study of Deaths Following Electro Muscular Disruption: Interim Report* (Washington DC, US Department of Justice, June 2008), p.3.
280. Ibid, p.3.
281. Ibid, p.3–4.
282. Brian Chasnoff, "Texas Chief Prohibits TASER Use Against Suspects on Drugs," *San Antonio Express-News*, quoted on Policeone.com (October 15, 2008): http://www.policeone.com/less-lethal/articles/1745789-Texas-chief-prohibits-TASER-use-against-suspects-on-drugs/
283. See Steve Hougland, Charlie Mesloh, and Mark Henych, "Use of Force, Civil Litigation, and the Taser – One Agency's Experience," *FBI Law Enforcement Bulletin* (March 2005), p.27.
284. Al Baker, "Report on City Police Shootings Urges More Use of Tasers Before Guns," *New York Times* (June 10, 2008).
285. Ibid, p.25.
286. See Thomas J. Aveni, "Obsolescence: The Police Firearms Training Dilemma," *Answering the Call* (Fall 2008), pp.11–15 (p.12).
287. Thomas J. Aveni, "Critical Deadly Force Training Perspectives," *Answering the Call* (Fall 2007), pp.16–19 (p.17).

288. Ibid, p.19.
289. Aveni, "Obsolescence," p.13.
290. Ibid, p.11.
291. Ibid, pp.11–12.
292. Ibid, p.13.
293. Interview with Gregory B. Morrison (September 10, 2008).
294. Aveni, "Obsolescence," p.14.
295. For example, see T. M. Dees, "Ethics & the Sipowicz Factor," *Law Enforcement Technology*, 23, 6 (June 1996), pp.58–60.
296. Bureau of Justice Statistics, Department of Justice, "Trends in Law Enforcement Officers Killed by Weapon Type, 1973–2005": http://www.ojp.usdoj.gov/bjs/homicide/tables/leokweaptab.htm
297. F. P. Rivara and C.D. Mack, "Motor Vehicle Crash Deaths Related to Police Pursuits in the United States," *Injury Prevention*, 10 (2004), pp.93–95 (p.93).
298. Pine Bluff Police Department, Policy and Procedures Manual, Policy no. 231, "Police Vehicle – Pursuit Driving" (February 19, 2008), p.1.
299. Geoffrey P. Alpert, "Police Pursuit: Policies and Training," National Institute of Justice (May 1997), p.4.
300. See Tanangachi Mfui and Alison Gendar, "Retired NY Sgt. Killed in Apparent 'Suicide-by-Cop'," *The Daily News* (July 22, 2008).
301. Gary Bush, taken from the Suicide by Cop web site: http://www.suicidebycop.com/7601.html
302. Interview with Rebecca Stincelli (October 27, 2008).

CHAPTER 6

303. BBC News, April 24, 2008: http://news.bbc.co.uk/1/hi/world/americas/7349759.stm
304. Peter Scharf and Arnold Binder, *The Badge and the Bullet – Police Use of Deadly Force* (New York, Praeger Publishing, 1983), p.32.
305. Ibid, p.41.
306. Jennifer Klinesmith et al., *Guns, Testosterone, and Aggression: An Experimental Test of a Mediational Hypothesis* (Galesburg, IL, Knox College, 2006), p.9.
307. There are numerous other variables that affect accuracy, including windage (the degree of "looseness" between bore and bullet), the type of rifling (the spiral grooves in the bore that impart spin to the bullet), and even weather conditions, but the fact remains that long barrels give better accuracy over short barrels when the barrels are of comparable quality.
308. "Shooting incidents" are classified as incidents in which the officer engaged a perpetrator, as opposed to simple "incidents" in which the officer discharged his firearm for reasons of accident, shooting animals etc. For the following data and more, see Aveni, "Officer Involved Shootings," p.5.
309. Ibid, p.7.

310. Ibid, p.6.
311. City of New York Police Department, *Firearms Discharge Report 2006* (Police Academy Firearms and Tactics Section, 2006), p.10.
312. Ibid, p.11.
313. For analysis of wound ballistics and other related themes in both military and police contexts, see Chris McNab and Hunter Keeter, *Tools of Violence – Guns, Tanks and Dirty Bombs* (Oxford, UK, Osprey Publishing, 2008), pp.42–56.
314. For some of the best analysis of wound ballistics myths and realities, see the following titles, all by Martin L. Fackler: "Gunshot Wound Review," *Annals of Emergency Medicine*, 28:2 (August 1996) pp.194–203; "Wound Ballistics and Soft-Tissue Wound Treatment," *Techniques in Orthopaedics*, 10:3 (1995) pp.163–70; and "What's Wrong with the Wound Ballistics Literature, and Why," Letterman Army Institute of Research, Division of Military Trauma Research, Report no.239 (July 1987).
315. Klinger, *Into the Kill Zone*, p.90.
316. Urey W. Patrick and John C. Hall, *In Defense of Self and Others... Issues, Facts, & Fallacies – the Realities of Law Enforcement's Use of Deadly Force* (Durham, NC, Carolina Academic Press, 2005), pp.63–64.
317. Firearms Tactical Institute, Tactical Briefs #7 (July 1998). Report W. French Anderson MD, *Forensic Analysis of the April 11, 1986, FBI Firefight* (1996). Note that the FTI and Anderson acknowledge that further study of the autopsy report and photographs shows that the bullet initially passed through the biceps muscle rather than the lower sections of the arm.
318. Martin L. Fackler MD, "Police Handgun Ammunition Selection," *Wound Ballistics Review* (Fall 1992), pp.32–37; p.37.
319. Patrick and Hall, *In Defense*, pp.108–09.
320. WKLY.com NewsChannel 32; transcript published online at: http://www.wlky.com/news/1957321/detail.html
321. Dave Spaulding, "What Really Happens in a Gunfight," *Guns and Ammo Handguns*, online: www.handgunsmag.com/tactics_training/what_happens_gunfight/
322. Firearms Tactical Institute, Tactical Briefs #3, "The Myth of Energy Transfer" (15 March 1998).
323. Urey W. Patrick, US Department of Justice, Federal Bureau of Investigation, "Handgun Wounding Factors and Effectiveness" (Quantico, Virginia, Firearms Training Unit, July 14, 1989), p.11.
324. Interview with Major Mike LoMonaco, Fairfax County Police (March 2008),
325. William B. Waegel, "How Police Justify the Use of Deadly Force," *Social Problems*, vol.32, no.2 (December 1984), pp.144–55 (p.151).
326. Testimony given by Stone in court, July 2006.
327. CBS News, The Early Show, interview with Harry Smith, transcript at: http://www.cbsnews.com/stories/2006/07/21/earlyshow/main1824357.shtml
328. Tyler Police Department News Release #06-03-051 (March 24, 2006).
329. Information from Policeone.com, "New study may 'radically alter' how police deadly force is viewed" (February 11, 2001): http://www.policeone.com/writers/columnists/Force-

Science/articles/1660208-New-study-may-radically-alter-how-police-deadly-force-is-viewed/

330. Ibid.

331. Ibid.

332. Ibid.

333. Data from Dr Bill Lewinski, "Why is the Suspect Shot in the Back?," *The Police Marksman*, vol. XXV, no.6 (November/December 2000), pp.20–28.

334. Results data contained in Dr Bill Lewinski and Dr Bill Hudson, "Time to Start Shooting? Time to Stop Shooting? The Tempe Study," in *The Police Marksman*, vol. XXVIII, no. 5 (September/October 2003), pp.26–29.

335. Ibid, p.26.

336. Patrick and Hall, *In Defense*, p.103.

337. Edward Mamet being interviewed by Brian Lehrer, WNCY radio (January 8, 2007).

338. Sean Gardiner, "Guns Gone Wild – NYPD gunfire goes up while crime goes down," *The Village Voice* online: http://www.villagevoice.com/news/0649.gardiner.75216.6.html

339. See Bernard D. Rostker et al, *Evaluation of the New York City Police Department Firearm Training and Firearm-Discharge Review Process* (Santa Monica, CA, Rand Corporation, 2008).

340. Thomas J. Aveni, "Contagious Fire: Fact or Fiction?," *Answering the Call*, Police Policy Studies Council (Summer 2007) pp.16–20 (pp.17–18).

341. Thomas J. Aveni and Edward Gidnig, "Surviving the Nightshift," *Answering the Call*, Police Policy Studies Council (Summer 2007) pp.8–14 (p.10).

342. Ibid, p.11.

343. Florida Department of Law Enforcement, Criminal Justice Standards & Training Commission, Technical Memo 2004-15 (September 10, 2004).

344. David Klinger, *Police Responses to Officer Involved Shootings*, US Department of Justice document #192286 (February 1, 2001) p.27.

345. Charles Remsberg, "Telling the Truth About Police Shootings," *The Police Marksman*, Vol. XXIX, no.6 (November/December 2004) pp.18–22 (pp.20–21).

346. "When Cops Shoot," *Chicago Tribune* (December 6, 2007).

347. Baker, *Cops*, p.157.

BIBLIOGRAPHY

ACLU, Illinois Branch statement, "A Fault of Reason" (1968)

Adams, Jim, "Police gunning to equal criminals' firepower with assault rifles," Star Tribune.com: http://www.startribune.com/local/17144341.html

Adler, Jeffrey S., "Shoot to Kill: The Use of Deadly Force by the Chicago Police, 1875–1920," *Journal of Interdisciplinary History*, XXXVIII (Autumn 2007), pp.233–54

Affidavit of Special Agent In Charge M. H. Purvis and S. P. Cowley, sworn to Division of Investigation, Department of Justice, Chicago, Illinois, on July 28, 1934. FBI file 62-29777-1-24

Alpert, Geoffrey P., "Police Pursuit: Policies and Training," National Institute of Justice (May 1997)

Alpert, Geoffrey P. and Lorie A. Fridell, *Police Vehicles and Firearms – Instruments of Deadly Force* (Prospect Heights, IL, Waveland Press, 1992)

Amnesty International, *Amnesty International's Continuing Concerns About Taser Use* (2006): http://www.amnestyusa.org/document.php?lang=e&id=ENGAMR510302006

Anderson, W. French, *Forensic Analysis of the April 11, 1986, FBI Firefight* (W. French Anderson, 1996)

Ann Arbor Police Department, "Ann Arbor's Outdoor Range": http://www.aadl.org/aapd/outdoorrange

Aveni, Thomas, "Contagious Fire: Fact or Fiction?," *Answering the Call*, Police Policy Studies Council (Summer 2007), pp.16–20

Aveni, Thomas, "Critical Deadly Force Training Perspectives," *Answering the Call* (Fall 2007), pp.16–19

Aveni, Thomas, "Obsolescence: The Police Firearms Training Dilemma," *Answering the Call* (Fall 2008), pp.11–15

Aveni, Thomas, "Officer-Involved Shootings: What We Don't Know Has Hurt Us," Police Policy Studies Council Document: http://www.theppsc.org/Staff_Views/Aveni/OIS.pdf

Aveni, Thomas and Edward Gidnig, "Surviving the Nightshift," *Answering the Call*, Police Policy Studies Council (Summer 2007), pp.8–14

Ayoob, Massad, "Guns 50th Police," *Guns Magazine* (Jan 2005)

Ayoob, Massad, "Hallway Firefight: The Amadou Diallo Shooting," *American Handgunner* (November 2000)

Ayoob, Massad, "Lessons of the Newhall Massacre," *Association News* (March 2001)

Baker, Mark, *Cops – Their Lives in Their Own Words* (New York, Simon & Schuster, 1985)

Bellesiles, Michael A., "The Origins of Gun Culture in the United States, 1760–1865," in Jan E. Dizard et al. (eds), *Guns in America – A Reader* (New York, New York University Press, 1999), pp.17–46

Brinkerhoff, John R., "The Posse Comitatus Act and Homeland Security" (February 2002): http://www.homelandsecurity.org/journal/Articles/brinkerhoffpossecomitatus.htm

Brown, Jodi M. and Patrick A. Langan, *Policing and Homicide, 1976-98: Justifiable Homicide by Police, Police Officers Murdered by Felons* (US Department of Justice, Office of Justice Programs, Bureau of Justice Statistics, March 2001)

Brown, Richard Maxwell, *No Duty to Retreat: Violence and Values in American History and Society* (New York, Oxford University Press, 1991)

Bryan Jones, Carole *Twentieth Century USA* (London, Hodder, 2005)

Bureau of Justice Statistics, US Department of Justice, "Trends in Law Enforcement Officers Killed by Weapon Type, 1973–2005": http://www.ojp.usdoj.gov/bjs/homicide/tables/leokweaptab.htm

Caffey, Detective Wayne, Los Angeles County Sheriff's Office, "Crips and Bloods": http://www.nagia.org/Gang%20Articles/Crips%20and%20Bloods.pdf

Caplan, David I., "Even Deadly Force: Fully Justifiable Homicide Vs. Barely Excusable Homicide," Second Amendment Foundation online: www.saf.org/JFPP12ch1.htm

Center for Research on Criminal Justice, *The Iron Fist and the Velvet Glove – An Analysis of the U.S. Police* (Berkeley, CA, 1975)

Chevigny, Paul, *Edge of the Knife – Police Violence in the Americas* (New York, The New York Press, 1995)

City of New York Police Department, *Firearms Discharge Report 2006* (Police Academy Firearms and Tactics Section, 2006)

Commission to Investigate Allegations of Police Corruption, *The Knapp Commission Report on Police Corruption* (New York, George Braziller, 1973)

Committee on Internal Security, *Symbionese Liberation Army – A Study Prepared for the Use of the Committee on Internal Security, House of Representatives, Ninety-Third Congress, Second Session* (Washington DC, US Government Printing Office, February 18, 1974)

Cook, David J., *Hands Up! or Twenty Years of Detective Life in the Mountains and on the Plains* (1882)

Crongeyer, Sven, *Six Gun Sound – The Early History of the Los Angeles County Sheriff's Department* (Fresno, CA, Linden Publishing, 2006)

Daniel, Lisa, "Lessons Applied," *National Guard* (May 2000)

Dees, T. M., "Ethics & the Sipowicz Factor," *Law Enforcement Technology*, 23, 6 (June 1996), pp.58–60

Delk, Major General (Ret.) James D., "Military Operations in Los Angeles, 1992," California State Military Department, The California Military Museum: www.militarymuseum.org/HistoryKingMilOps.html; previously published in *Military Review* (September 1992)

Fackler, Martin L., "Gunshot Wound Review," *Annals of Emergency Medicine*, 28:2 (August 1996), pp.194–203

Fackler, Martin L., "Police Handgun Ammunition Selection," *Wound Ballistics Review* (Fall 1992), pp.32–37

Fackler, Martin L., "What's Wrong with the Wound Ballistics Literature, and Why," Letterman Army Institute of Research, Division of Military Trauma Research, Report no.239 (July 1987)

Fackler, Martin L., "Wound Ballistics and Soft-Tissue Wound Treatment," *Techniques in Orthopaedics*, 10:3 (1995), pp.163–70

Fast, Howard, "Memorial Day Massacre": http://www.trussel.com/hf/memorial.htm

Faulkner, Samuel D. and Larry P. Danaher, "Controlling Subjects: Realistic Training vs. Magic Bullets," *FBI Law Enforcement Bulletin* (February 1997)

Firearms Tactical Institute, Tactical Briefs #7 (July 1998). Report W. French Anderson MD, *Forensic Analysis of the April 11, 1986, FBI Firefight* (1996)

Florida Department of Law Enforcement, Criminal Justice Standards & Training Commission, Technical Memo 2004-15 (September 10, 2004)

Franklin, Benjamin, *Memoirs* (Philadelphia, PA,1788)

Fyfe, James, "Shots Fired: Examination of New York City Police Firearms Discharges," (Unpublished dissertation, State University of New York, 1978)

Gabor, Tom, "Rethinking SWAT – Police Special Weapons and Tactics," FBI Law Enforcement Bulletin (April 1993)

Garner, Joel H. and Christopher D. Maxwell, "Measuring the Amount of Force Used By and Against the Police in Six Jurisdictions," National Criminal Justice Reference Service: http://www.ncjrs.gov/pdffiles1/nij/176330-2.pdf#page=13

Garrett, Pat, *The Authentic Life of Billy the Kid* (1884)

Gates, Daryl F., with Diane K. Shah, *Chief – My Life in the LAPD* (New York, Bantam Books, 1992)

Geller, William A. and Kevin J. Karales, *Split-Second Decisions: Shootings of and by Chicago Police* (Chicago, IL, Chicago Law Enforcement Study Group, 1981)

Gompers, Samuel, *Seventy Years of Life and Labor* (E. P. Dutton & Company, 1925)

Hall, John C., "FBI Training on the New Federal Deadly Force Policy," *FBI Law Enforcement Bulletin* (April 1996)

Handbook of Texas Online: http://www.tshaonline.org

Henry, Patrick and J. Elliot, *Debates in the Several State Conventions 45*, 2nd ed. (Philadelphia, PA, 1836)

Hickey, John J., *Our Police Guardians* (New York, 1925)

Higgins, Lois Lundell, *Policewoman's Manual* (Springfield, IL., Charles C. Thomas, 1961)

Hopkins, Ernest Jerome, *Our Lawless Police: A Study of the Unlawful Enforcement of the Law* (New York, Viking, 1931; reprint De Capo, 1972)

Horvath, Frank, "The Police Use of Deadly Force: A Description of Selected Characteristics of Intrastate Incidents," *Journal of Police Science and Administration*, 15 (1987), pp.226–38

Hougland, Steve and Mesloh, Charlie and Henych, Mark, "Use of Force, Civil Litigation, and the Taser – One Agency's Experience," *FBI Law Enforcement Bulletin* (March 2005)

Investigation into the Activities of Federal Law Enforcement Agencies toward the Branch Davidians; Thirteenth Report by the Committee on Government Reform and Oversight, Section IIb

James, Steve, "TASER Today: Controversy, Credibility and Control Considerations,"

Policeone.com (May 14, 2005): http://www.policeone.com/police-products/less-lethal/taser/articles/100546-TASER-today-Controversy-credibility-control-considerations/

Jennings, N. A., *Texas Ranger* (1882)

Johnson, Marilynn S., *Street Justice – A History of Police Violence in New York City* (Boston, MA, Beacon Press, 2003)

Klinesmith, Jennifer et al, *Guns, Testosterone, and Aggression: An Experimental Test of a Mediational Hypothesis* (Galesburg, IL, Knox College, 2006)

Klinger, David, *Into the Kill Zones – A Cop's Eye View of Deadly Force* (San Francisco, CA, Jossey-Bass, 2004)

Klinger, David, *Police Responses to Officer Involved Shootings*, US Department of Justice document #192286 (February 1, 2001)

Kopel, David B., "Rational Basis Analysis of 'Assault Weapon' Prohibition," *Journal of Contemporary Law*, 20 (1994), pp.381–417

Kraska, Peter B. and Victor E. Kappeler, "Militarizing American Police: The Rise and Normalization of Paramilitary Units," *Social Problems*, vol.44, no.1 (February 1997)

Laurie, Clayton D. and Ronald H. Cole, *The Role of Federal Military Forces in Civil Disturbances 1877–1945* (Darby, PA, Diane Publishing, 1999)

Lawrence, Regina G., *The Politics of Force* (Berkeley, CA, University of California Press, 2000)

Lewinski, Bill, "Why is the Suspect Shot in the Back?," *The Police Marksman*, vol. XXV, no. 6 (November/December 2000), pp.20–28

Lewinski, Bill and Bill Hudson, "Time to Start Shooting? Time to Stop Shooting? The Tempe Study," in *The Police Marksman*, vol. XXVIII, no. 5 (September/October 2003), pp.26–29

Los Angeles Police Department, *The Symbionese Liberation Army in Los Angeles* (July 19, 1974)

Martinez, Ramiro "Ray," *They Call me Ranger Ray* (New Braunfels, TX, Rio Bravo Publishing, 2004)

McGrath, Roger D., "A Violent Birth: Disorder, Crime and Law Enforcement, 1849–1890," in *California History* (Winter 2003)

McGrath, Roger D., *Gunfighters, Highwaymen, & Vigilantes – Violence on the Frontier* (Berkeley and Los Angeles, CA, University of California Press, 1984)

McNab, Chris (ed.), *Gunfighters – The Outlaws and their Weapons* (San Diego, CA, Thunder Bay Press, 2005)

McNab, Chris and Hunter Keeter, *Tools of Violence – Guns, Tanks and Dirty Bombs* (Oxford, UK, Osprey Publishing, 2008)

Metz, Leon Claire, *The Encyclopedia of Lawmen, Outlaws, and Gunfighters* (New York, Checkmark Books, 2003)

Metz, Leon Claire, *The Shooters – A Gallery of Notorious Gunmen from the American West* (New York, Berkley Books, 1996)

Meyer, Marshall W., "Police Shootings at Minorities: The Case of Los Angeles," *The Annals of the American Academy of Political and Social Science*, vol. 452, no. 1 (1980), pp.98–110

Morrison, Gregory B. and Bryan J. Vila, "Police Handgun Qualification: Practical Measure or Aimless Activity?" *Policing: An International Journal of Police Strategies & Management*, vol. 21, no.3 (1993), pp.510–33

National Commission on the Causes and Prevention of Violence, Daniel Walker, *Rights in Conflict:*

The Violent Confrontation of Demonstrators and Police in the Parks and Streets of Chicago During the Week of the Democratic National Convention of 1968 (released December 1, 1968)

National Institute of Justice, "The Effectiveness and Safety of Pepper Spray," (Washington DC, US Department of Justice, April 2003), pp.2–7

National Institute of Justice, *Study of Deaths Following Electro Muscular Disruption: Interim Report* (Washington DC, US Department of Justice, June 2008)

National Law Enforcement Officers Memorial Fund website: http://www.nleomf.org/TheMemorial/Facts/history.htm

O'Neal, Bill, *The Pimlico Encyclopedia of Western Gunfighters* (London, Pimlico, 1998)

Ohio History Central web site: www.ohiohistorycentral.org/entry.php?rec=488

Patrick, Urey W., US Department of Justice, Federal Bureau of Investigation, "Handgun Wounding Factors and Effectiveness," (Quantico, Virginia, Firearms Training Unit, July 14, 1989)

Patrick, Urey W. and John C. Hall, *In Defense of Self and Others ... Issues, Facts, & Fallacies – the Realities of Law Enforcement's Use of Deadly Force* (Durham, NC, Carolina Academic Press, 2005)

Pennsylvania Historical and Museum Commission, "The Lattimer Massacre": http://www.phmc.state.pa.us/ppet/lattimer/page2.asp?secid=31

Peters Jr., John G. and Michael A. Brave, "Force Continuums: Are They Still Needed?" *Police and Security News*, 22:1 (January/February 2006)

Pine Bluff Police Department, Policy and Procedures Manual, Policy no. 231, "Police Vehicle – Pursuit Driving" (February 19, 2008)

Policeone.com, "New Study May 'Radically Alter' How Police Deadly Force is Viewed" (February 11, 2001):

http://www.policeone.com/writers/columnists/Force-Science/articles/1660208-New-study-may-radically-alter-how-police-deadly-force-is-viewed/

Rawick, George P. (ed.), *The American Slave: A Composite Autobiography*, vol. 9 (Westport, CT, Greenwood Press, 1979)

Remsberg, Charles, "Telling the Truth About Police Shootings," *The Police Marksman*, vol. XXIX, no.6 (November/December 2004), pp.18–22

Report and proceedings of the Senate committee appointed to investigate the police department of the city of New York (1895)

Report House of Representatives 104th Congress, 2nd Session, Union Calendar no. 395 (August 2, 1996)

Richardson, James F., *The New York Police: Colonial Times to 1901* (New York, Oxford University Press, 1970)

Riders, Randy, "Graham v. Connor: Gauging Excessive Force," Officer.com: http://www.officer.com/web/online/Investigation/Graham-v-Connor/18$40765

Rigg, Nancy J., "Shoot-out in North Hollywood – Command and Communications": http://www.9-1-1magazine.com/magazine/1997/0997/features/rigg.html

Rivara, F. P. and C. D. Mack, "Motor Vehicle Crash Deaths Related to Police Pursuits in the United States," *Injury Prevention*, 10 (2004), pp.93–95

Robinson III, Charles M., *American Frontier Lawmen 1850–1930* (Oxford, UK, Osprey Publishing, 2005)

Rosa, J. G., *The Gunfighter: Man or Myth?* (Norman, OK, and London, University of Oklahoma

Press, 1969)

Rostker, Bernard D. et al, *Evaluation of the New York City Police Department Firearm Training and Firearm-Discharge Review Process* (Santa Monica, CA, Rand Corporation, 2008)

Roth, Jeffrey A. and Christopher S. Koper, "Impacts of the 1994 Assault Weapons Ban: 1994–96," *National Institute of Justice – Research in Brief* (March 1999), p.2

Rubenstein, Jonathan, *City Police* (New York, Farrar, Straus and Giroux, 1973)

Scharf, Peter and Arnold Binder, *The Badge and the Bullet – Police Use of Deadly Force* (New York, Praeger Publishing, 1983)

Schnaubelt, Lieutenant Colonel Christopher M., "Lessons in Command and Control from the Los Angeles Riots," California State Military Department, The California Military Museum: www.militarymuseum.org/LARiots1.html; previously published in *Parameters* (Summer 1997), pp.88–109

Schneider, John C., *Detroit and the Problem of Order, 1830–1880: A Geography of Crime, Riot, and Policing* (Lincoln, NE, University of Nebraska Press, 1980)

Sherman, Lawrence W. et al., *Citizens Killed by Big City Police, 1970–84* (Washington DC, Crime Control Institute, 1986)

Skolnick, Jerome H. and James J. Fyfe, *Above the Law – Police and the Excessive Use of Force* (New York, Simon & Schuster, 1993)

Solari, Jenna and John Bostain, "Use of Force Continuum (podcast transcript)," Federal Law Enforcement Training Center, Department of Homeland Security web site: http://www.fletc.gov/training/programs/legal-division/podcasts/hot-issues-podcasts/hot-issues-transcripts/use-of-force-continuum-podcast-transcript.html

Spaulding, Dave, "What Really Happens in a Gunfight," *Guns and Ammo Handguns*, online: www.handgunsmag.com/tactics_training/what_happens_gunfight/

Stincelli, Rebecca, *Suicide by Cop – Victims From Both Sides of the Badge* (Placerville, CA, Kele Publishing, rev. ed. March 2004)

Sylvester, Richard, "A History of the 'Sweat Box' and 'Third Degree'," in *International Association of Chiefs of Police: Seventeenth Annual Session* (May 10–13, 1910)

Symbionese Liberation Army, Communique #3 (February 4, 1974)

Texas Department of Public Safety: http://www.txdps.state.tx.us

Unger, Robert, *Union Station Massacre: The Original Sin of J. Edgar Hoover's FBI* (Andrew McMeel, 1997)

US Bureau of the Census, Foreign Trade Division, FT246U.S. Imports for Consumption 1964–73

US Department of Justice, Bureau of Justice Statistics, "Percent of Murders, Robberies and Aggravated Assaults in which Firearms were Used, 1973 to 2006" (data revised January 25, 2008)

US Department of Justice, Civil Rights Division, Summary of FBI reports into Kent State (July 1970): http://www.may4archive.org/appendices.shtml#FBI

US Department of Justice, "Justifiable Homicides by Police and Citizens, 1976–2005": www.ojp.usdoj.gov/bjs/homicde/d_justifyreason.htm

US Department of Justice, *Report to the Deputy Attorney General on the Events at Waco, Texas February 28 to April 19, 1993* (October 8, 1993) Section VIII/A

US Department of Justice, Resolution 14b, Policy Statement "Use of Deadly Force": http://www.usdoj.gov/ag/readingroom/resolution14b.htm

Utley, Robert M., *Lone Star Justice: The First Century of the Texas Rangers* (New York, Oxford University Press, 2002)

Vance, Cyrus R., *Final Report Of Cyrus R. Vance, Special Assistant To The Secretary Of Defense Concerning The Detroit Riots July 23 through August 2, 1967* (1968): http://www.lbjlib.utexas.edu/johnson/archives.hom/oralhistory.hom/Vance-C/DetroitReport.asp#LL

Vila, Bryan and Cynthia Morris (eds), *The Role of Police in American Society: A Documentary History* (Westport, CT, Greenwood Press, 1999)

Virginia Police and Deputy Sheriffs, "NYPD SOP 9 – Analysis of Police Combat": www.virginiacops.org/Articles/Shooting/Combat.htm

Vollmer, August, "The Policeman as a Social Worker," in *International Association of Chiefs of Police: Proceedings 26th Convention* (April 14–16, 1919)

Waegel, William B., "How Police Justify the Use of Deadly Force," *Social Problems*, vol.32, no.2 (December 1984), pp.144–55

Williams, Kristian, *Our Enemies in Blue: Police and Power in America* (Soft Skull Press, 2003)

Wilson, James Q., *Varieties of Police Behavior* (Harvard University Press, 1978)

Wilson, Orlando W., *Police Administration* (New York, McGraw Hill, 1950)

Woods, Arthur, *Policeman and Public* (New Haven, CT, Yale University Press, 1919)

Zentner, Joe, "Western Gunslinger Myths": www.desertusa.com/mag05/jul/myths.html

Zawitz, Marianne W., *Guns Used in Crime* (Washington, D.C., US Department of Justice, July 1995)

Zimring, Franklin E., "Firearms and Federal Law: The Gun Control Act Of 1968," *Journal of Legal Studies*, 4 (1975), pp.134–200

INDEX